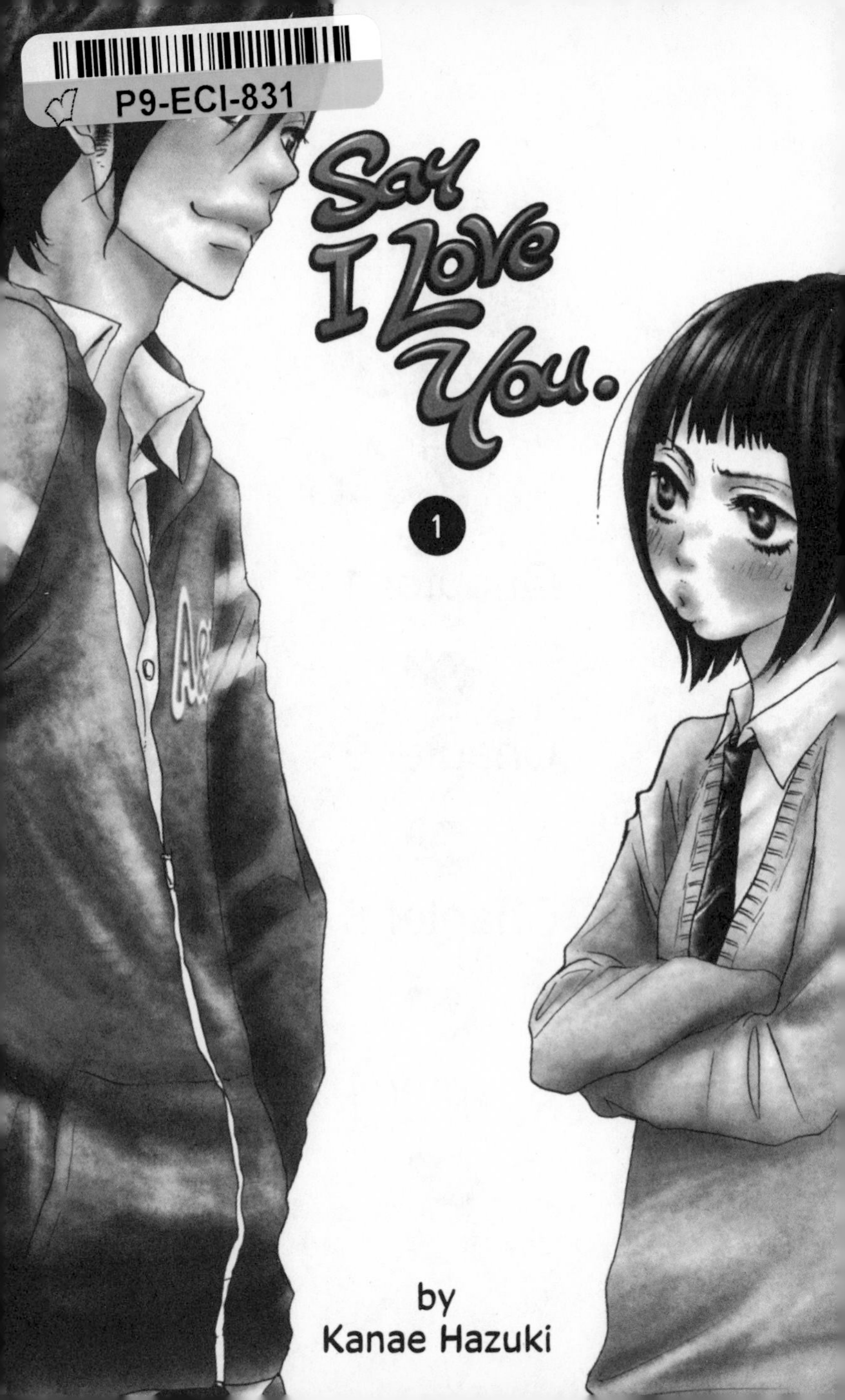

Say I Love You.

1

by

Kanae Hazuki

Kanae Hazuki
presents

Chapter 1

4

Chapter 2

49

Chapter 3

89

Chapter 4

129

Say
"I love you".

Kanae Hazuki

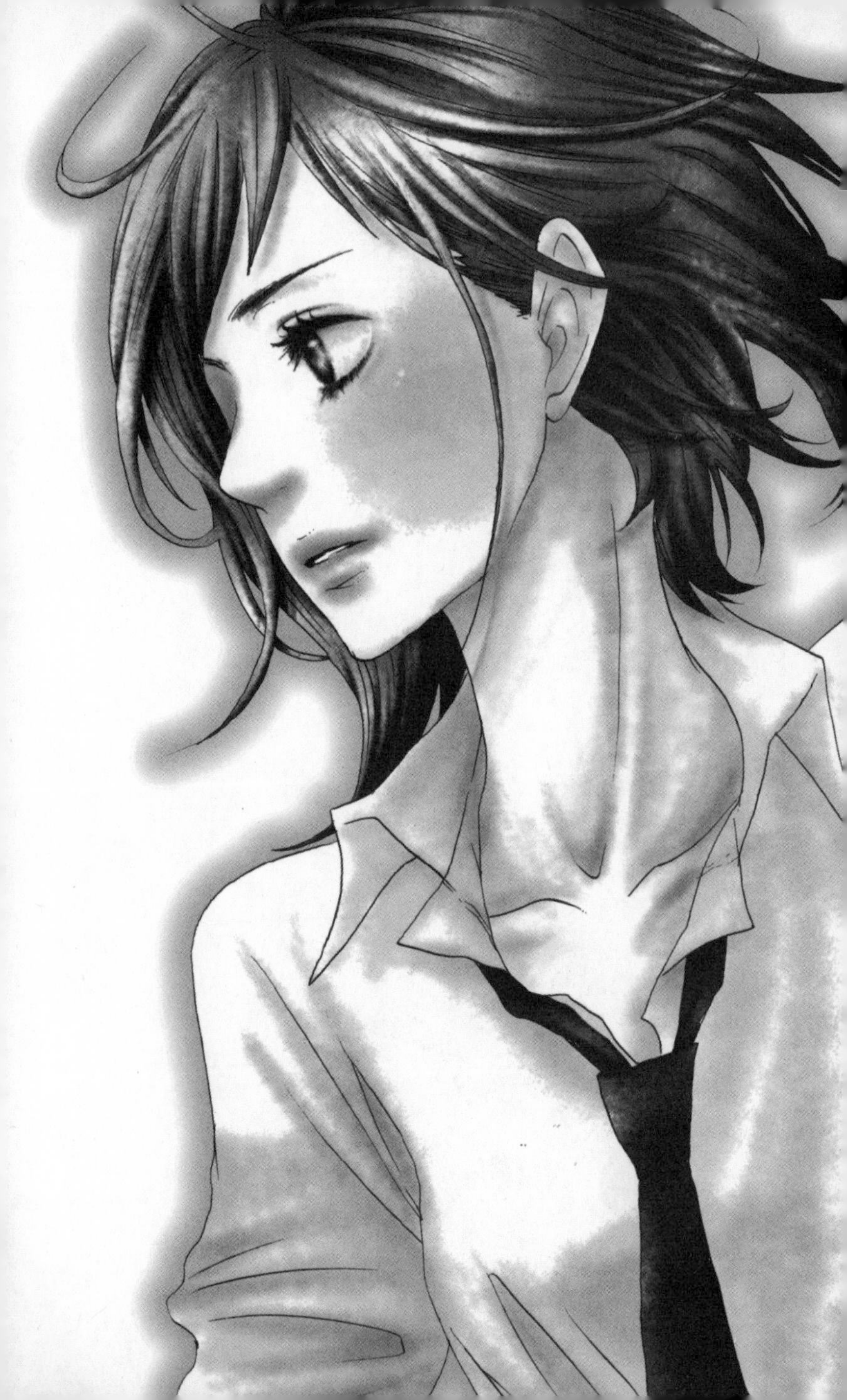

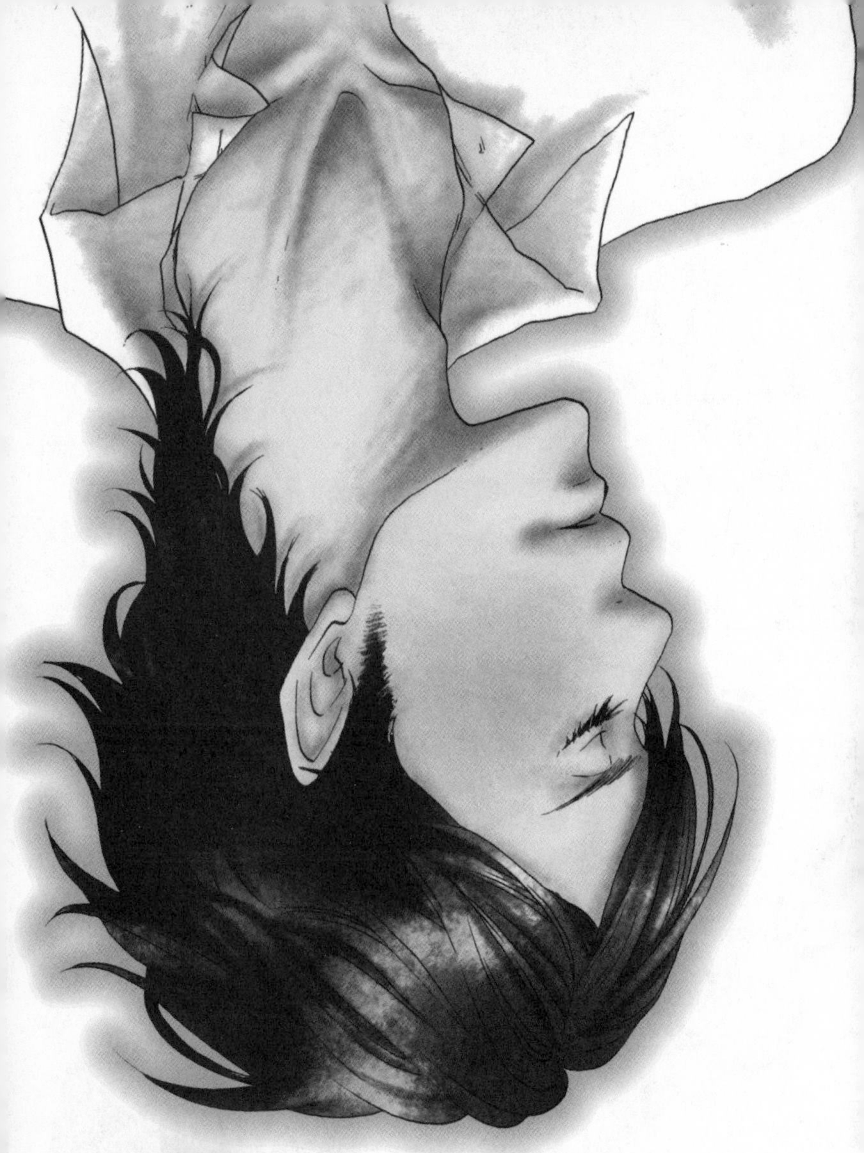

Chapter 1

Say
"I love you".
Kanae Hazuki

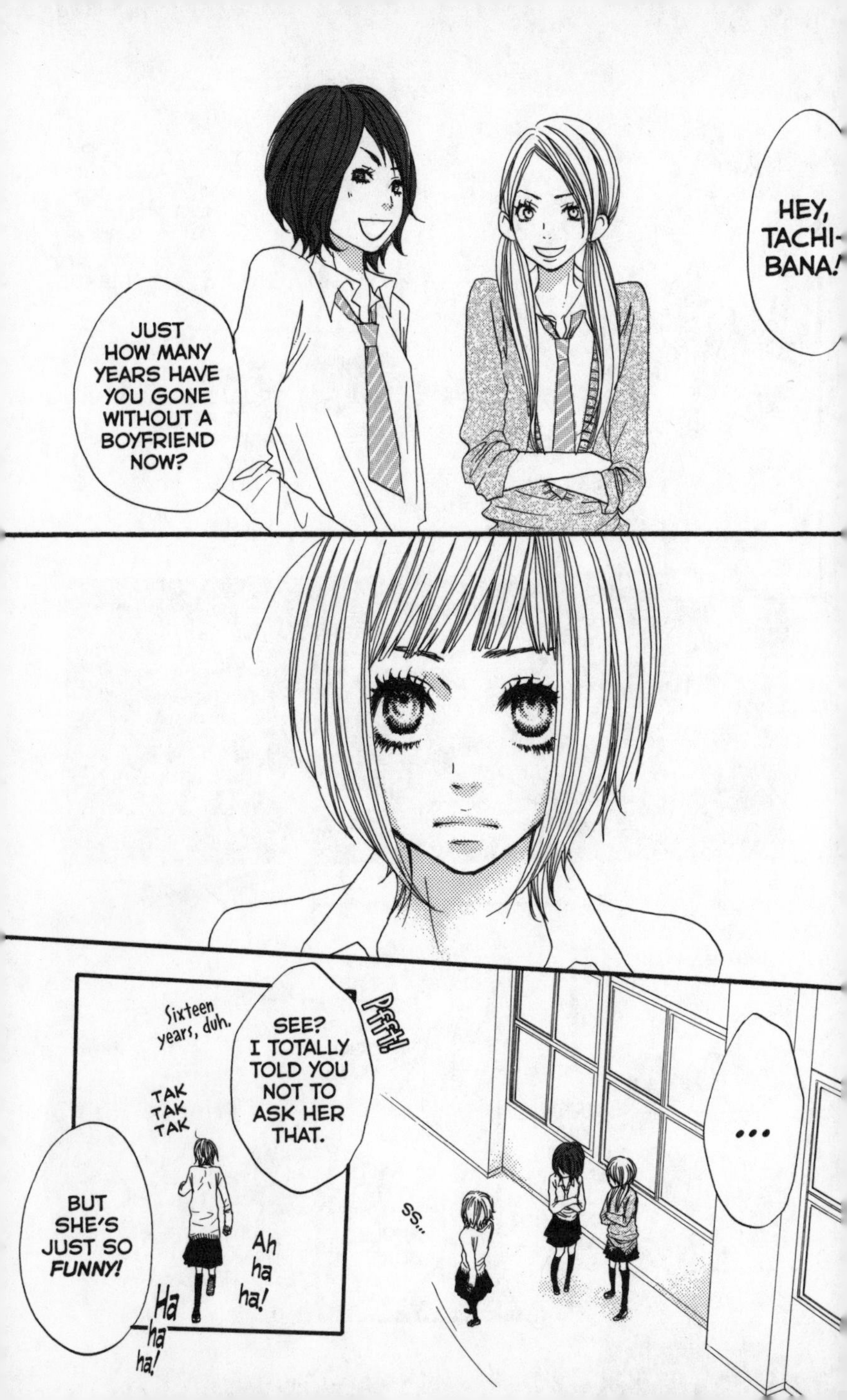
HEY, TACHI-BANA!
JUST HOW MANY YEARS HAVE YOU GONE WITHOUT A BOYFRIEND NOW?
...
SS...
Pffft!
SEE? I TOTALLY TOLD YOU NOT TO ASK HER THAT.
Sixteen years, duh.
TAK TAK TAK
Ah ha ha!
BUT SHE'S JUST SO *FUNNY!*
Ha ha ha ha!

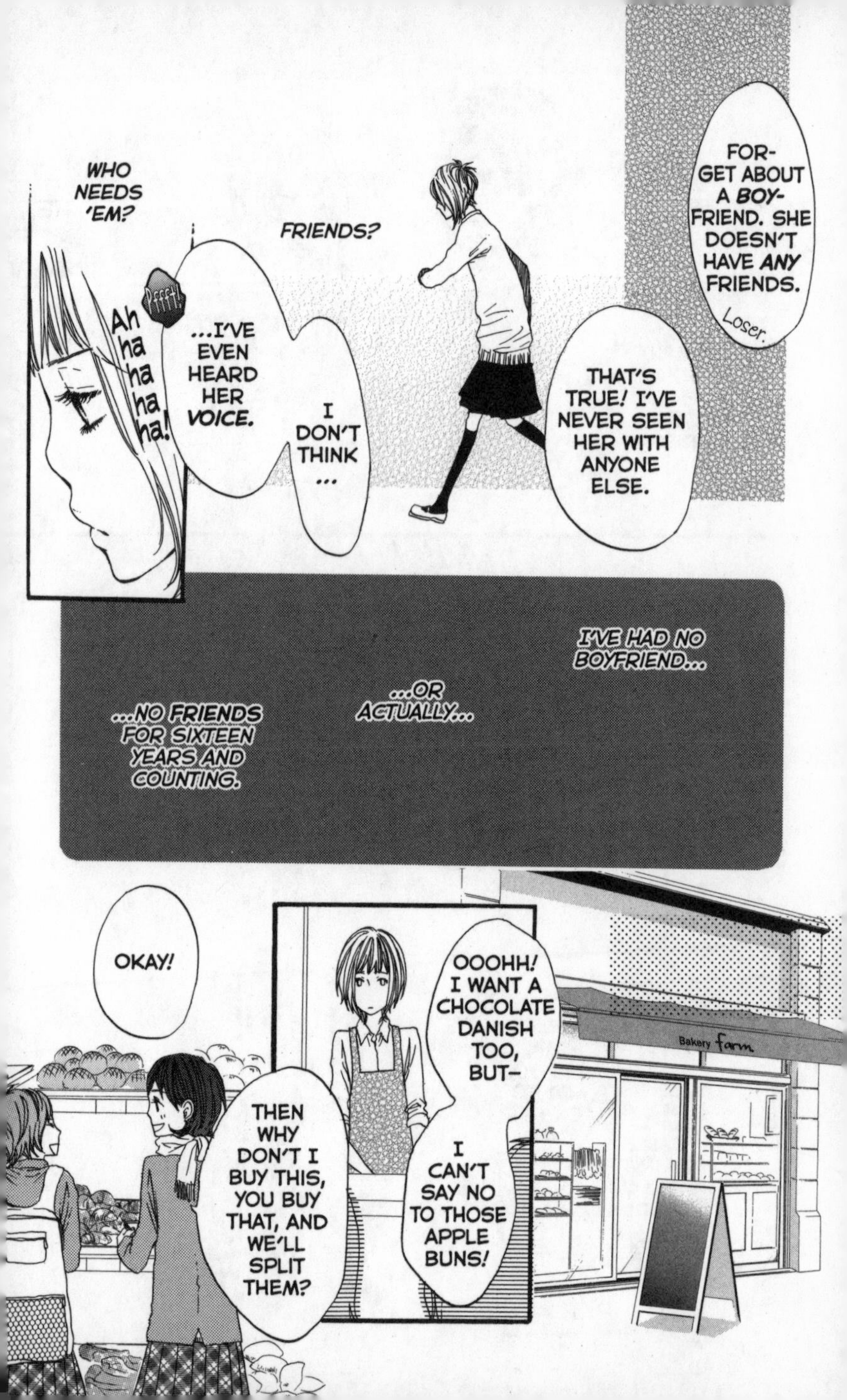
FOR-GET ABOUT A BOY-FRIEND. SHE DOESN'T HAVE ANY FRIENDS.
Loser.
THAT'S TRUE! I'VE NEVER SEEN HER WITH ANYONE ELSE.
FRIENDS?
WHO NEEDS 'EM?
I DON'T THINK...
...I'VE EVEN HEARD HER VOICE.
Pffft!
Ah ha ha ha ha!
I'VE HAD NO BOYFRIEND...
...OR ACTUALLY...
...NO FRIENDS FOR SIXTEEN YEARS AND COUNTING.
Bakery farm
OOOHH! I WANT A CHOCOLATE DANISH TOO, BUT–
I CAN'T SAY NO TO THOSE APPLE BUNS!
THEN WHY DON'T I BUY THIS, YOU BUY THAT, AND WE'LL SPLIT THEM?
OKAY!

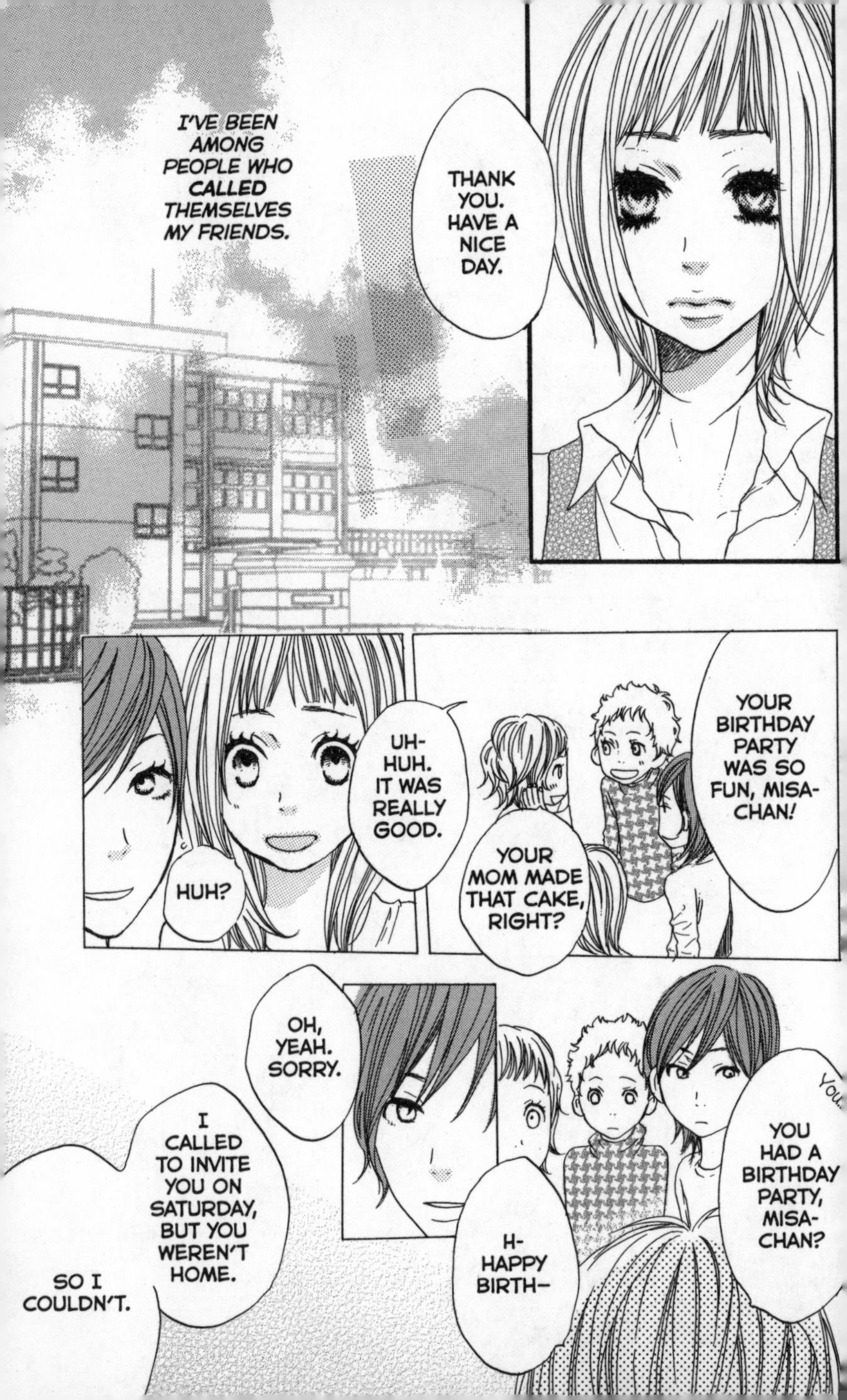
THANK YOU. HAVE A NICE DAY.
I'VE BEEN AMONG PEOPLE WHO CALLED THEMSELVES MY FRIENDS.
YOUR BIRTHDAY PARTY WAS SO FUN, MISA-CHAN!
YOUR MOM MADE THAT CAKE, RIGHT?
UH-HUH. IT WAS REALLY GOOD.
HUH?
YOU...
YOU HAD A BIRTHDAY PARTY, MISA-CHAN?
H-HAPPY BIRTH-
OH, YEAH. SORRY.
I CALLED TO INVITE YOU ON SATURDAY, BUT YOU WEREN'T HOME.
SO I COULDN'T.

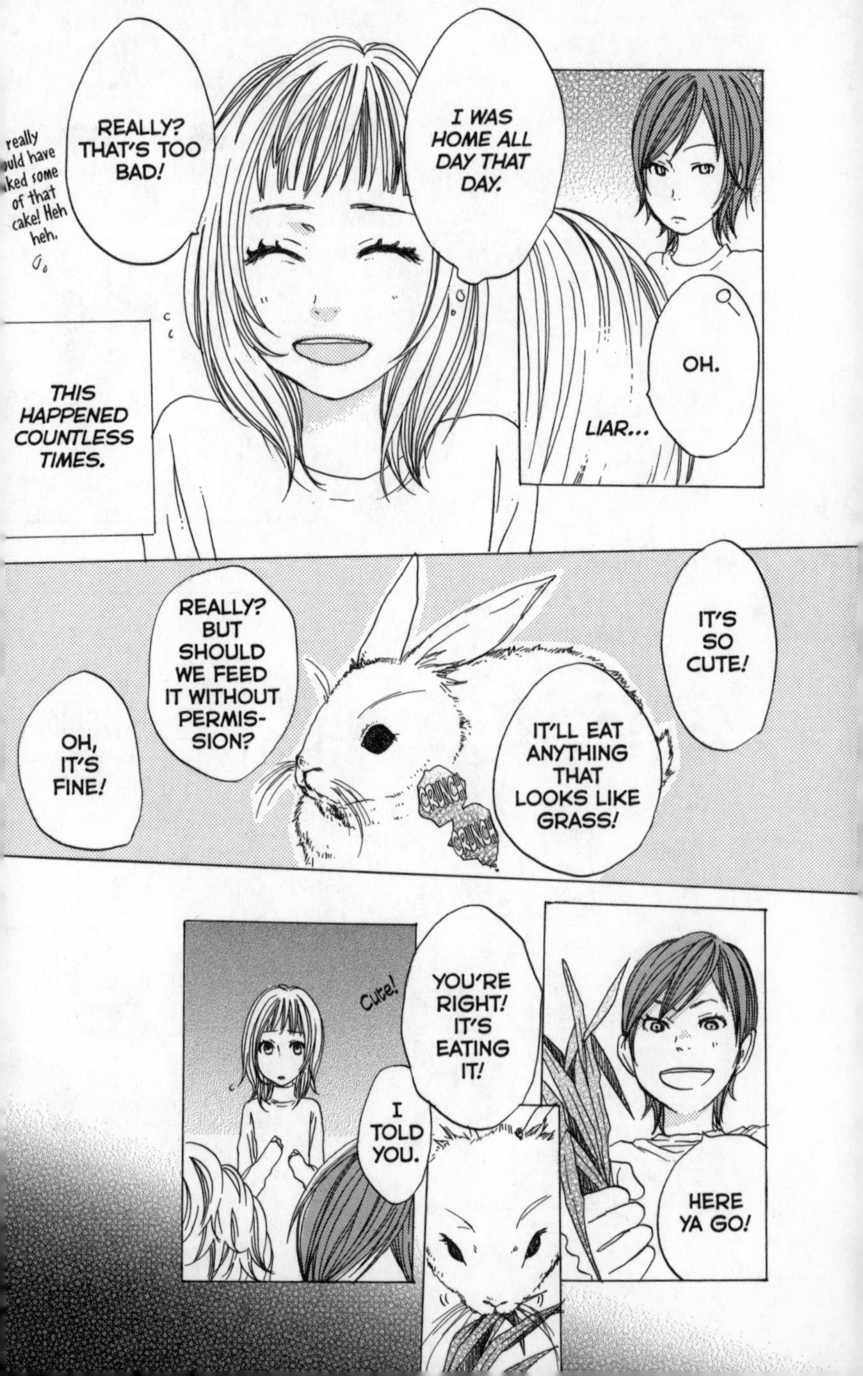
I WAS HOME ALL DAY THAT DAY.
OH.
LIAR...
REALLY? THAT'S TOO BAD!
really ould have ked some of that cake! Heh heh.
THIS HAPPENED COUNTLESS TIMES.
IT'S SO CUTE!
IT'LL EAT ANYTHING THAT LOOKS LIKE GRASS!
CRUNCH CRUNCH
REALLY? BUT SHOULD WE FEED IT WITHOUT PERMISSION?
OH, IT'S FINE!
HERE YA GO!
YOU'RE RIGHT! IT'S EATING IT!
Cute!
I TOLD YOU.

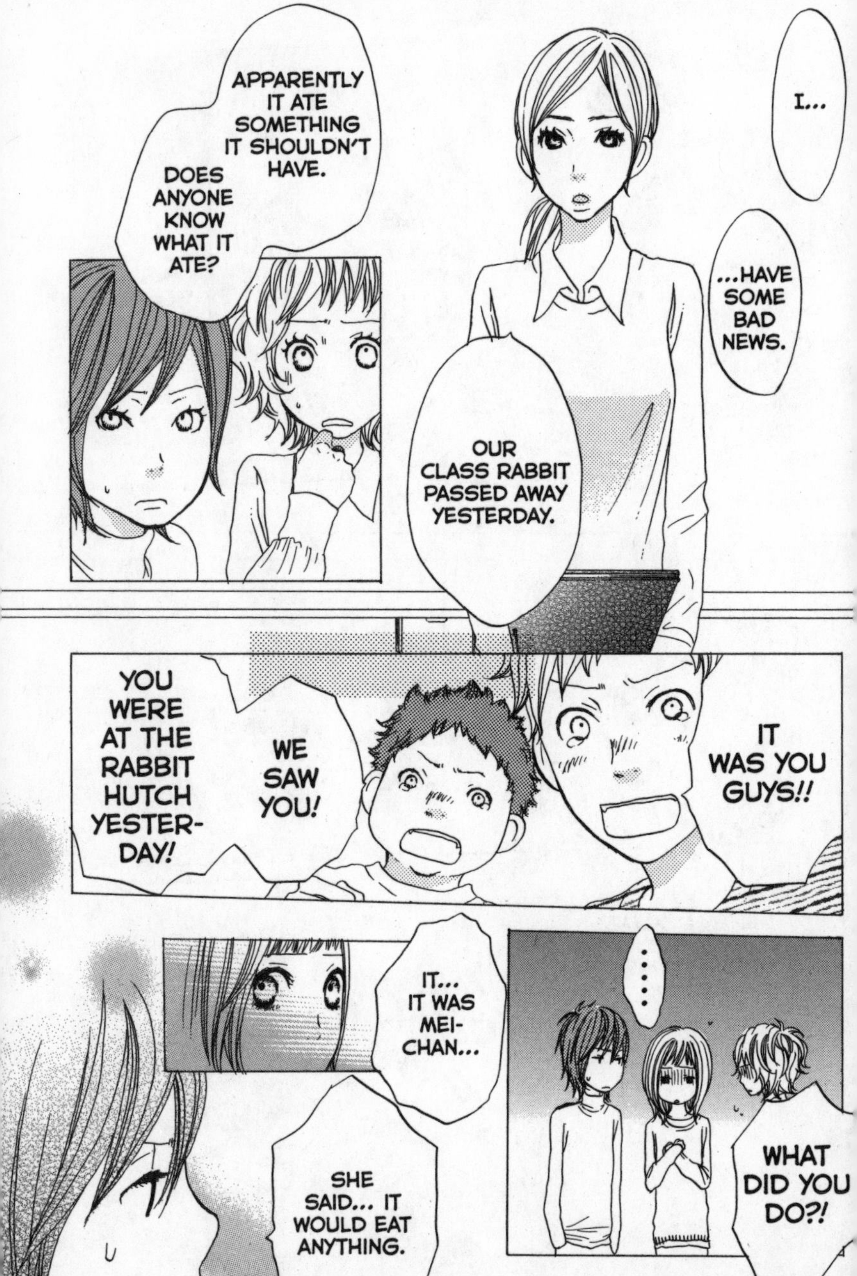
I...
...HAVE SOME BAD NEWS.
OUR CLASS RABBIT PASSED AWAY YESTERDAY.
APPARENTLY IT ATE SOMETHING IT SHOULDN'T HAVE.
DOES ANYONE KNOW WHAT IT ATE?
IT WAS YOU GUYS!!
WE SAW YOU!
YOU WERE AT THE RABBIT HUTCH YESTER-DAY!
.....
WHAT DID YOU DO?!
IT... IT WAS MEI-CHAN...
SHE SAID... IT WOULD EAT ANYTHING.

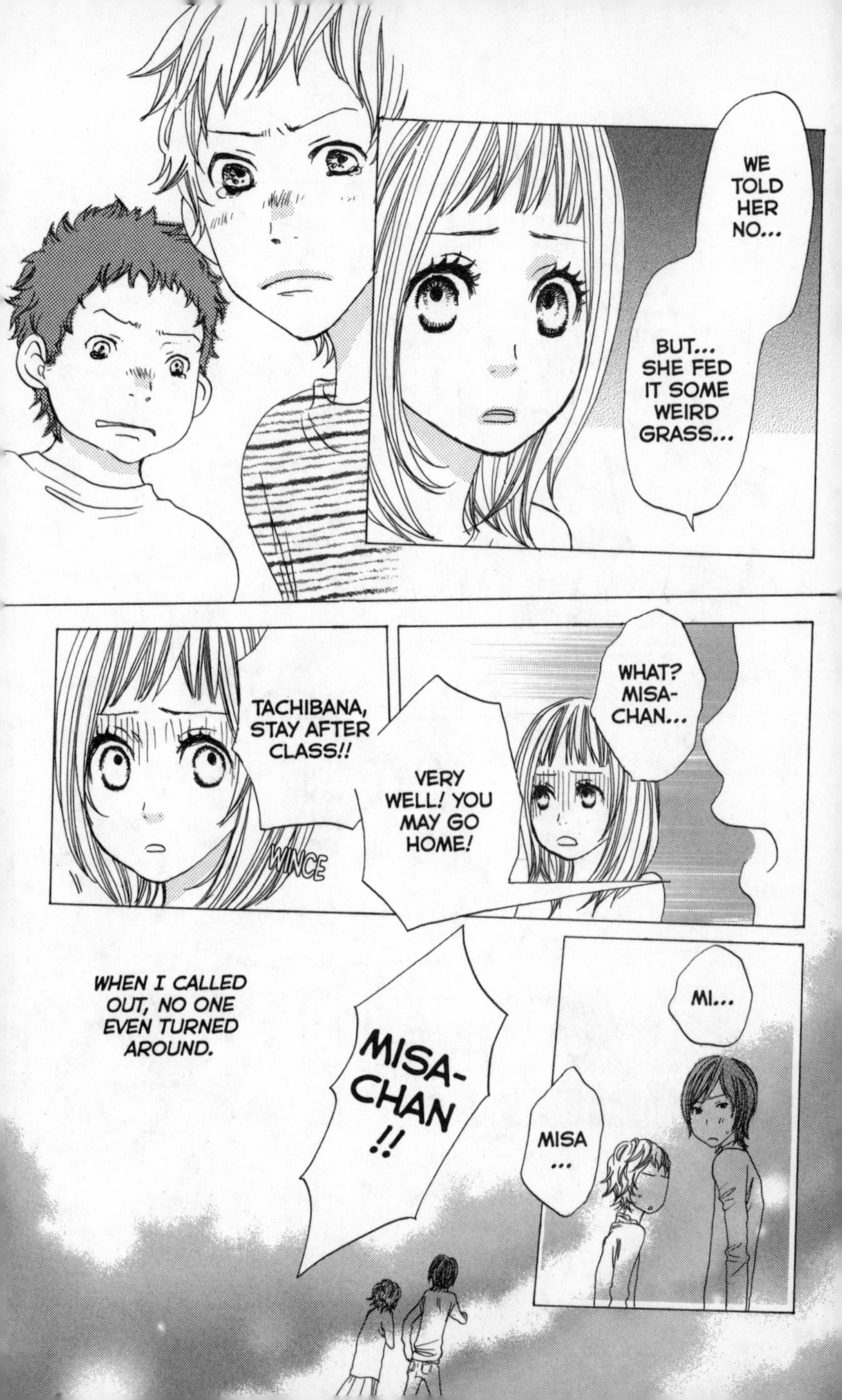
WE TOLD HER NO...
BUT... SHE FED IT SOME WEIRD GRASS...
WHAT? MISA-CHAN...
VERY WELL! YOU MAY GO HOME!
TACHIBANA, STAY AFTER CLASS!!
WINCE
MI...
MISA ...
MISA-CHAN !!
WHEN I CALLED OUT, NO ONE EVEN TURNED AROUND.

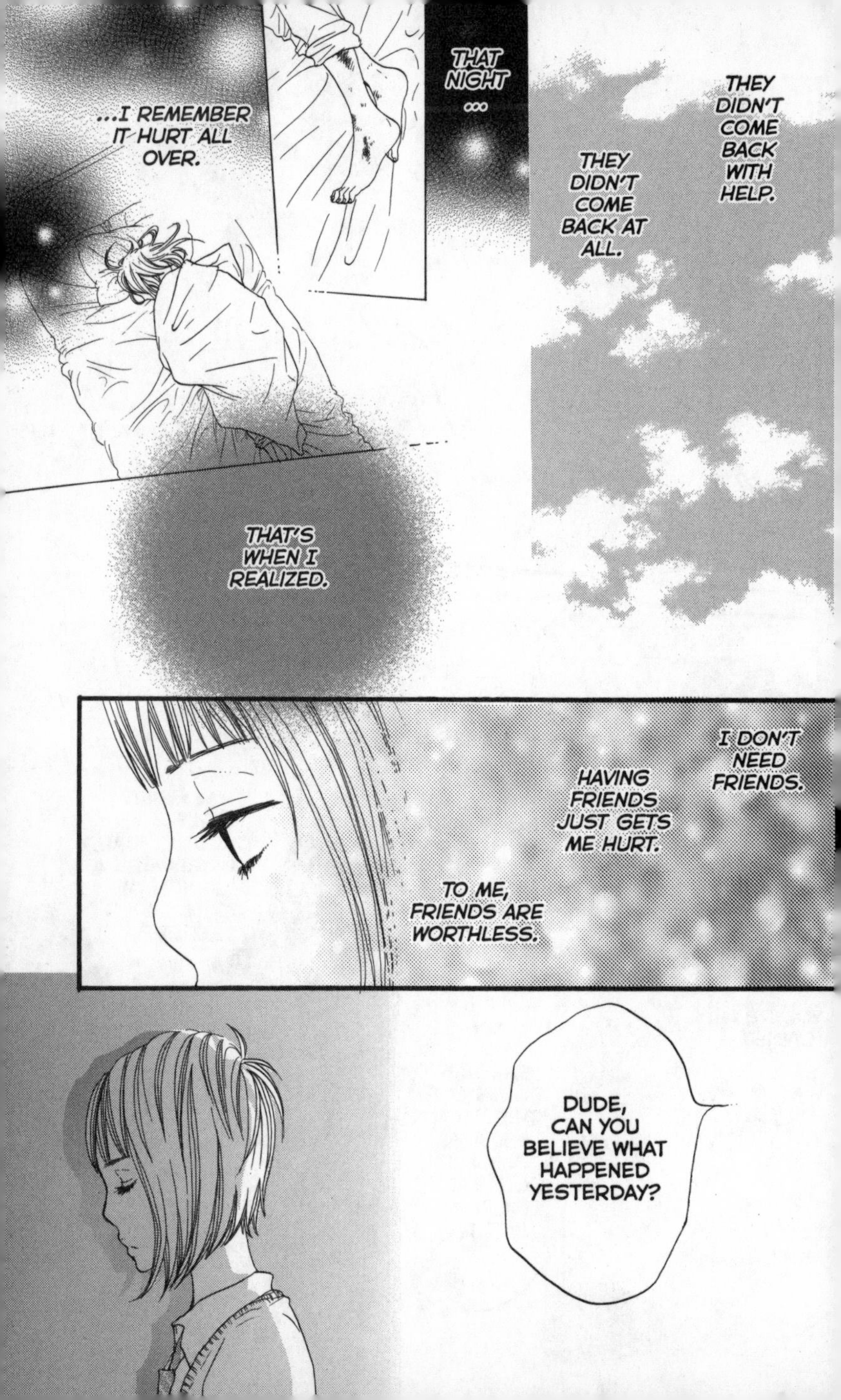
THEY DIDN'T COME BACK WITH HELP.
THEY DIDN'T COME BACK AT ALL.
THAT NIGHT...
...I REMEMBER IT HURT ALL OVER.
THAT'S WHEN I REALIZED.
I DON'T NEED FRIENDS.
HAVING FRIENDS JUST GETS ME HURT.
TO ME, FRIENDS ARE WORTHLESS.
DUDE, CAN YOU BELIEVE WHAT HAPPENED YESTERDAY?

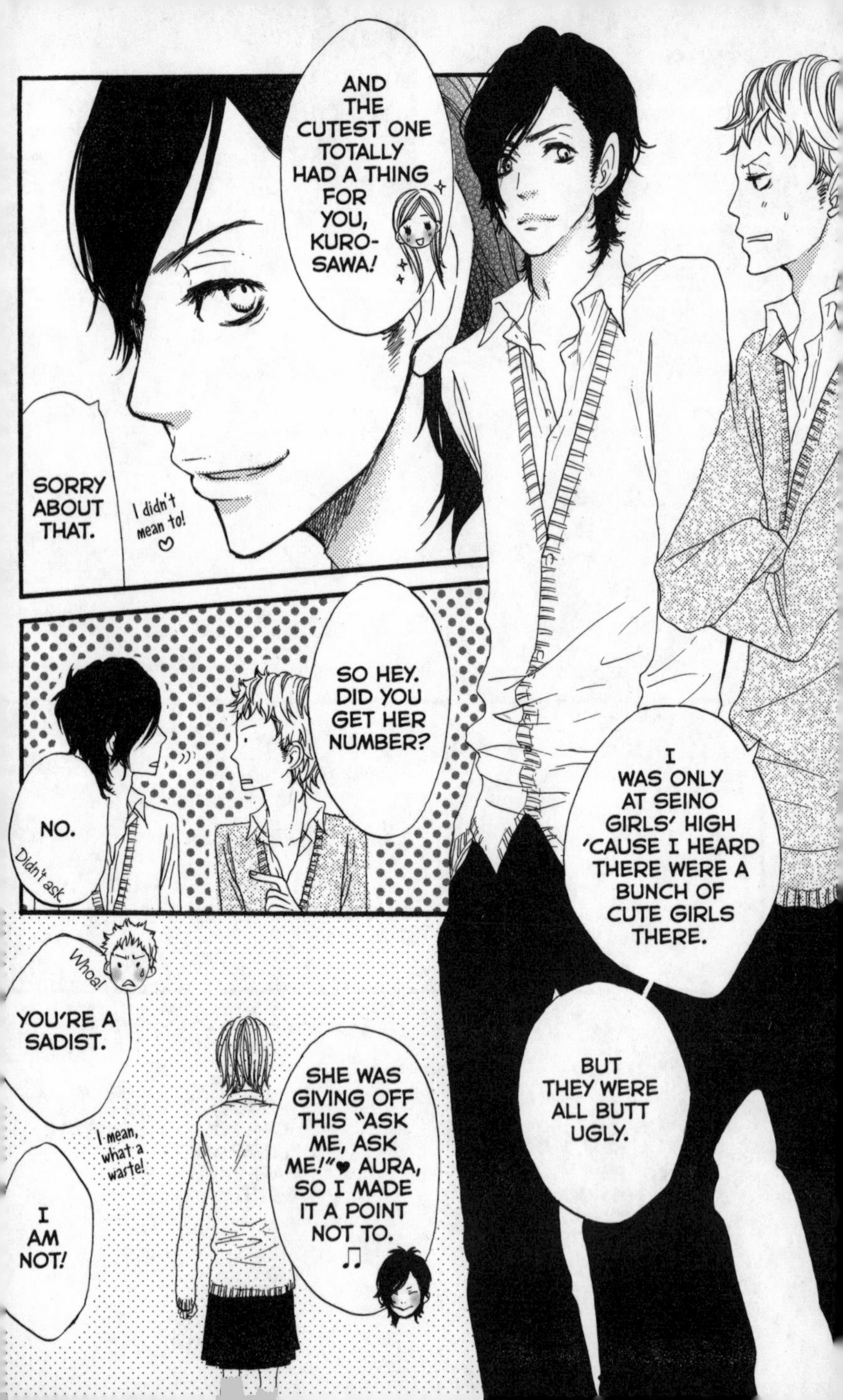

I WAS ONLY AT SEINO GIRLS' HIGH 'CAUSE I HEARD THERE WERE A BUNCH OF CUTE GIRLS THERE.
BUT THEY WERE ALL BUTT UGLY.
AND THE CUTEST ONE TOTALLY HAD A THING FOR YOU, KURO-SAWA!
SORRY ABOUT THAT.
I didn't mean to! ♡
SO HEY. DID YOU GET HER NUMBER?
NO.
Didn't ask
SHE WAS GIVING OFF THIS "ASK ME, ASK ME!"♥ AURA, SO I MADE IT A POINT NOT TO. ♫
YOU'RE A SADIST.
Whoa!
I mean, what a waste!
I AM NOT!

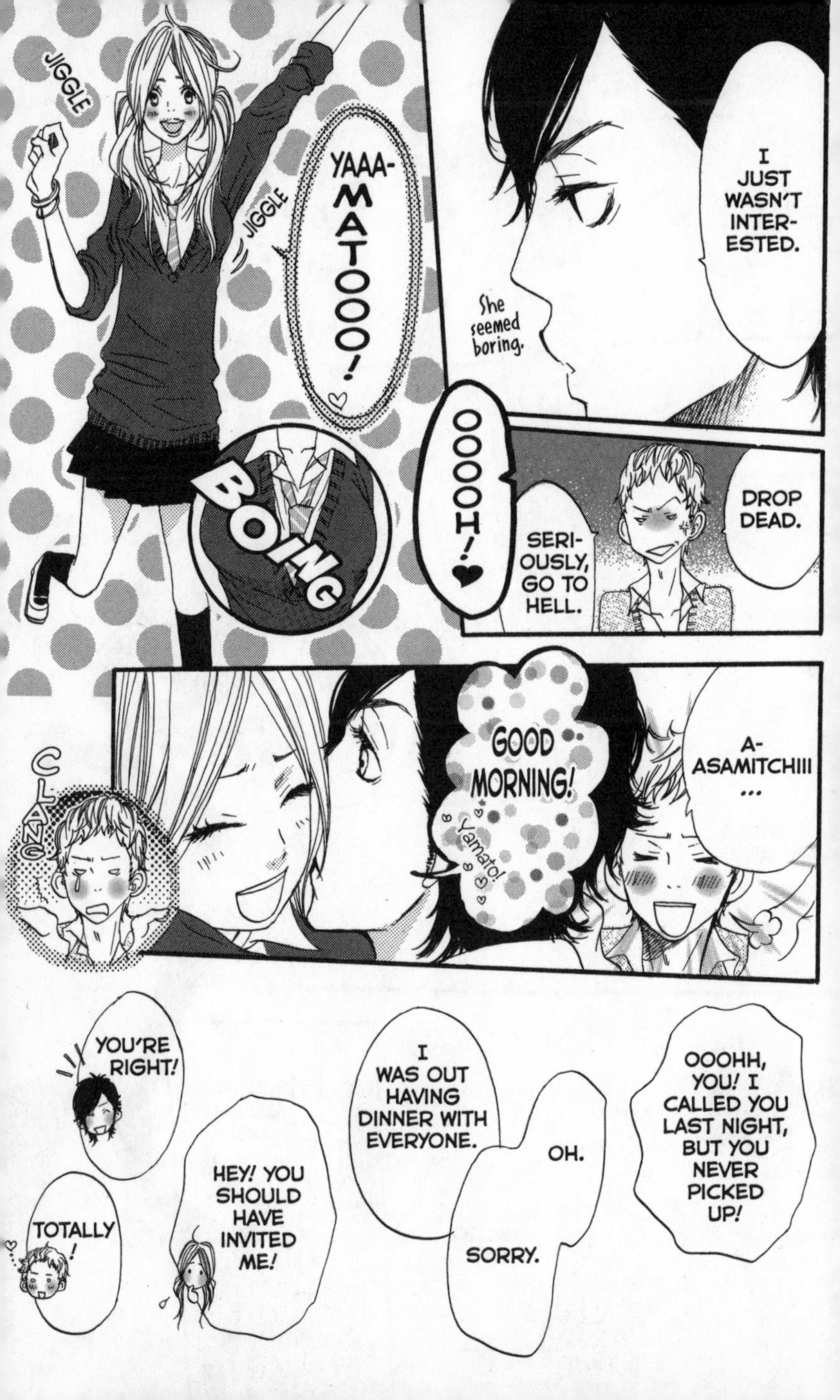
I JUST WASN'T INTER-ESTED.
She seemed boring.
DROP DEAD.
SERI-OUSLY, GO TO HELL.
OOOOH! ♥
YAAA-MATOOOO! ♥
JIGGLE
JIGGLE
BOING
A-ASAMITCHIII...
GOOD MORNING!
Yamato!
CLANG
OOOHH, YOU! I CALLED YOU LAST NIGHT, BUT YOU NEVER PICKED UP!
OH.
SORRY.
I WAS OUT HAVING DINNER WITH EVERYONE.
HEY! YOU SHOULD HAVE INVITED ME!
YOU'RE RIGHT!
TOTALLY!

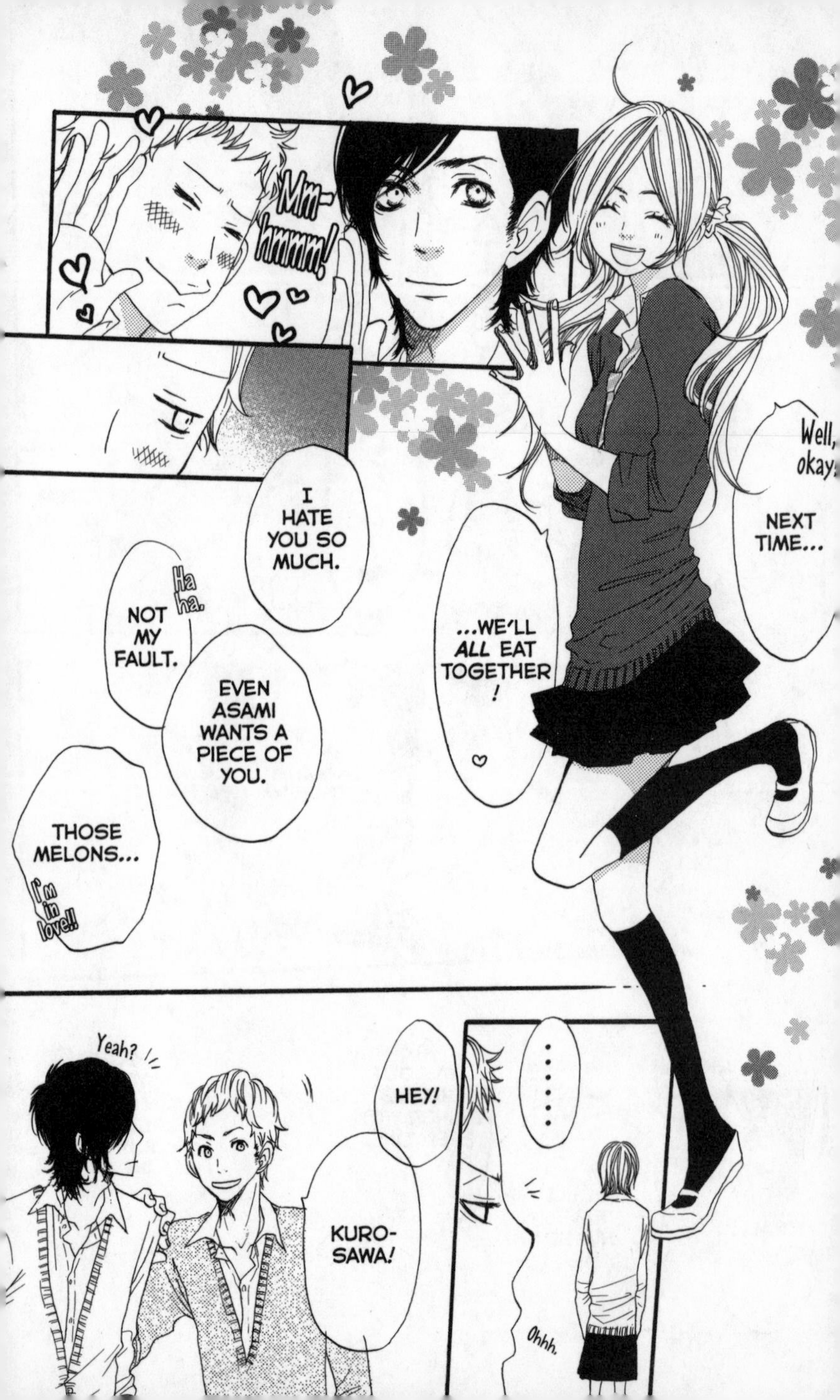
Well, okay.
NEXT TIME...
...WE'LL ALL EAT TOGETHER!
Mm-hmmm!
I HATE YOU SO MUCH.
Ha ha.
NOT MY FAULT.
EVEN ASAMI WANTS A PIECE OF YOU.
THOSE MELONS...
I'm in love!!
......
Ohhh.
HEY!
KURO-SAWA!
Yeah?

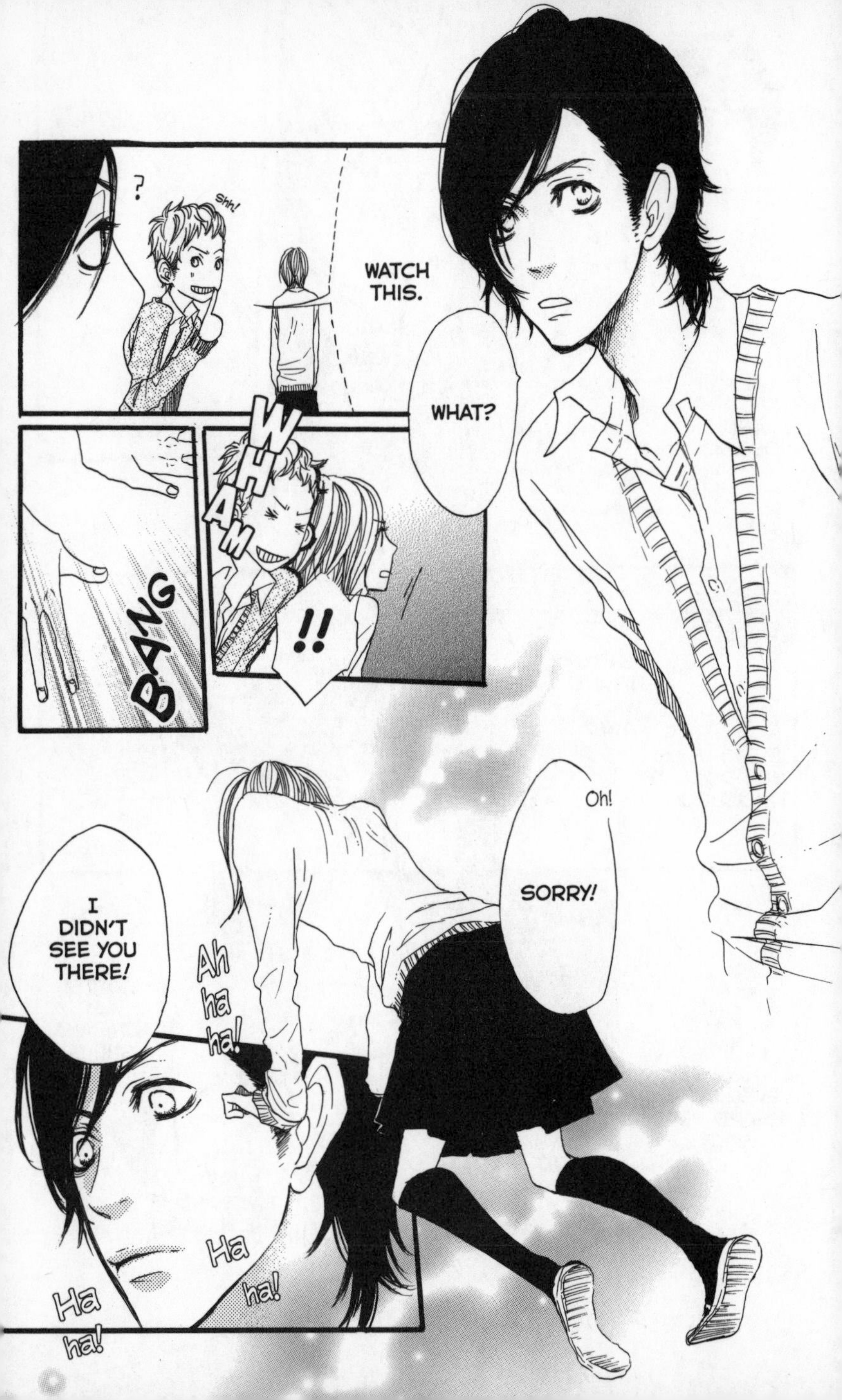
WATCH THIS.
Shh!
?
WHAM
!!
BANG
WHAT?
Oh!
SORRY!
I DIDN'T SEE YOU THERE!
Ah ha ha!
Ha ha!
Ha ha!

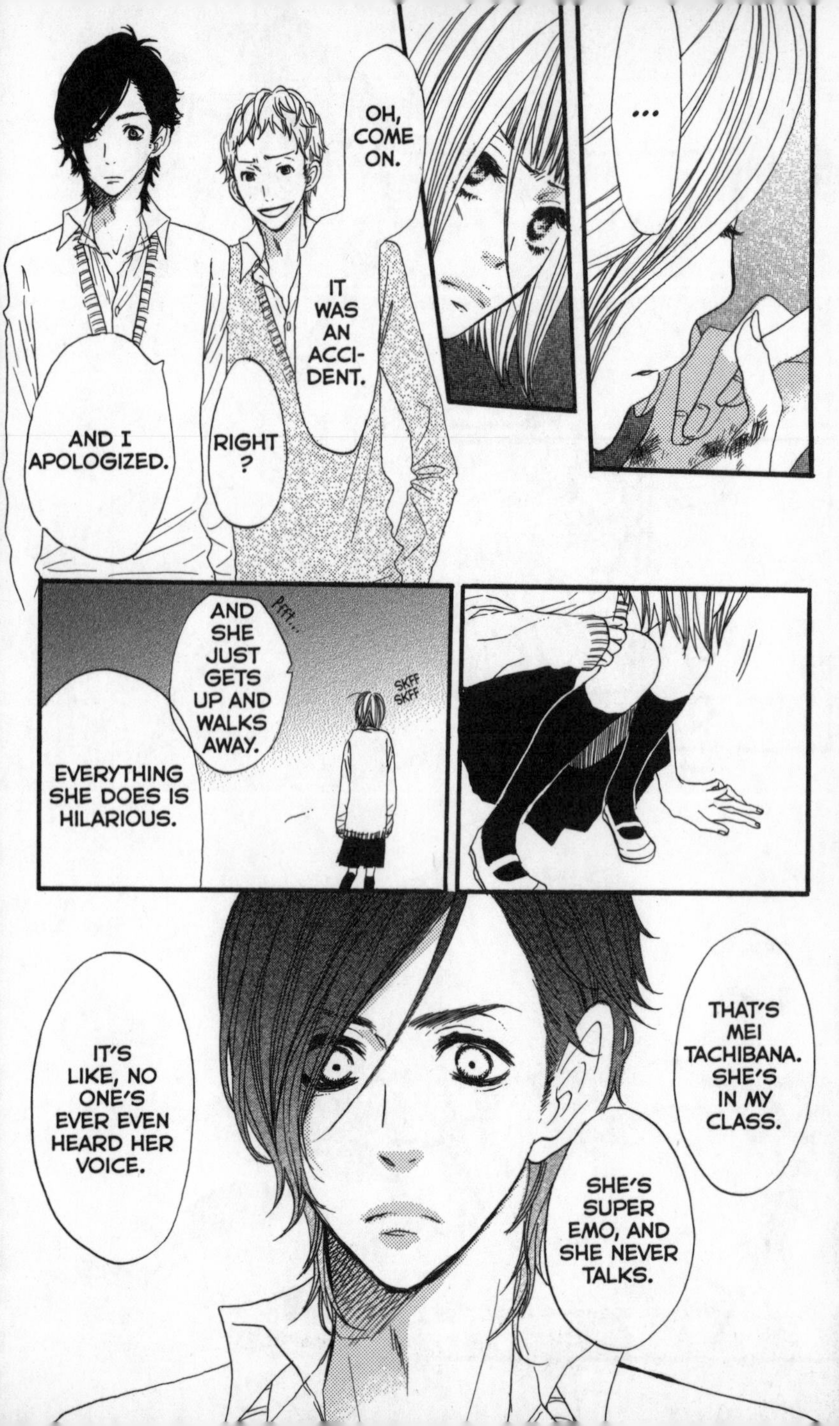
...
OH, COME ON.
IT WAS AN ACCIDENT.
RIGHT?
AND I APOLOGIZED.
SKFF SKFF
Pfft...
AND SHE JUST GETS UP AND WALKS AWAY.
EVERYTHING SHE DOES IS HILARIOUS.
THAT'S MEI TACHIBANA. SHE'S IN MY CLASS.
SHE'S SUPER EMO, AND SHE NEVER TALKS.
IT'S LIKE, NO ONE'S EVER EVEN HEARD HER VOICE.

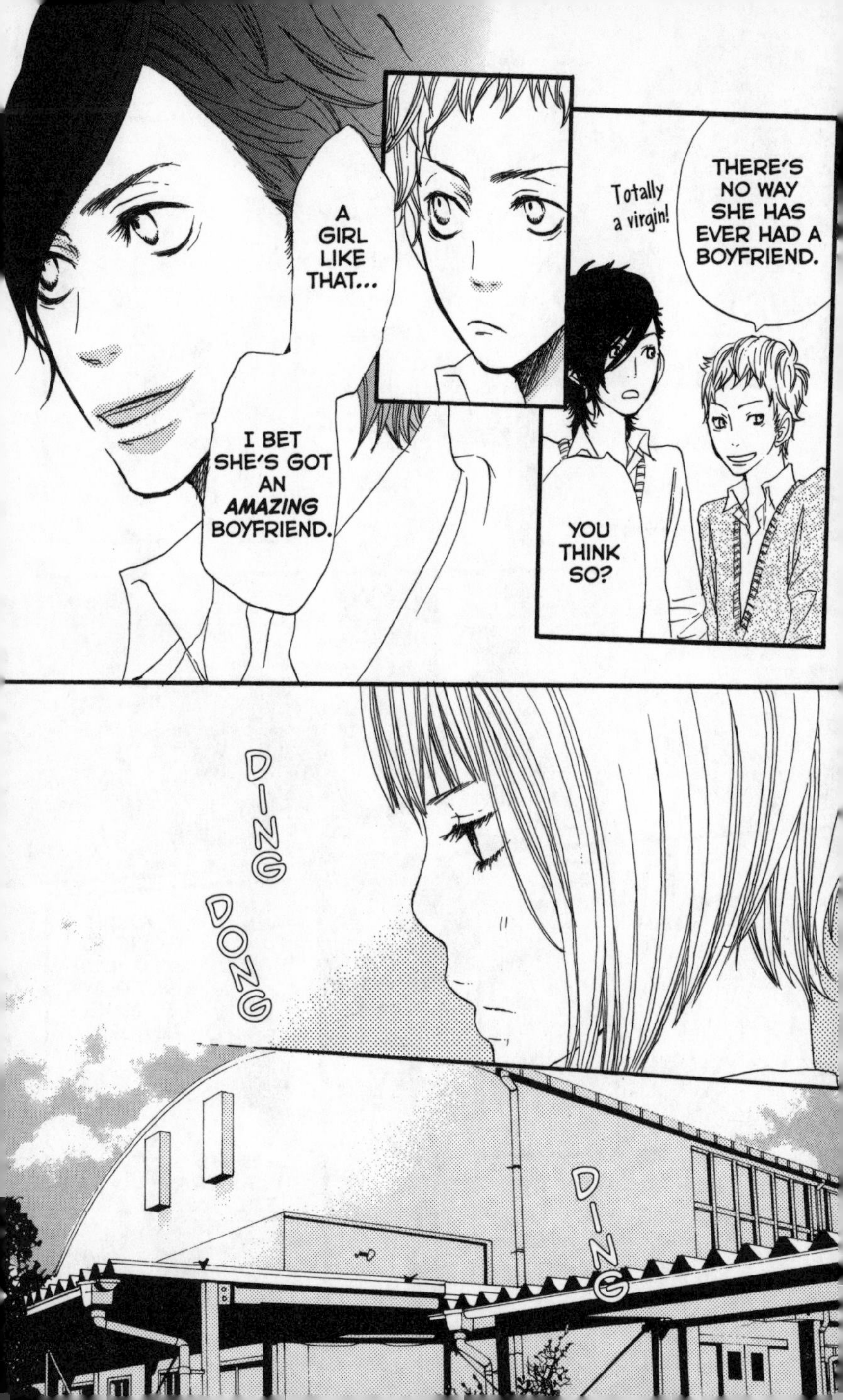
THERE'S NO WAY SHE HAS EVER HAD A BOYFRIEND.
Totally a virgin!
YOU THINK SO?
A GIRL LIKE THAT...
I BET SHE'S GOT AN *AMAZING* BOYFRIEND.
DING DONG
DING

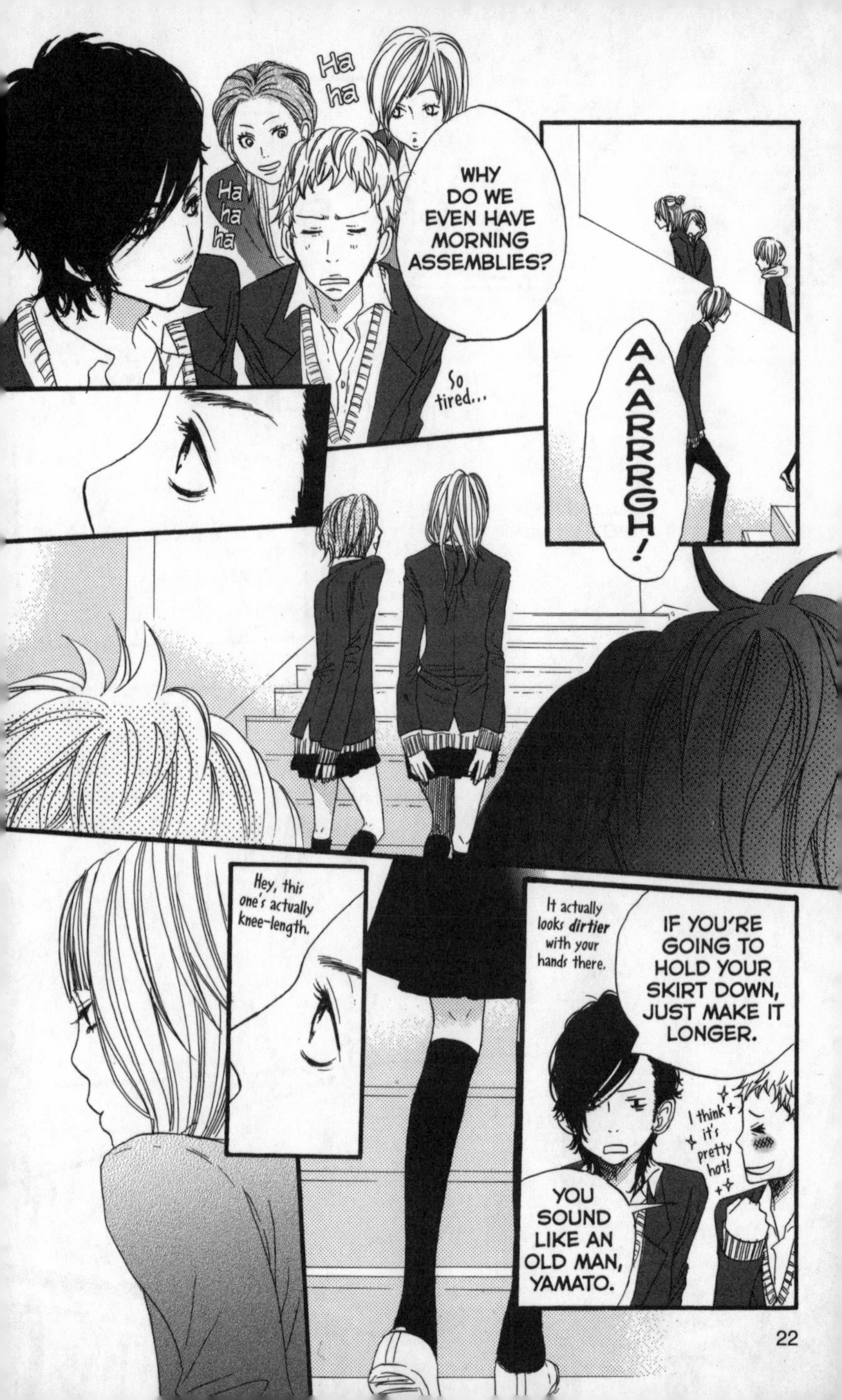

AAARRGH!
WHY DO WE EVEN HAVE MORNING ASSEMBLIES?
Ha ha
Ha ha ha
So tired...
It actually looks **dirtier** with your hands there.
IF YOU'RE GOING TO HOLD YOUR SKIRT DOWN, JUST MAKE IT LONGER.
I think it's pretty hot!
YOU SOUND LIKE AN OLD MAN, YAMATO.
Hey, this one's actually knee-length.

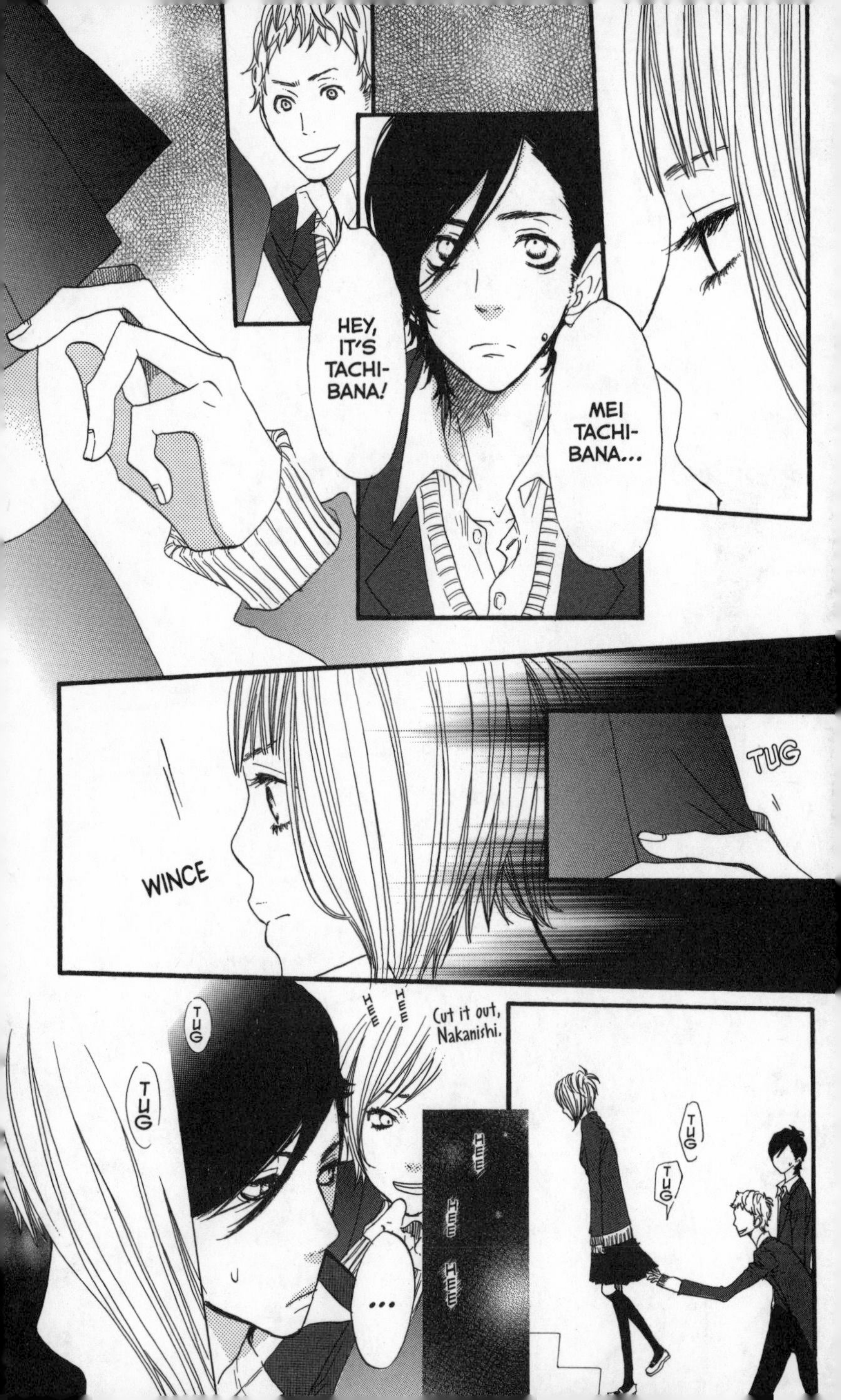
HEY, IT'S TACHI-BANA!
MEI TACHI-BANA...
TUG
WINCE
TUG
TUG
Cut it out, Nakanishi.
HEE HEE
TUG
TUG
HEE HEE HEE HEE
...

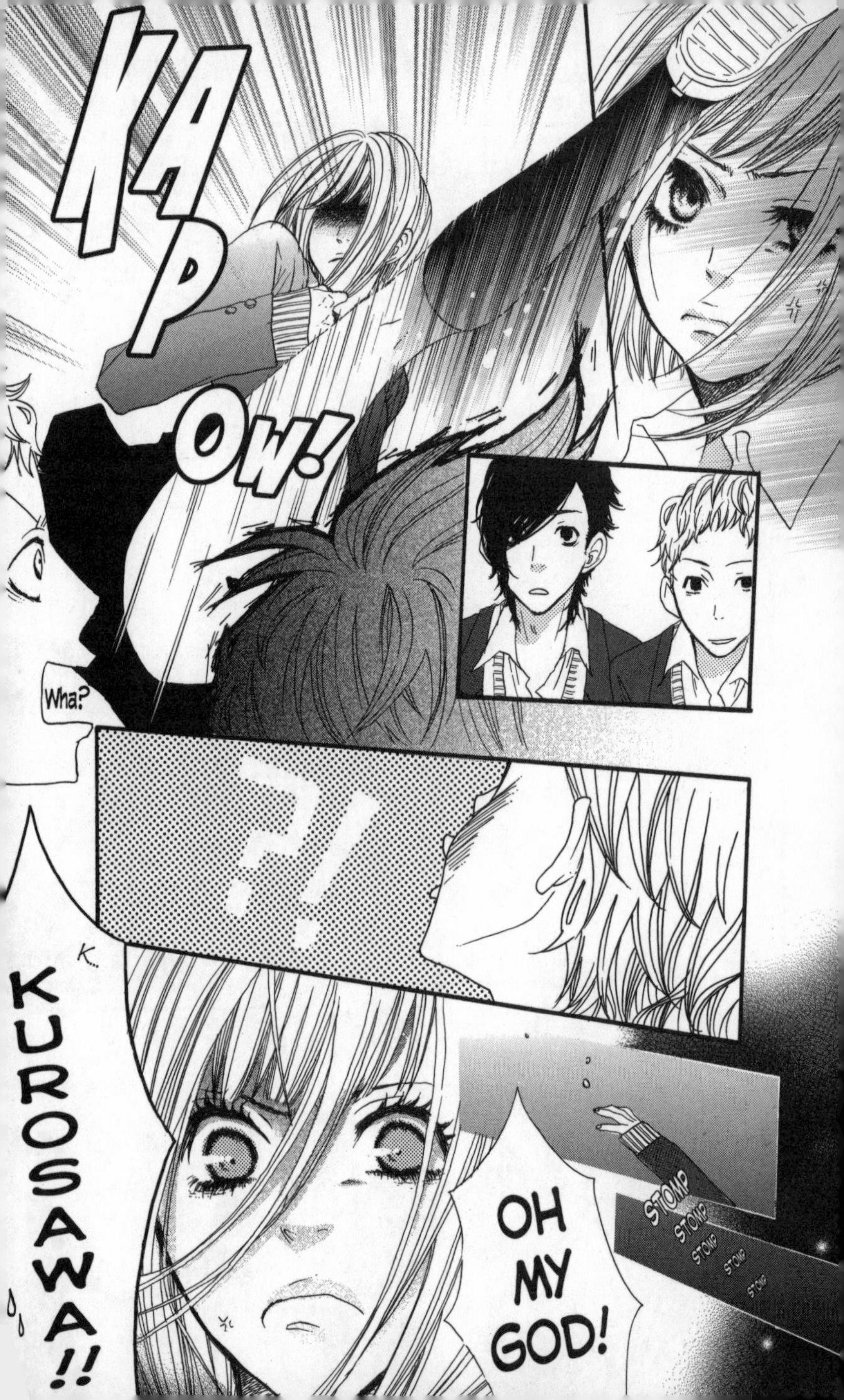
KAPOW
OW!
Wha?
?!
STOMP STOMP STOMP STOMP STOMP
OH MY GOD!
K...
KUROSAWA!!

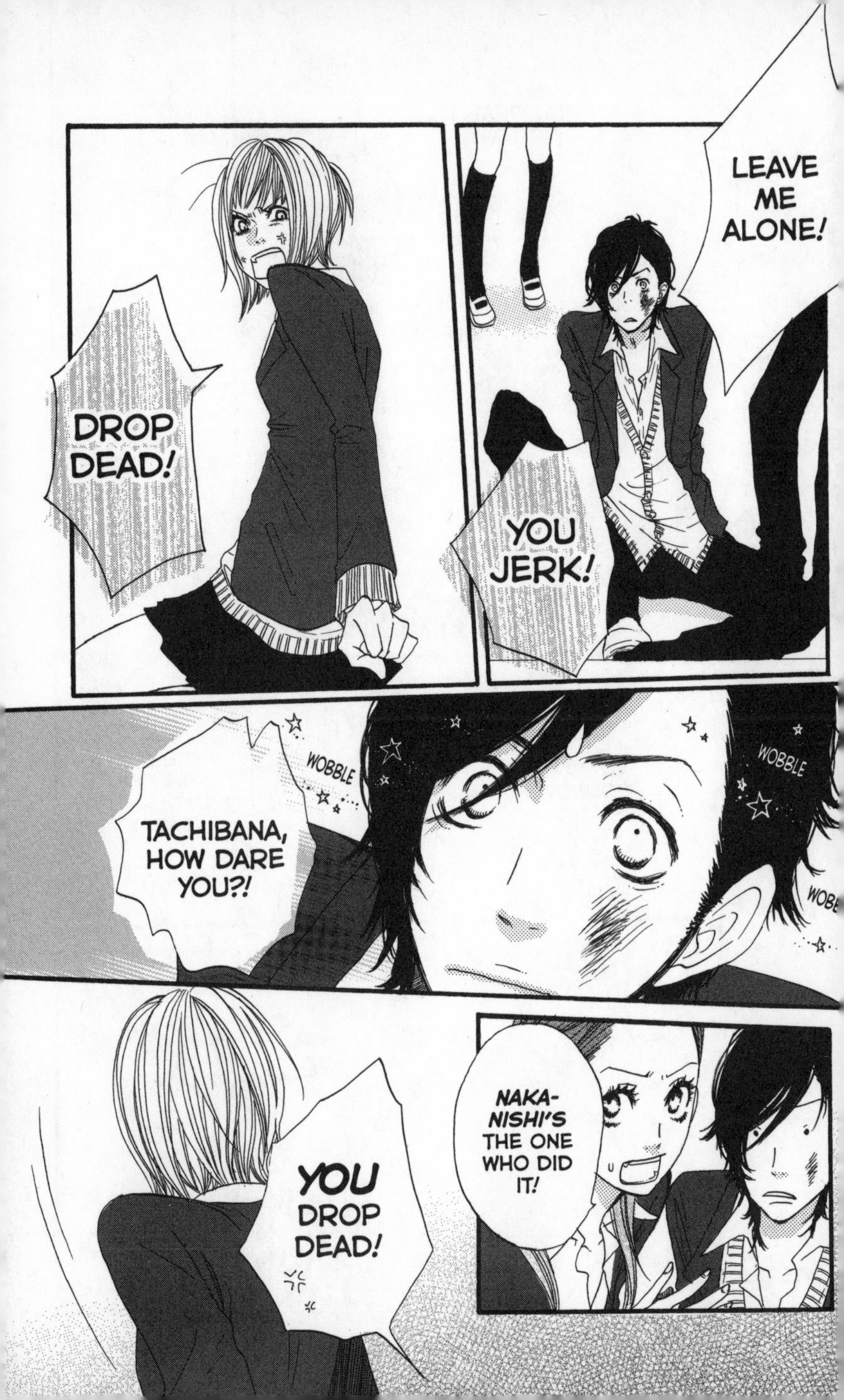
LEAVE ME ALONE!
YOU JERK!
DROP DEAD!
WOBBLE
WOBBLE
TACHIBANA, HOW DARE YOU?!
NAKA-NISHI'S THE ONE WHO DID IT!
YOU DROP DEAD!

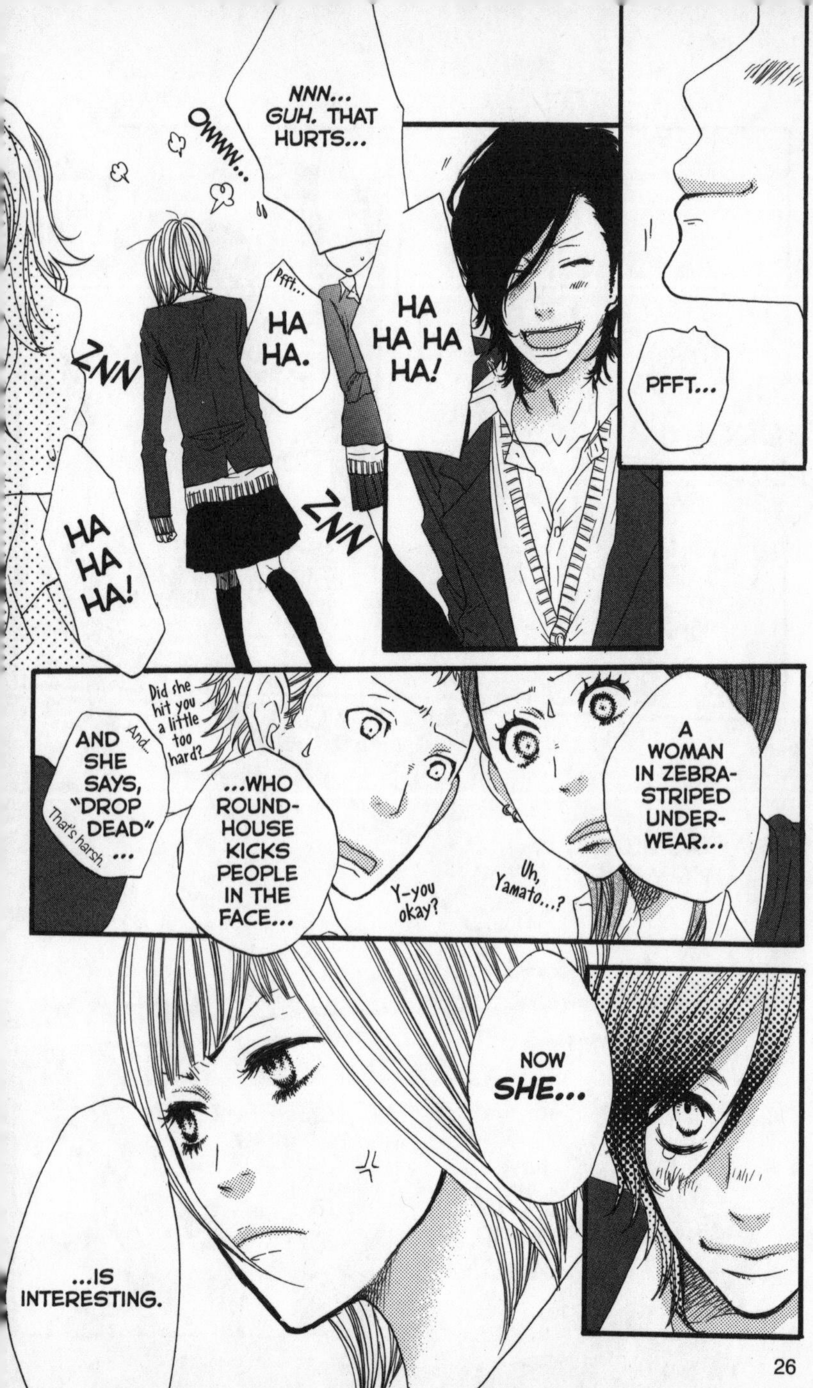
PFFT...
HA HA HA HA!
NNN... GUH. THAT HURTS...
OWWW...
Pfft...
HA HA.
ZNN
ZNN
HA HA HA!
A WOMAN IN ZEBRA-STRIPED UNDERWEAR...
Uh, Yamato...?
Y-you okay?
...WHO ROUNDHOUSE KICKS PEOPLE IN THE FACE...
Did she hit you a little too hard?
And...
AND SHE SAYS, "DROP DEAD"...
That's harsh.
NOW SHE...
...IS INTERESTING.

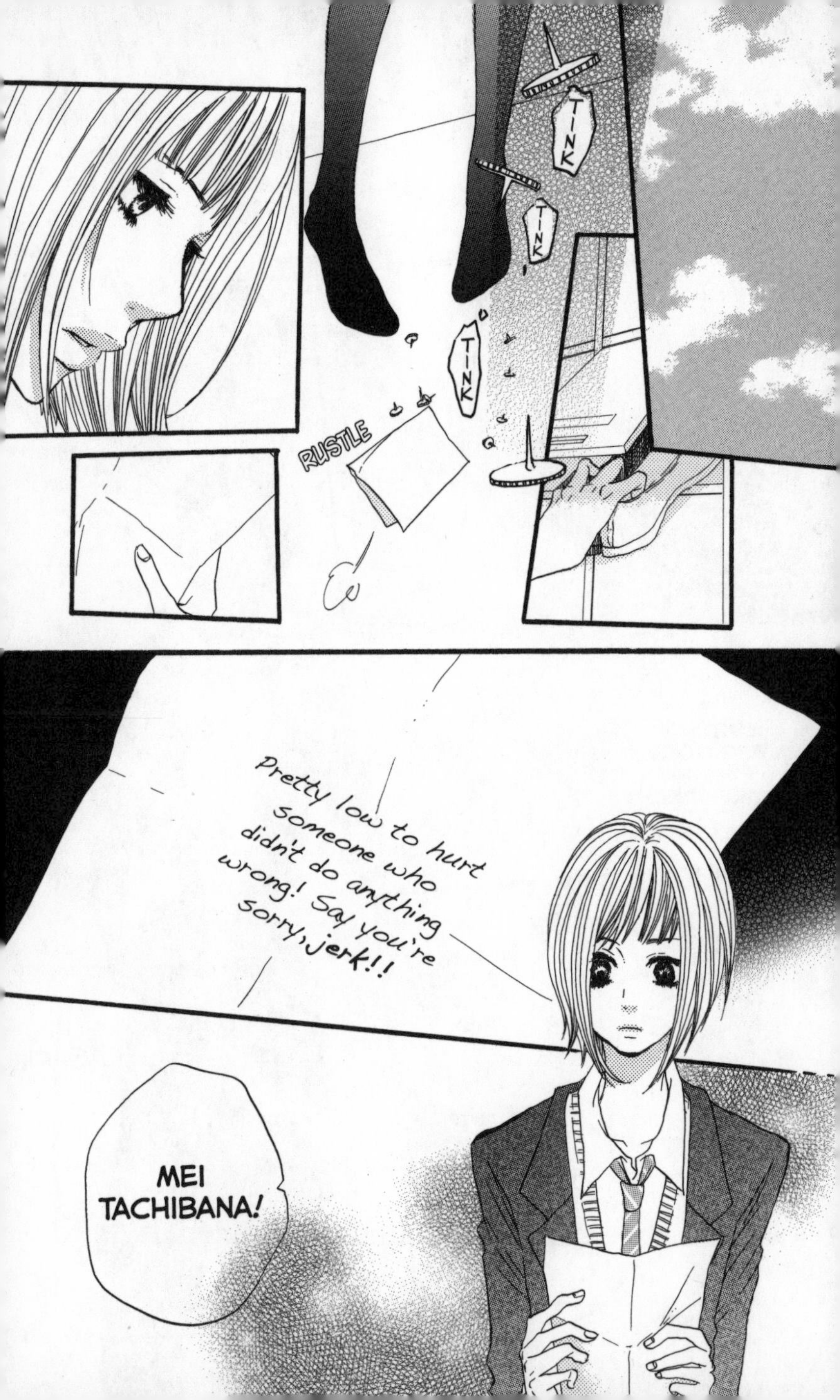
TINK
TINK
TINK
RUSTLE
Pretty low to hurt someone who didn't do anything wrong! Say you're sorry, jerk!!
MEI TACHIBANA!

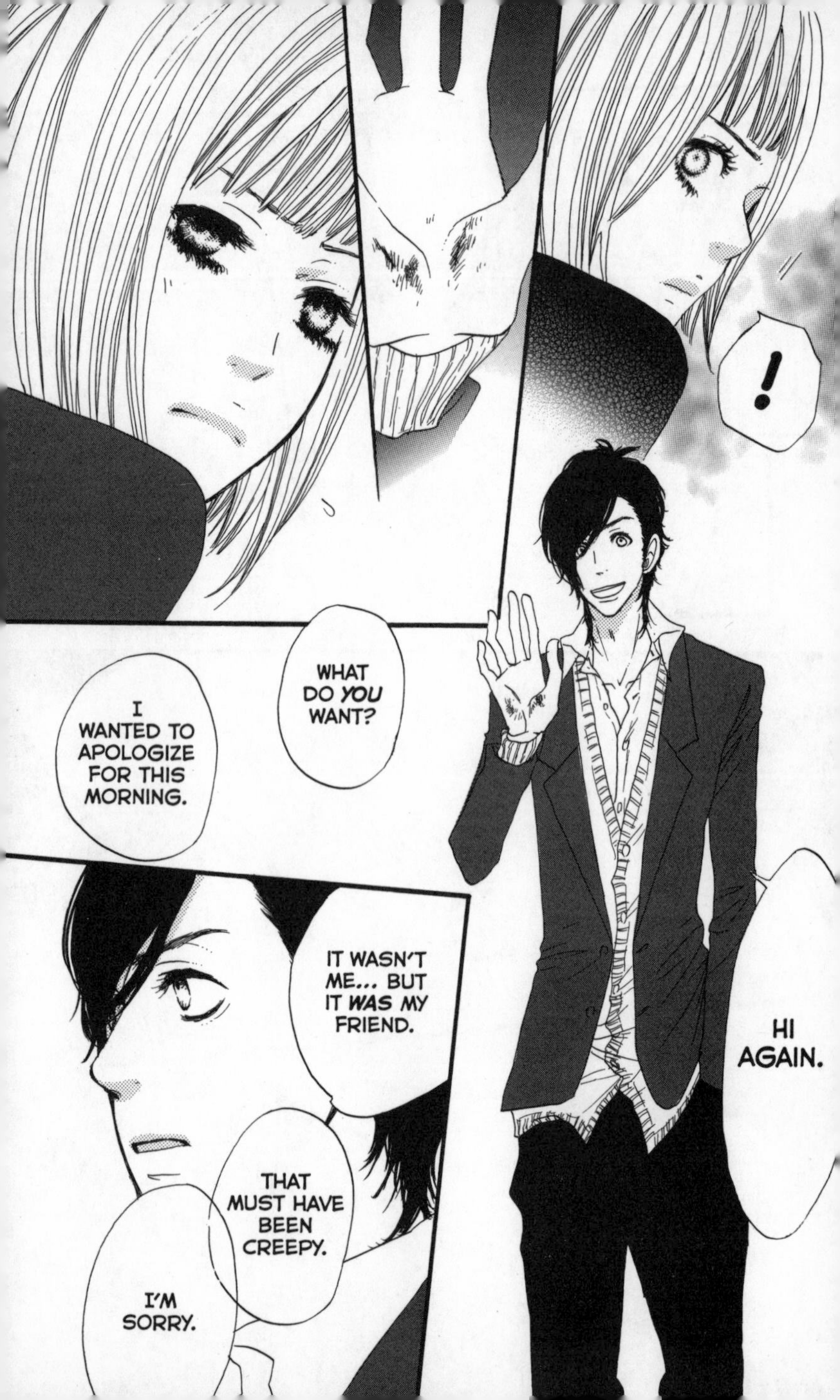
!
HI AGAIN.
WHAT DO *YOU* WANT?
I WANTED TO APOLOGIZE FOR THIS MORNING.
IT WASN'T ME... BUT IT *WAS* MY FRIEND.
THAT MUST HAVE BEEN CREEPY.
I'M SORRY.

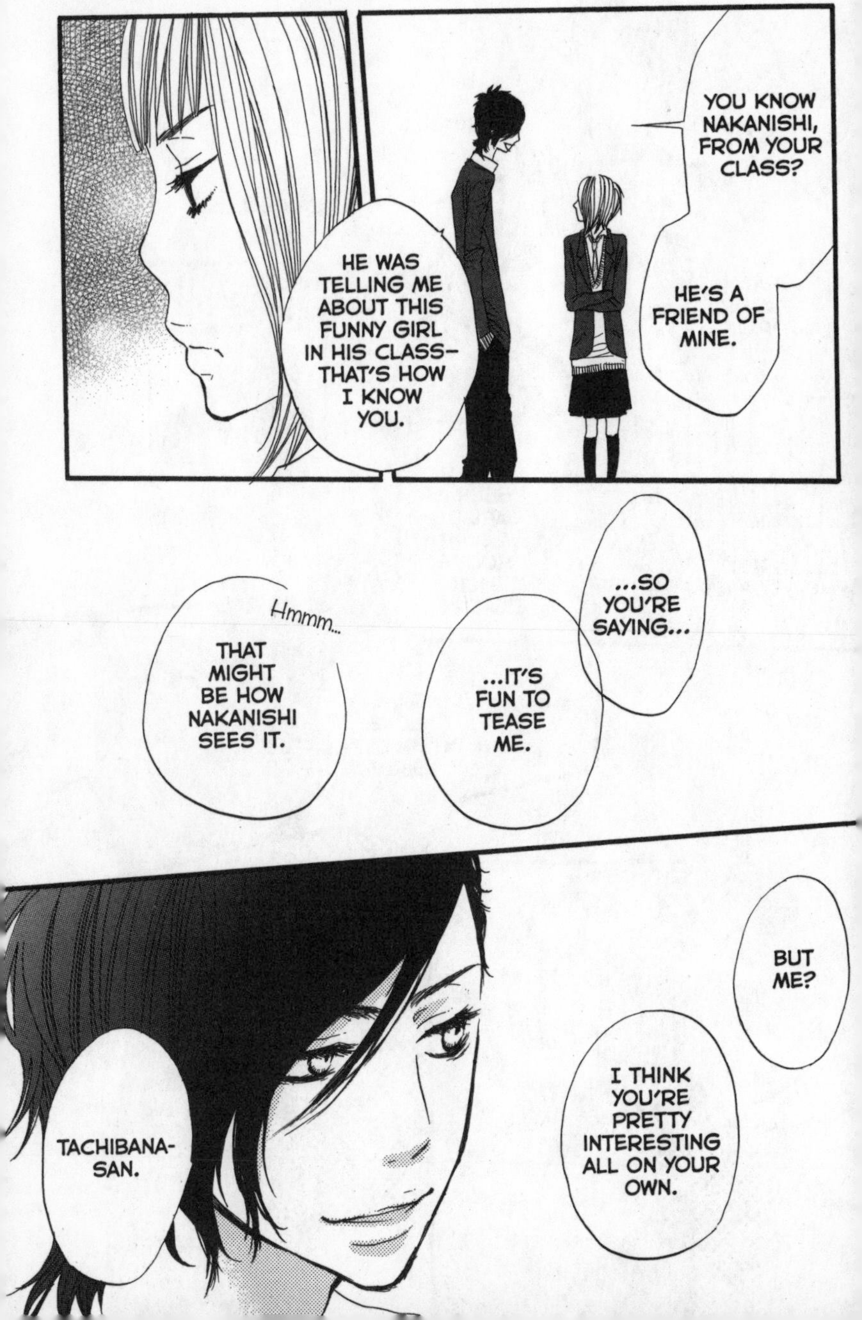
YOU KNOW NAKANISHI, FROM YOUR CLASS?
HE'S A FRIEND OF MINE.
HE WAS TELLING ME ABOUT THIS FUNNY GIRL IN HIS CLASS— THAT'S HOW I KNOW YOU.
...SO YOU'RE SAYING...
...IT'S FUN TO TEASE ME.
Hmmm...
THAT MIGHT BE HOW NAKANISHI SEES IT.
BUT ME?
I THINK YOU'RE PRETTY INTERESTING ALL ON YOUR OWN.
TACHIBANA-SAN.

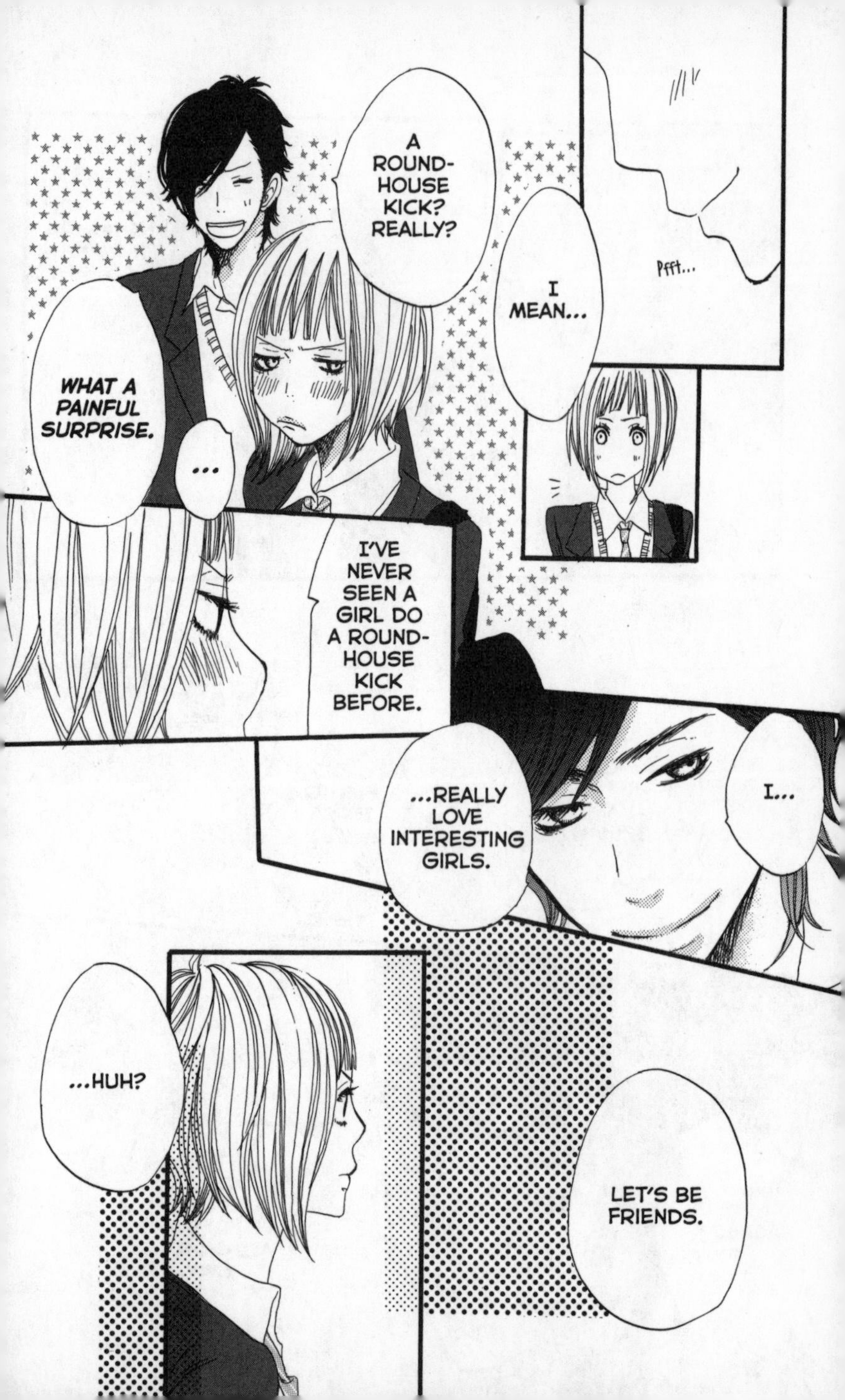
Pfft...
I MEAN...
A ROUND-HOUSE KICK? REALLY?
WHAT A PAINFUL SURPRISE.
...
I'VE NEVER SEEN A GIRL DO A ROUND-HOUSE KICK BEFORE.
I...
...REALLY LOVE INTERESTING GIRLS.
LET'S BE FRIENDS.
...HUH?

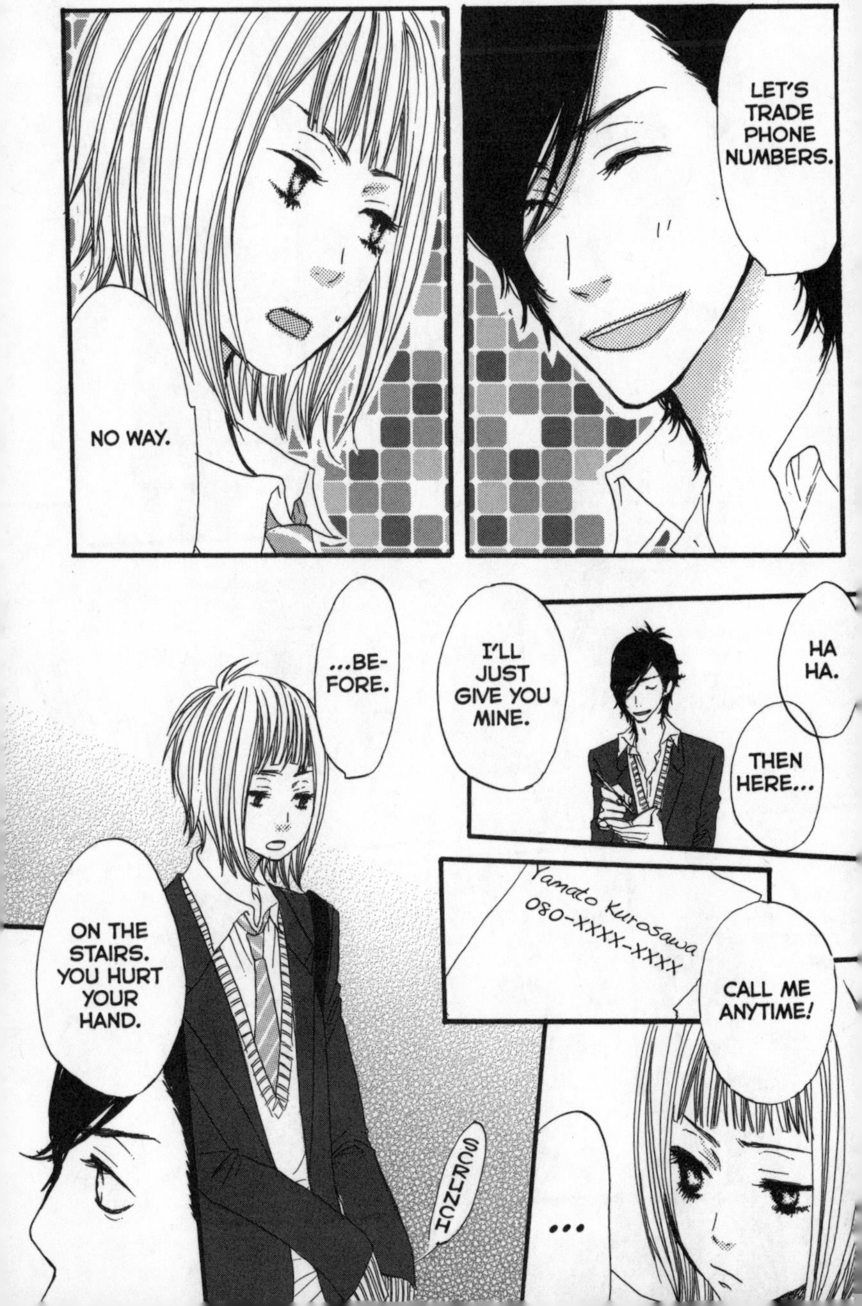
LET'S TRADE PHONE NUMBERS.
NO WAY.
HA HA.
THEN HERE...
I'LL JUST GIVE YOU MINE.
Yamato Kurosawa
080-XXXX-XXXX
CALL ME ANYTIME!
...
...BE-FORE.
ON THE STAIRS. YOU HURT YOUR HAND.
SCRUNCH

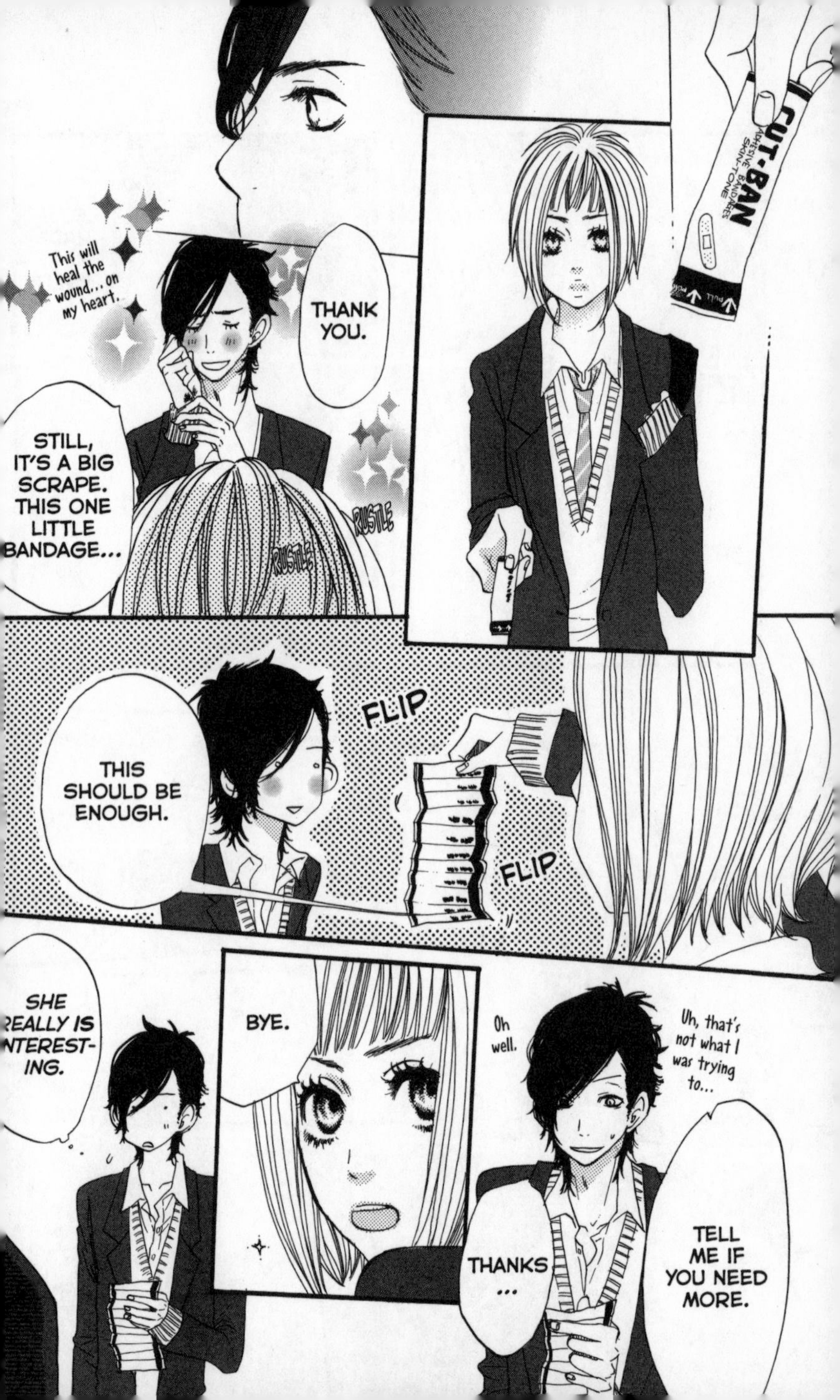
CUT-BAN
THANK YOU.
This will heal the wound... on my heart.
STILL, IT'S A BIG SCRAPE. THIS ONE LITTLE BANDAGE...
RUSTLE
RUSTLE
FLIP
THIS SHOULD BE ENOUGH.
FLIP
Uh, that's not what I was trying to...
Oh well.
TELL ME IF YOU NEED MORE.
THANKS...
BYE.
SHE
EALLY IS
NTEREST-
ING.

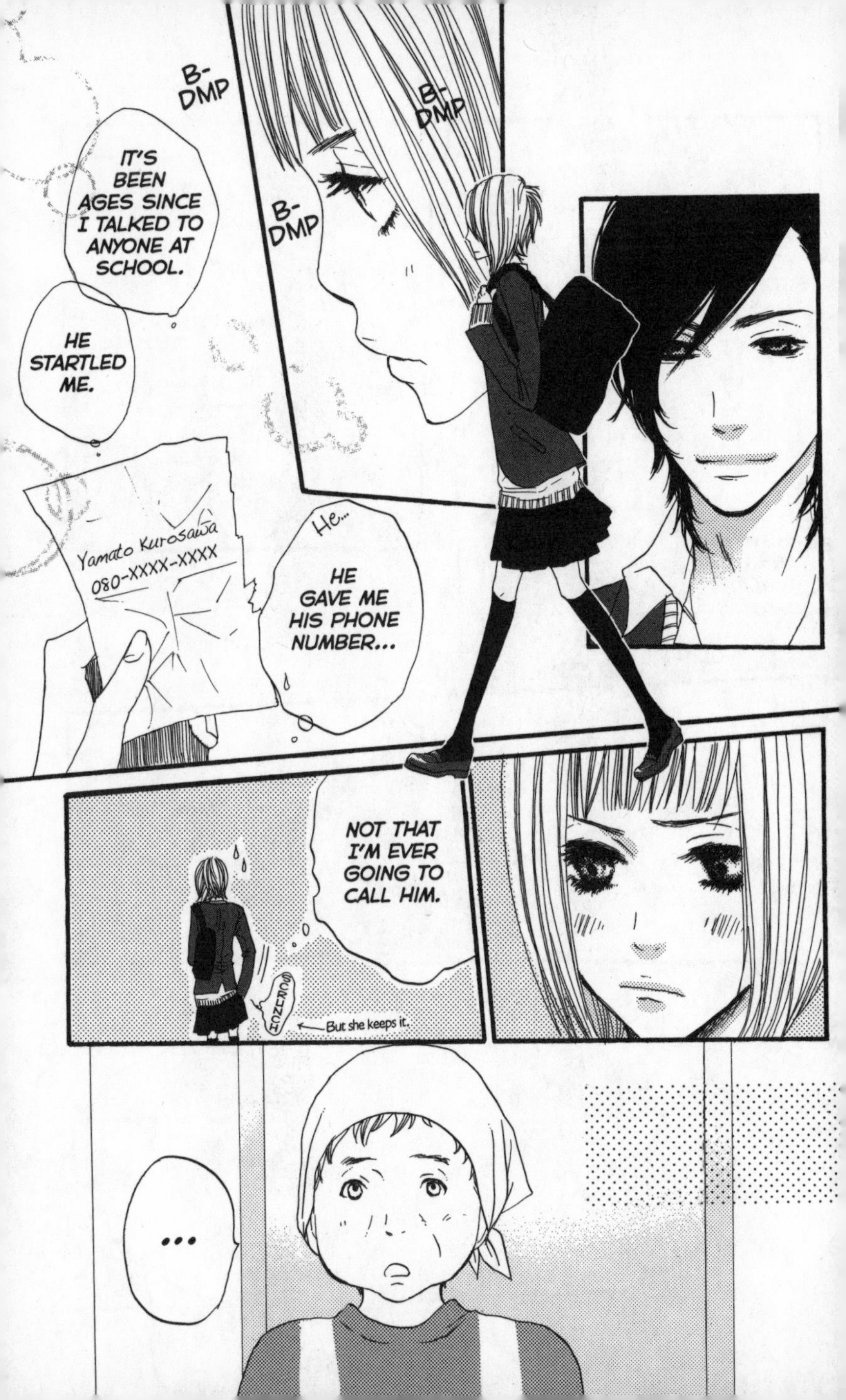
B-DMP
B-DMP
B-DMP
IT'S BEEN AGES SINCE I TALKED TO ANYONE AT SCHOOL.
HE STARTLED ME.
He...
HE GAVE ME HIS PHONE NUMBER...
Yamato Kurosawa
080-XXXX-XXXX
NOT THAT I'M EVER GOING TO CALL HIM.
SCRUNCH
But she keeps it.
...

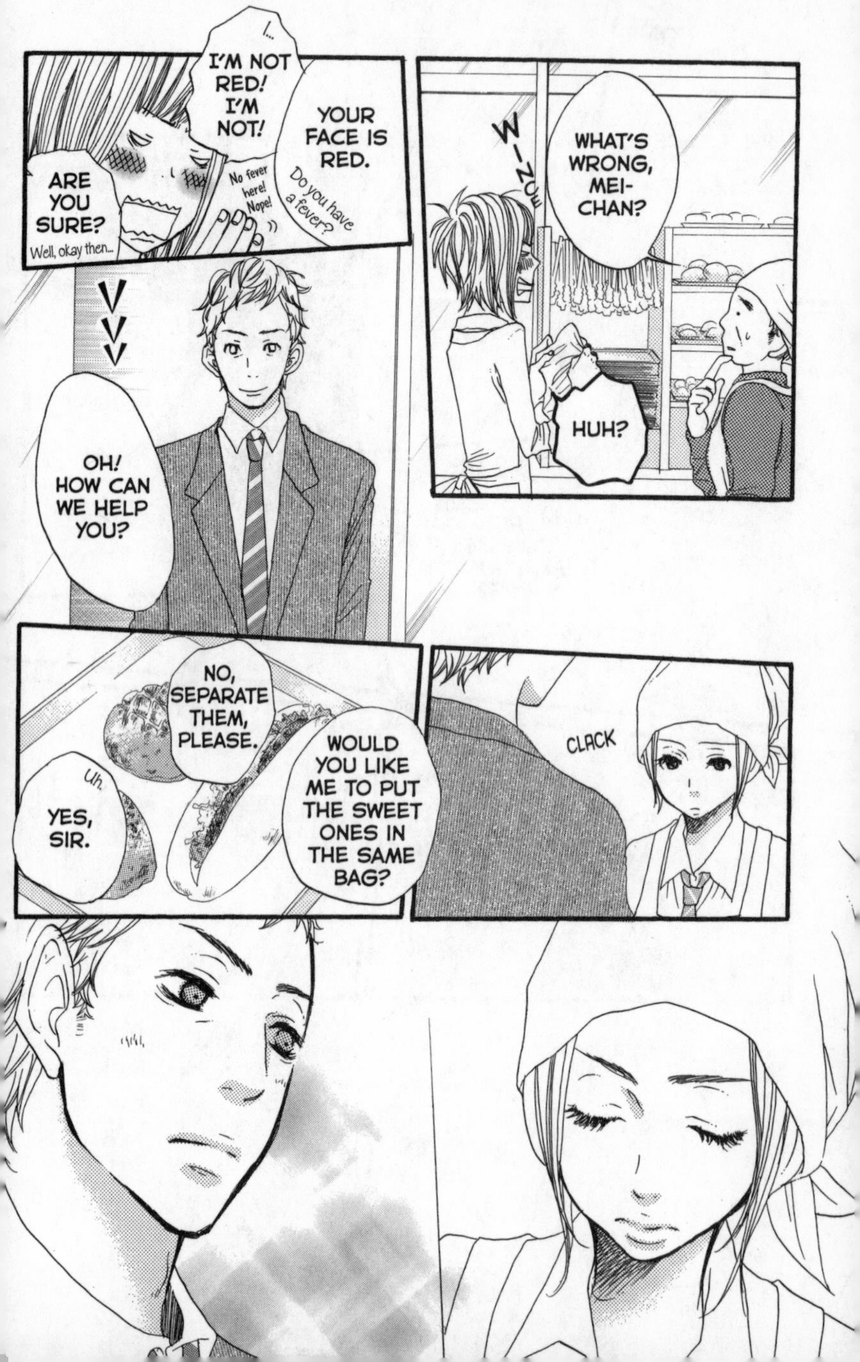
WHAT'S WRONG, MEI-CHAN?
W-ZOE
HUH?
YOUR FACE IS RED.
Do you have a fever?
I... I'M NOT RED! I'M NOT!
No fever here! Nope!
ARE YOU SURE?
Well, okay then...
OH! HOW CAN WE HELP YOU?
CLACK
WOULD YOU LIKE ME TO PUT THE SWEET ONES IN THE SAME BAG?
NO, SEPARATE THEM, PLEASE.
Uh.
YES, SIR.

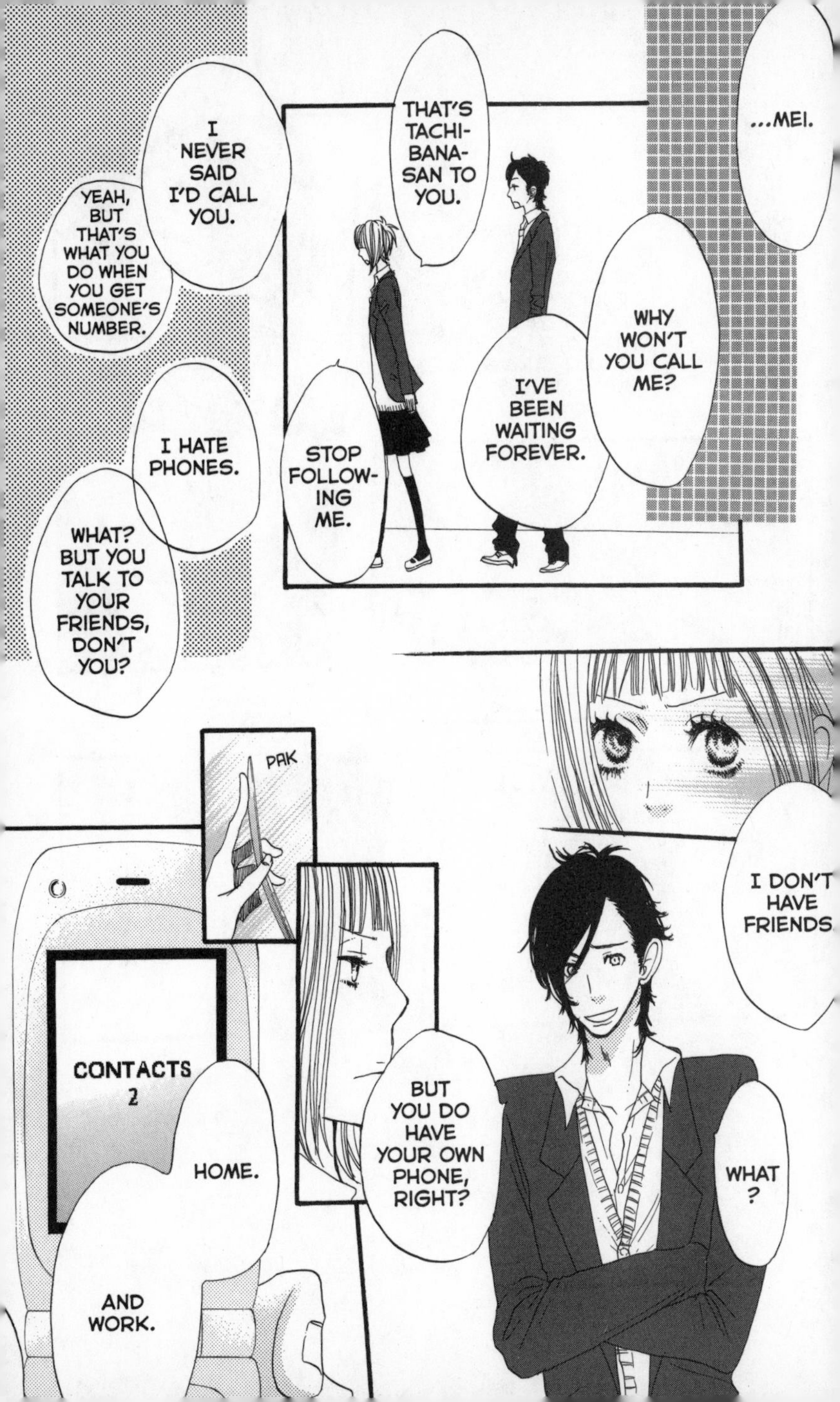
...MEI.
THAT'S TACHIBANA-SAN TO YOU.
WHY WON'T YOU CALL ME?
I'VE BEEN WAITING FOREVER.
STOP FOLLOWING ME.
I NEVER SAID I'D CALL YOU.
YEAH, BUT THAT'S WHAT YOU DO WHEN YOU GET SOMEONE'S NUMBER.
I HATE PHONES.
WHAT? BUT YOU TALK TO YOUR FRIENDS, DON'T YOU?
PAK
I DON'T HAVE FRIENDS.
WHAT?
BUT YOU DO HAVE YOUR OWN PHONE, RIGHT?
CONTACTS 2
HOME.
AND WORK.

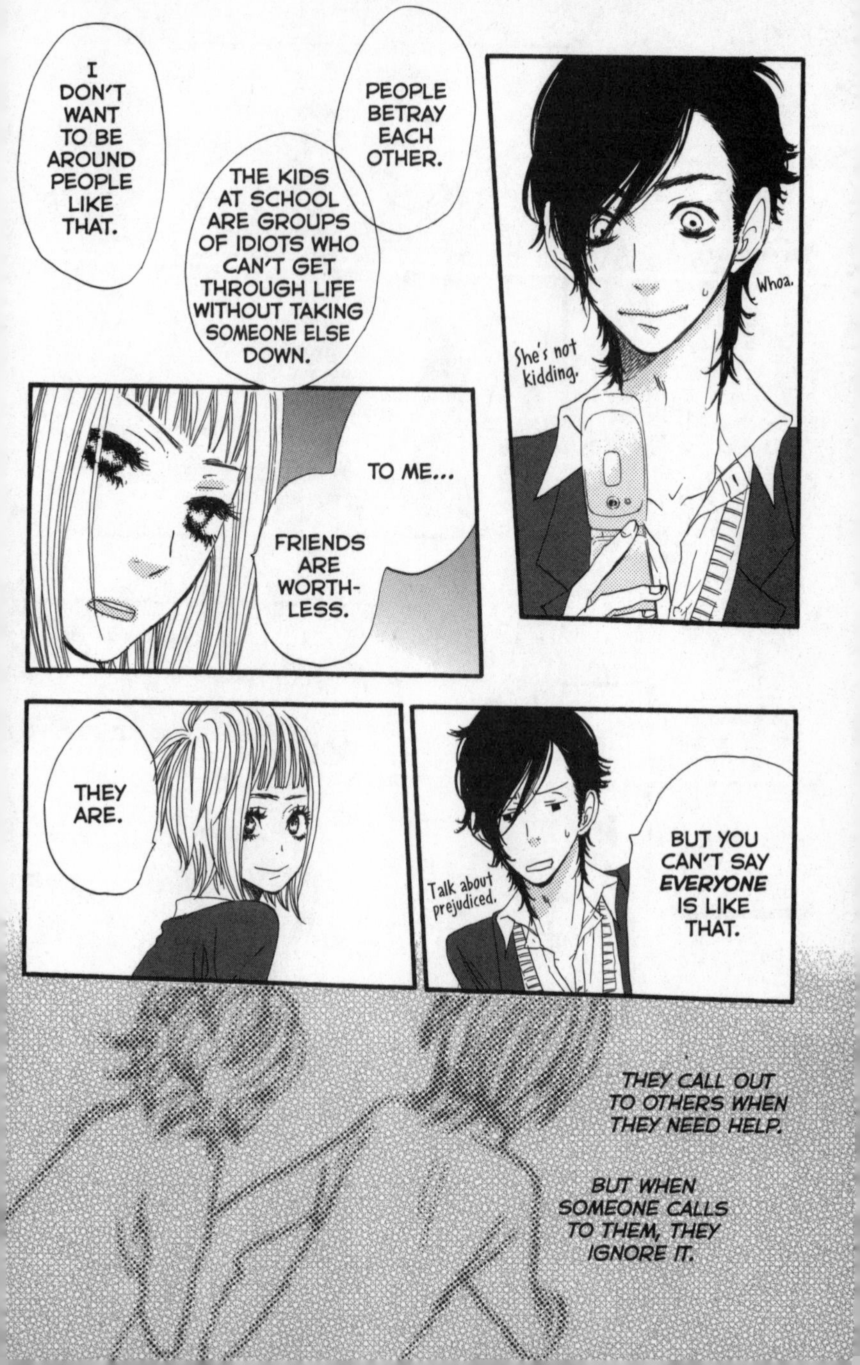

Whoa.
She's not kidding.
PEOPLE BETRAY EACH OTHER.
THE KIDS AT SCHOOL ARE GROUPS OF IDIOTS WHO CAN'T GET THROUGH LIFE WITHOUT TAKING SOMEONE ELSE DOWN.
I DON'T WANT TO BE AROUND PEOPLE LIKE THAT.
TO ME...
FRIENDS ARE WORTHLESS.
BUT YOU CAN'T SAY **EVERYONE** IS LIKE THAT.
Talk about prejudiced.
THEY ARE.
THEY CALL OUT TO OTHERS WHEN THEY NEED HELP.
BUT WHEN SOMEONE CALLS TO THEM, THEY IGNORE IT.

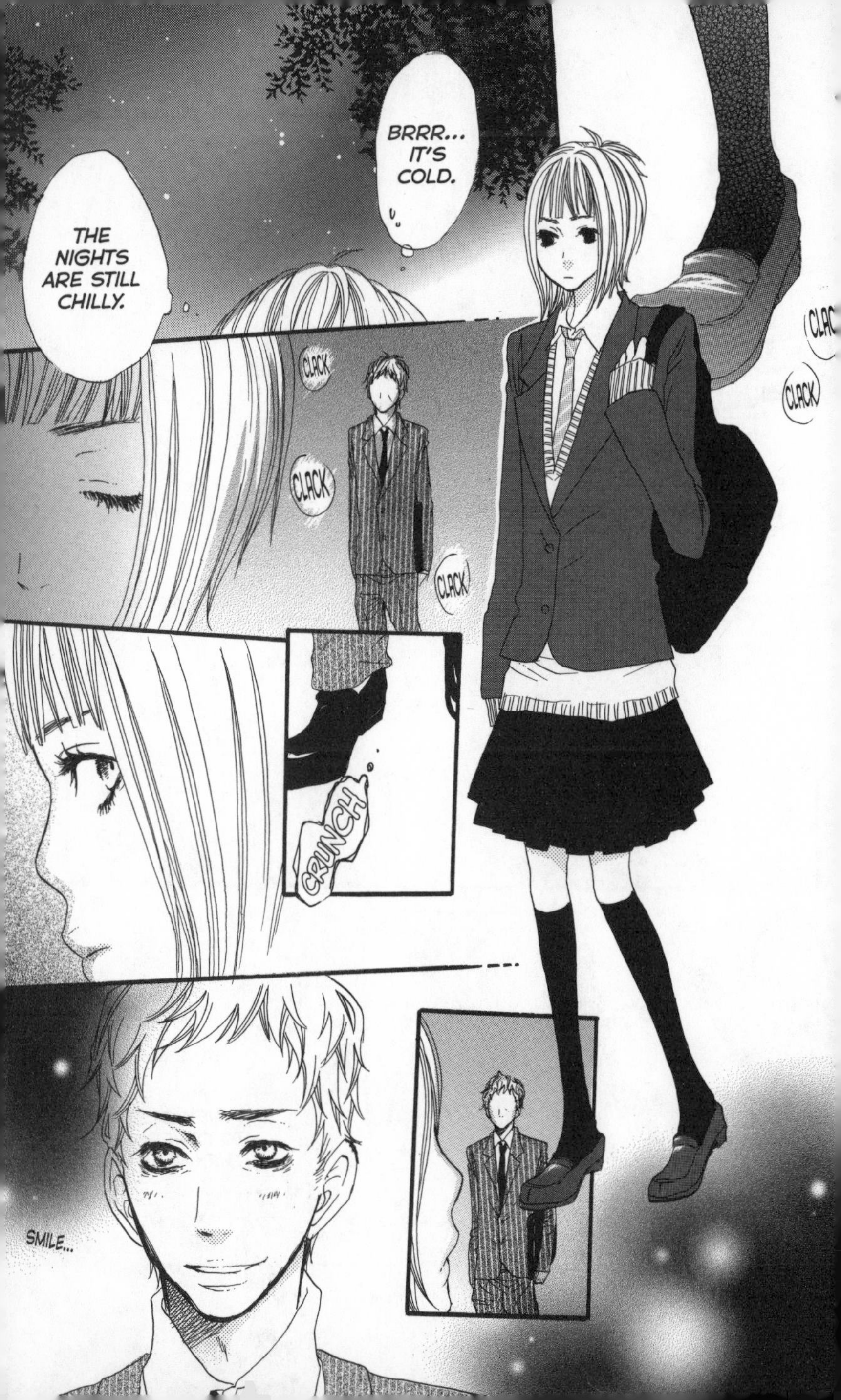

BRRR... IT'S COLD.
THE NIGHTS ARE STILL CHILLY.
CLAC
CLACK
CLACK
CLACK
CLACK
CRUNCH
SMILE...

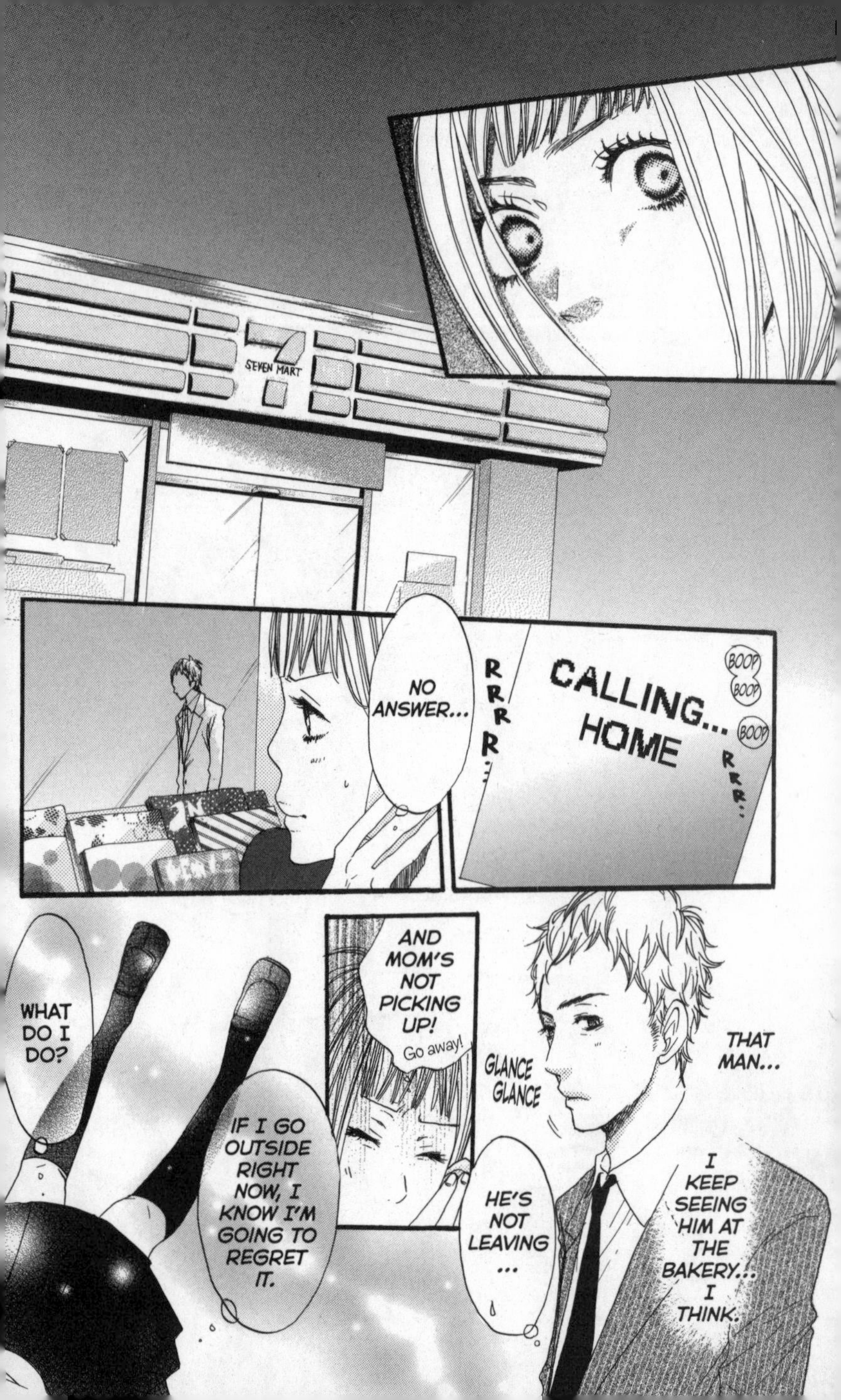
SEVEN MART
CALLING... HOME
BOOP BOOP BOOP
RRR...
NO ANSWER...
RRRR...
THAT MAN...
I KEEP SEEING HIM AT THE BAKERY... I THINK.
GLANCE GLANCE
HE'S NOT LEAVING...
AND MOM'S NOT PICKING UP!
Go away!
WHAT DO I DO?
IF I GO OUTSIDE RIGHT NOW, I KNOW I'M GOING TO REGRET IT.

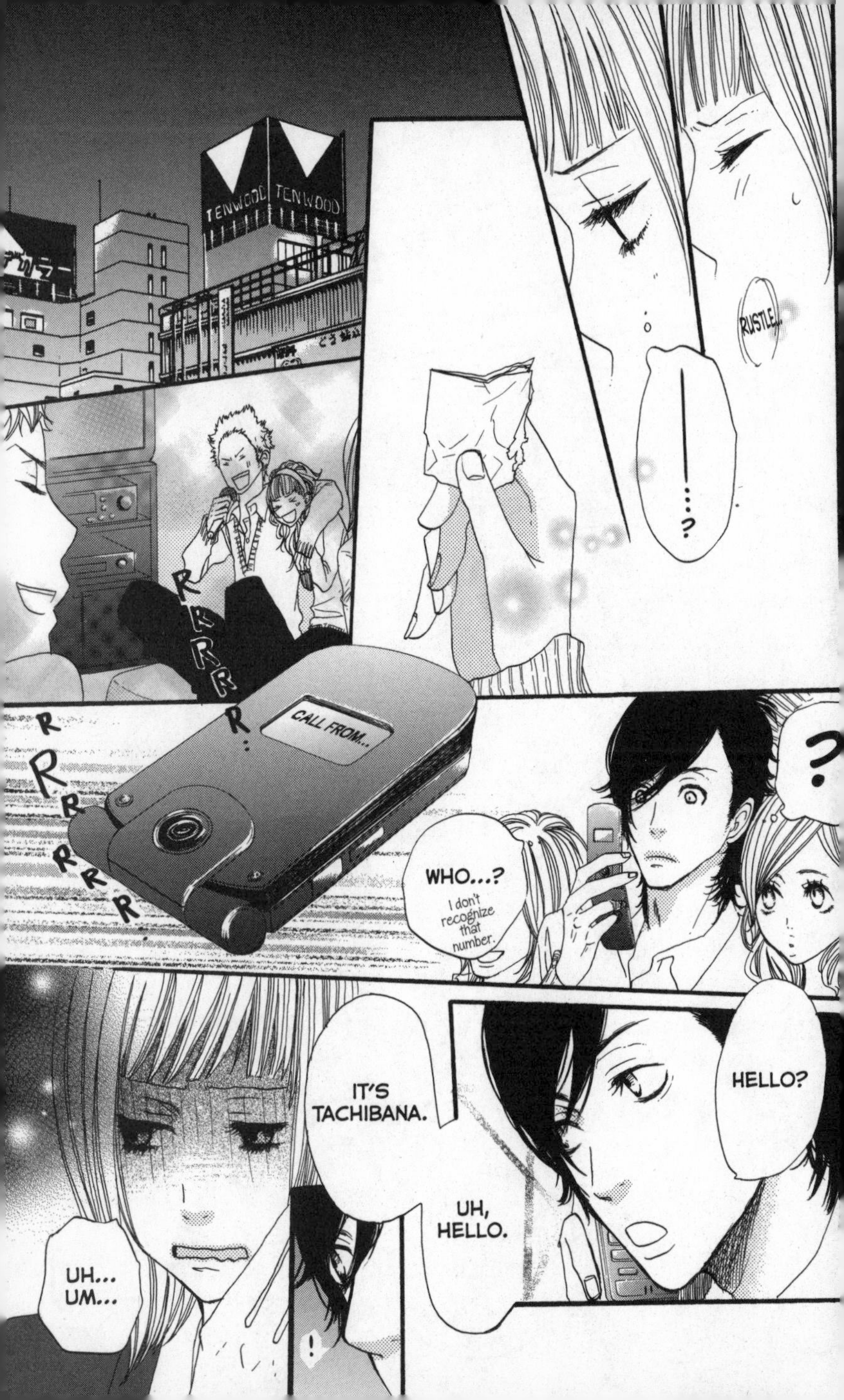
RUSTLE...
......?
TENWOOD
TENWOOD
RRRR
?
WHO...?
I don't recognize that number.
CALL FROM...
RRRRRR
HELLO?
UH... UM...
IT'S TACHIBANA.
!
UH, HELLO.

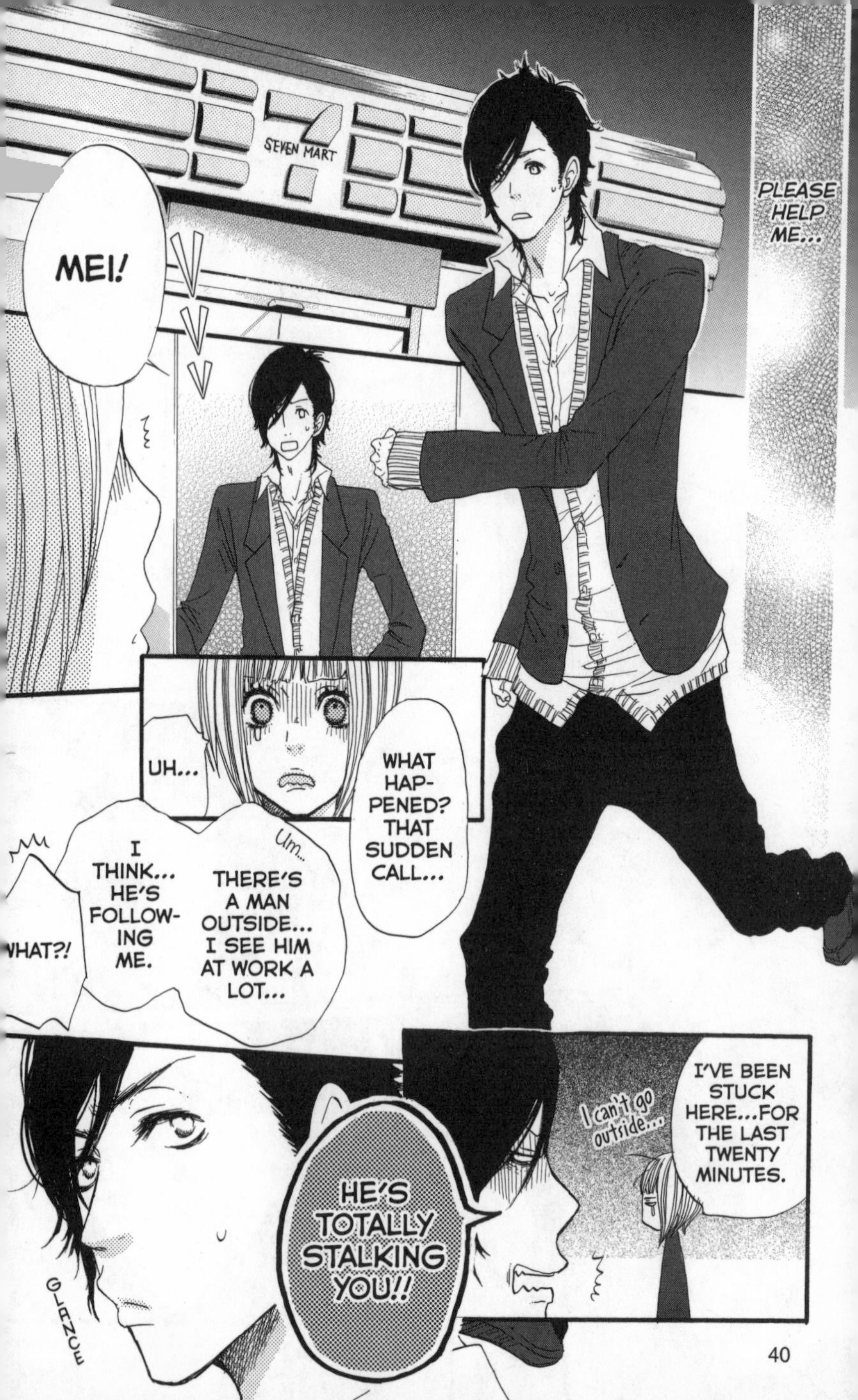

PLEASE HELP ME...
STEVEN MART
MEI!
WHAT HAPPENED? THAT SUDDEN CALL...
UH...
Um..
THERE'S A MAN OUTSIDE... I SEE HIM AT WORK A LOT...
I THINK... HE'S FOLLOWING ME.
WHAT?!
I'VE BEEN STUCK HERE...FOR THE LAST TWENTY MINUTES.
I can't go outside...
HE'S TOTALLY STALKING YOU!!
GLANCE

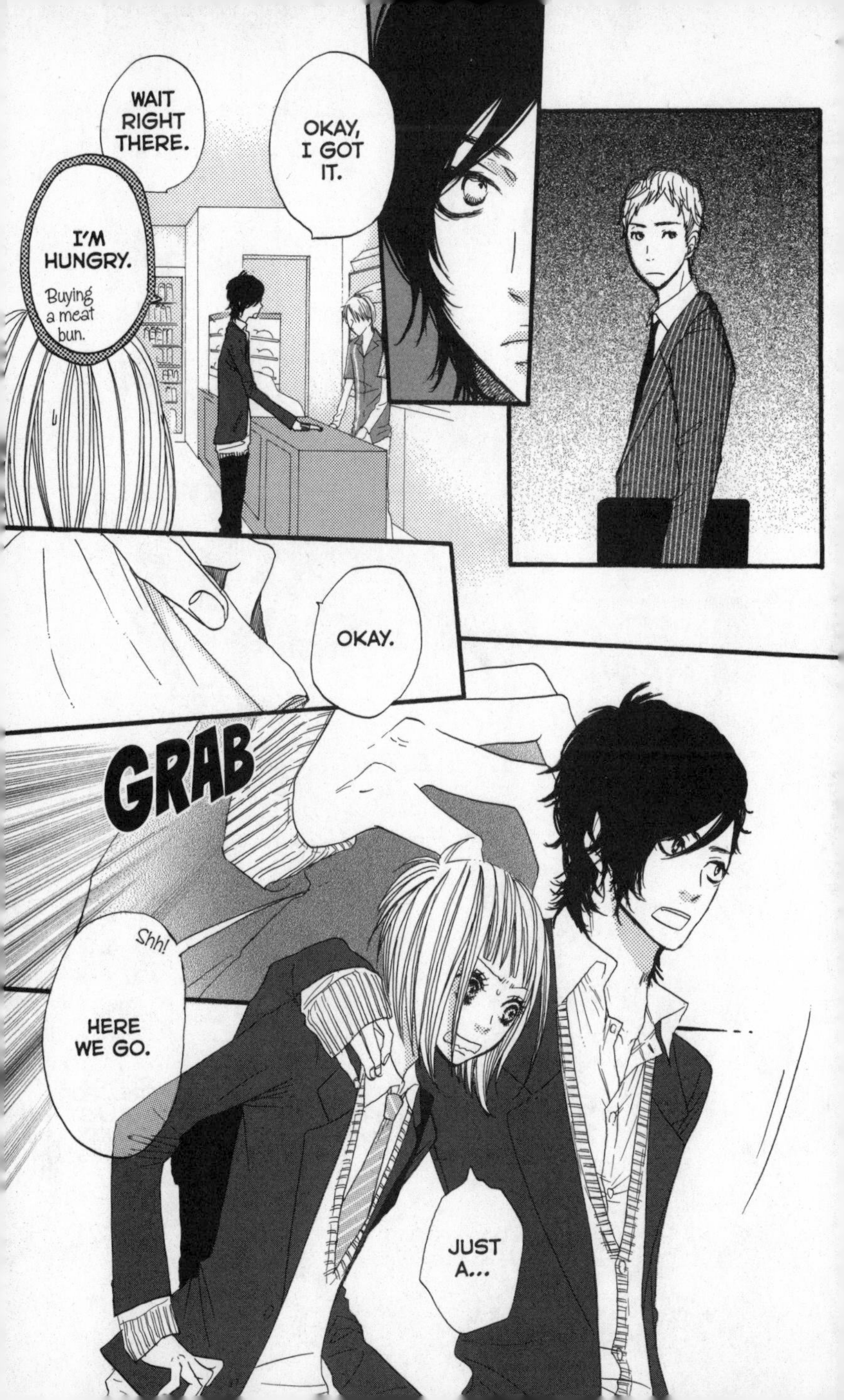

OKAY, I GOT IT.
WAIT RIGHT THERE.
I'M HUNGRY.
Buying a meat bun.
OKAY.
GRAB
Shh!
HERE WE GO.
JUST A...

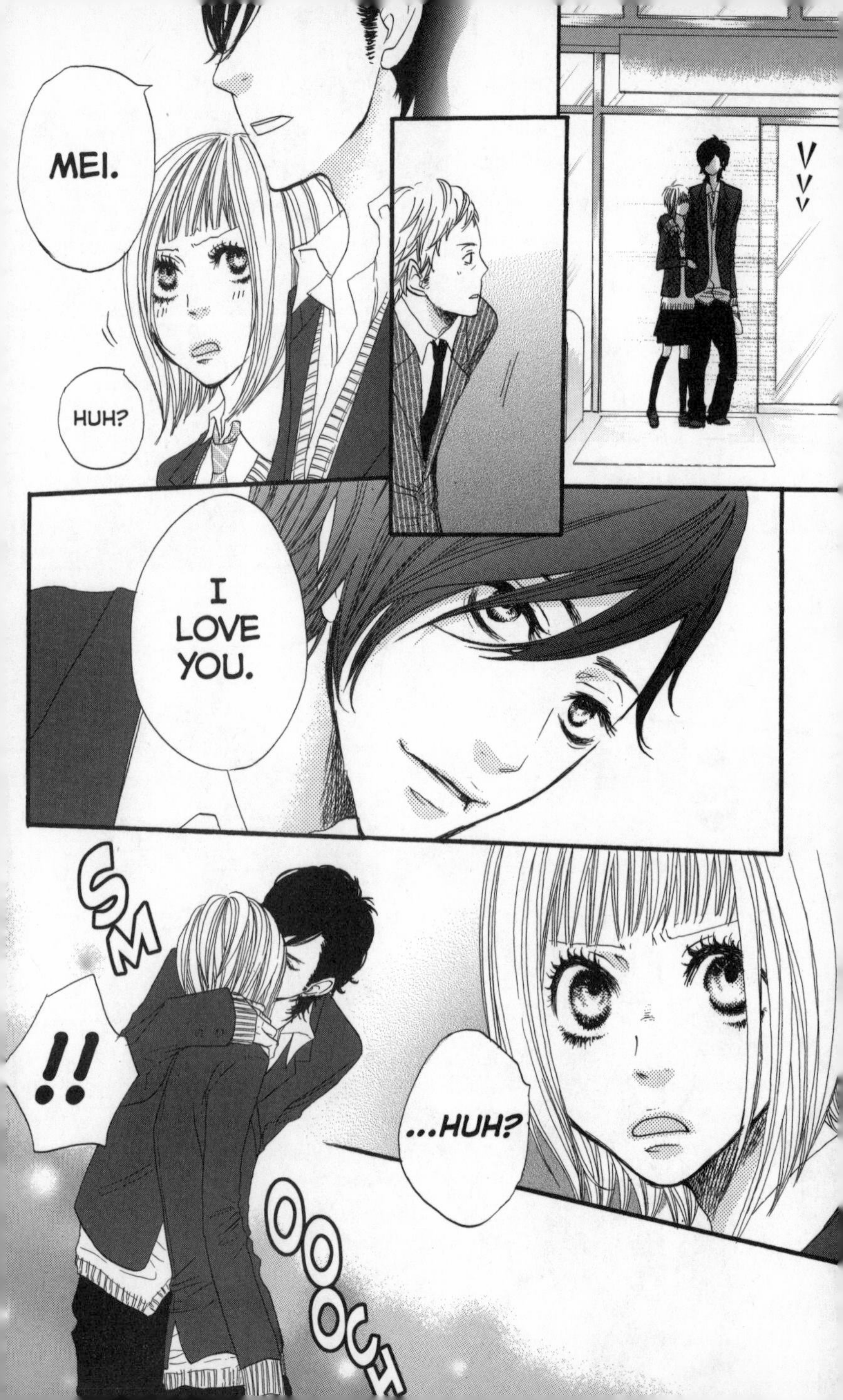
MEI.
HUH?
I LOVE YOU.
...HUH?
SMOOOCH
!!

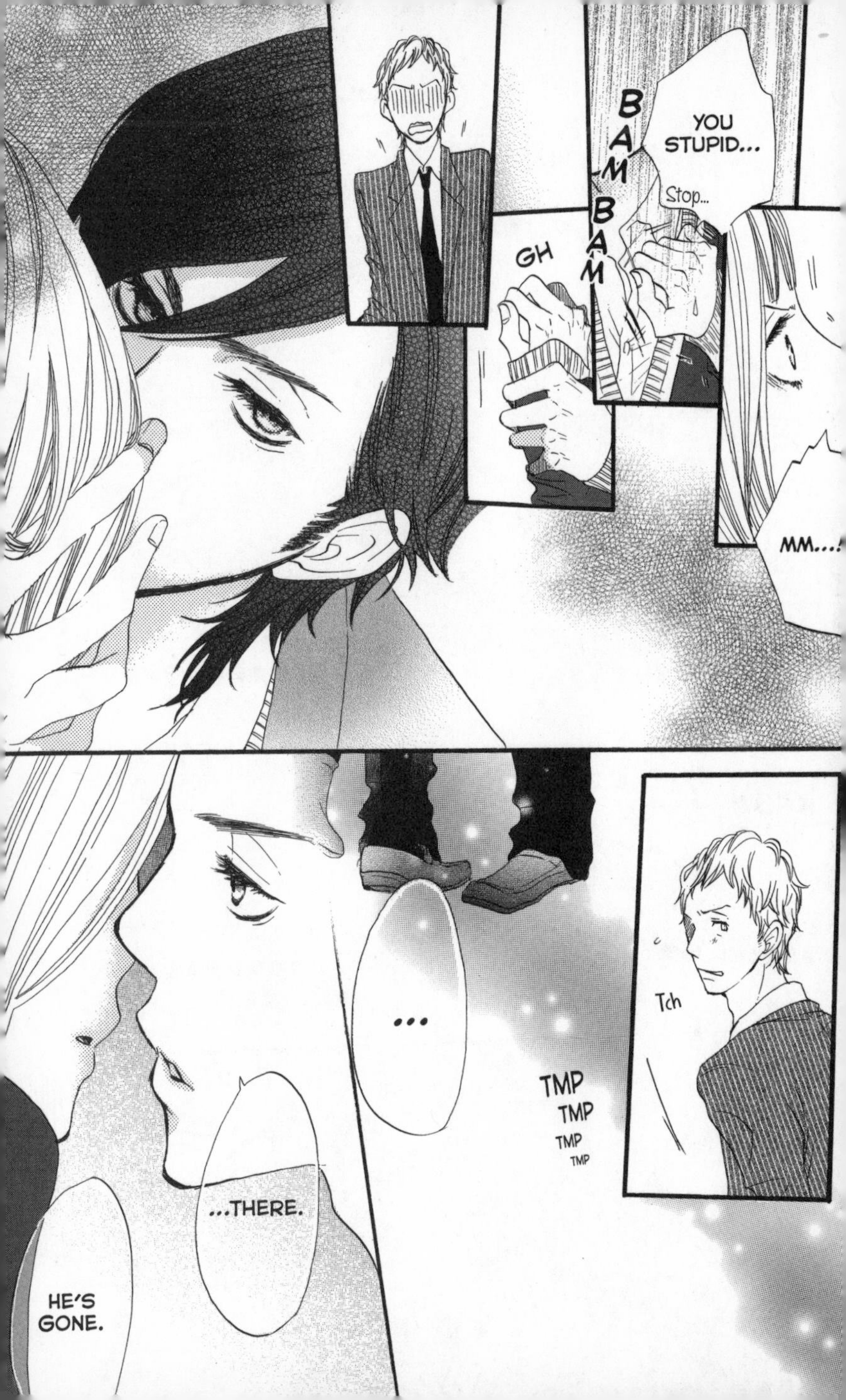

YOU STUPID...
BAM BAM
Stop...
MM...!
GH
Tch
TMP TMP TMP TMP
...
...THERE.
HE'S GONE.

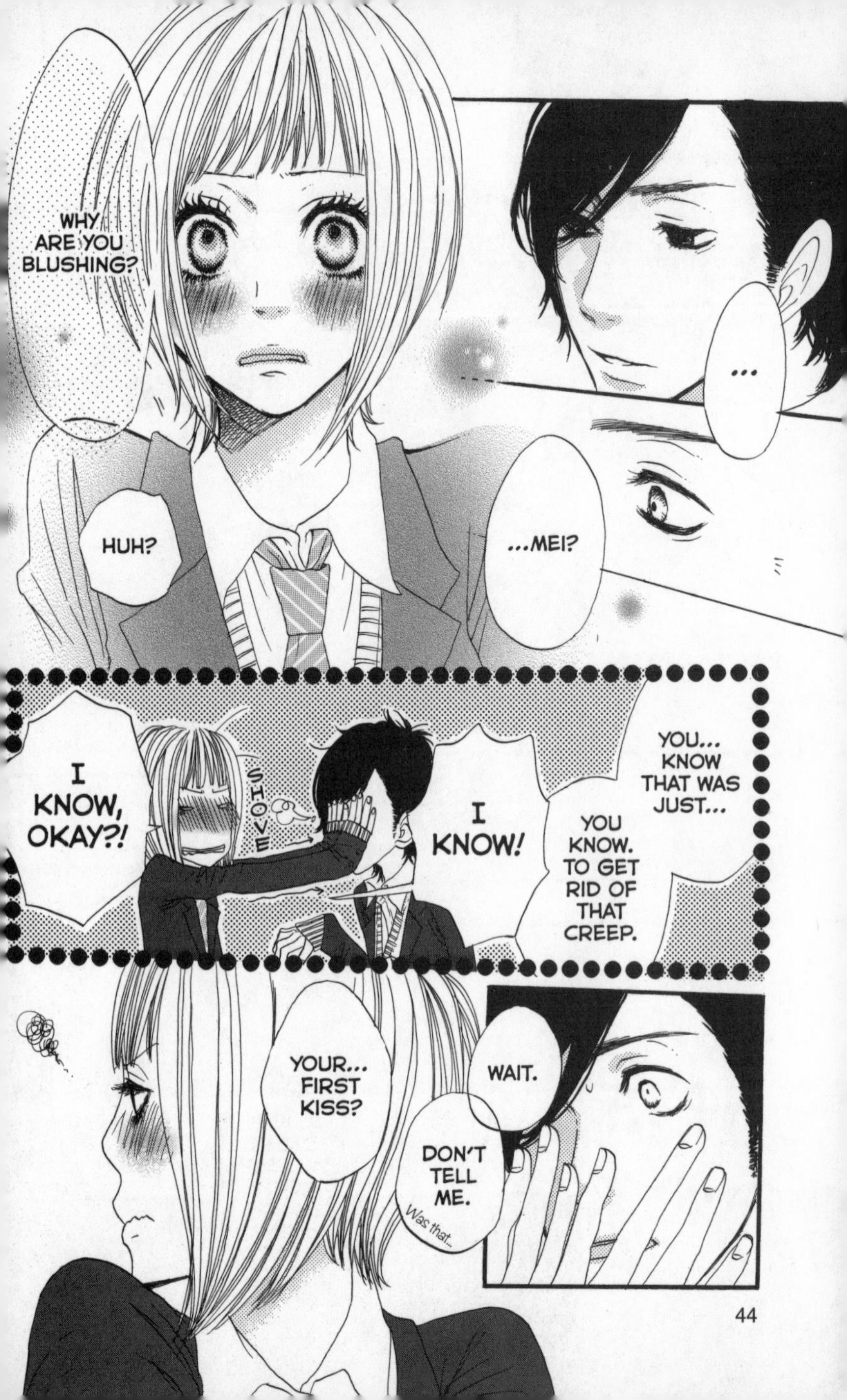
...
...MEI?
WHY ARE YOU BLUSHING?
HUH?
YOU... KNOW THAT WAS JUST...
YOU KNOW. TO GET RID OF THAT CREEP.
I KNOW!
SHOVE
I KNOW, OKAY?!
WAIT.
DON'T TELL ME.
Was that...
YOUR... FIRST KISS?

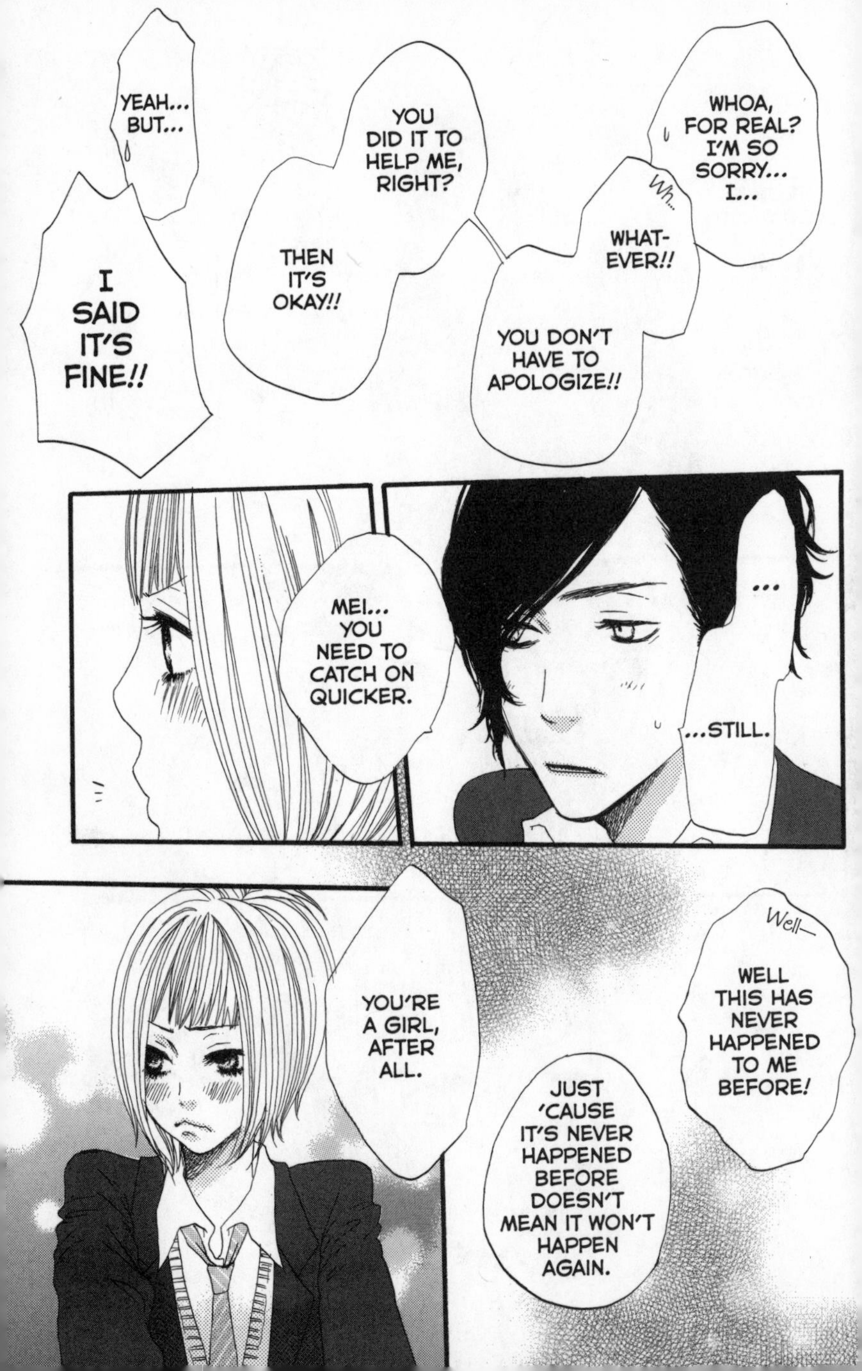
WHOA, FOR REAL? I'M SO SORRY... I...
Wh...
WHAT-EVER!!
YOU DON'T HAVE TO APOLOGIZE!!
YOU DID IT TO HELP ME, RIGHT?
THEN IT'S OKAY!!
YEAH... BUT...
I SAID IT'S FINE!!
...
...STILL.
MEI... YOU NEED TO CATCH ON QUICKER.
Well—
WELL THIS HAS NEVER HAPPENED TO ME BEFORE!
JUST 'CAUSE IT'S NEVER HAPPENED BEFORE DOESN'T MEAN IT WON'T HAPPEN AGAIN.
YOU'RE A GIRL, AFTER ALL.

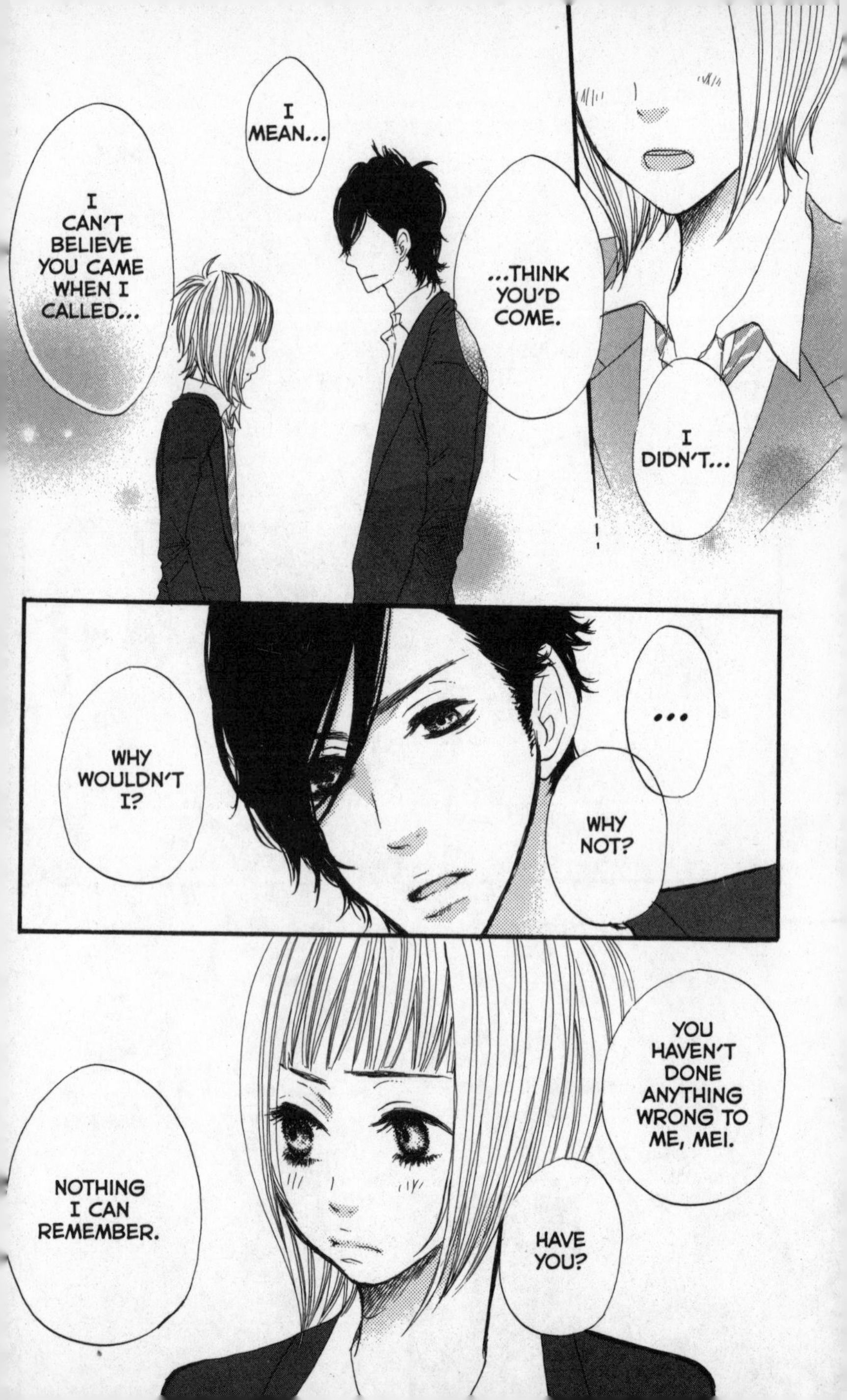
I DIDN'T...
...THINK YOU'D COME.
I MEAN...
I CAN'T BELIEVE YOU CAME WHEN I CALLED...
...
WHY NOT?
WHY WOULDN'T I?
YOU HAVEN'T DONE ANYTHING WRONG TO ME, MEI.
HAVE YOU?
NOTHING I CAN REMEMBER.

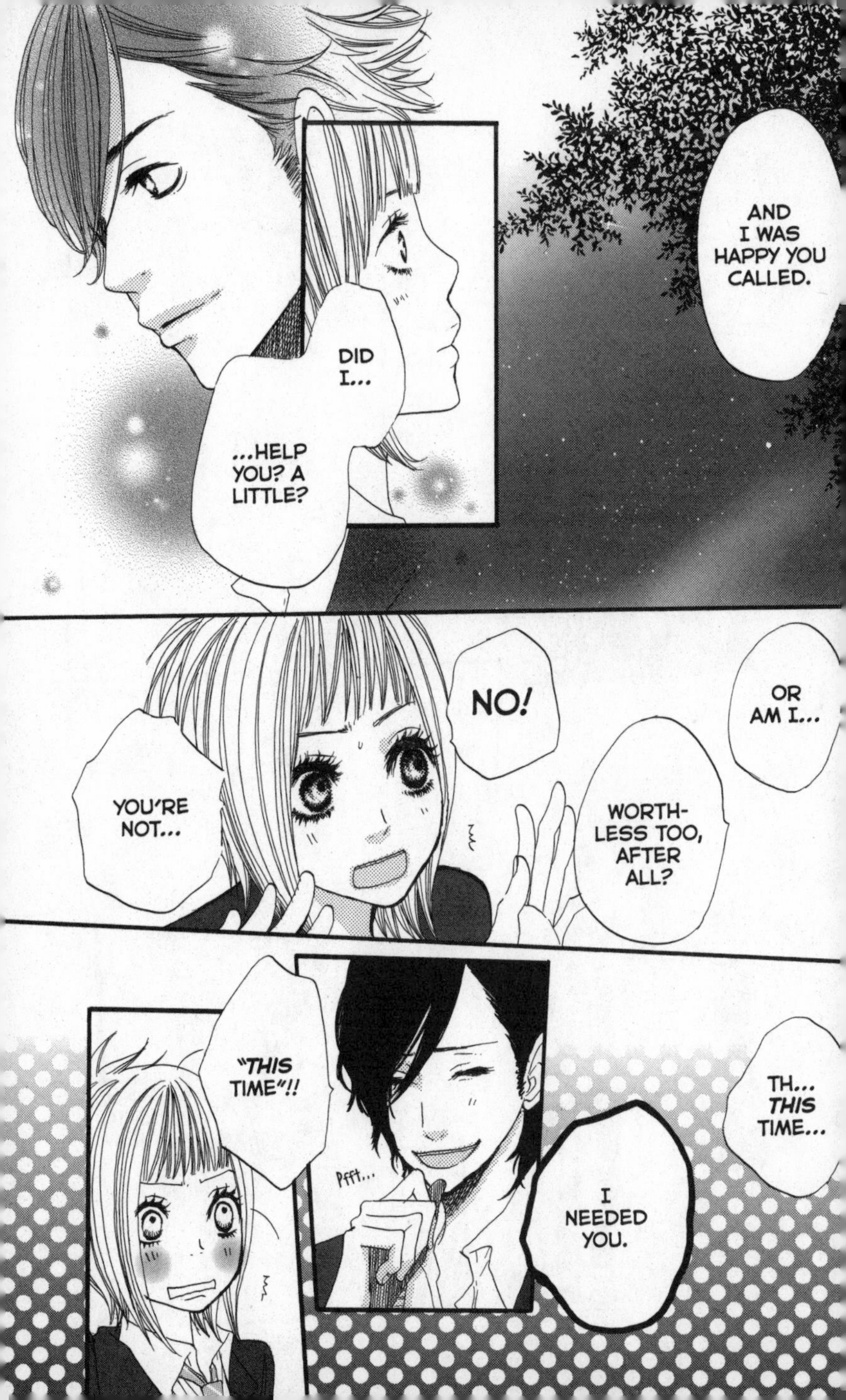
AND I WAS HAPPY YOU CALLED.
DID I...
...HELP YOU? A LITTLE?
OR AM I...
WORTH-LESS TOO, AFTER ALL?
NO!
YOU'RE NOT...
TH... *THIS* TIME...
I NEEDED YOU.
Pfft...
"*THIS* TIME"!!

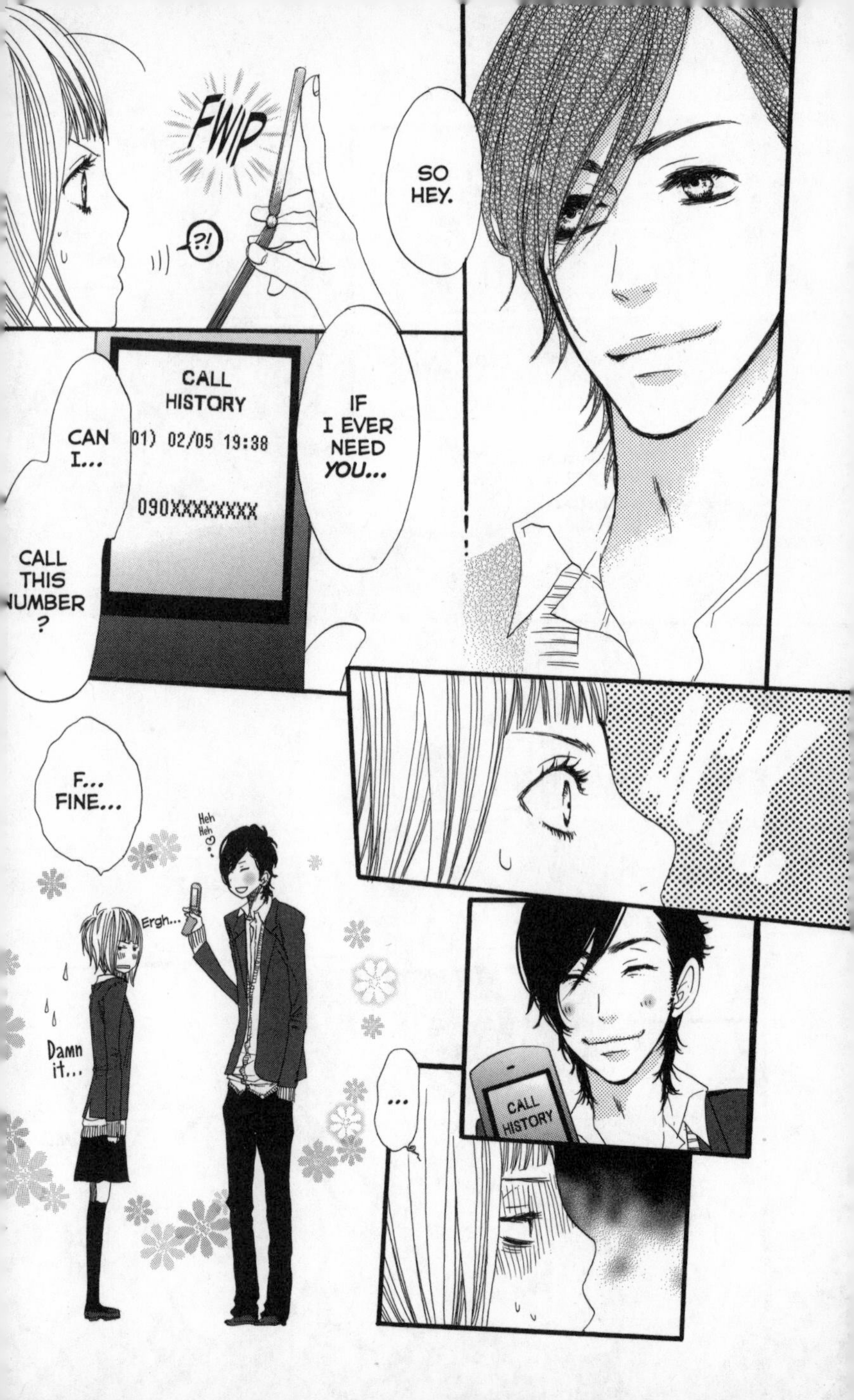
SO HEY.
FWIP
?!
IF I EVER NEED YOU...
CALL HISTORY
01) 02/05 19:38
090XXXXXXXX
CAN I...
CALL THIS NUMBER?
CALL HISTORY
...
F... FINE...
Heh Heh
Ergh...
Damn it...

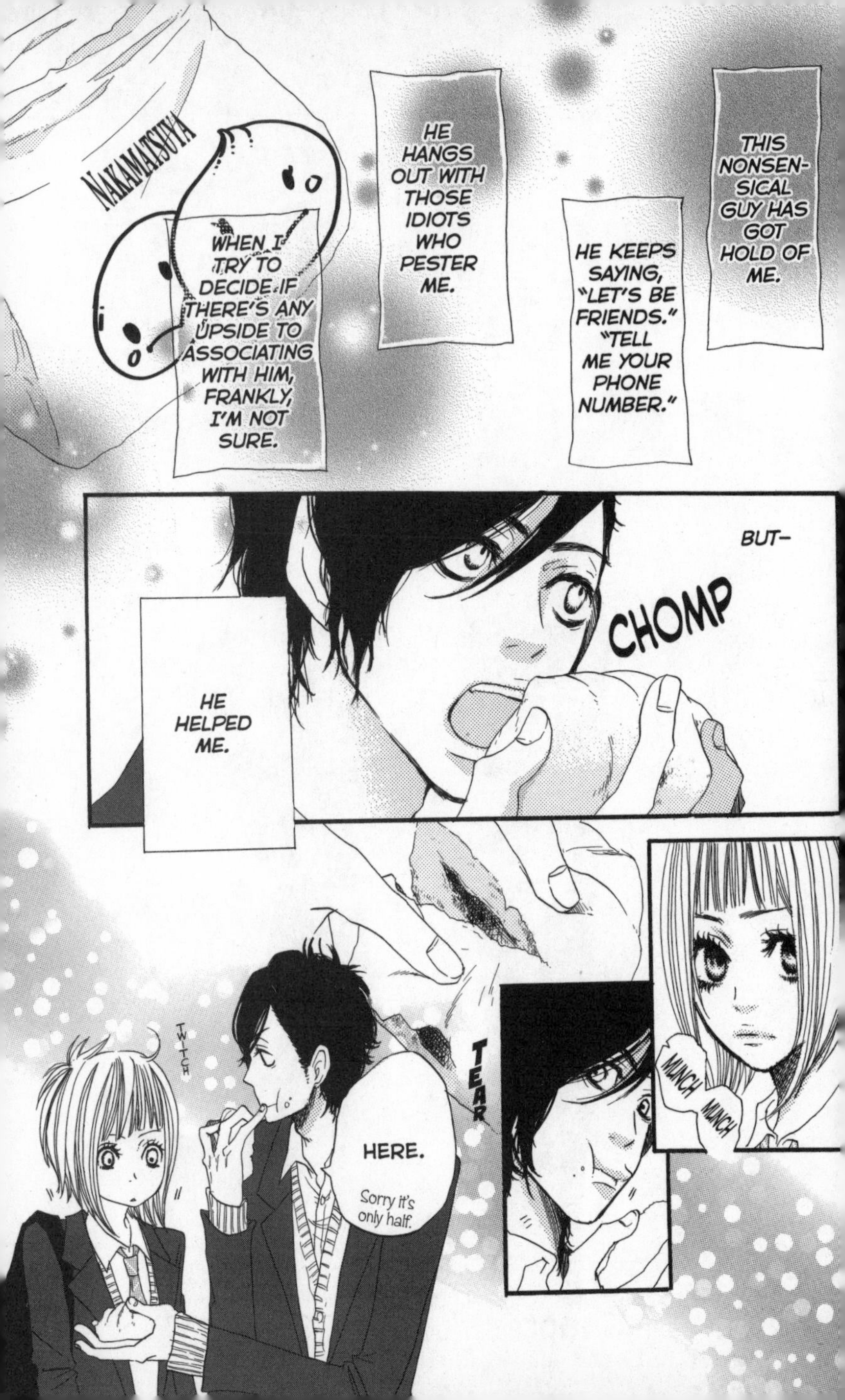
THIS NONSEN-SICAL GUY HAS GOT HOLD OF ME.
HE KEEPS SAYING, "LET'S BE FRIENDS." "TELL ME YOUR PHONE NUMBER."
HE HANGS OUT WITH THOSE IDIOTS WHO PESTER ME.
NAKAMATSUYA
WHEN I TRY TO DECIDE IF THERE'S ANY UPSIDE TO ASSOCIATING WITH HIM, FRANKLY, I'M NOT SURE.
BUT–
CHOMP
HE HELPED ME.
MUNCH
MUNCH
TEAR
TWITCH
HERE.
Sorry it's only half.

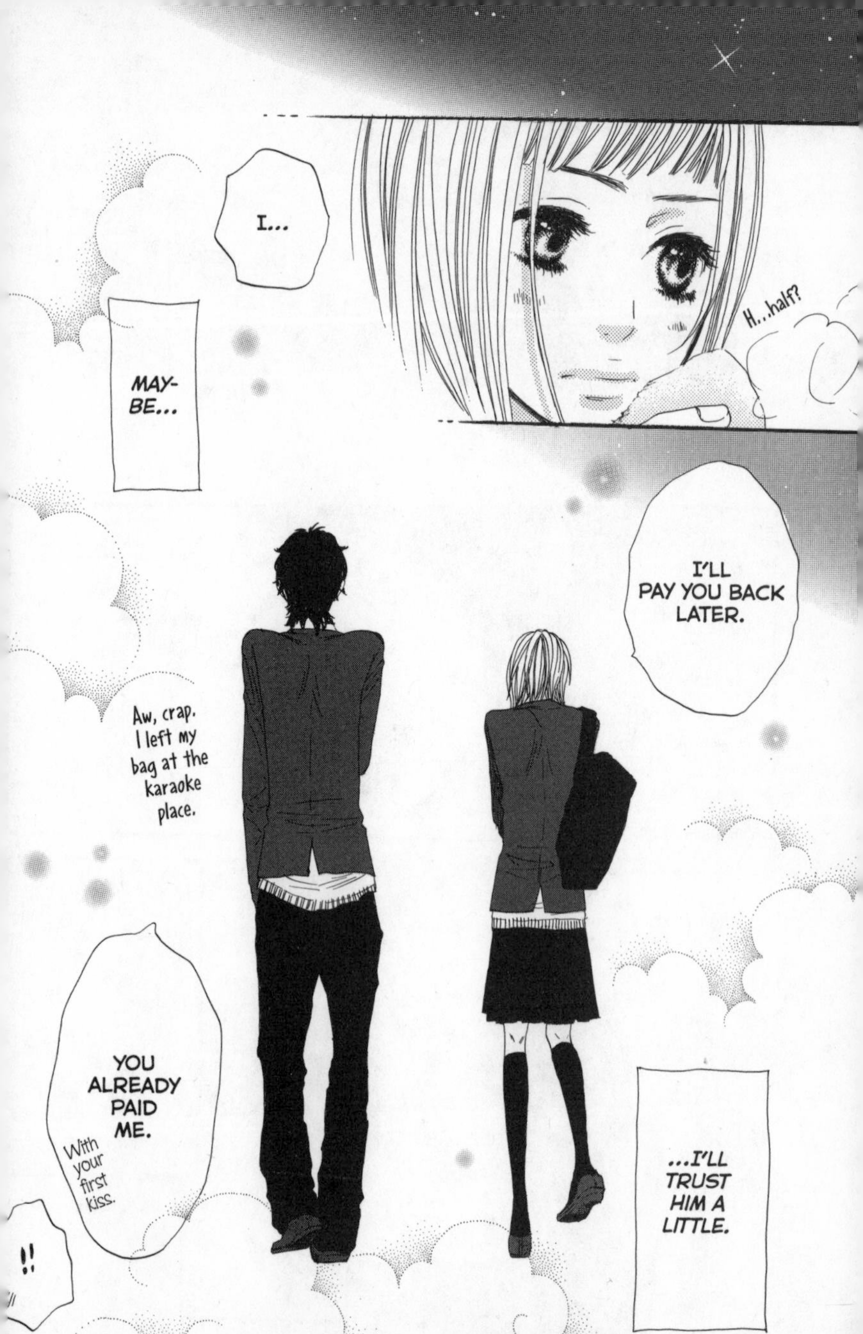
H..half?
I...
MAY-BE...
I'LL PAY YOU BACK LATER.
Aw, crap. I left my bag at the karaoke place.
...I'LL TRUST HIM A LITTLE.
YOU ALREADY PAID ME.
With your first kiss.
!!

Chapter 1 — The End

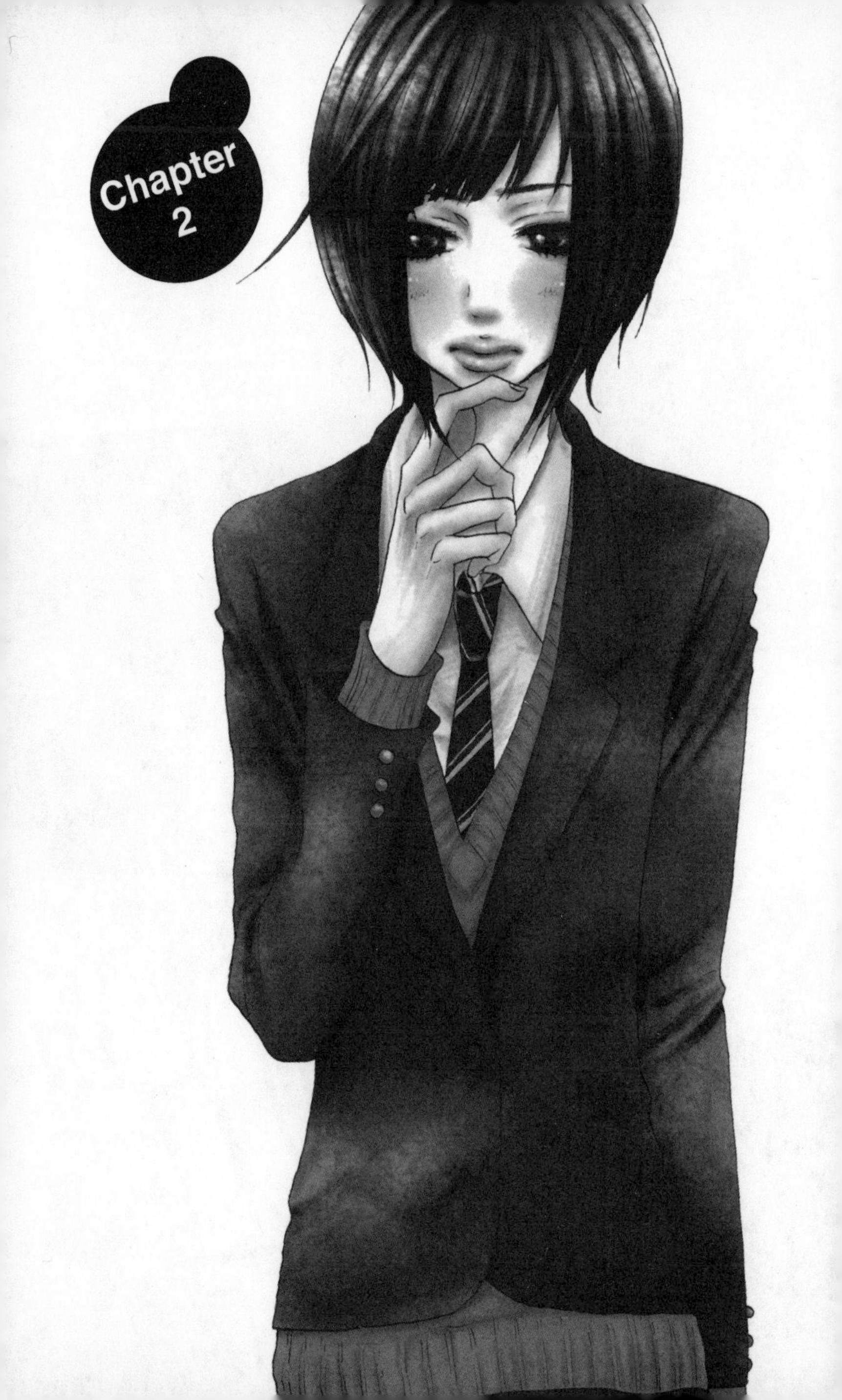
Chapter
2

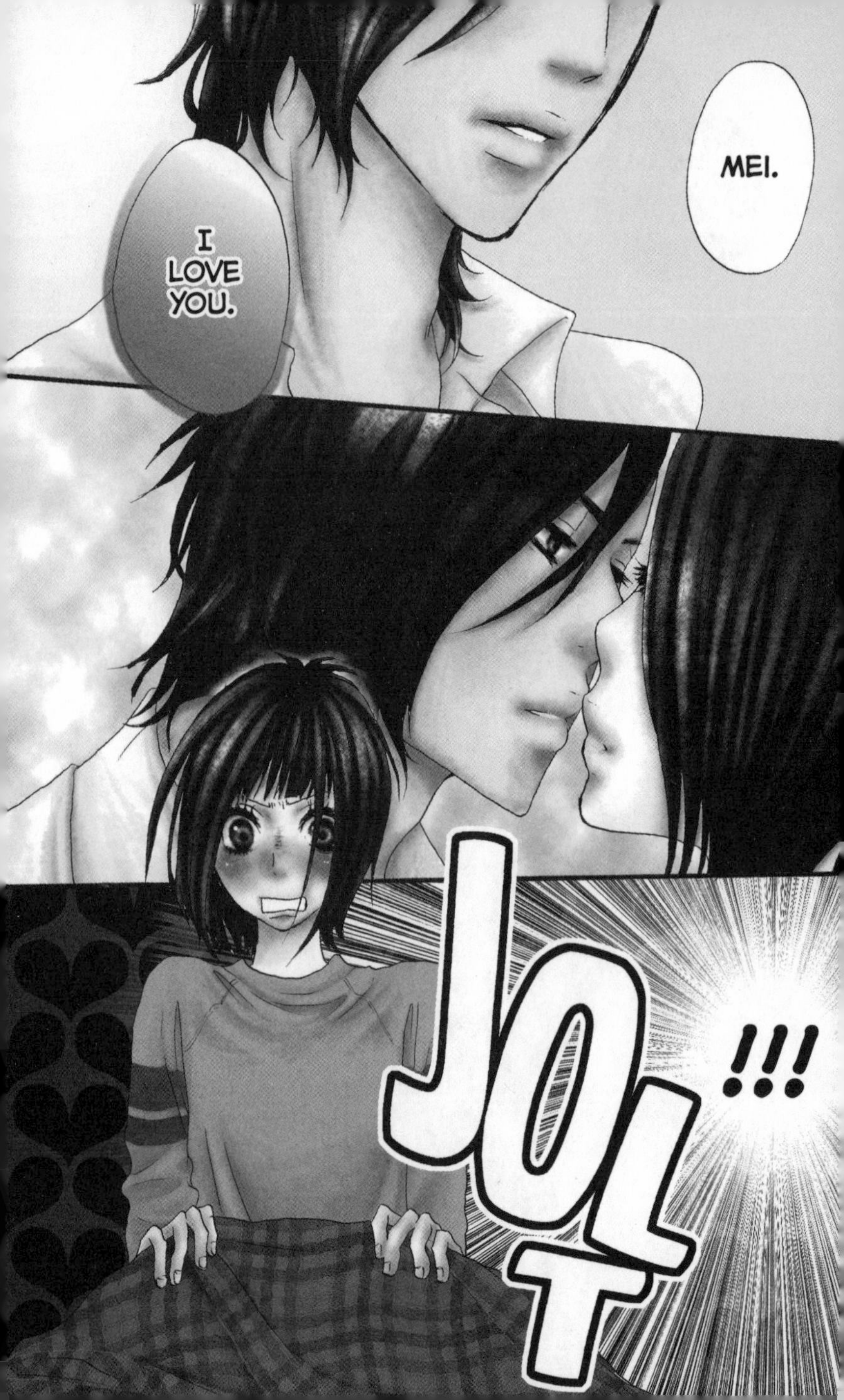
MEI.
I LOVE YOU.
JOLT !!!

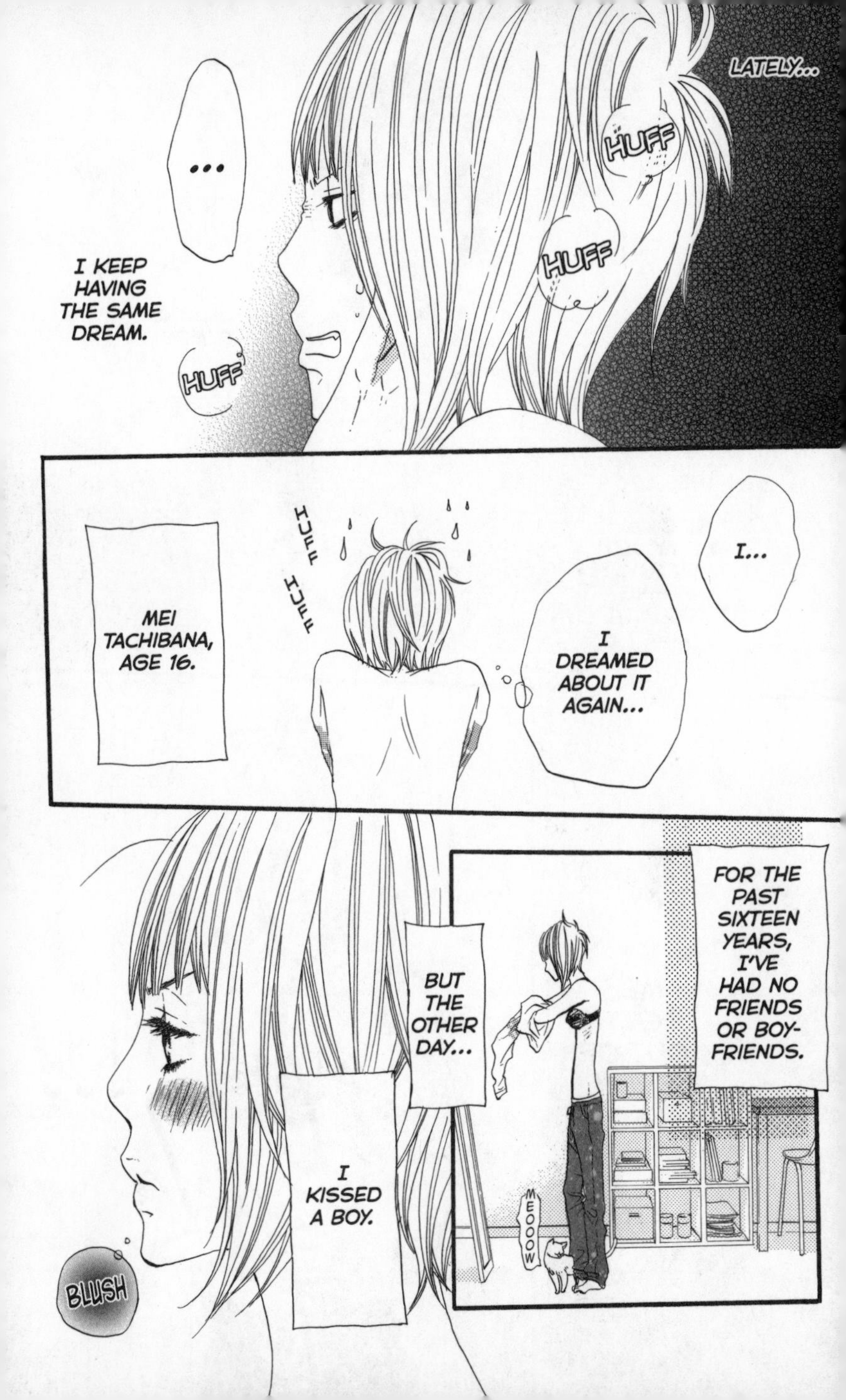
LATELY...
HUFF
HUFF
...
I KEEP HAVING THE SAME DREAM.
HUFF
I...
I DREAMED ABOUT IT AGAIN...
HUFF HUFF
MEI TACHIBANA, AGE 16.
FOR THE PAST SIXTEEN YEARS, I'VE HAD NO FRIENDS OR BOY-FRIENDS.
MEOOOW
BUT THE OTHER DAY...
I KISSED A BOY.
BLUSH

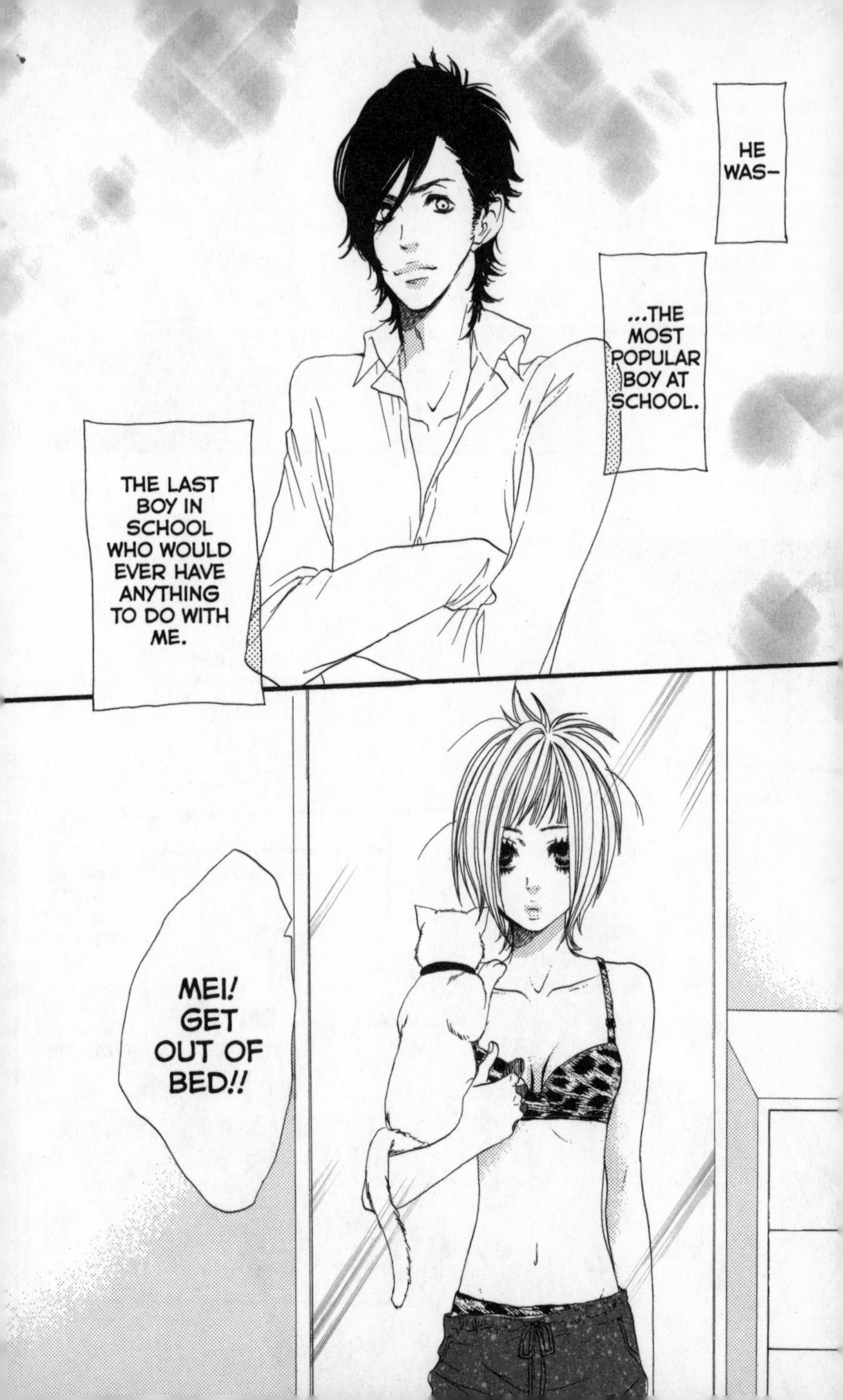
HE WAS—
...THE MOST POPULAR BOY AT SCHOOL.
THE LAST BOY IN SCHOOL WHO WOULD EVER HAVE ANYTHING TO DO WITH ME.
MEI! GET OUT OF BED!!

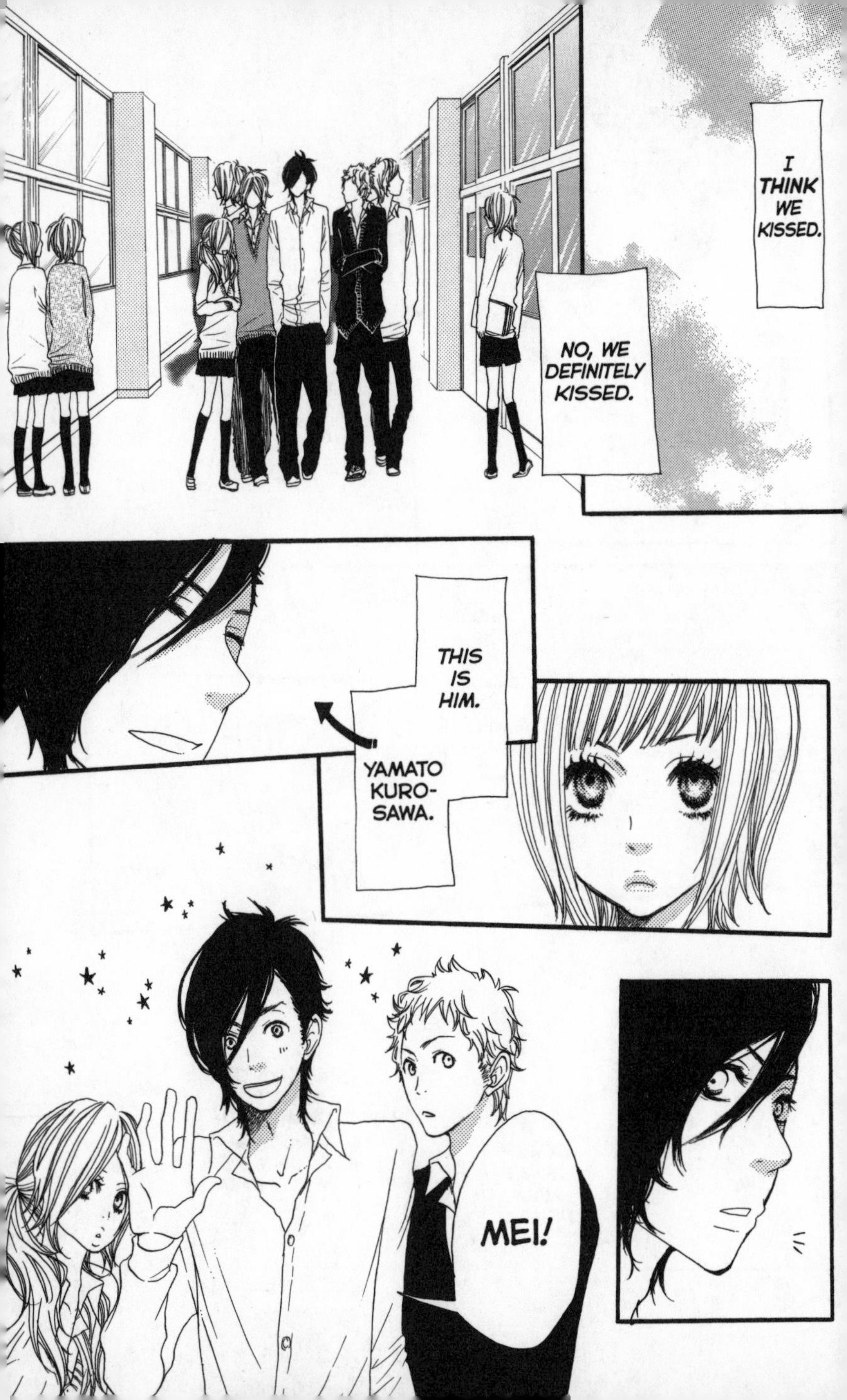
I THINK WE KISSED.
NO, WE DEFINITELY KISSED.
THIS IS HIM.
YAMATO KURO-SAWA.
MEI!

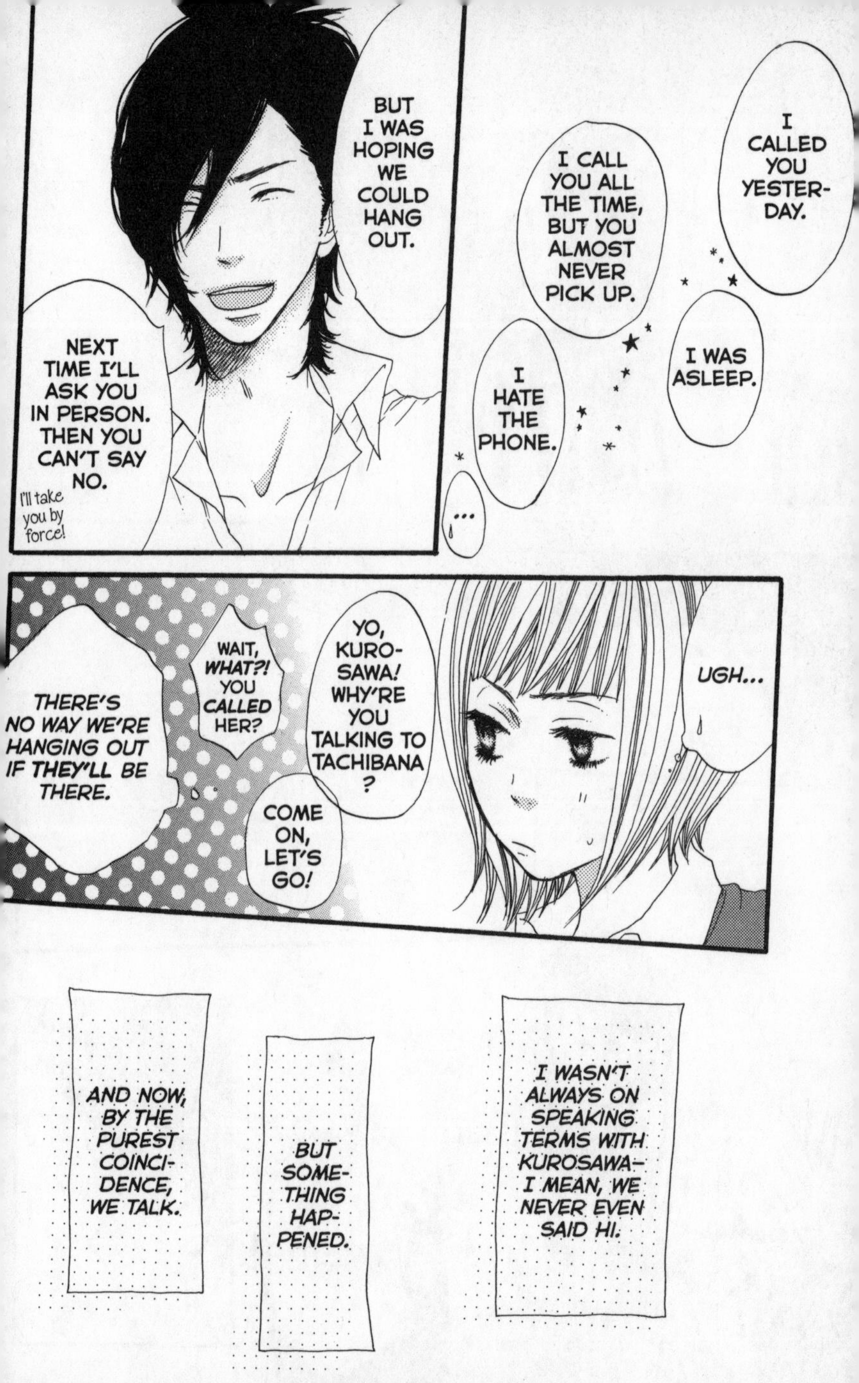
I CALLED YOU YESTER-DAY.
I WAS ASLEEP.
I CALL YOU ALL THE TIME, BUT YOU ALMOST NEVER PICK UP.
I HATE THE PHONE.
...
BUT I WAS HOPING WE COULD HANG OUT.
NEXT TIME I'LL ASK YOU IN PERSON. THEN YOU CAN'T SAY NO.
I'll take you by force!
UGH...
YO, KURO-SAWA! WHY'RE YOU TALKING TO TACHIBANA?
COME ON, LET'S GO!
WAIT, WHAT?! YOU CALLED HER?
THERE'S NO WAY WE'RE HANGING OUT IF THEY'LL BE THERE.
I WASN'T ALWAYS ON SPEAKING TERMS WITH KUROSAWA— I MEAN, WE NEVER EVEN SAID HI.
BUT SOME-THING HAP-PENED.
AND NOW, BY THE PUREST COINCI-DENCE, WE TALK.

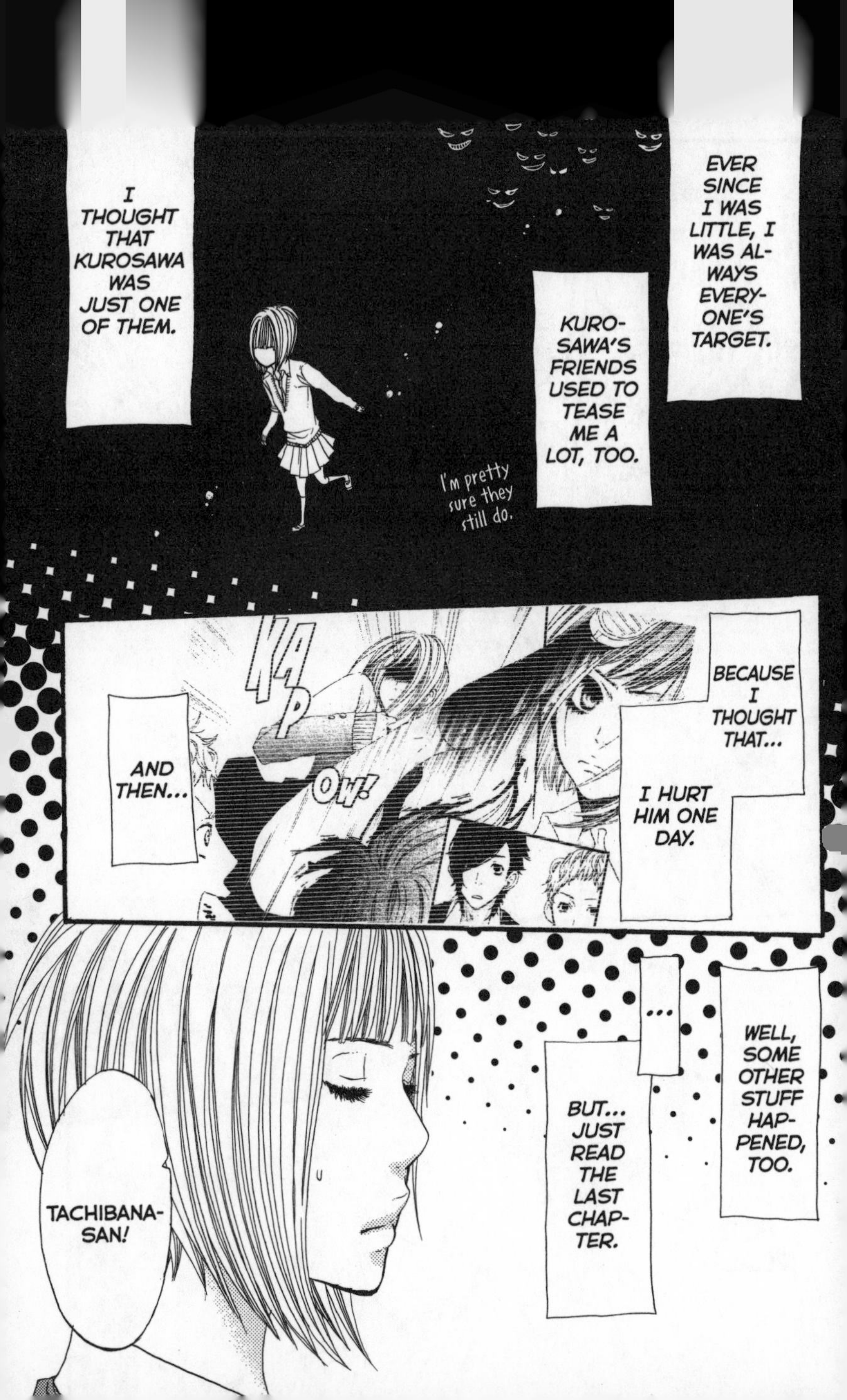
EVER SINCE I WAS LITTLE, I WAS ALWAYS EVERYONE'S TARGET.
KUROSAWA'S FRIENDS USED TO TEASE ME A LOT, TOO.
I'm pretty sure they still do.
I THOUGHT THAT KUROSAWA WAS JUST ONE OF THEM.
BECAUSE I THOUGHT THAT...
I HURT HIM ONE DAY.
WAP
OW!
AND THEN...
WELL, SOME OTHER STUFF HAPPENED, TOO.
...
BUT... JUST READ THE LAST CHAPTER.
TACHIBANA-SAN!

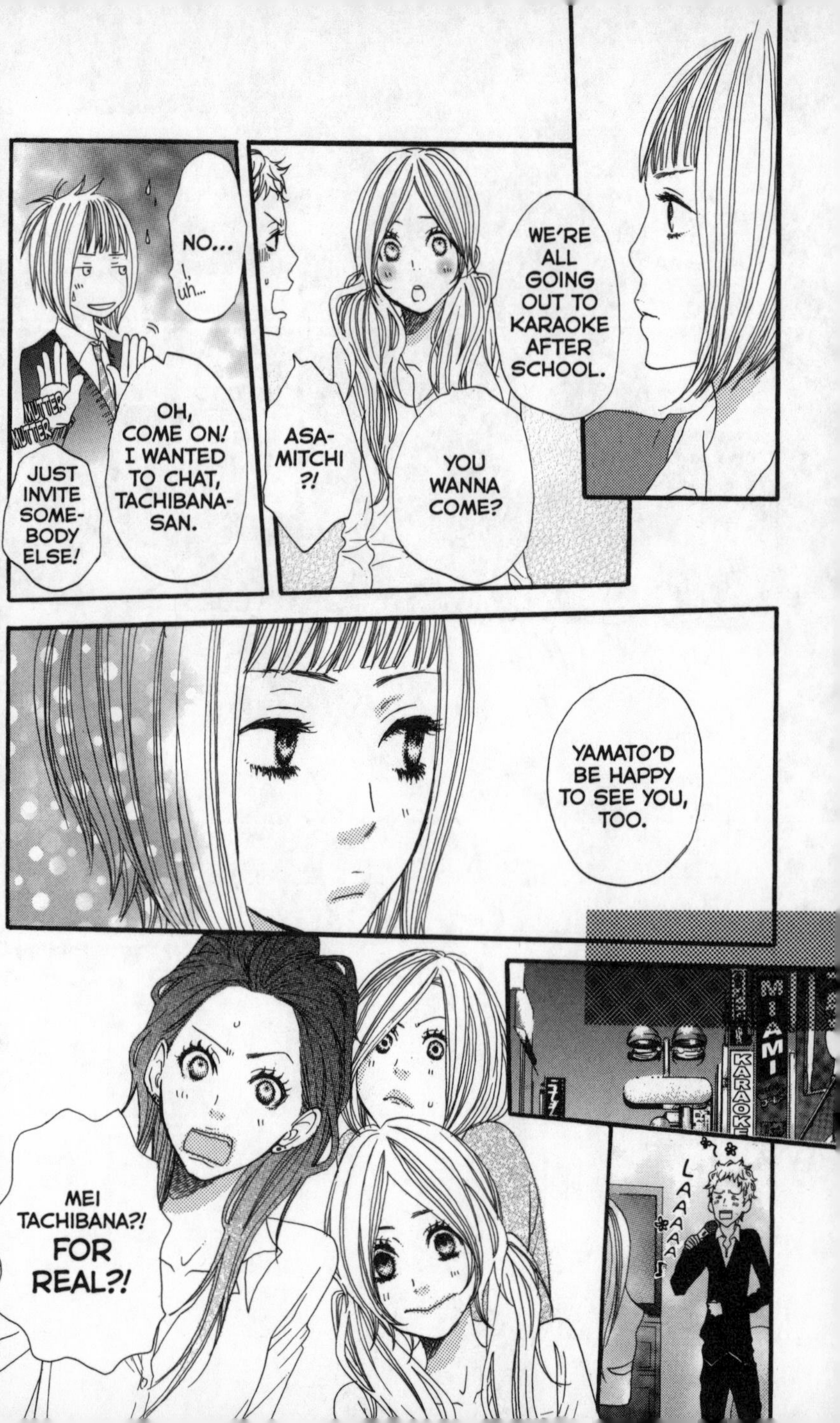
WE'RE ALL GOING OUT TO KARAOKE AFTER SCHOOL.
YOU WANNA COME?
ASA-MITCHI?!
NO... I, uh...
OH, COME ON! I WANTED TO CHAT, TACHIBANA-SAN.
MUTTER MUTTER
JUST INVITE SOMEBODY ELSE!
YAMATO'D BE HAPPY TO SEE YOU, TOO.
MIAMI
KARAOKE
LAAAAA
MEI TACHIBANA?! FOR REAL?!

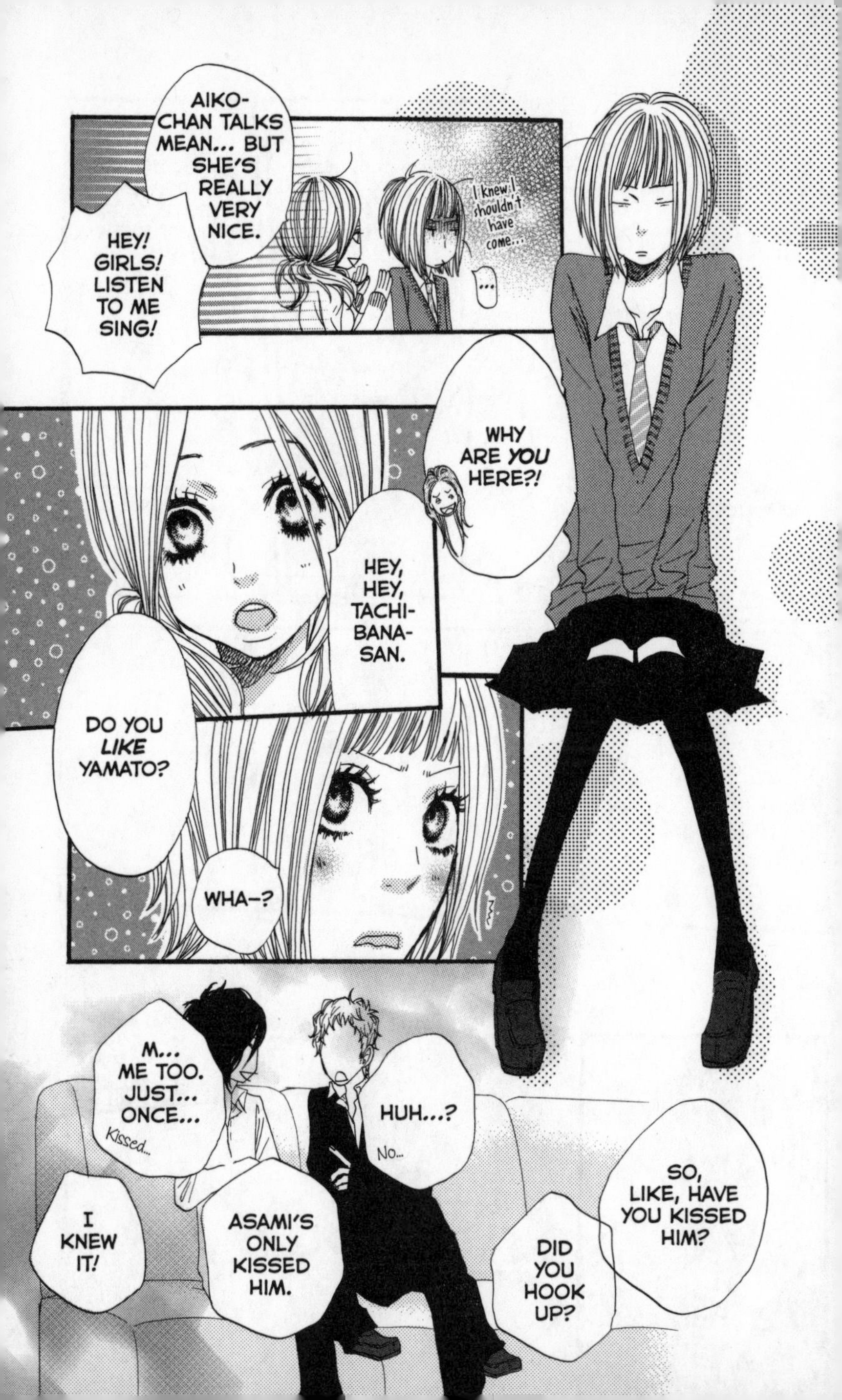
AIKO-CHAN TALKS MEAN... BUT SHE'S REALLY VERY NICE.
I knew I shouldn't have come...
...
HEY! GIRLS! LISTEN TO ME SING!
WHY ARE *YOU* HERE?!
HEY, HEY, TACHIBANA-SAN.
DO YOU *LIKE* YAMATO?
WHA–?
SO, LIKE, HAVE YOU KISSED HIM?
DID YOU HOOK UP?
HUH...?
No...
M... ME TOO. JUST... ONCE...
Kissed...
ASAMI'S ONLY KISSED HIM.
I KNEW IT!

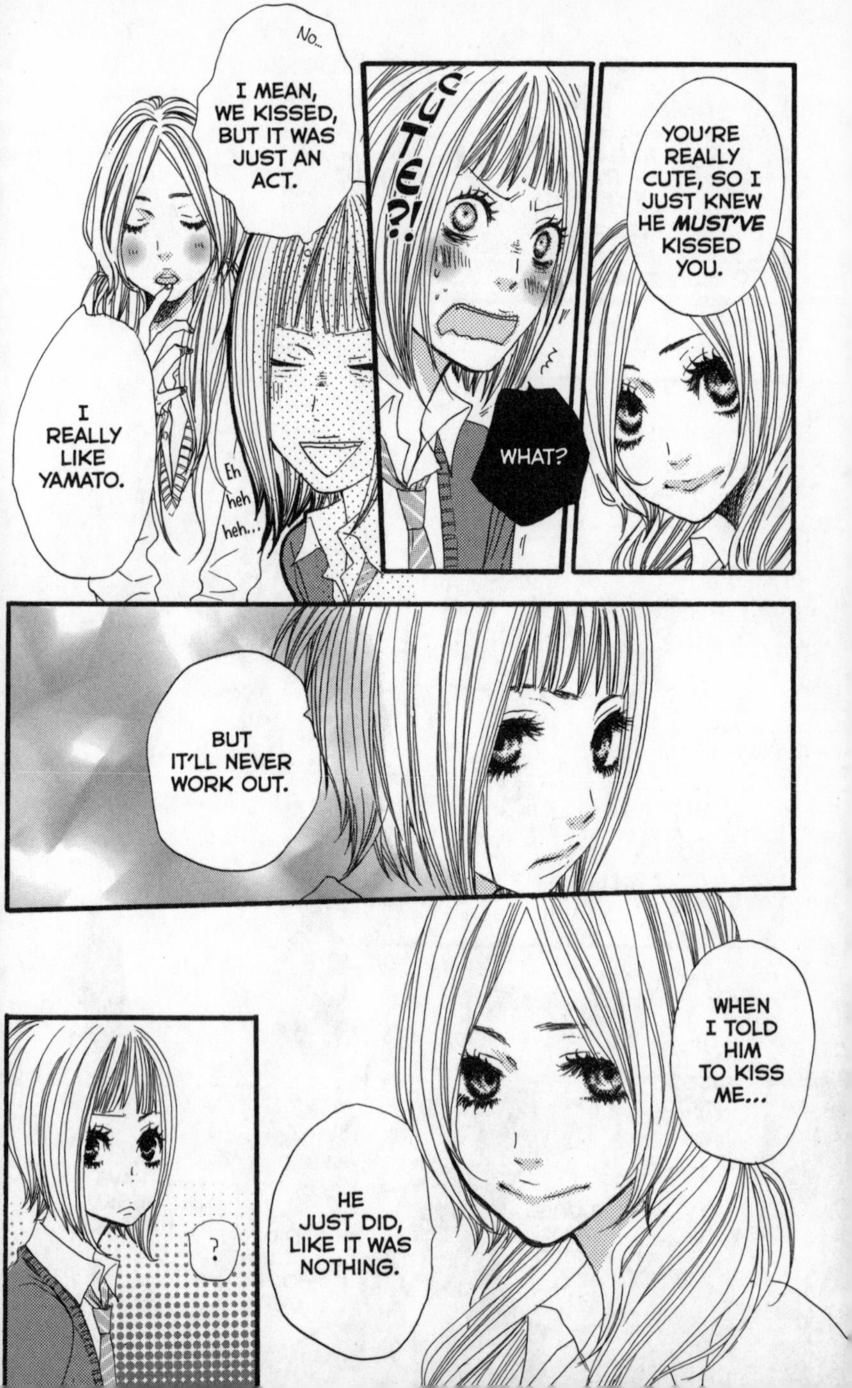
YOU'RE REALLY CUTE, SO I JUST KNEW HE *MUST'VE* KISSED YOU.
CUTE?!
WHAT?
No...
I MEAN, WE KISSED, BUT IT WAS JUST AN ACT.
Eh heh heh...
I REALLY LIKE YAMATO.
BUT IT'LL NEVER WORK OUT.
WHEN I TOLD HIM TO KISS ME...
HE JUST DID, LIKE IT WAS NOTHING.
?

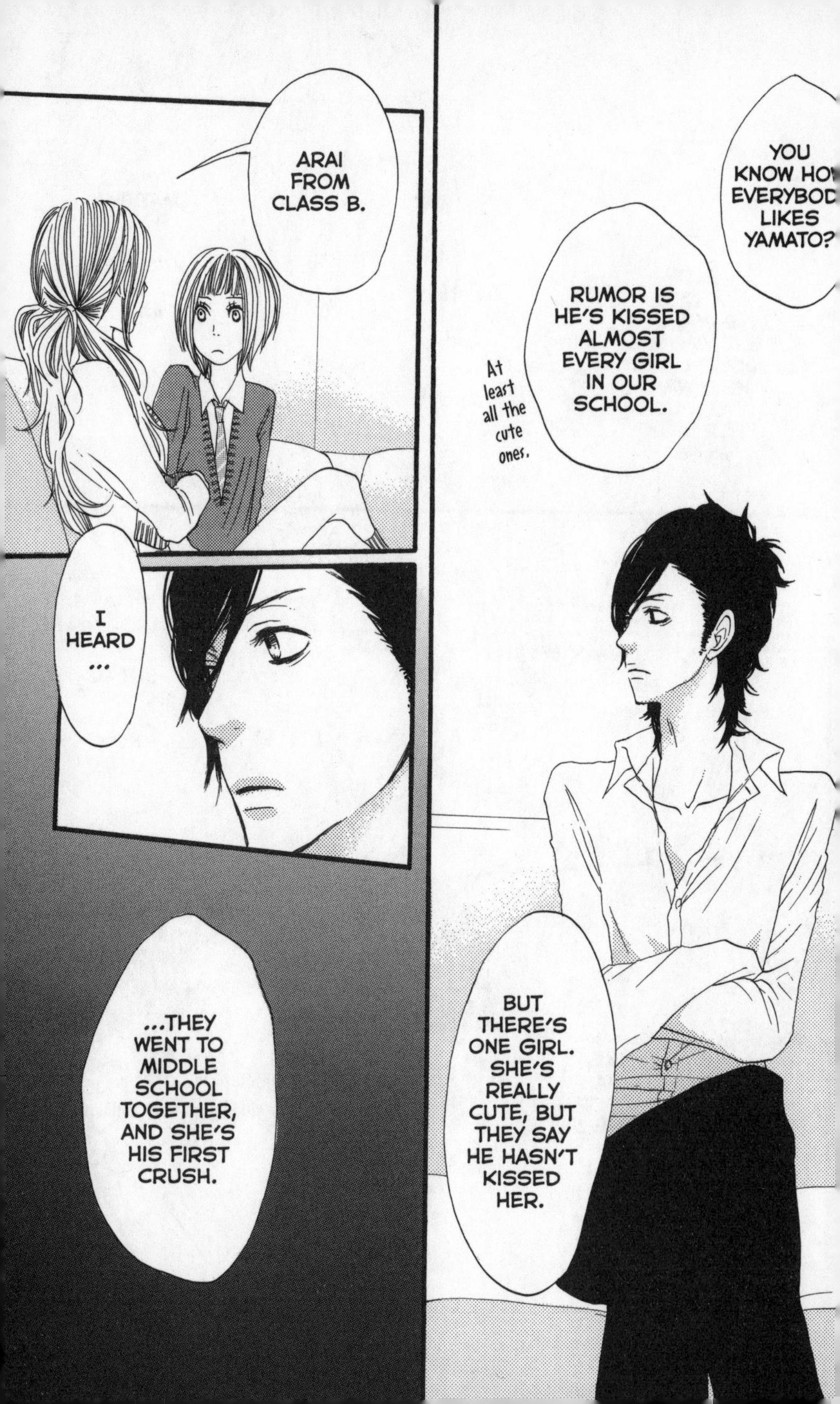
YOU KNOW HO EVERYBOD LIKES YAMATO?
RUMOR IS HE'S KISSED ALMOST EVERY GIRL IN OUR SCHOOL.
At least all the cute ones.
BUT THERE'S ONE GIRL. SHE'S REALLY CUTE, BUT THEY SAY HE HASN'T KISSED HER.
ARAI FROM CLASS B.
I HEARD...
...THEY WENT TO MIDDLE SCHOOL TOGETHER, AND SHE'S HIS FIRST CRUSH.

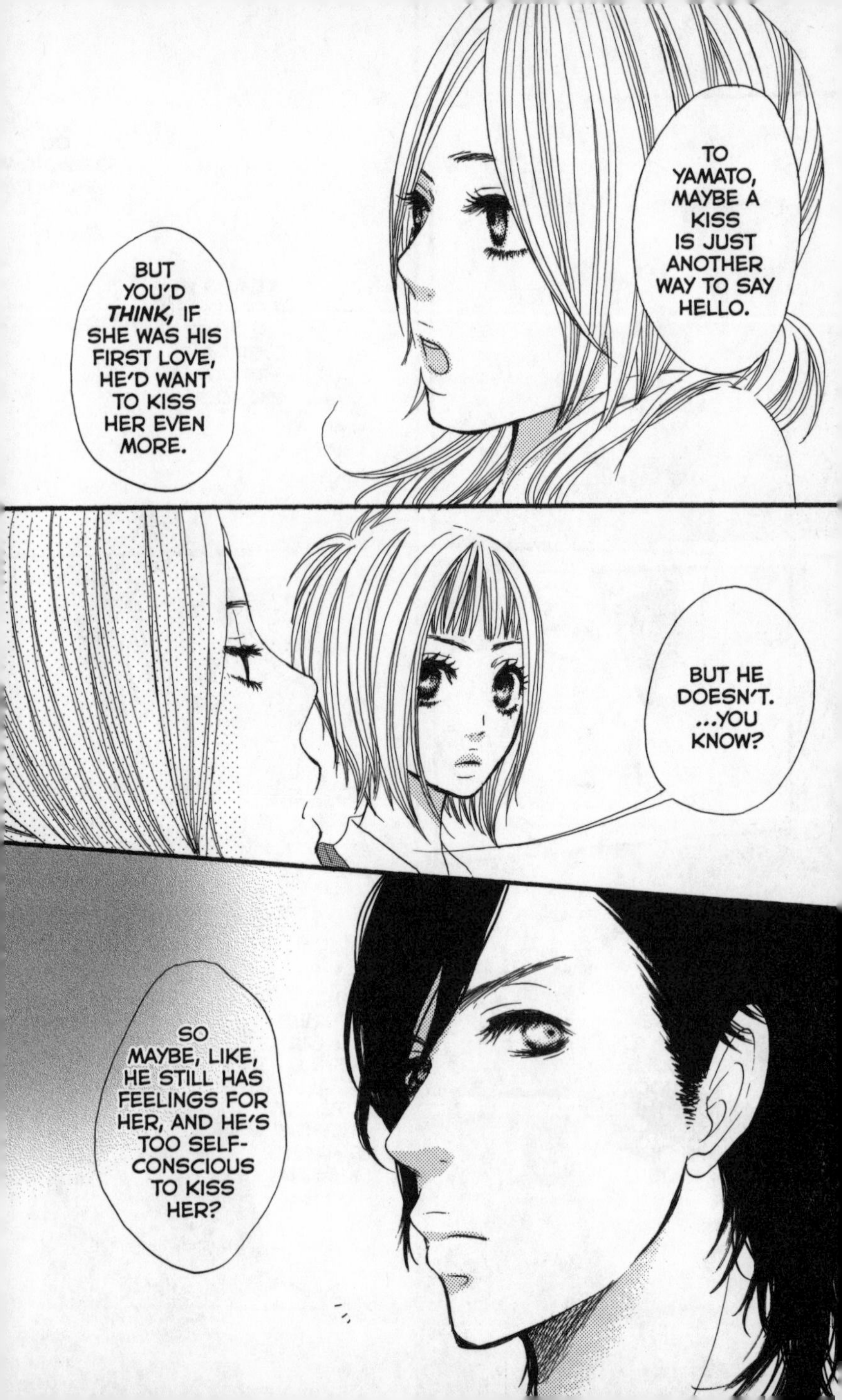
TO YAMATO, MAYBE A KISS IS JUST ANOTHER WAY TO SAY HELLO.
BUT YOU'D *THINK,* IF SHE WAS HIS FIRST LOVE, HE'D WANT TO KISS HER EVEN MORE.
BUT HE DOESN'T. ...YOU KNOW?
SO MAYBE, LIKE, HE STILL HAS FEELINGS FOR HER, AND HE'S TOO SELF-CONSCIOUS TO KISS HER?

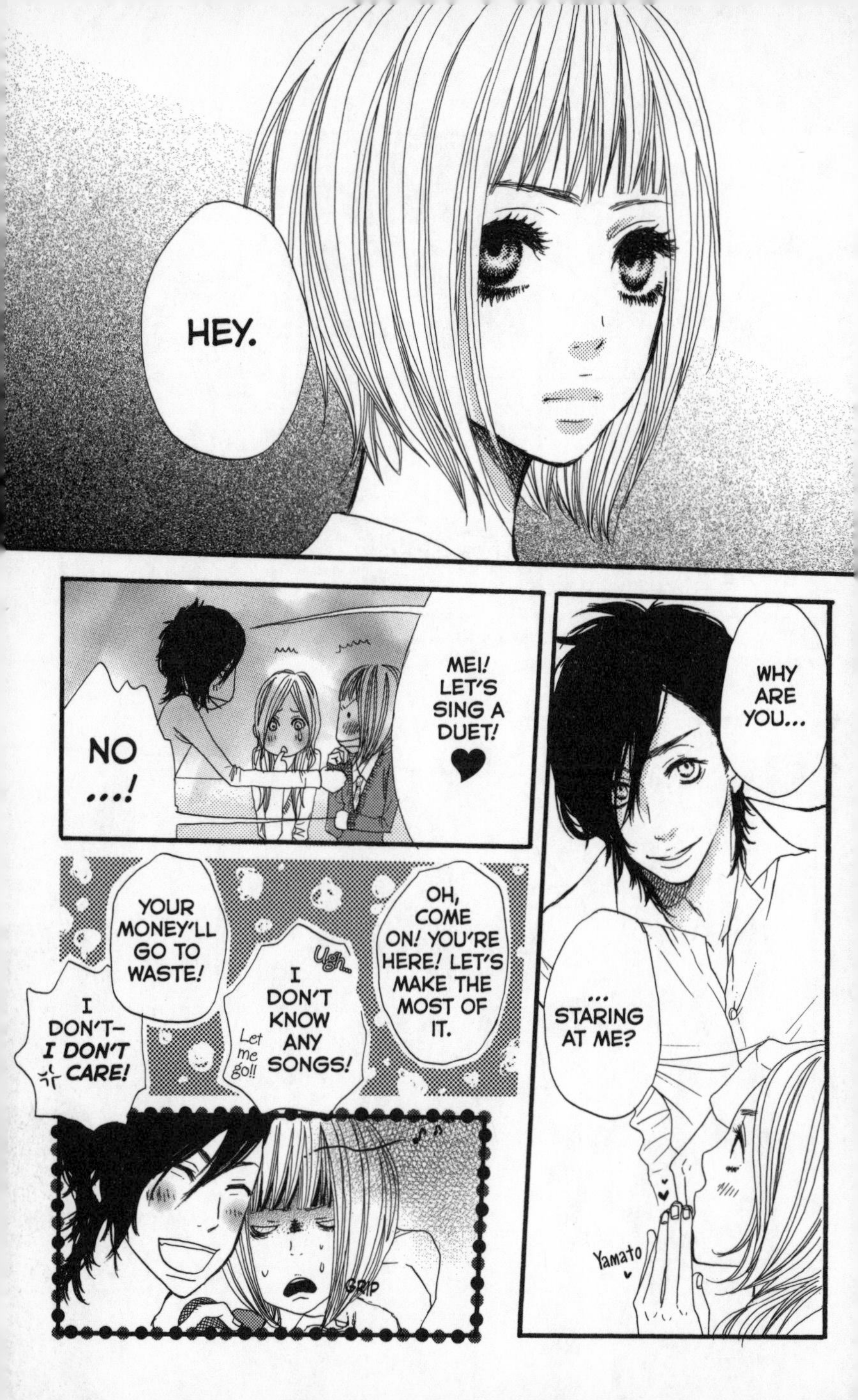
HEY.
WHY ARE YOU...
...STARING AT ME?
Yamato ♥
MEI! LET'S SING A DUET! ♥
NO ...!
OH, COME ON! YOU'RE HERE! LET'S MAKE THE MOST OF IT.
Ugh...
I DON'T KNOW ANY SONGS!
Let me go!!
YOUR MONEY'LL GO TO WASTE!
I DON'T— I DON'T CARE!
GRIP

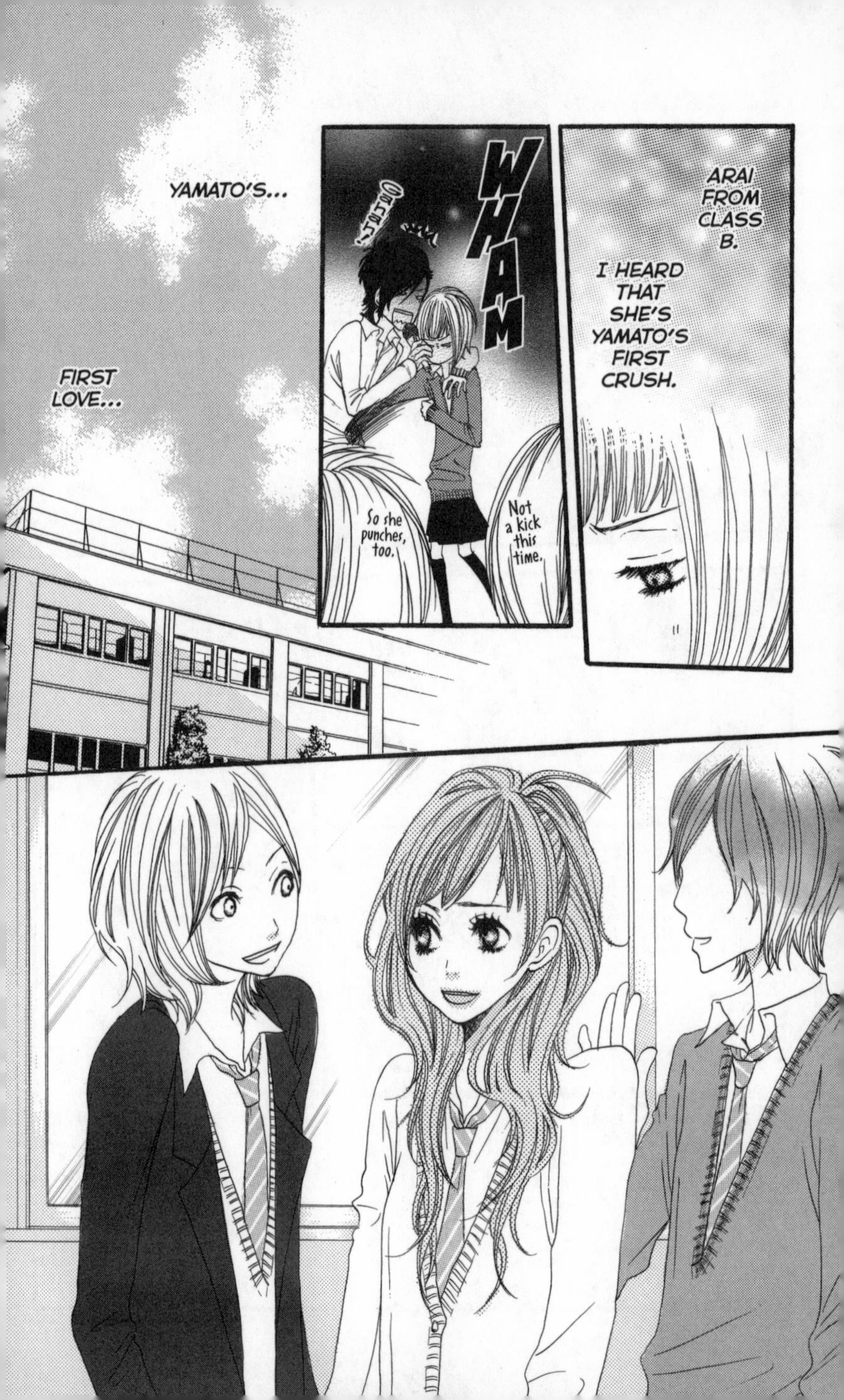
ARAI FROM CLASS B.
I HEARD THAT SHE'S YAMATO'S FIRST CRUSH.
WHAM
Not a kick this time.
So she punches, too.
YAMATO'S...
FIRST LOVE...

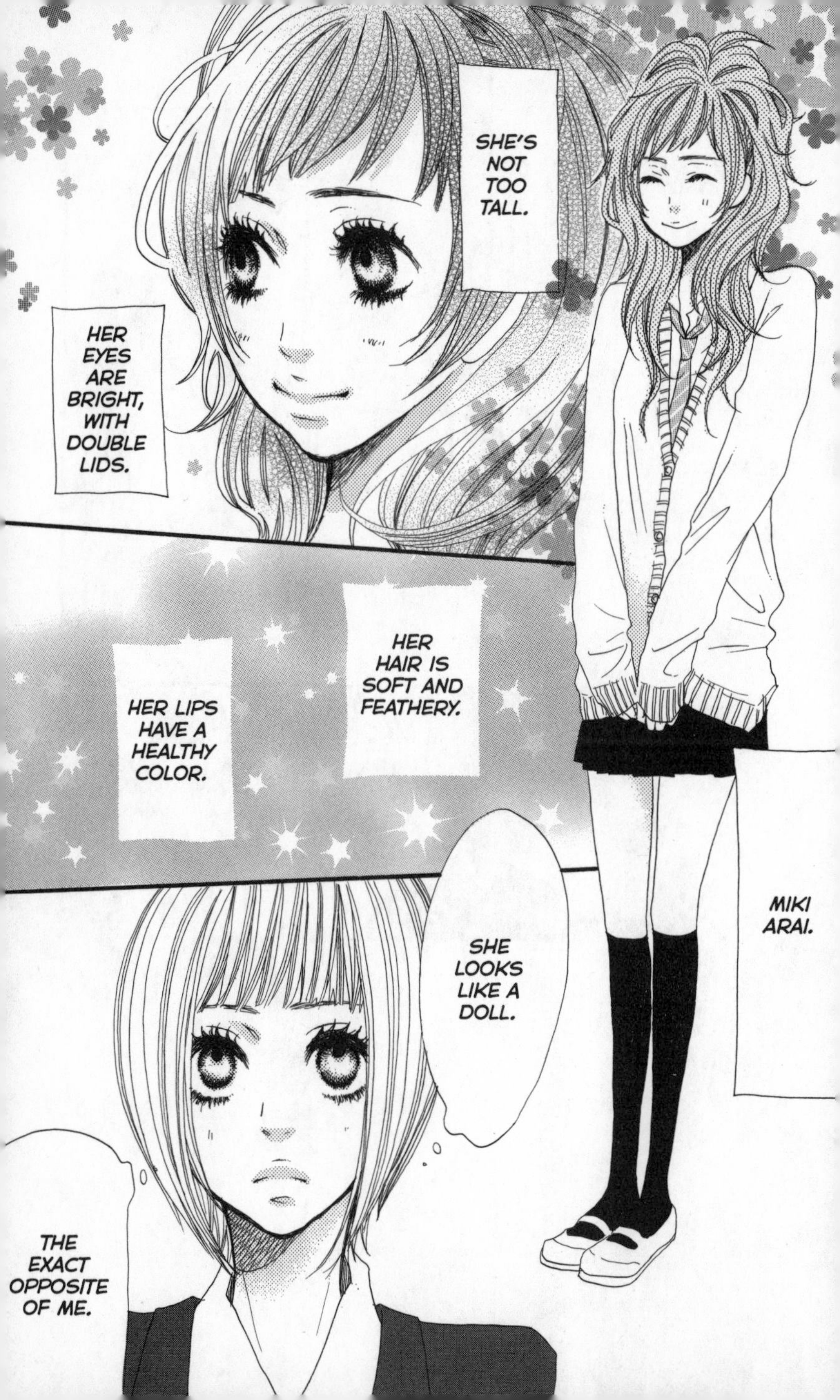
MIKI ARAI.
SHE'S NOT TOO TALL.
HER EYES ARE BRIGHT, WITH DOUBLE LIDS.
HER HAIR IS SOFT AND FEATHERY.
HER LIPS HAVE A HEALTHY COLOR.
SHE LOOKS LIKE A DOLL.
THE EXACT OPPOSITE OF ME.

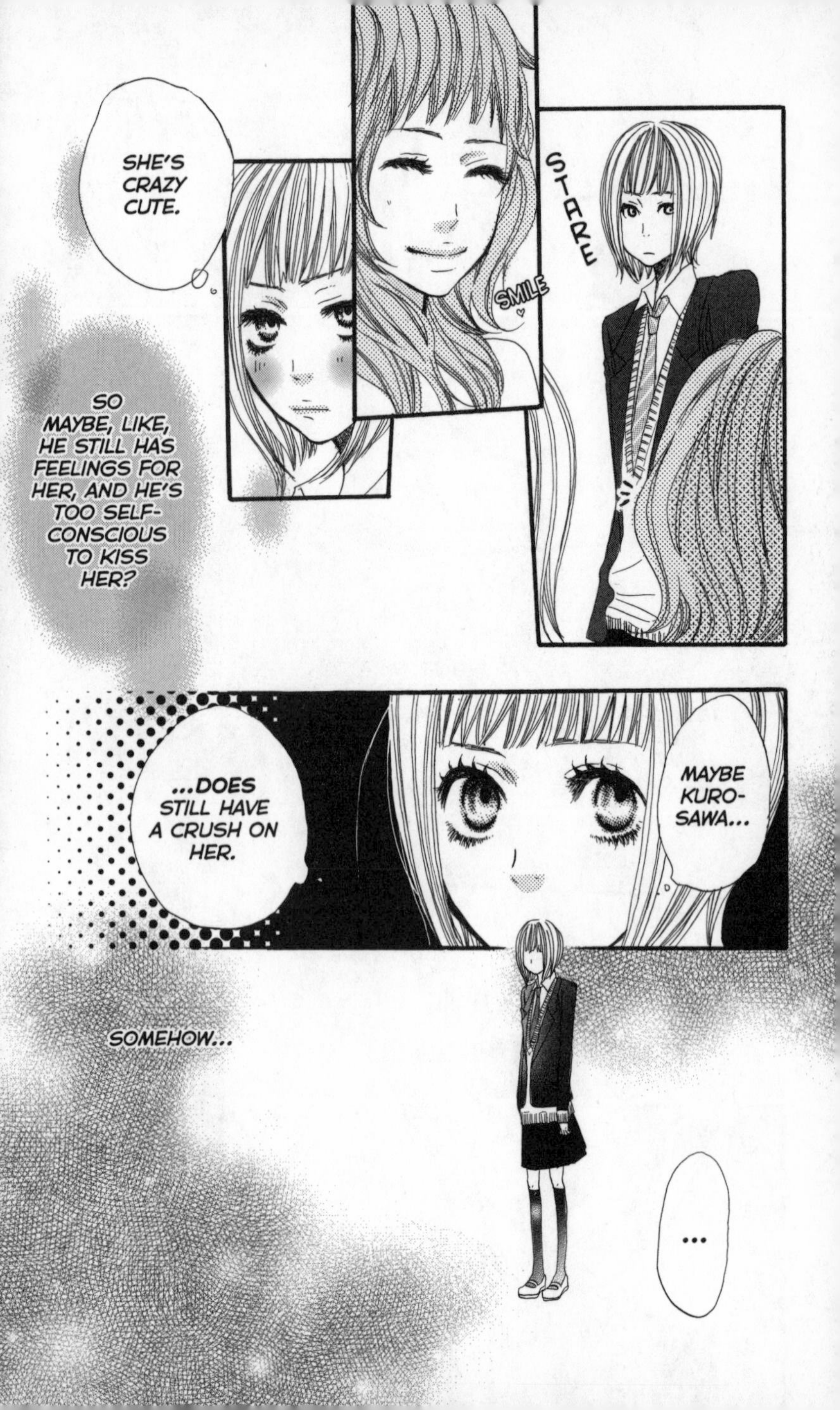
STARE
SMILE
SHE'S CRAZY CUTE.
SO MAYBE, LIKE, HE STILL HAS FEELINGS FOR HER, AND HE'S TOO SELF-CONSCIOUS TO KISS HER?
MAYBE KURO-SAWA...
...DOES STILL HAVE A CRUSH ON HER.
...
SOMEHOW...

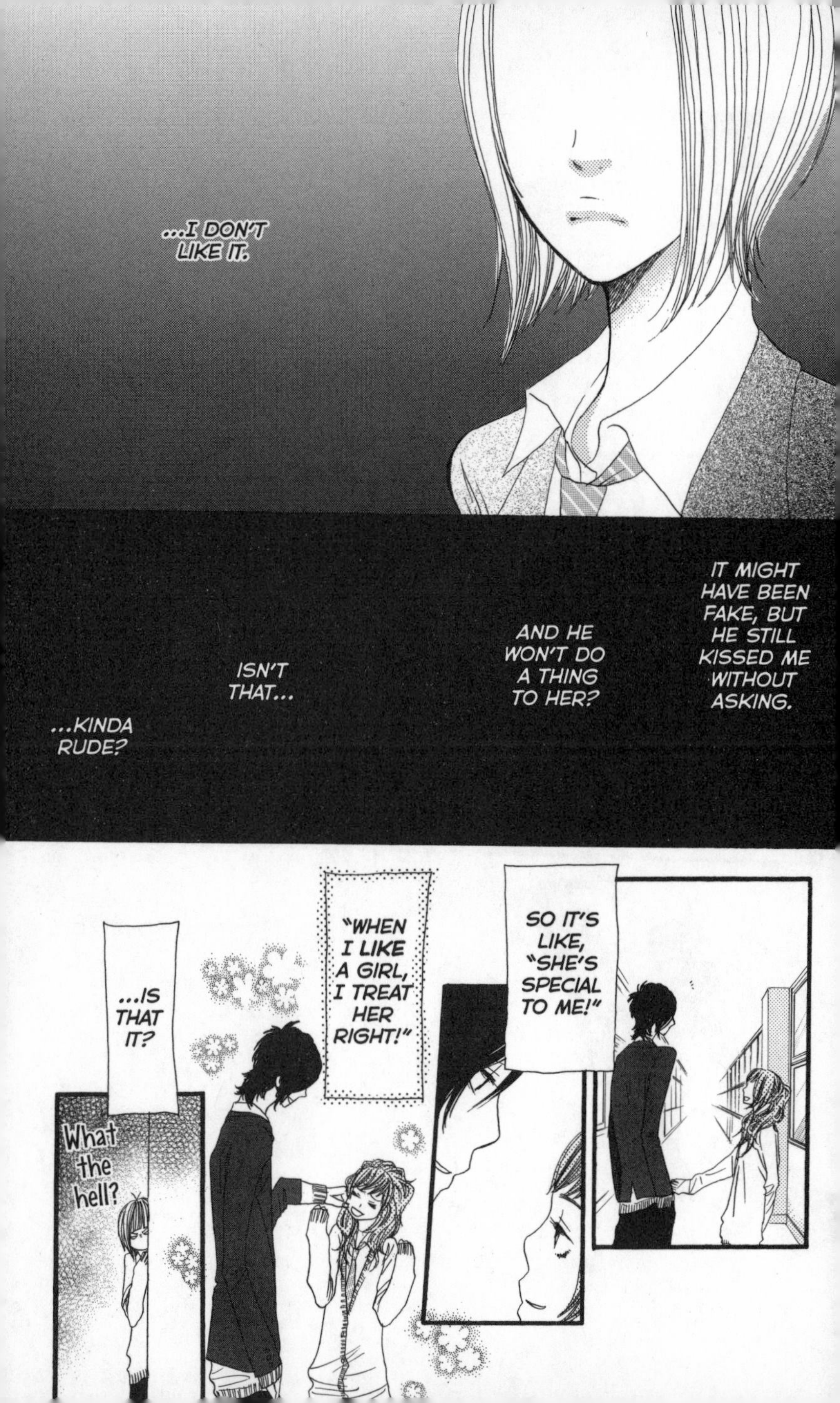
...I DON'T LIKE IT.
IT MIGHT HAVE BEEN FAKE, BUT HE STILL KISSED ME WITHOUT ASKING.
AND HE WON'T DO A THING TO HER?
ISN'T THAT...
...KINDA RUDE?
SO IT'S LIKE, "SHE'S SPECIAL TO ME!"
"WHEN I LIKE A GIRL, I TREAT HER RIGHT!"
...IS THAT IT?
What the hell?

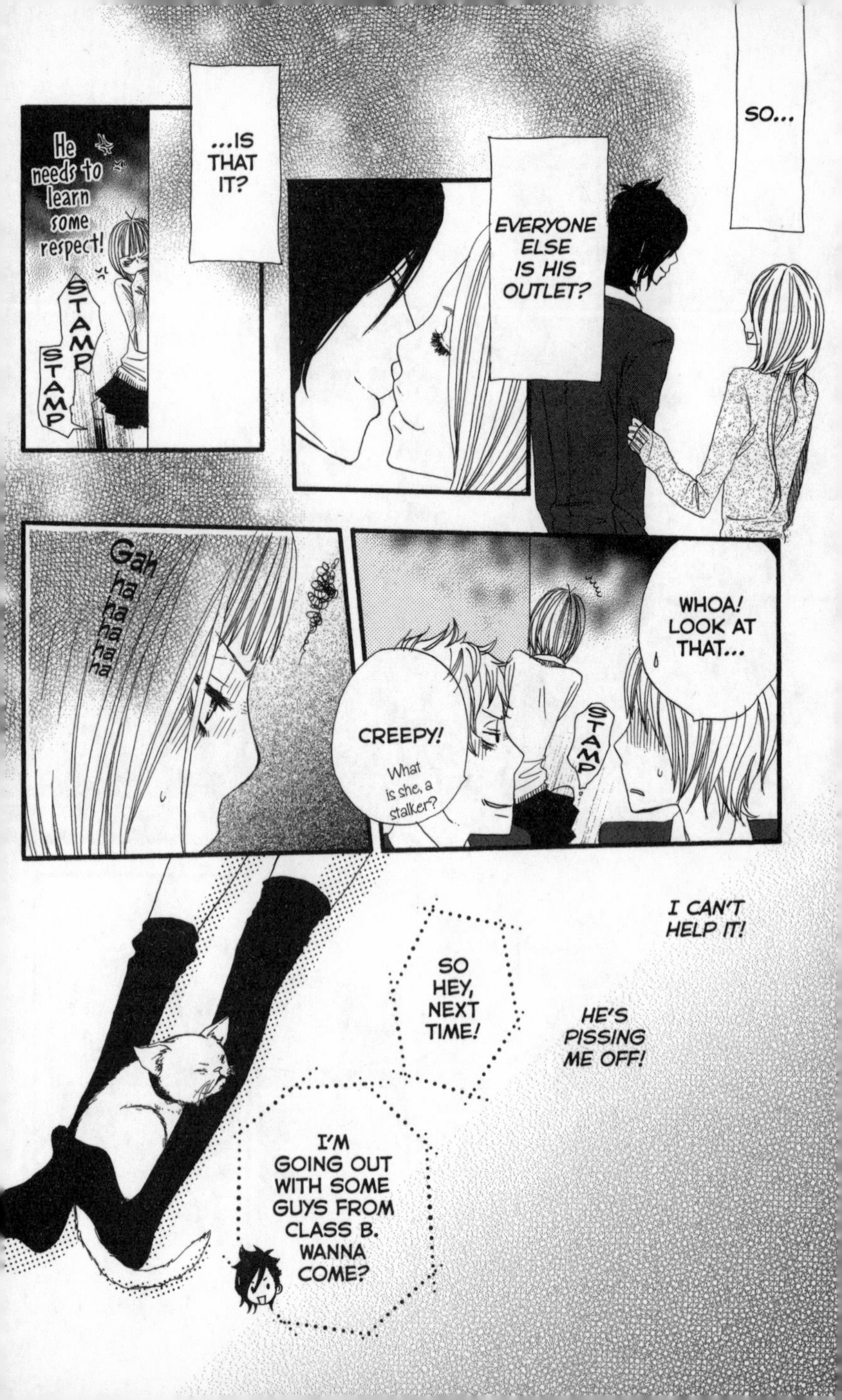
SO...
EVERYONE ELSE IS HIS OUTLET?
...IS THAT IT?
He needs to learn some respect!
STAMP STAMP STAMP
WHOA! LOOK AT THAT...
STAMP
CREEPY!
What is she, a stalker?
Gah ha ha ha ha ha
I CAN'T HELP IT!
HE'S PISSING ME OFF!
SO HEY, NEXT TIME!
I'M GOING OUT WITH SOME GUYS FROM CLASS B. WANNA COME?

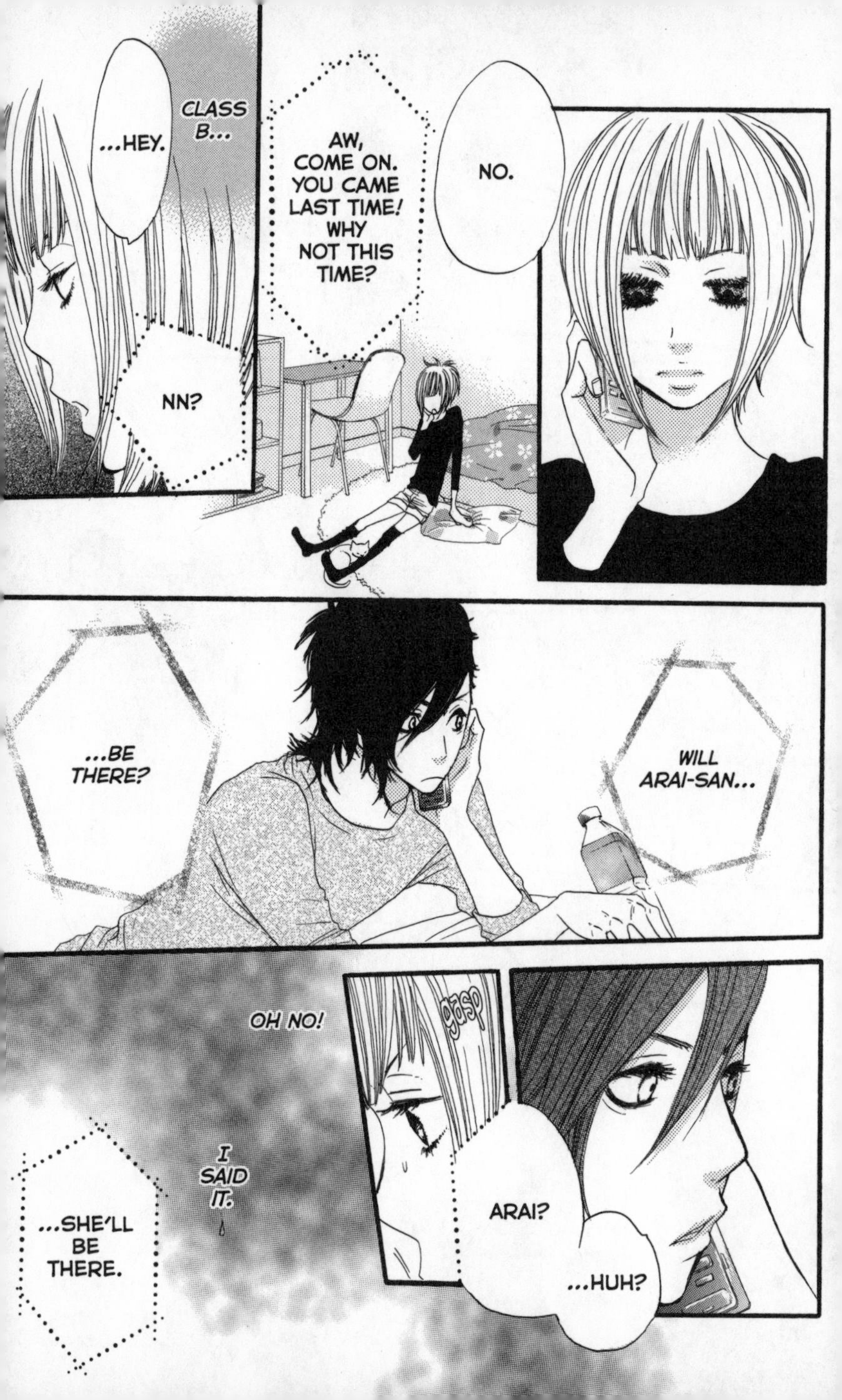
NO.
AW, COME ON. YOU CAME LAST TIME! WHY NOT THIS TIME?
CLASS B...
...HEY.
NN?
WILL ARAI-SAN...
...BE THERE?
...HUH?
ARAI?
gasp
OH NO!
I SAID IT.
...SHE'LL BE THERE.

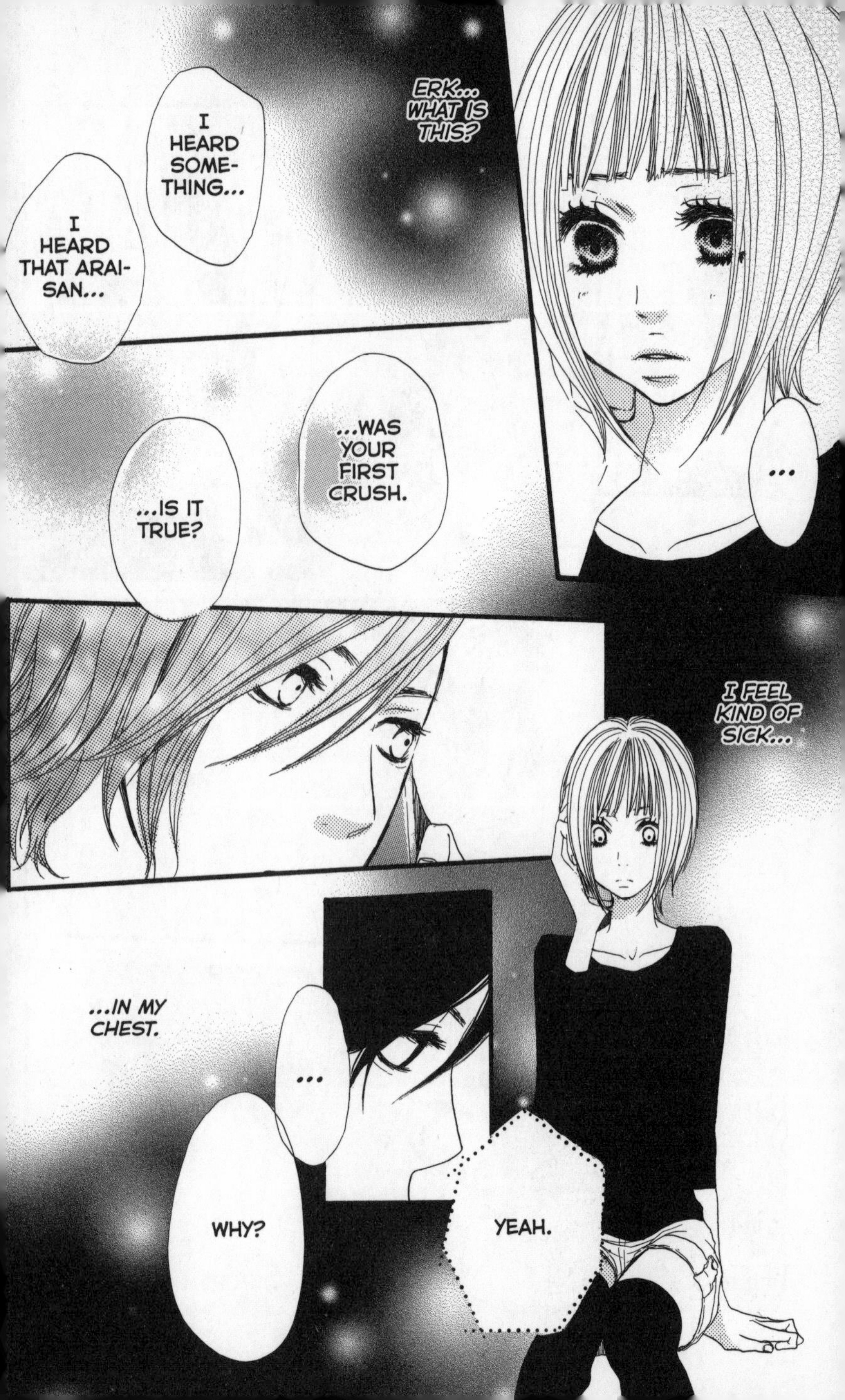
ERK... WHAT IS THIS?
I HEARD SOME-THING...
I HEARD THAT ARAI-SAN...
...WAS YOUR FIRST CRUSH.
...IS IT TRUE?
...
I FEEL KIND OF SICK...
...IN MY CHEST.
...
YEAH.
WHY?

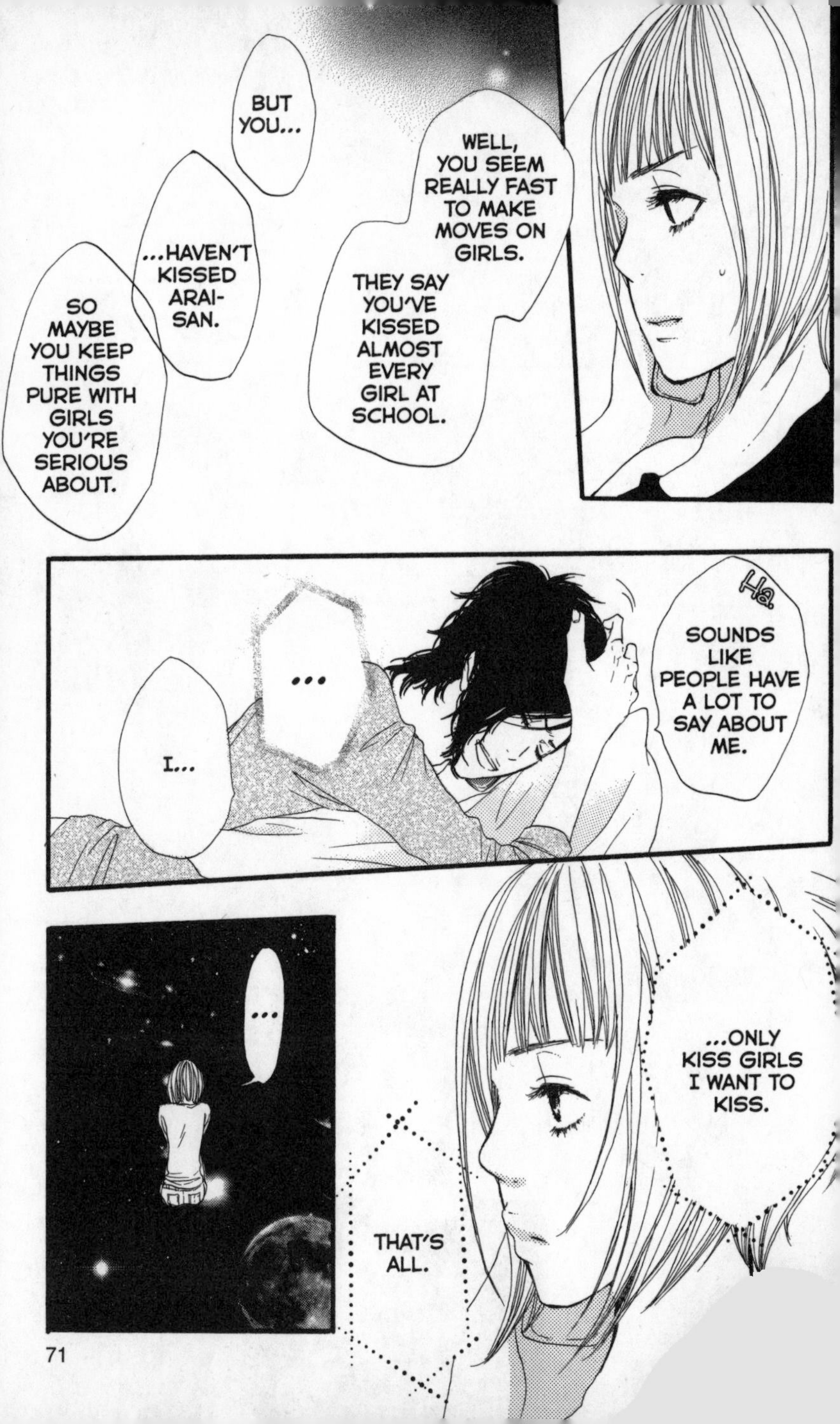
WELL, YOU SEEM REALLY FAST TO MAKE MOVES ON GIRLS.
THEY SAY YOU'VE KISSED ALMOST EVERY GIRL AT SCHOOL.
BUT YOU...
...HAVEN'T KISSED ARAI-SAN.
SO MAYBE YOU KEEP THINGS PURE WITH GIRLS YOU'RE SERIOUS ABOUT.
Ha.
SOUNDS LIKE PEOPLE HAVE A LOT TO SAY ABOUT ME.
...
I...
...ONLY KISS GIRLS I WANT TO KISS.
THAT'S ALL.
...

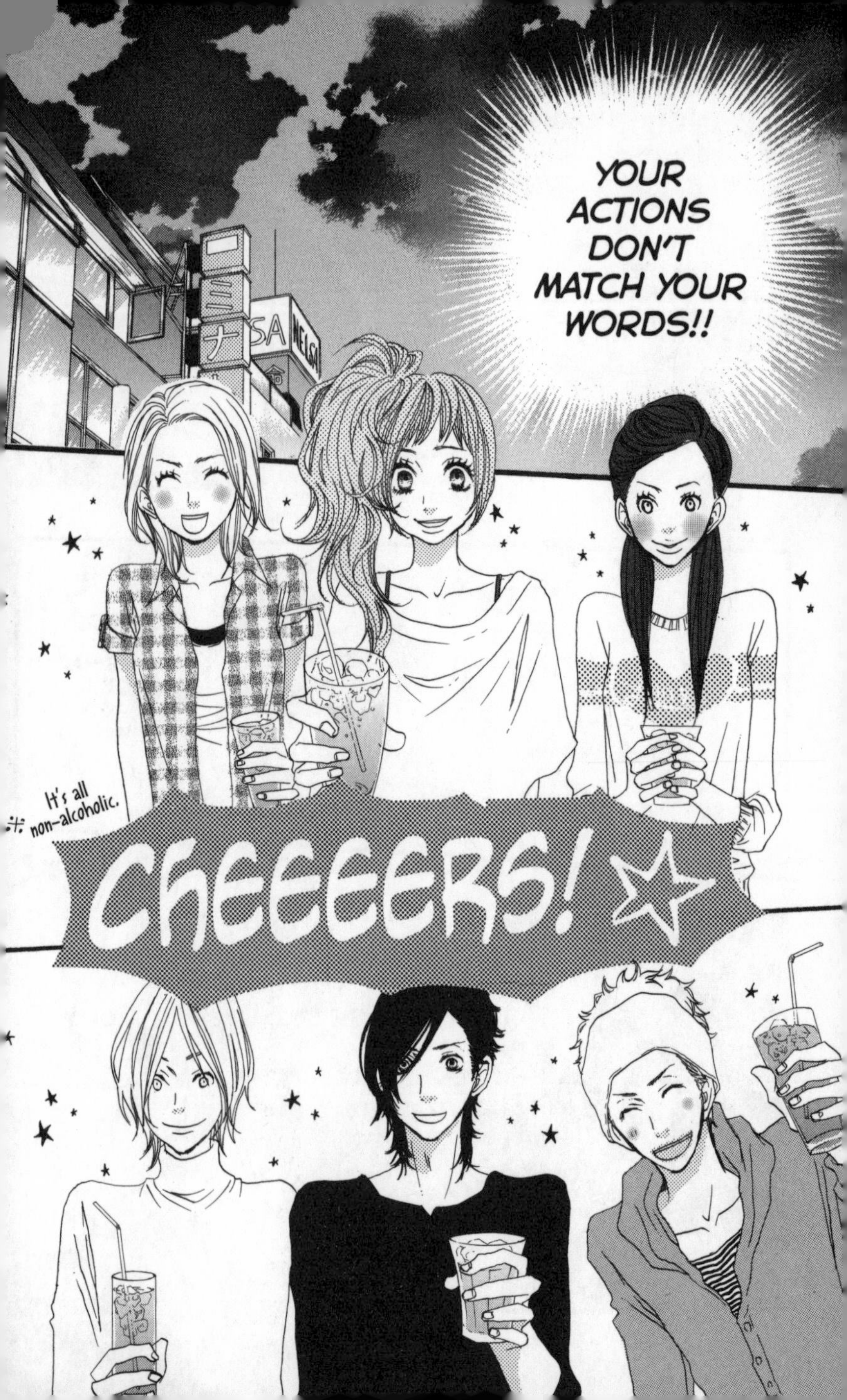
YOUR ACTIONS DON'T MATCH YOUR WORDS!!
※ It's all non-alcoholic.
CHEEEERS! ☆

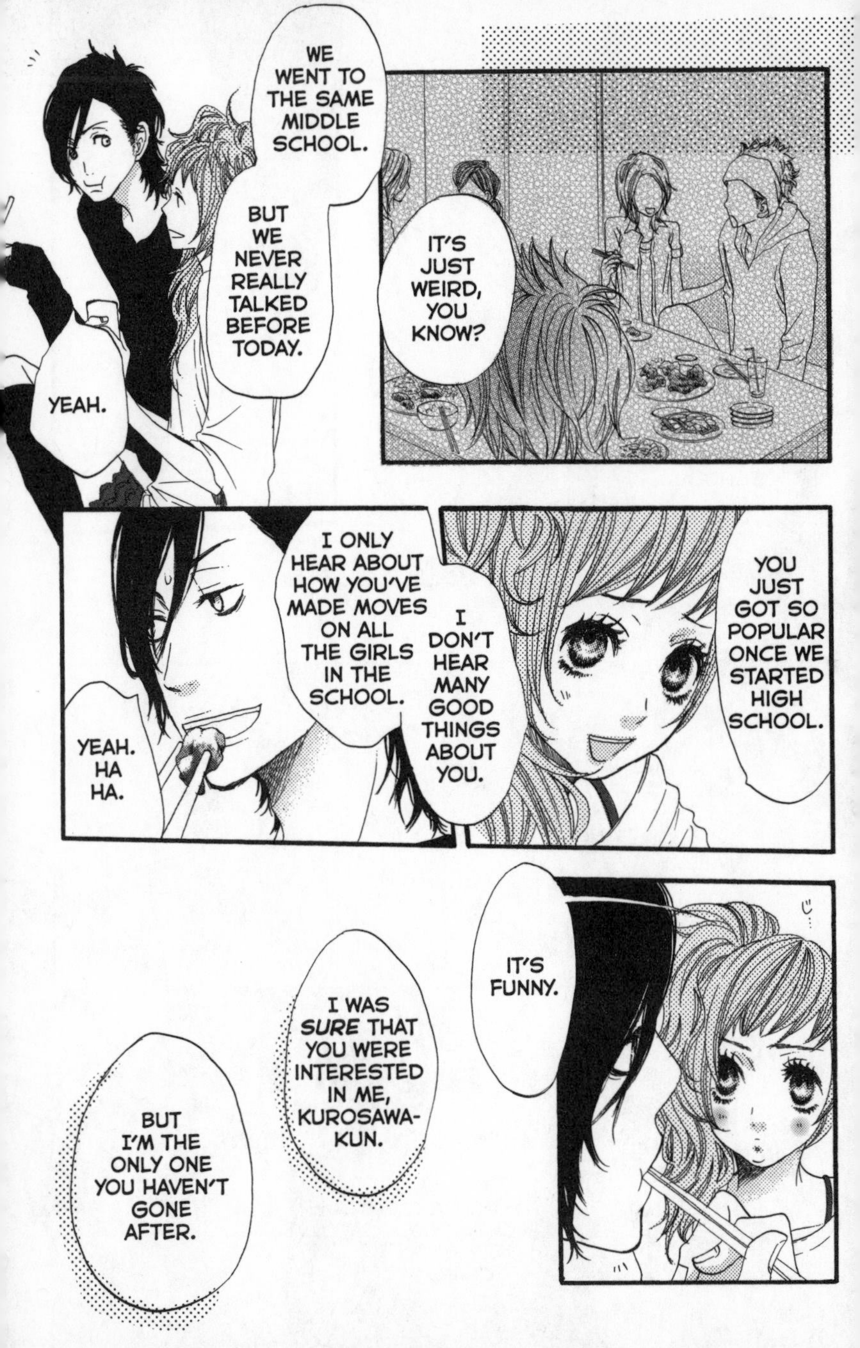
IT'S JUST WEIRD, YOU KNOW?
WE WENT TO THE SAME MIDDLE SCHOOL.
BUT WE NEVER REALLY TALKED BEFORE TODAY.
YEAH.
YOU JUST GOT SO POPULAR ONCE WE STARTED HIGH SCHOOL.
I DON'T HEAR MANY GOOD THINGS ABOUT YOU.
I ONLY HEAR ABOUT HOW YOU'VE MADE MOVES ON ALL THE GIRLS IN THE SCHOOL.
YEAH. HA HA.
じ…
IT'S FUNNY.
I WAS *SURE* THAT YOU WERE INTERESTED IN ME, KUROSAWA-KUN.
BUT I'M THE ONLY ONE YOU HAVEN'T GONE AFTER.

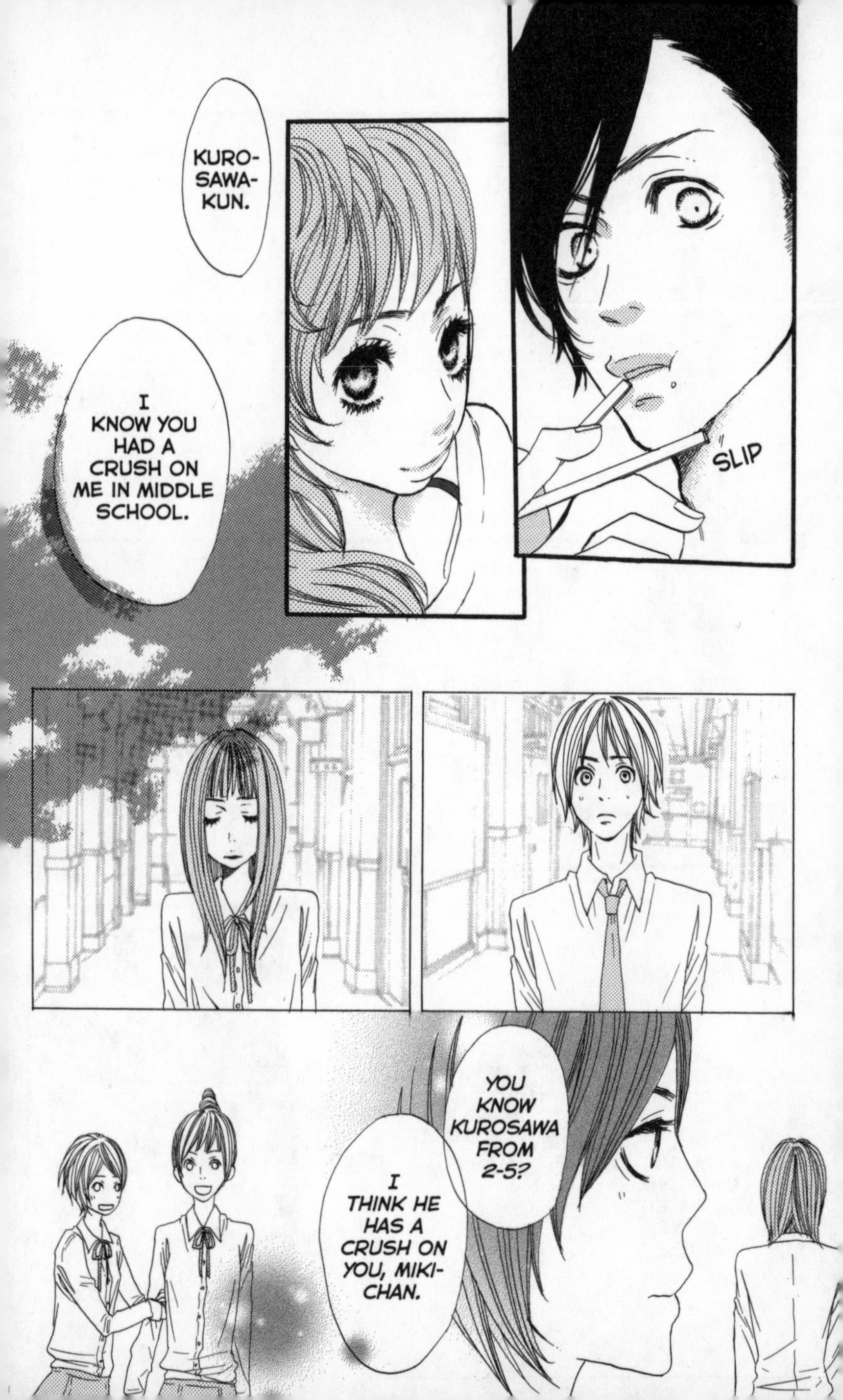
SLIP
KURO-SAWA-KUN.
I KNOW YOU HAD A CRUSH ON ME IN MIDDLE SCHOOL.
YOU KNOW KUROSAWA FROM 2-5?
I THINK HE HAS A CRUSH ON YOU, MIKI-CHAN.

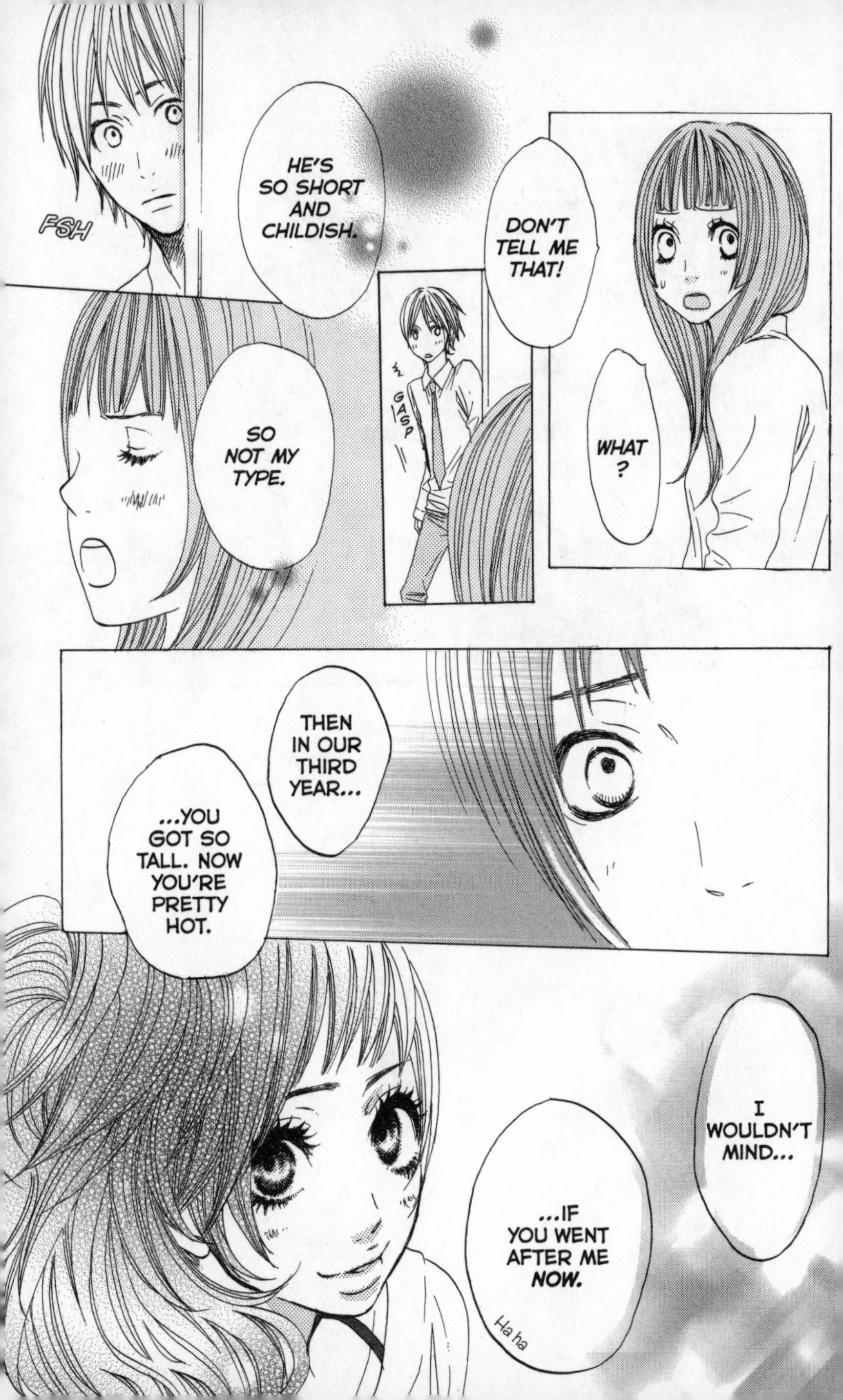
DON'T TELL ME THAT!
WHAT?
HE'S SO SHORT AND CHILDISH.
FSH
GASP
SO NOT MY TYPE.
THEN IN OUR THIRD YEAR...
...YOU GOT SO TALL. NOW YOU'RE PRETTY HOT.
I WOULDN'T MIND...
...IF YOU WENT AFTER ME NOW.
Ha ha

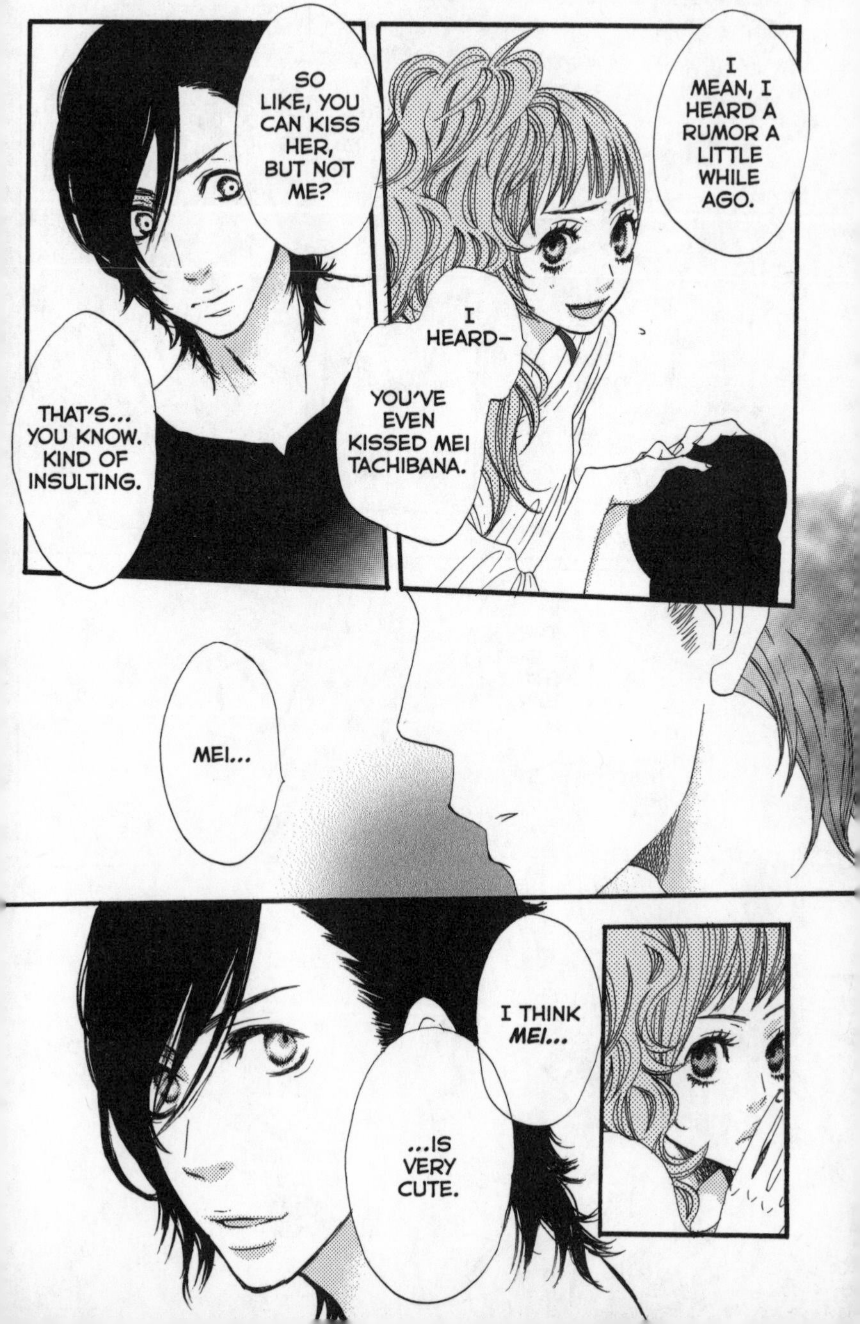
I MEAN, I HEARD A RUMOR A LITTLE WHILE AGO.
I HEARD—
YOU'VE EVEN KISSED MEI TACHIBANA.
SO LIKE, YOU CAN KISS HER, BUT NOT ME?
THAT'S... YOU KNOW. KIND OF INSULTING.
MEI...
I THINK *MEI...*
...IS VERY CUTE.

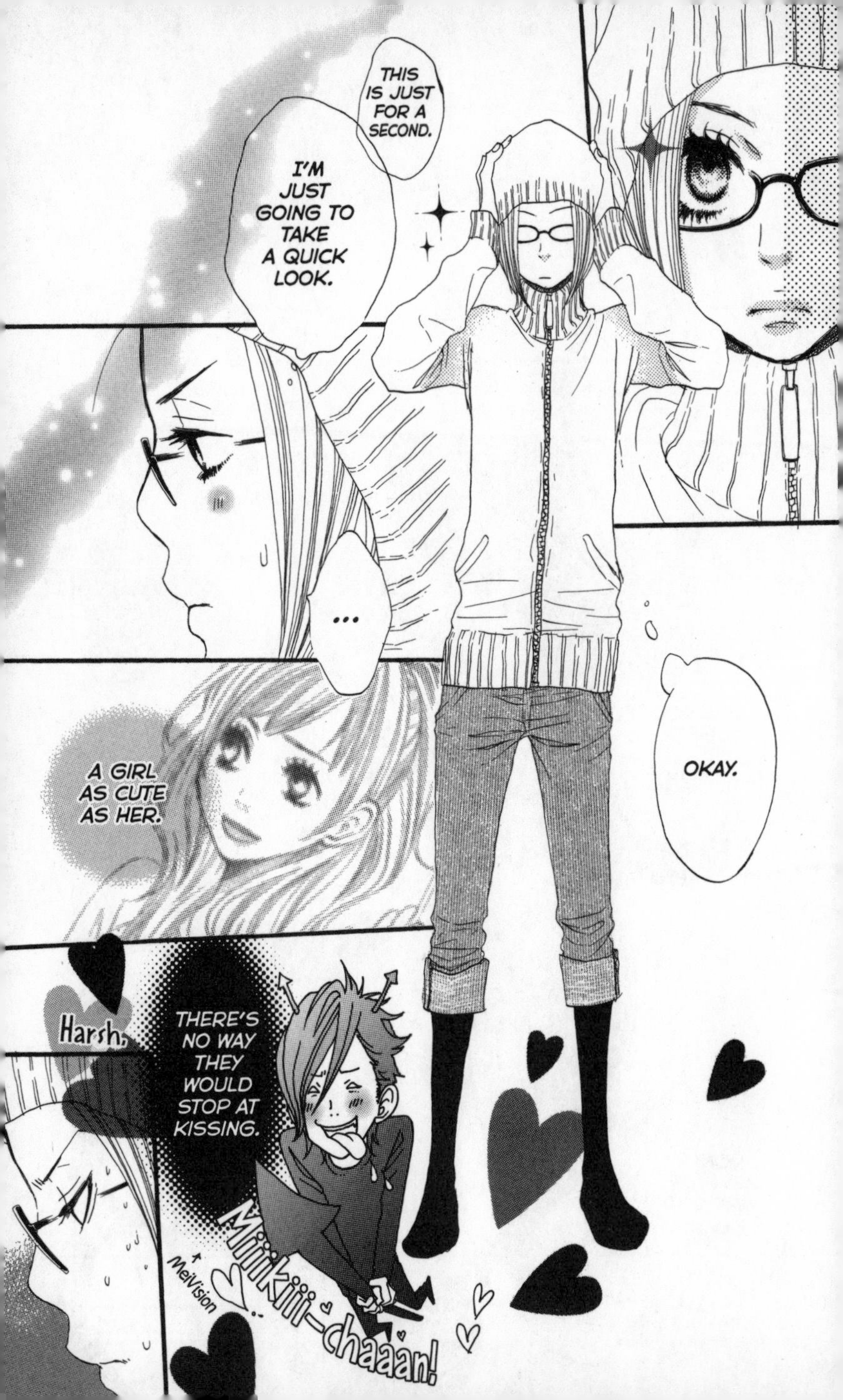
THIS IS JUST FOR A SECOND.
I'M JUST GOING TO TAKE A QUICK LOOK.
OKAY.
...
A GIRL AS CUTE AS HER.
THERE'S NO WAY THEY WOULD STOP AT KISSING.
Miiikiii-chaaan!
MeiVision
Harsh.

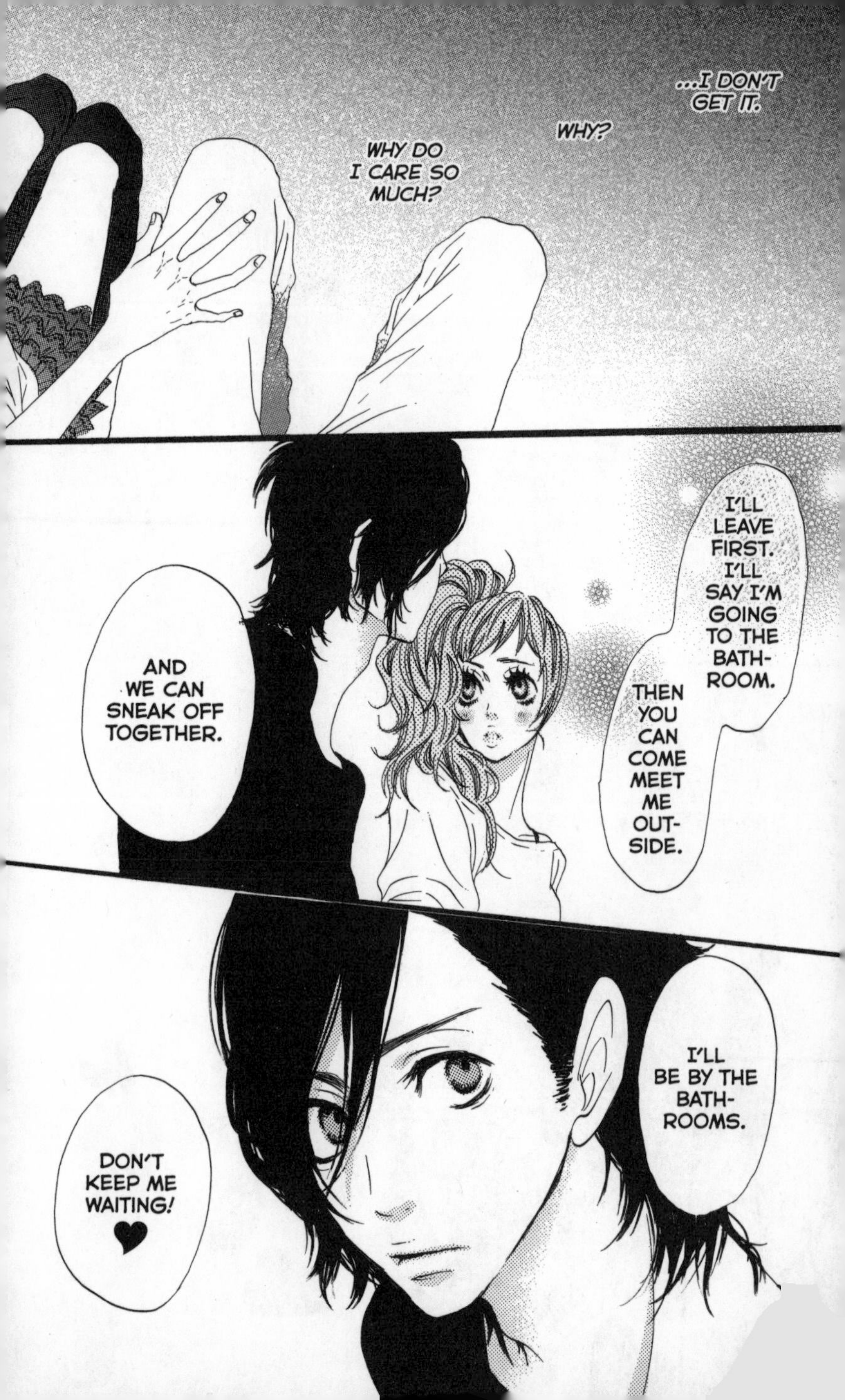
...I DON'T GET IT.
WHY?
WHY DO I CARE SO MUCH?
I'LL LEAVE FIRST. I'LL SAY I'M GOING TO THE BATHROOM.
THEN YOU CAN COME MEET ME OUTSIDE.
AND WE CAN SNEAK OFF TOGETHER.
I'LL BE BY THE BATHROOMS.
DON'T KEEP ME WAITING! ♥

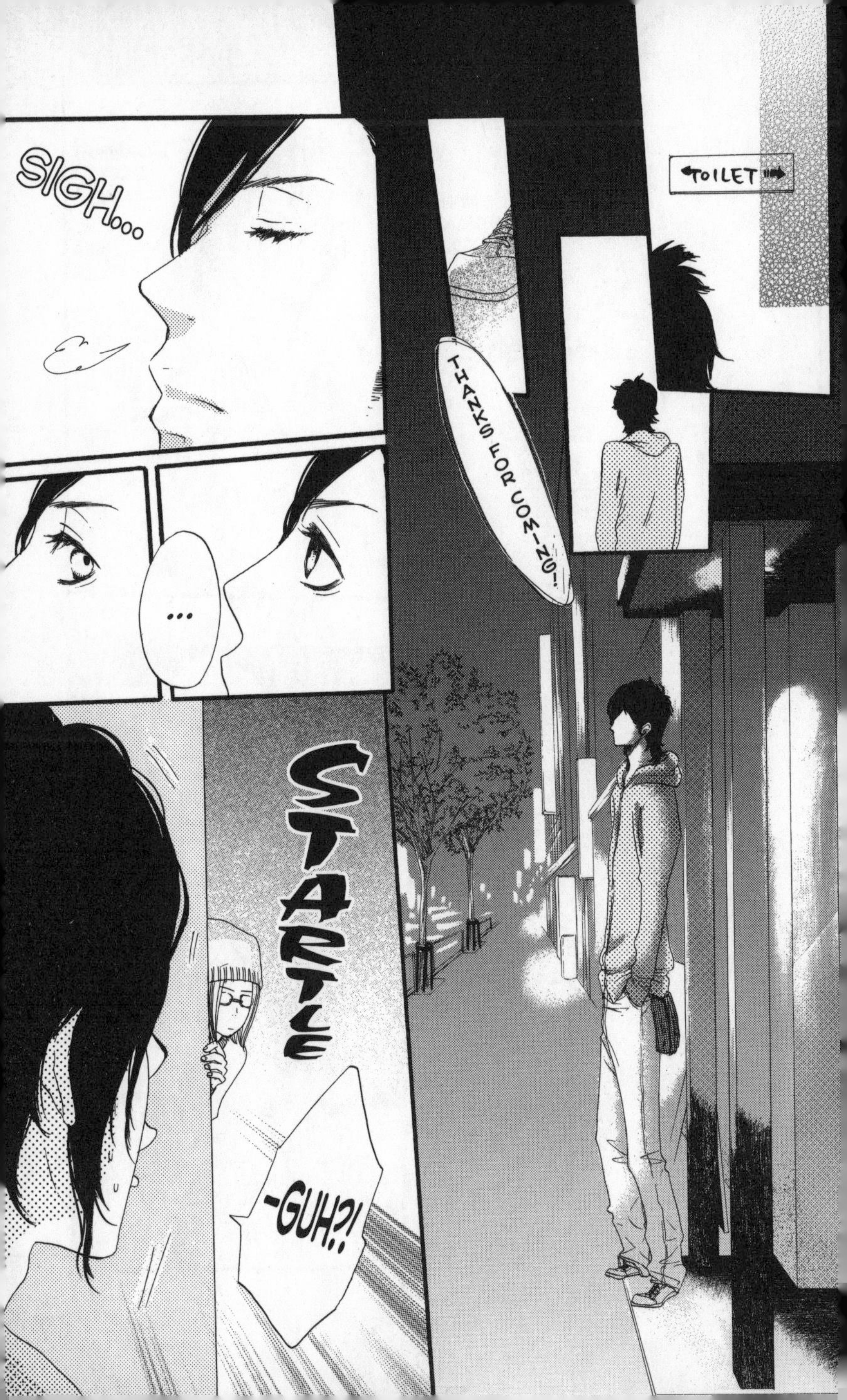
TOILET
THANKS FOR COMING!
SIGH...
...
STARTLE
-GUH?!

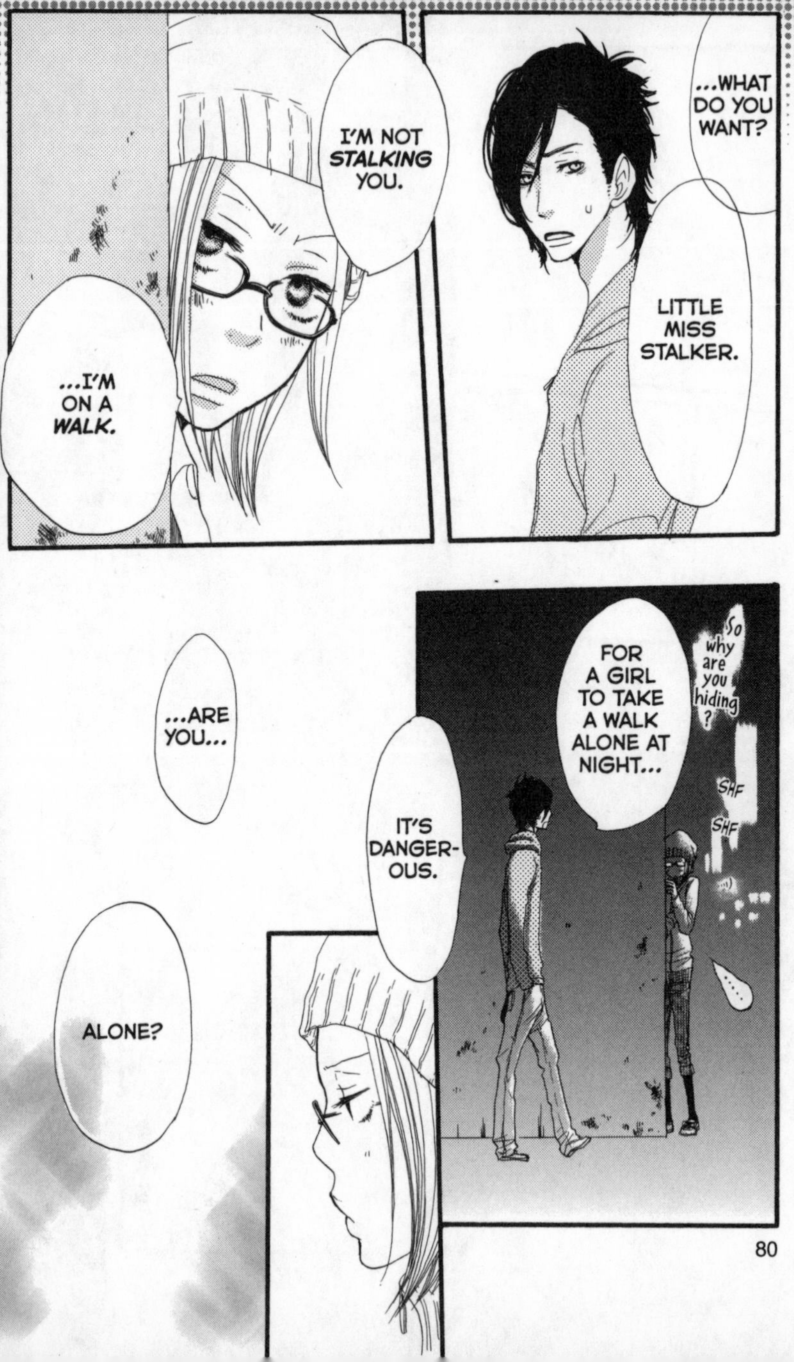
...WHAT DO YOU WANT?
LITTLE MISS STALKER.
I'M NOT *STALKING* YOU.
...I'M ON A *WALK*.
So why are you hiding?
FOR A GIRL TO TAKE A WALK ALONE AT NIGHT...
SHF
SHF
IT'S DANGER-OUS.
...
...ARE YOU...
ALONE?

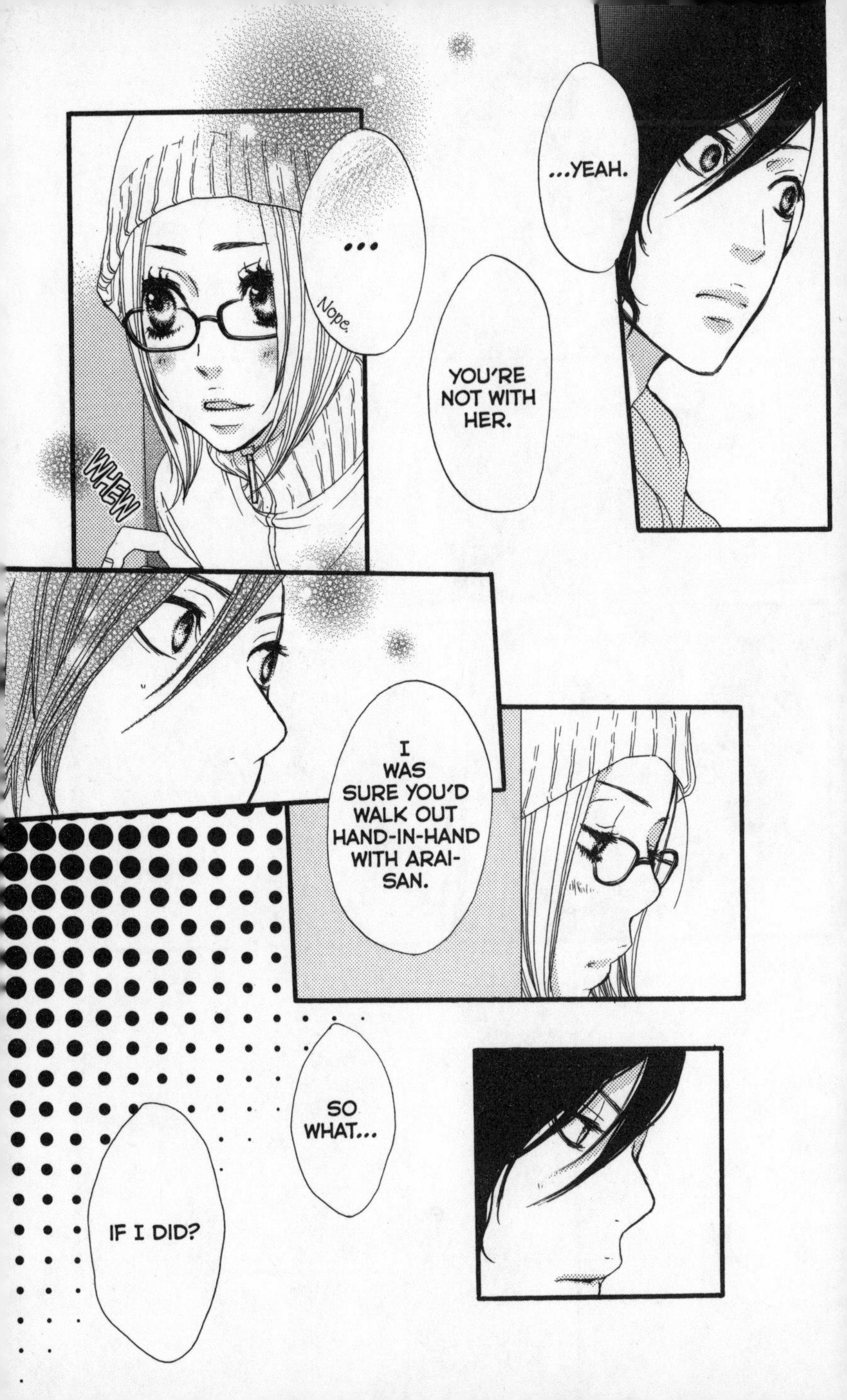
...YEAH.
YOU'RE NOT WITH HER.
...
Nope.
WHEW
I WAS SURE YOU'D WALK OUT HAND-IN-HAND WITH ARAI-SAN.
SO WHAT...
IF I DID?

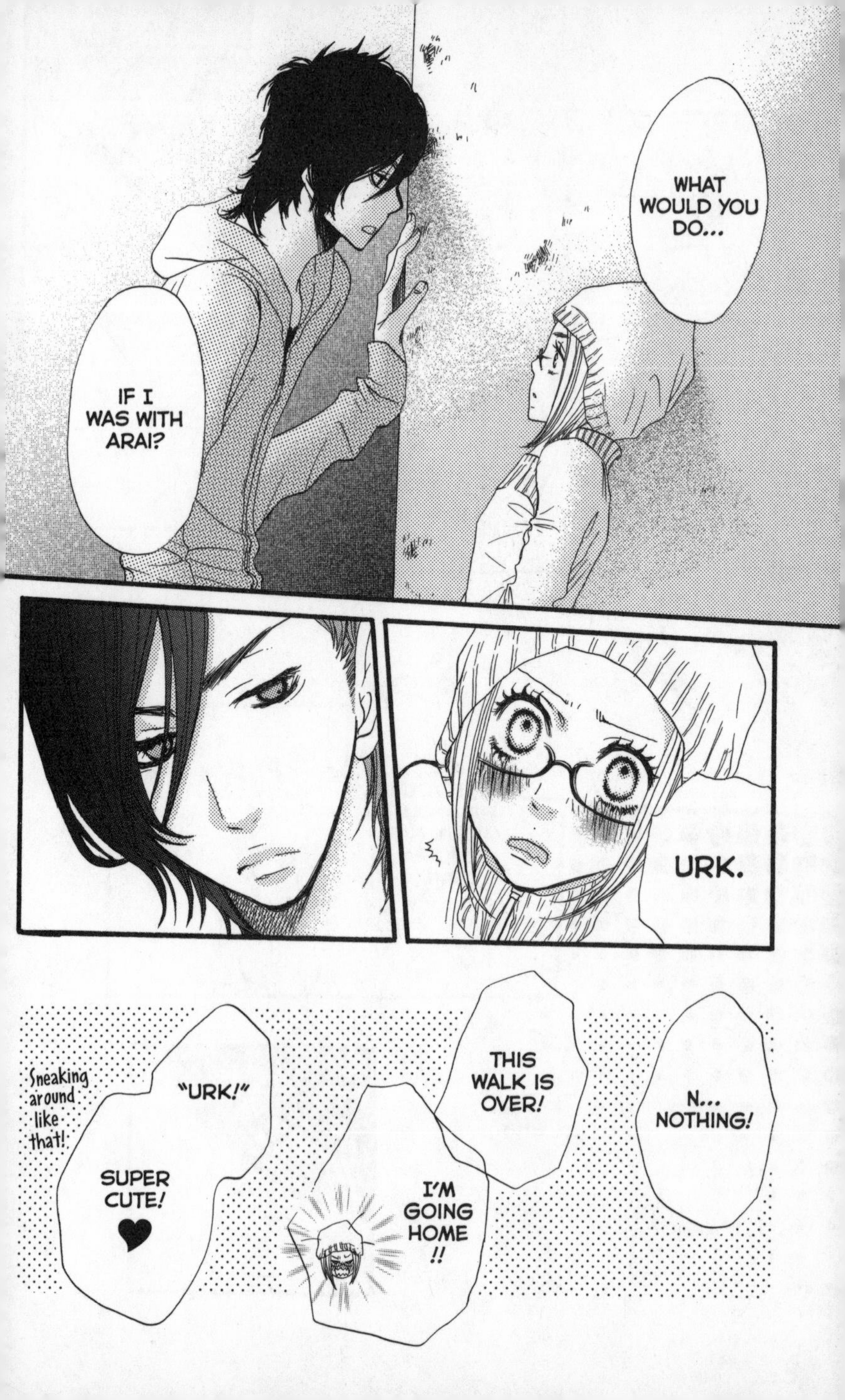
WHAT WOULD YOU DO...
IF I WAS WITH ARAI?
URK.
N... NOTHING!
THIS WALK IS OVER!
I'M GOING HOME !!
"URK!"
SUPER CUTE! ♥
Sneaking around like that!

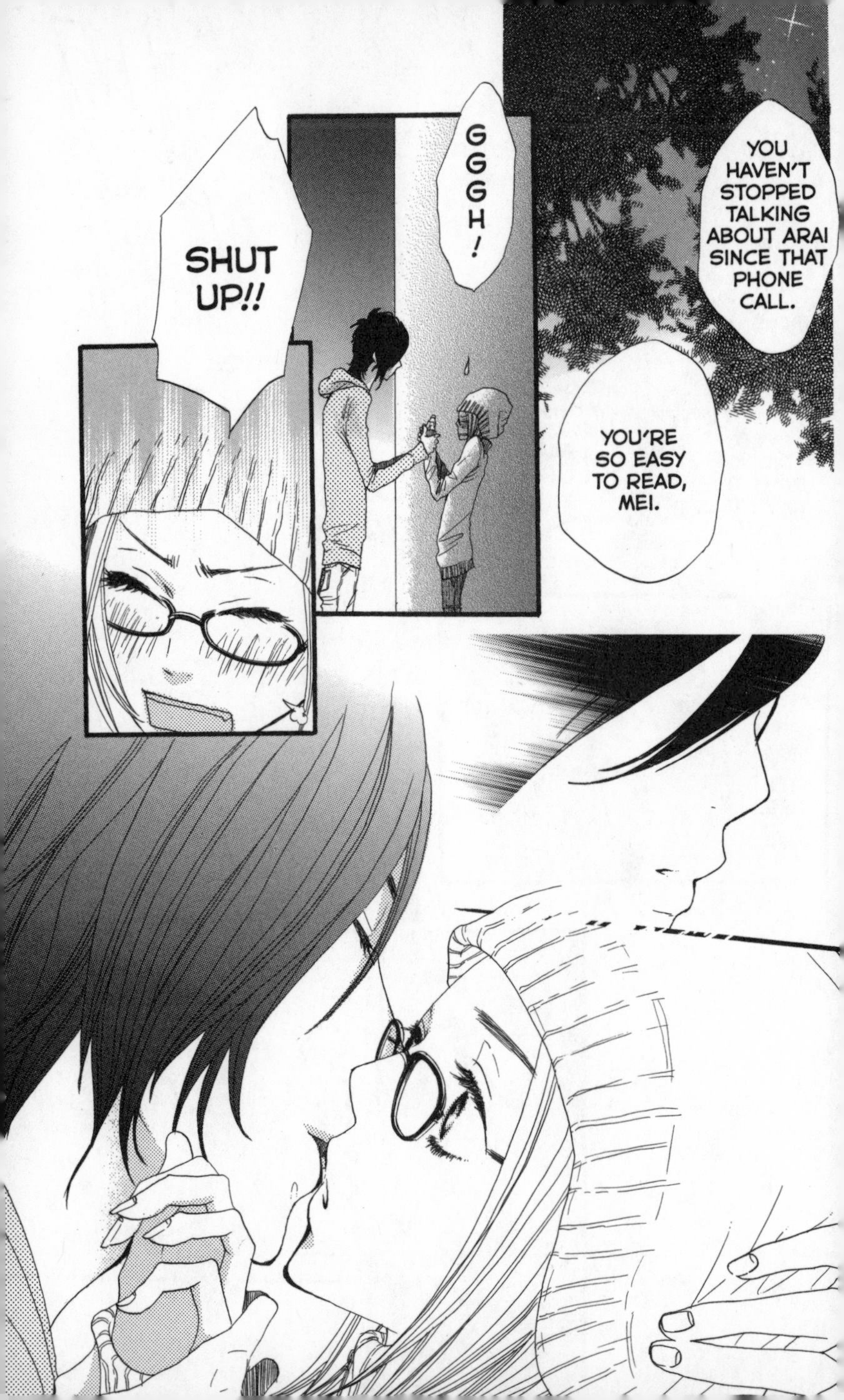
YOU HAVEN'T STOPPED TALKING ABOUT ARAI SINCE THAT PHONE CALL.
YOU'RE SO EASY TO READ, MEI.
GGGH!
SHUT UP!!

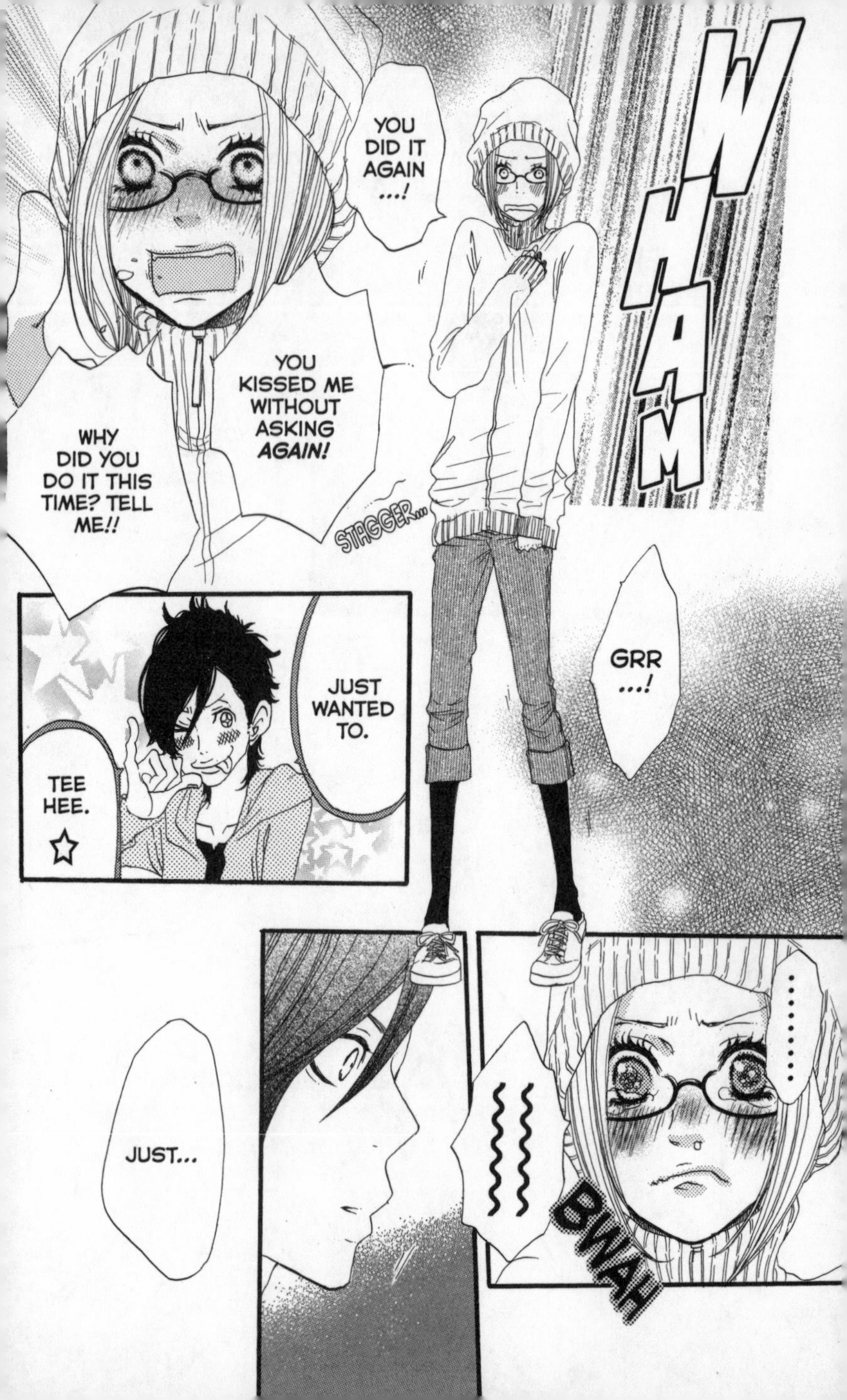
WHAM
YOU DID IT AGAIN ...!
STAGGER...
YOU KISSED ME WITHOUT ASKING *AGAIN!*
WHY DID YOU DO IT THIS TIME? TELL ME!!
GRR ...!
JUST WANTED TO.
TEE HEE. ☆
......
BWAH
JUST...

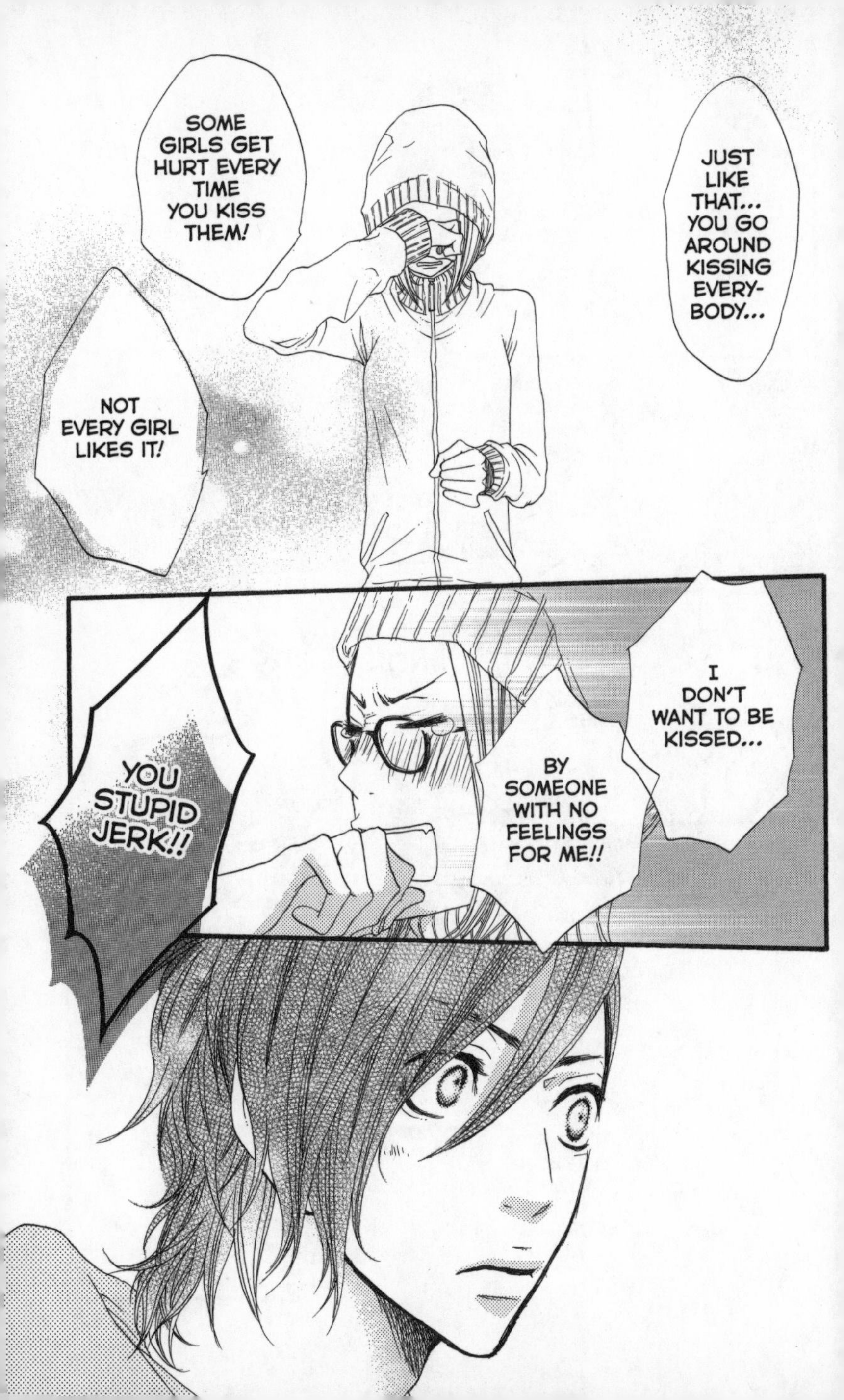
JUST LIKE THAT... YOU GO AROUND KISSING EVERY-BODY...
SOME GIRLS GET HURT EVERY TIME YOU KISS THEM!
NOT EVERY GIRL LIKES IT!
I DON'T WANT TO BE KISSED...
BY SOMEONE WITH NO FEELINGS FOR ME!!
YOU STUPID JERK!!

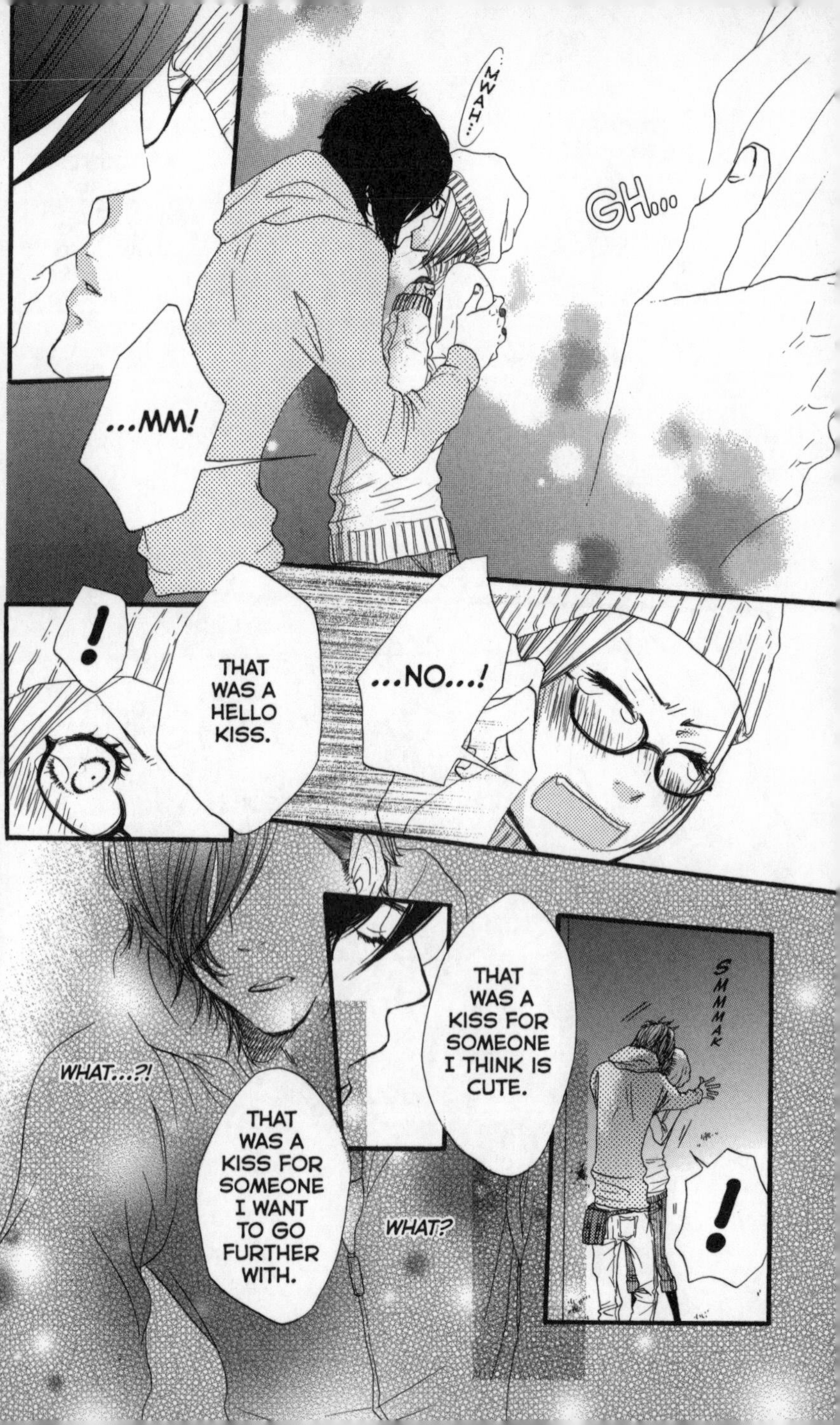
...MWAH...
GH...
...MM!
...NO...!
!
THAT WAS A HELLO KISS.
SMMMAK
!
THAT WAS A KISS FOR SOMEONE I THINK IS CUTE.
THAT WAS A KISS FOR SOMEONE I WANT TO GO FURTHER WITH.
WHAT?
WHAT...?!

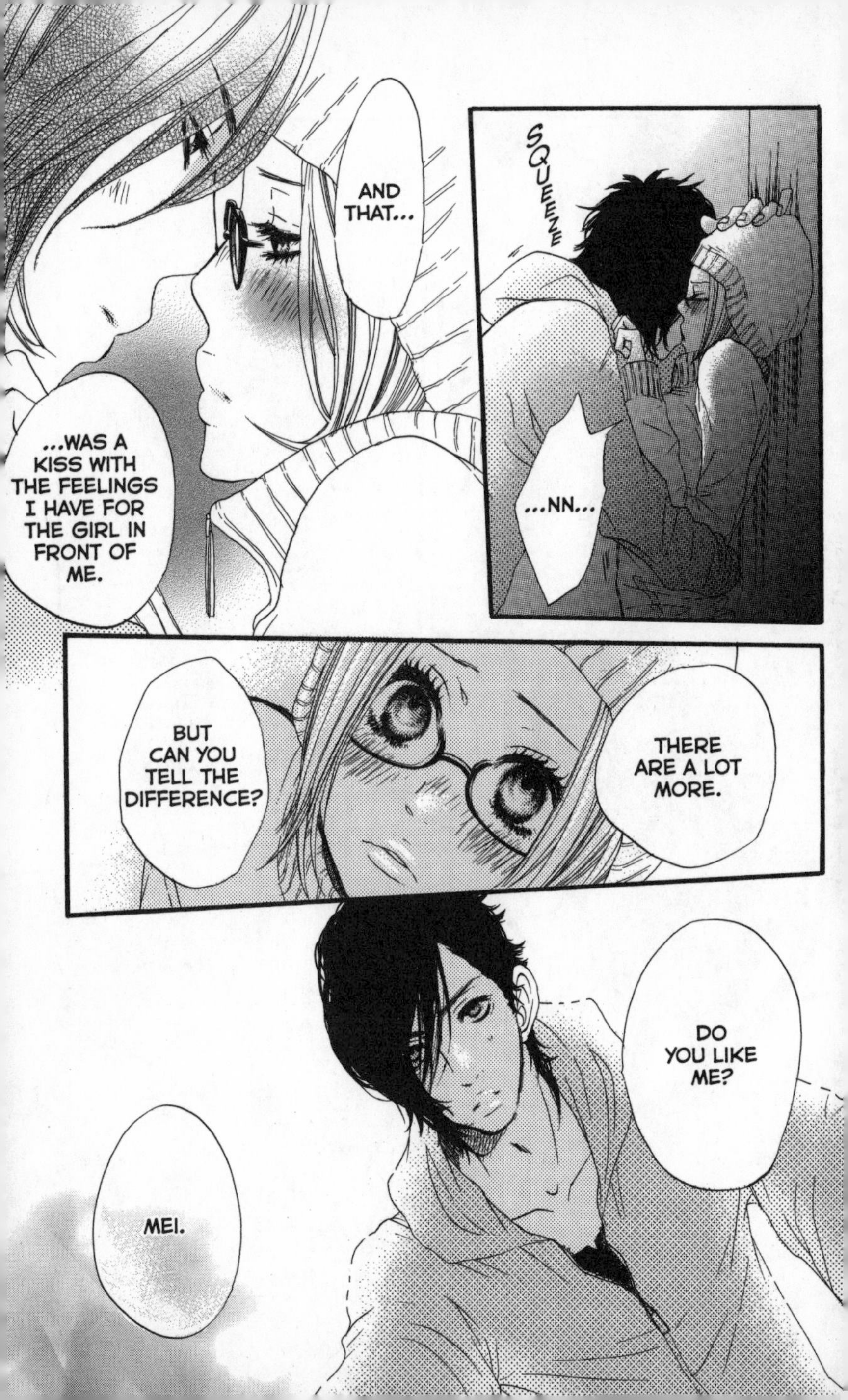
SQUEEZE
...NN...
AND THAT...
...WAS A KISS WITH THE FEELINGS I HAVE FOR THE GIRL IN FRONT OF ME.
THERE ARE A LOT MORE.
BUT CAN YOU TELL THE DIFFERENCE?
DO YOU LIKE ME?
MEI.

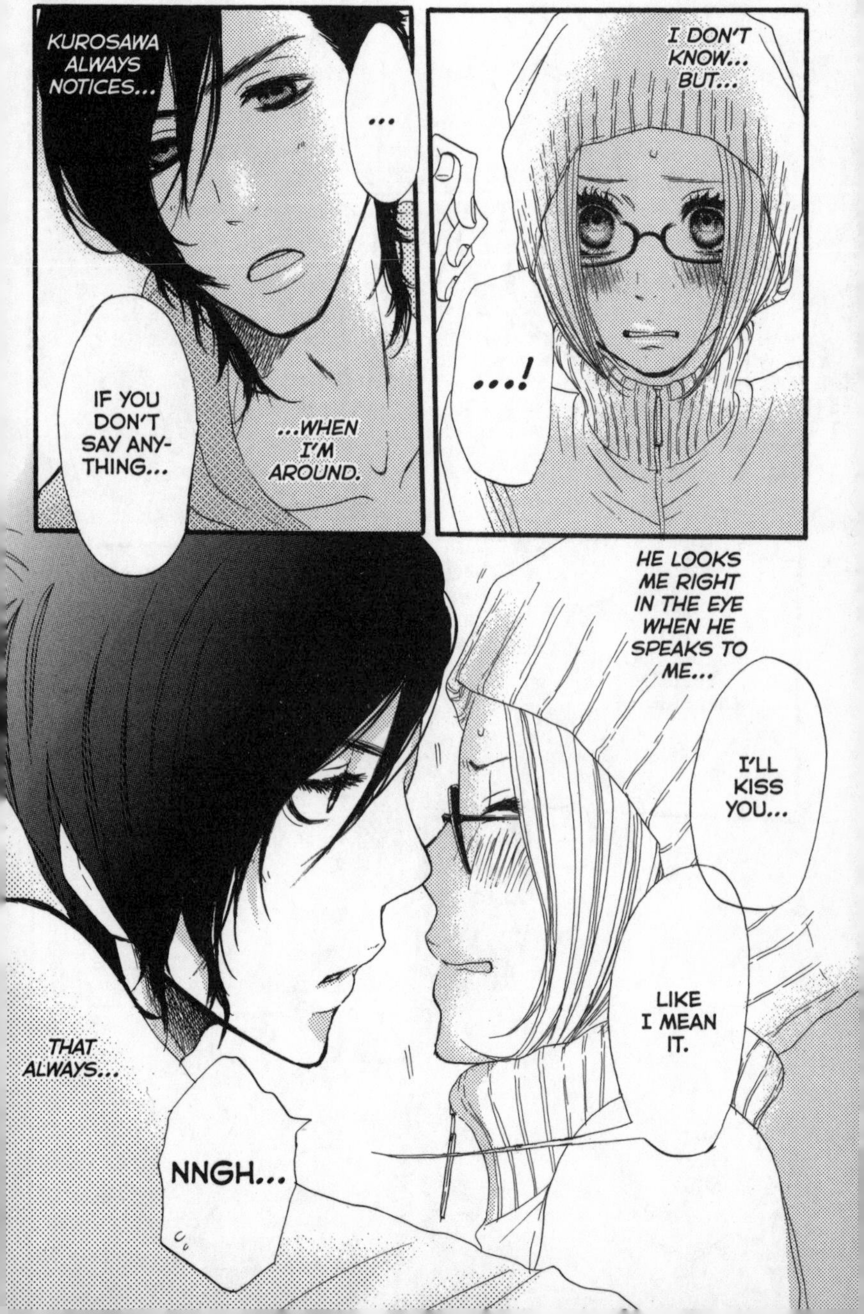

I DON'T KNOW... BUT...
...!
...
KUROSAWA ALWAYS NOTICES...
...WHEN I'M AROUND.
IF YOU DON'T SAY ANY-THING...
HE LOOKS ME RIGHT IN THE EYE WHEN HE SPEAKS TO ME...
I'LL KISS YOU...
LIKE I MEAN IT.
THAT ALWAYS...
NNGH...

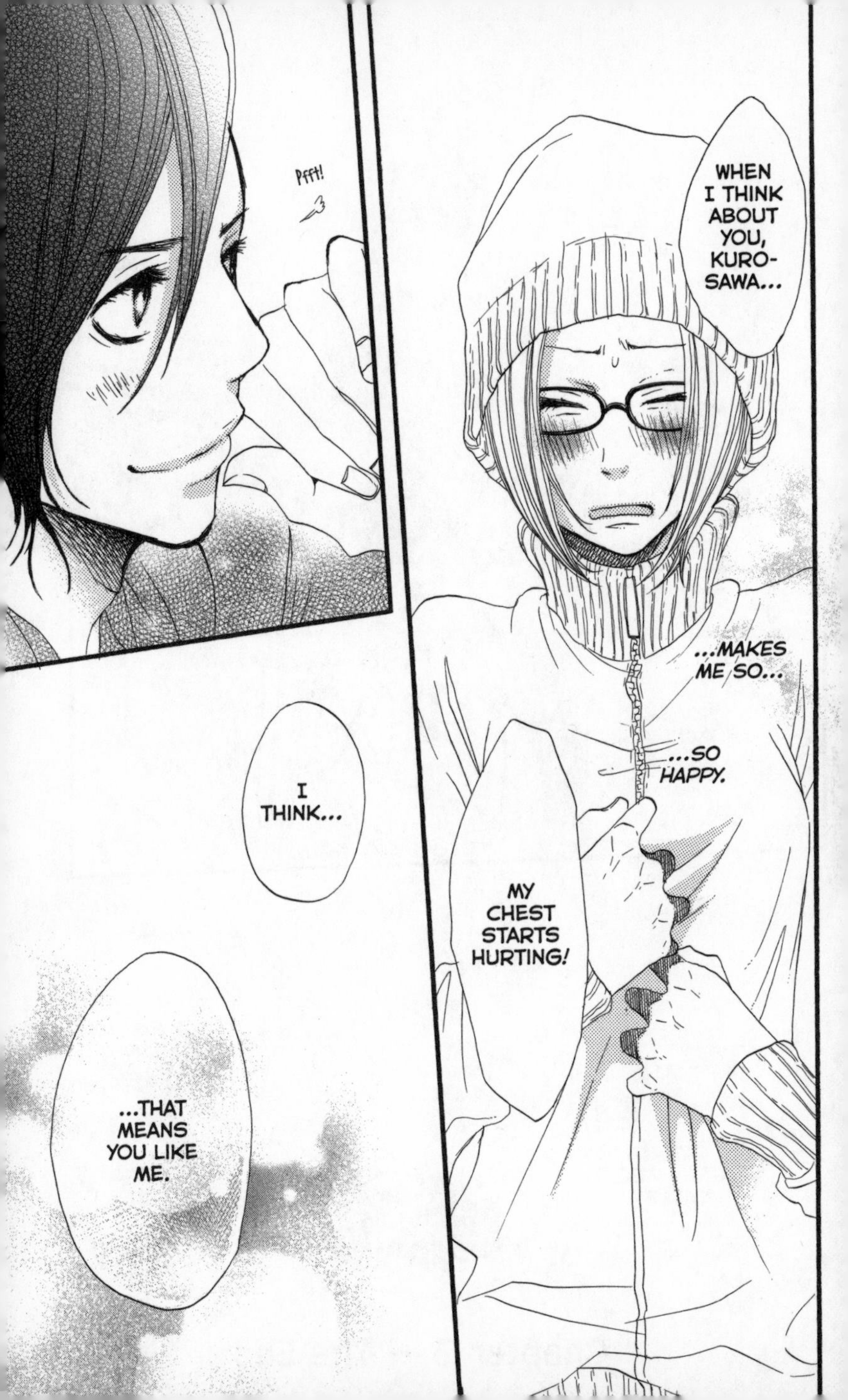
WHEN I THINK ABOUT YOU, KURO-SAWA...
...MAKES ME SO...
...SO HAPPY.
MY CHEST STARTS HURTING!
Pfft!
I THINK...
...THAT MEANS YOU LIKE ME.

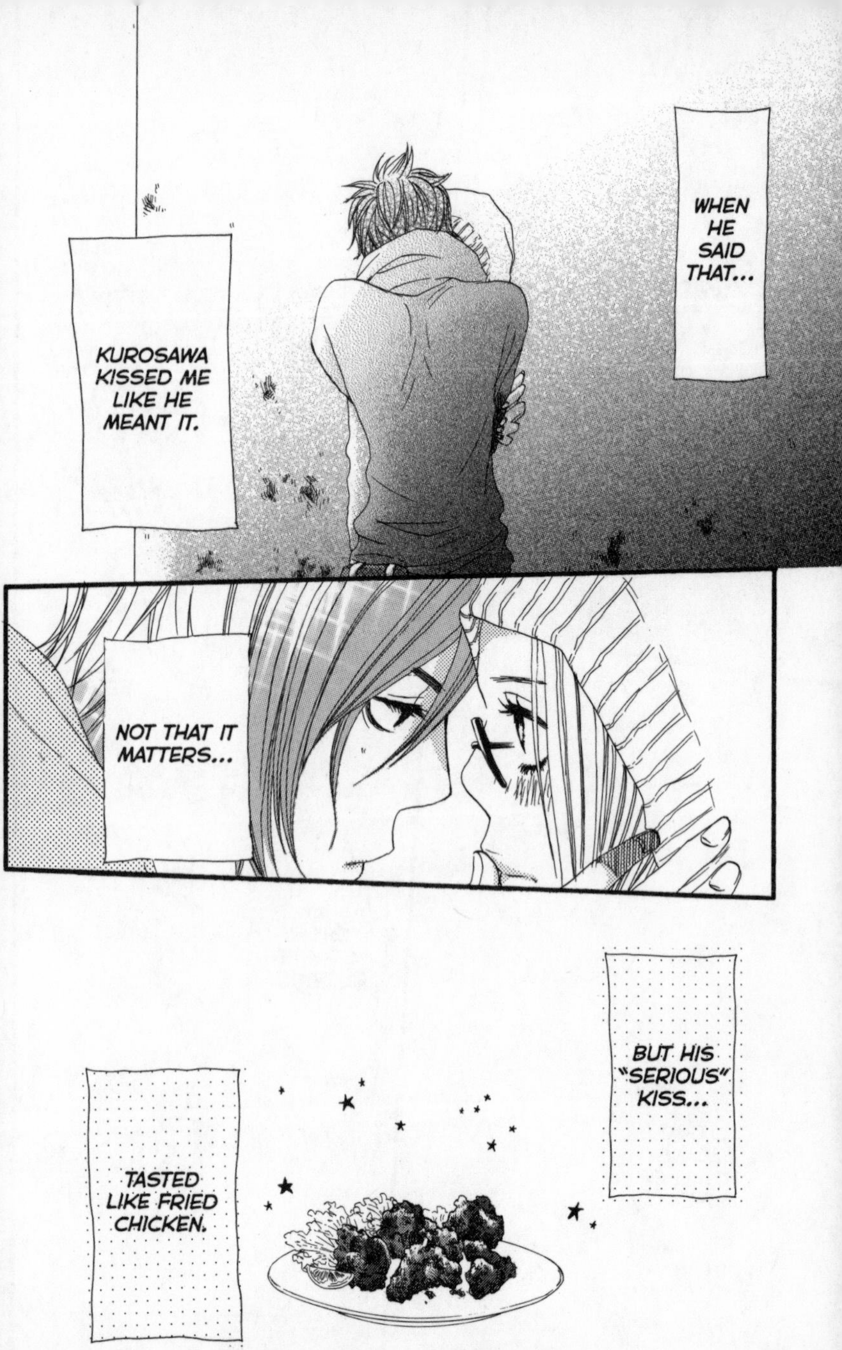
WHEN HE SAID THAT...
KUROSAWA KISSED ME LIKE HE MEANT IT.
NOT THAT IT MATTERS...
BUT HIS "SERIOUS" KISS...
TASTED LIKE FRIED CHICKEN.

Chapter 2 — The End

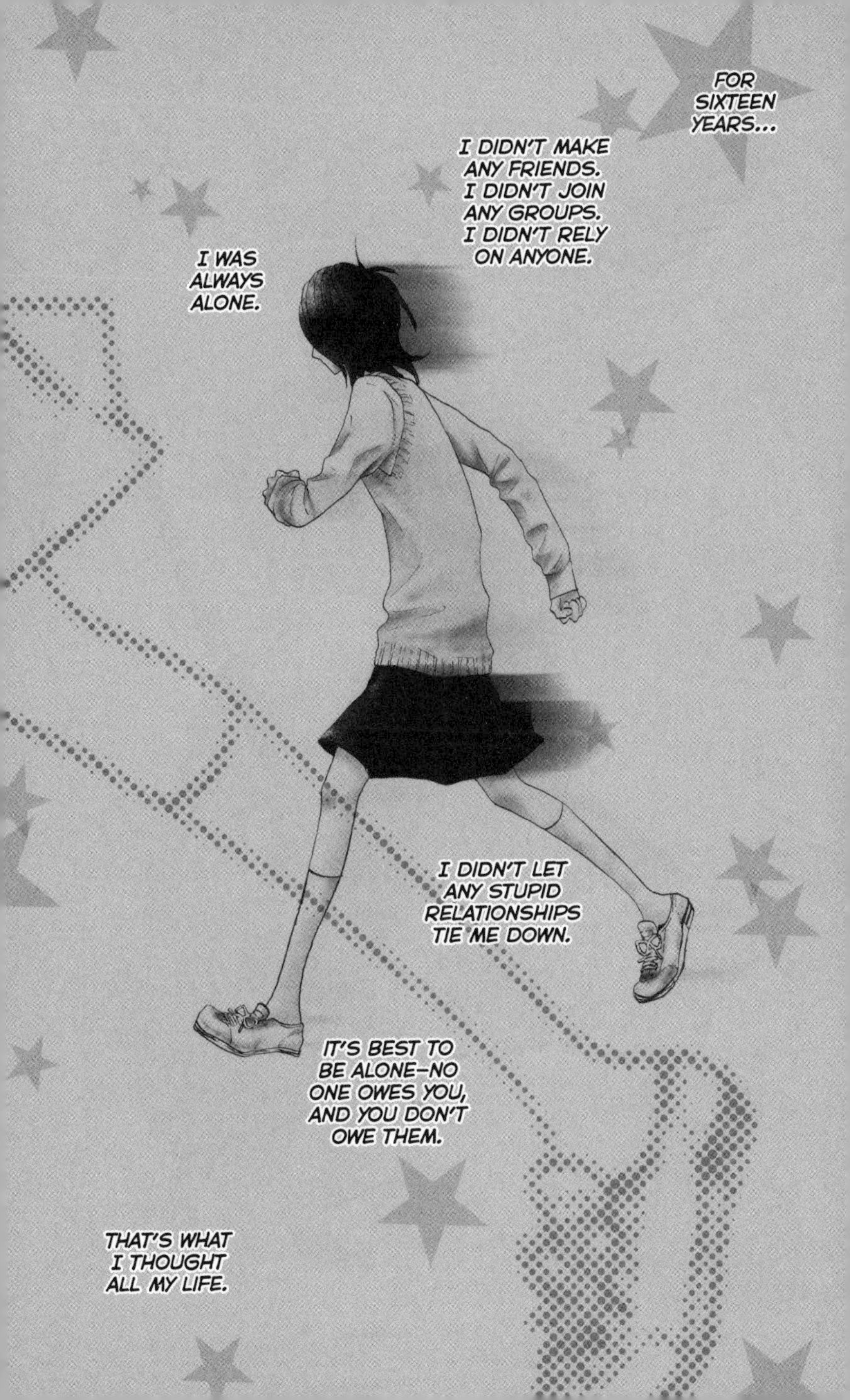
FOR SIXTEEN YEARS...
I DIDN'T MAKE ANY FRIENDS. I DIDN'T JOIN ANY GROUPS. I DIDN'T RELY ON ANYONE.
I WAS ALWAYS ALONE.
I DIDN'T LET ANY STUPID RELATIONSHIPS TIE ME DOWN.
IT'S BEST TO BE ALONE—NO ONE OWES YOU, AND YOU DON'T OWE THEM.
THAT'S WHAT I THOUGHT ALL MY LIFE.

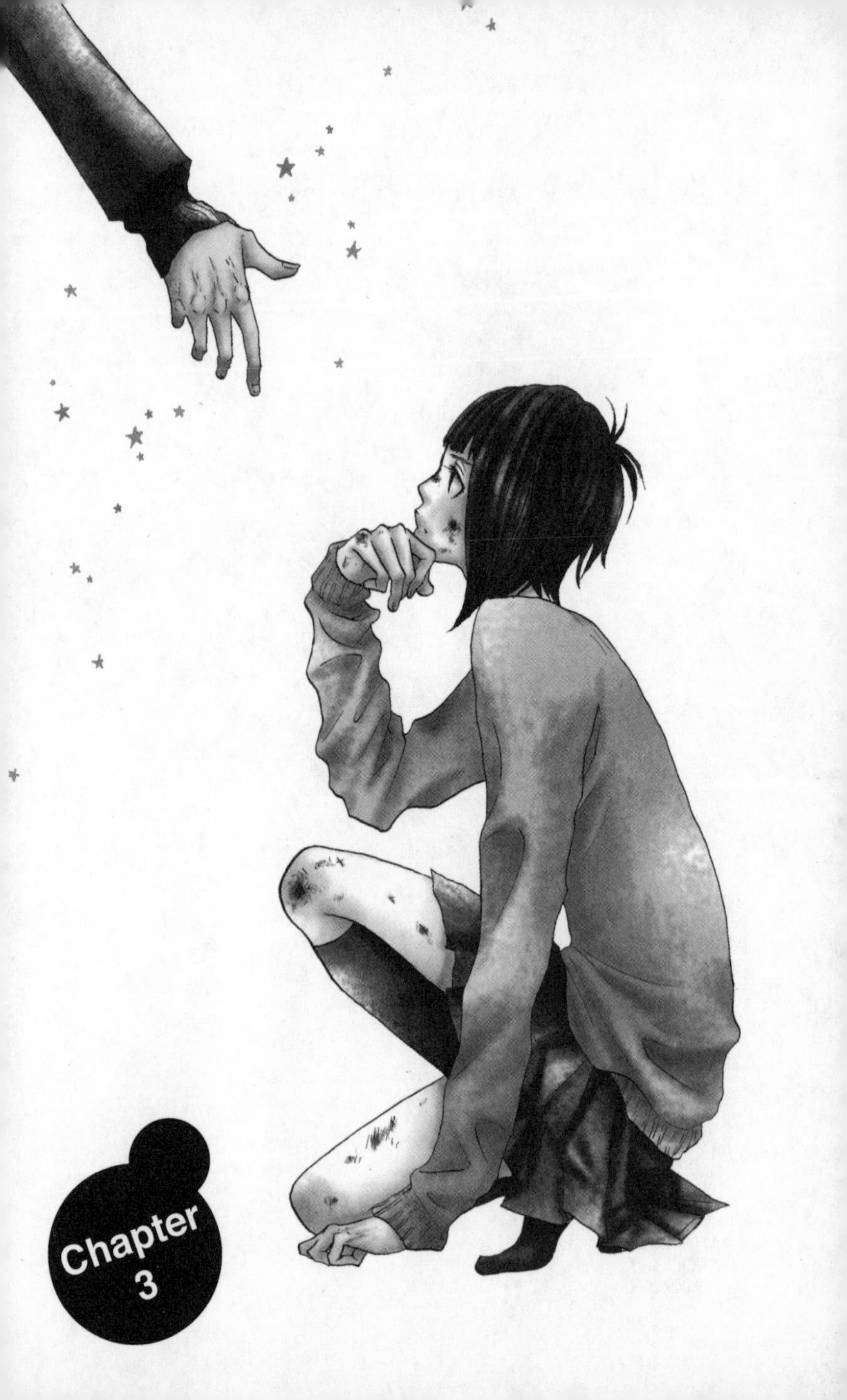
Chapter
3

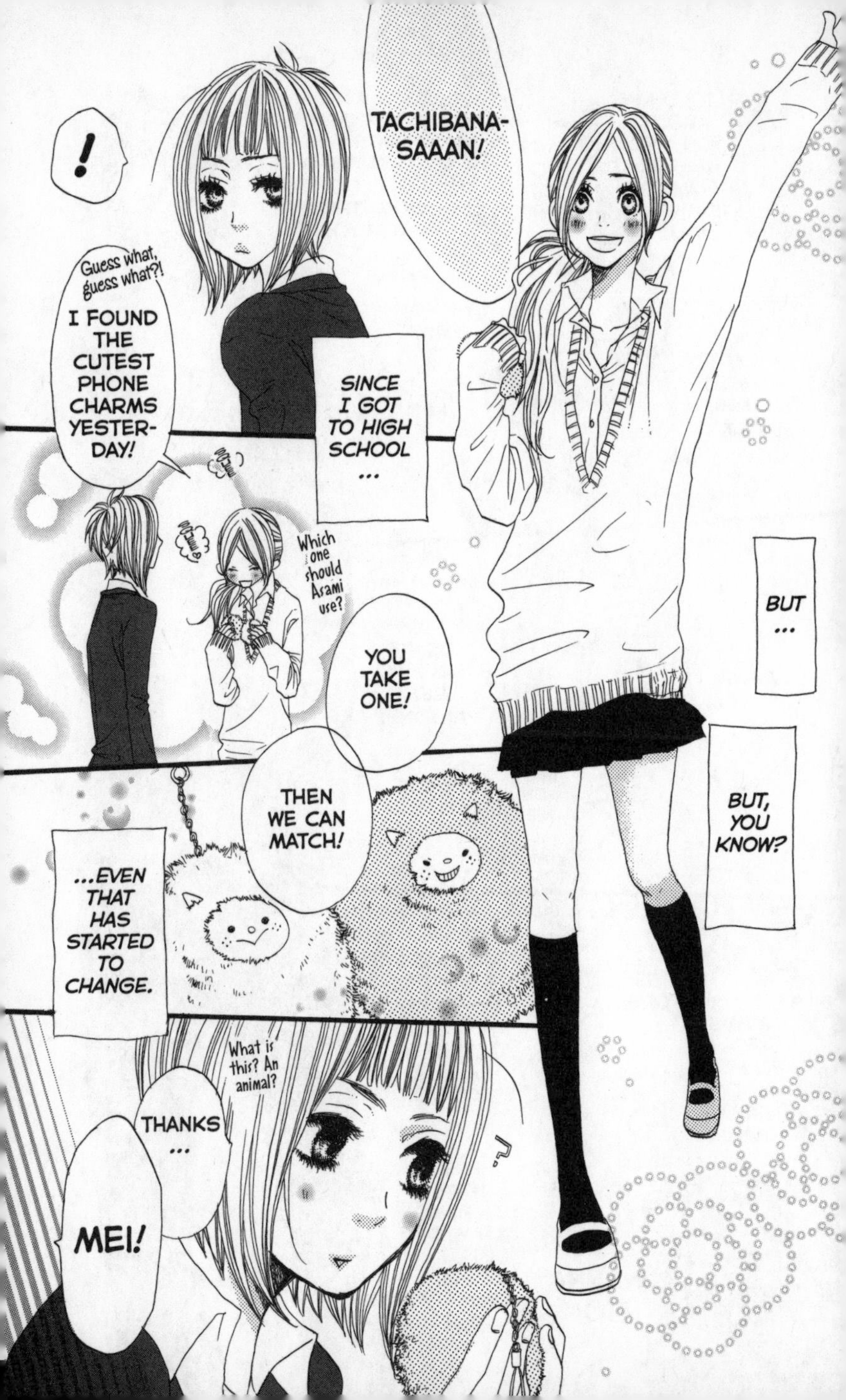

TACHIBANA-SAAAN!
SINCE I GOT TO HIGH SCHOOL ...
BUT ...
BUT, YOU KNOW?
!
Guess what, guess what?!
I FOUND THE CUTEST PHONE CHARMS YESTER-DAY!
Which one should Asami use?
YOU TAKE ONE!
THEN WE CAN MATCH!
...EVEN THAT HAS STARTED TO CHANGE.
What is this? An animal?
THANKS ...
MEI!

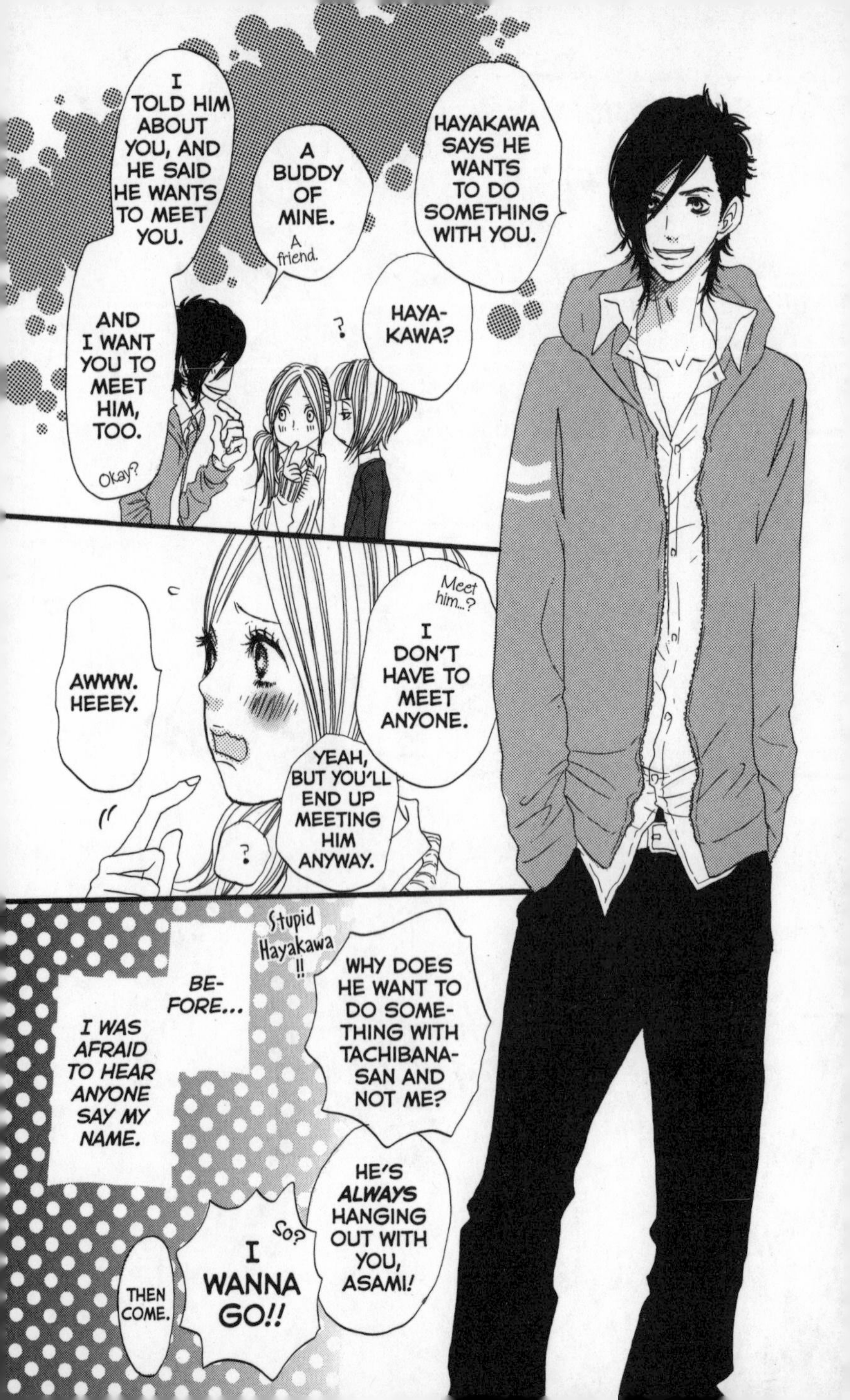
HAYAKAWA SAYS HE WANTS TO DO SOMETHING WITH YOU.
HAYA-KAWA?
?
A BUDDY OF MINE.
A friend.
I TOLD HIM ABOUT YOU, AND HE SAID HE WANTS TO MEET YOU.
AND I WANT YOU TO MEET HIM, TOO.
Okay?
Meet him...?
I DON'T HAVE TO MEET ANYONE.
YEAH, BUT YOU'LL END UP MEETING HIM ANYWAY.
?
AWWW. HEEEY.
Stupid Hayakawa!!
WHY DOES HE WANT TO DO SOME-THING WITH TACHIBANA-SAN AND NOT ME?
BE-FORE...
I WAS AFRAID TO HEAR ANYONE SAY MY NAME.
HE'S ALWAYS HANGING OUT WITH YOU, ASAMI!
So?
I WANNA GO!!
THEN COME.

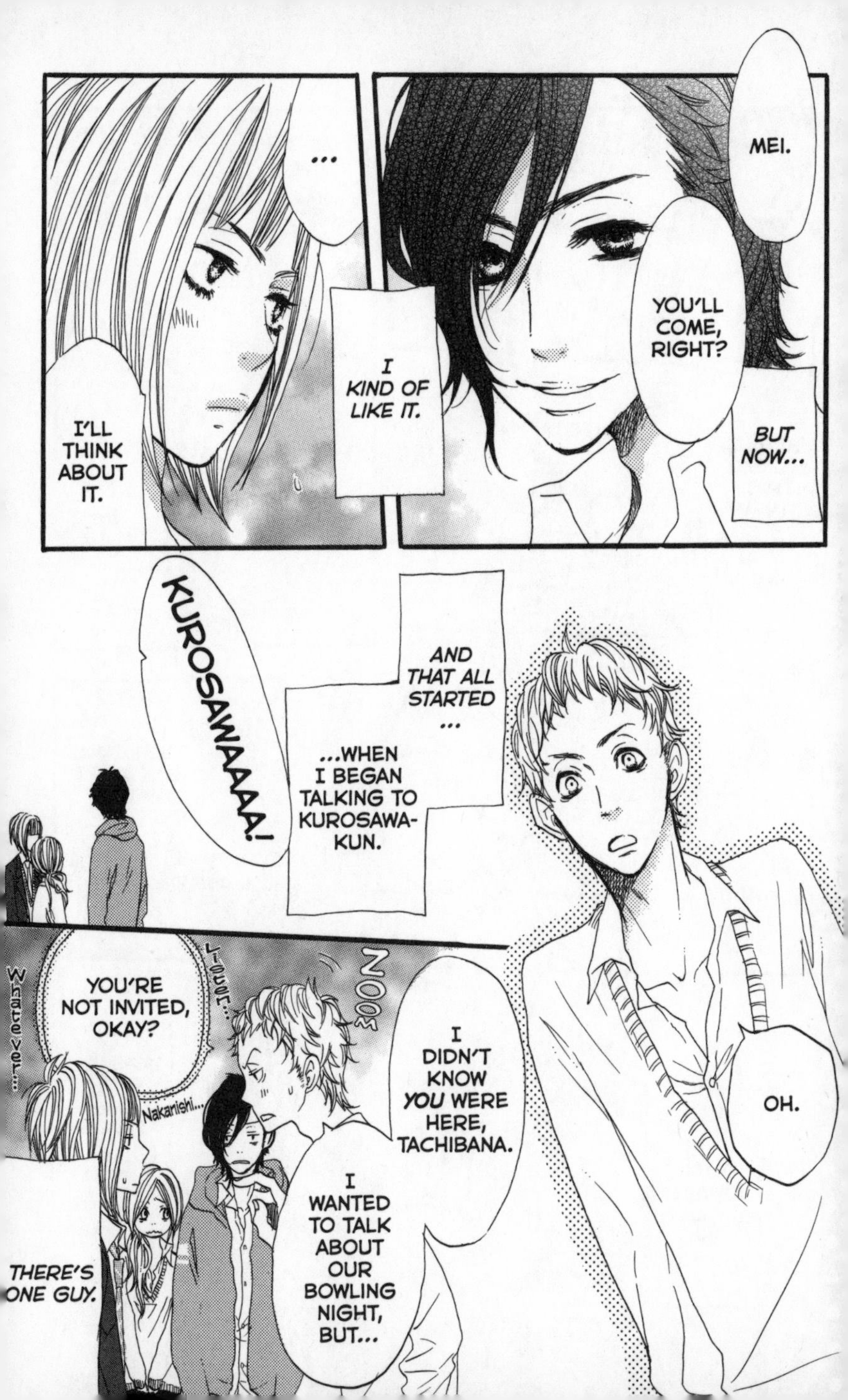
MEI.
YOU'LL COME, RIGHT?
BUT NOW...
I KIND OF LIKE IT.
...
I'LL THINK ABOUT IT.
AND THAT ALL STARTED ...
...WHEN I BEGAN TALKING TO KUROSAWA-KUN.
KUROSAWAAAA!
OH.
I DIDN'T KNOW YOU WERE HERE, TACHIBANA.
I WANTED TO TALK ABOUT OUR BOWLING NIGHT, BUT...
ZOOM
Listen...
YOU'RE NOT INVITED, OKAY?
Nakanishi...
Whatever...
THERE'S ONE GUY.

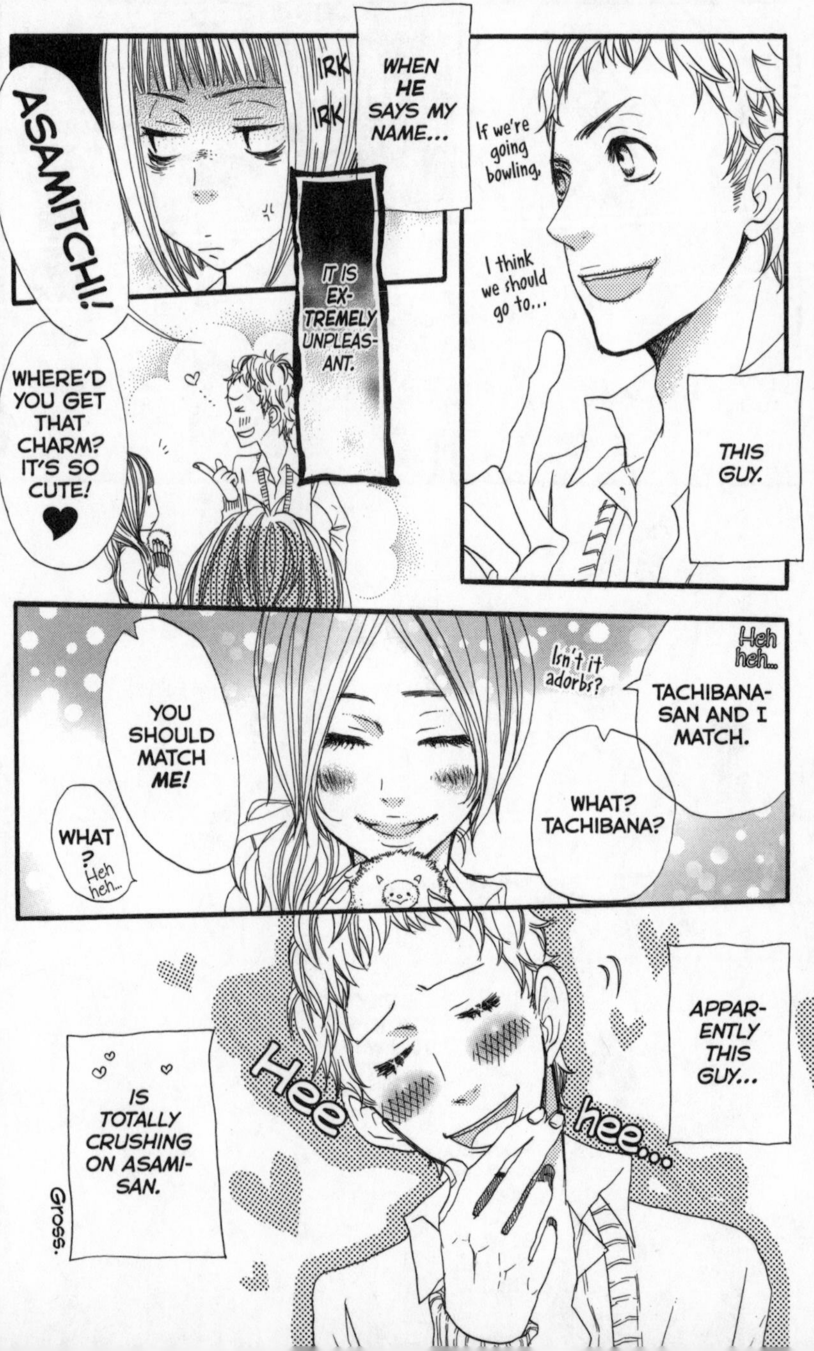
If we're going bowling,
I think we should go to...
THIS GUY.
WHEN HE SAYS MY NAME...
IRK
IRK
IT IS EXTREMELY UNPLEASANT.
ASAMITCHI!
WHERE'D YOU GET THAT CHARM? IT'S SO CUTE! ♥
Heh heh...
TACHIBANA-SAN AND I MATCH.
Isn't it adorbs?
WHAT? TACHIBANA?
YOU SHOULD MATCH ME!
WHAT?
Heh heh...
APPARENTLY THIS GUY...
Hee hee...
IS TOTALLY CRUSHING ON ASAMI-SAN.
Gross.

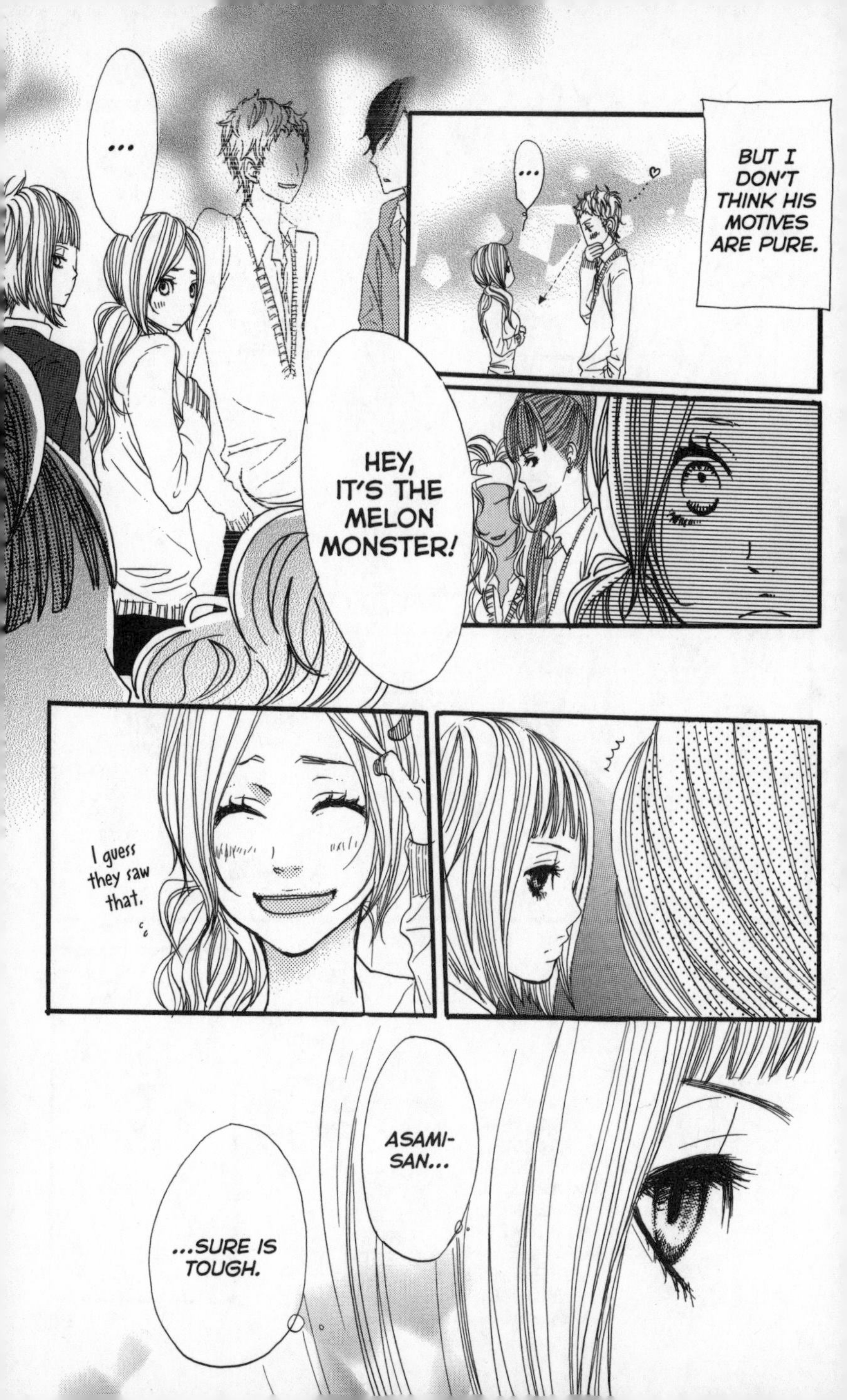
BUT I DON'T THINK HIS MOTIVES ARE PURE.
...
HEY, IT'S THE MELON MONSTER!
...
I guess they saw that.
ASAMI-SAN...
...SURE IS TOUGH.

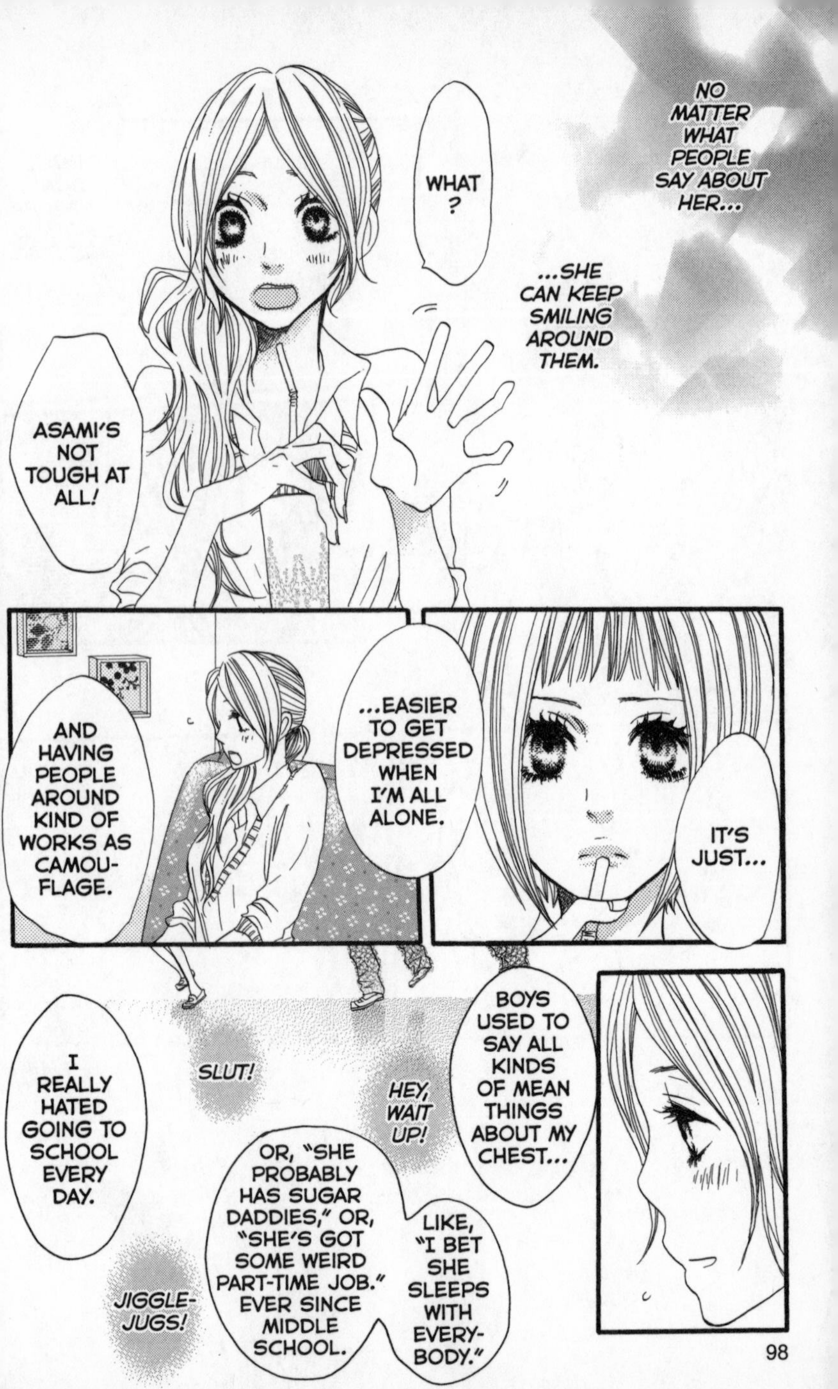
NO MATTER WHAT PEOPLE SAY ABOUT HER...
...SHE CAN KEEP SMILING AROUND THEM.
WHAT?
ASAMI'S NOT TOUGH AT ALL!
IT'S JUST...
...EASIER TO GET DEPRESSED WHEN I'M ALL ALONE.
AND HAVING PEOPLE AROUND KIND OF WORKS AS CAMOU-FLAGE.
BOYS USED TO SAY ALL KINDS OF MEAN THINGS ABOUT MY CHEST...
LIKE, "I BET SHE SLEEPS WITH EVERY-BODY."
OR, "SHE PROBABLY HAS SUGAR DADDIES," OR, "SHE'S GOT SOME WEIRD PART-TIME JOB." EVER SINCE MIDDLE SCHOOL.
HEY, WAIT UP!
SLUT!
JIGGLE-JUGS!
I REALLY HATED GOING TO SCHOOL EVERY DAY.

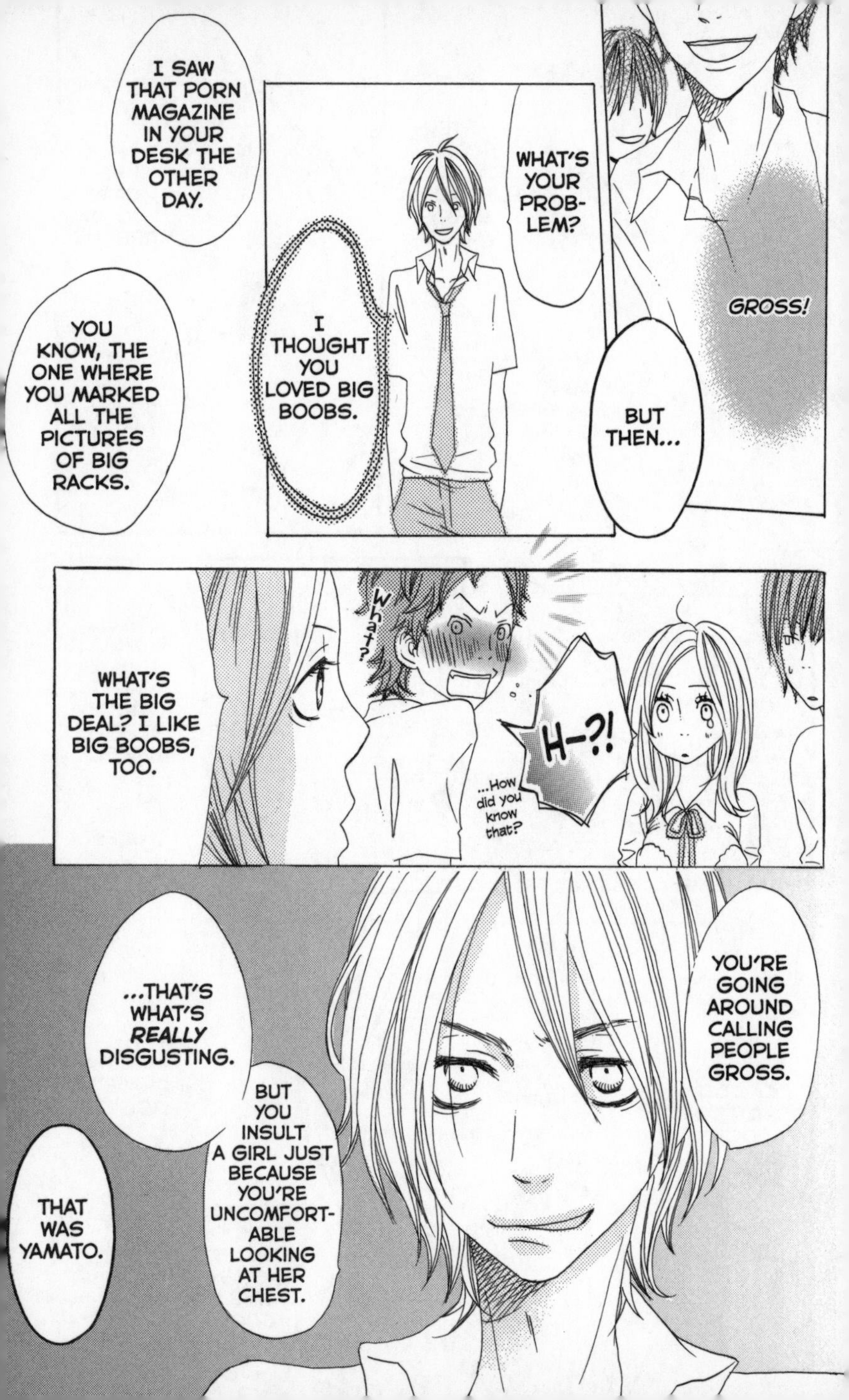
GROSS!
BUT THEN...
WHAT'S YOUR PROB-LEM?
I THOUGHT YOU LOVED BIG BOOBS.
I SAW THAT PORN MAGAZINE IN YOUR DESK THE OTHER DAY.
YOU KNOW, THE ONE WHERE YOU MARKED ALL THE PICTURES OF BIG RACKS.
H-?!
...How did you know that?
What?
WHAT'S THE BIG DEAL? I LIKE BIG BOOBS, TOO.
YOU'RE GOING AROUND CALLING PEOPLE GROSS.
BUT YOU INSULT A GIRL JUST BECAUSE YOU'RE UNCOMFORT-ABLE LOOKING AT HER CHEST.
...THAT'S WHAT'S *REALLY* DISGUSTING.
THAT WAS YAMATO.

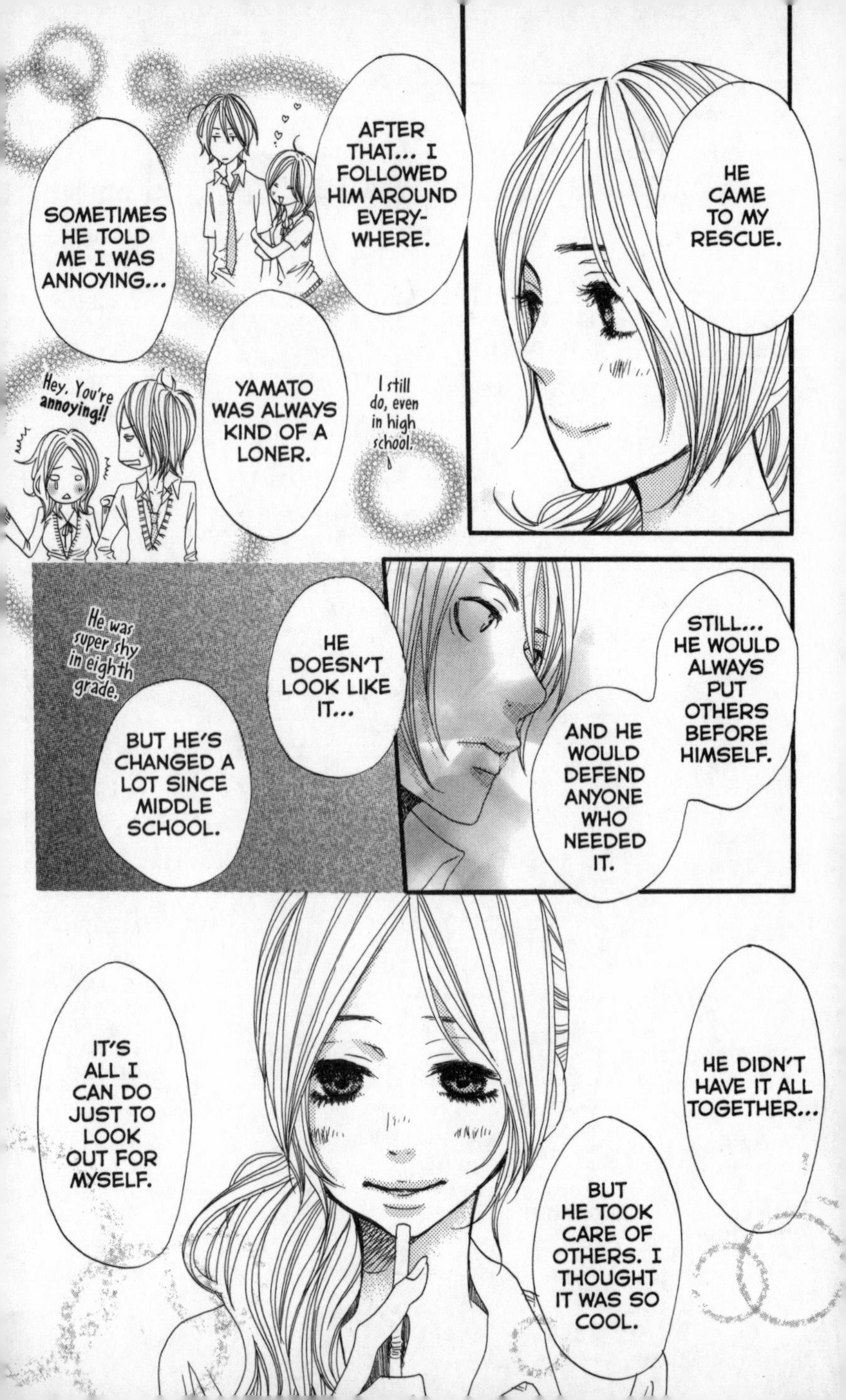
HE CAME TO MY RESCUE.
AFTER THAT... I FOLLOWED HIM AROUND EVERYWHERE.
SOMETIMES HE TOLD ME I WAS ANNOYING...
I still do, even in high school.
YAMATO WAS ALWAYS KIND OF A LONER.
Hey, You're **annoying!!**
STILL... HE WOULD ALWAYS PUT OTHERS BEFORE HIMSELF.
AND HE WOULD DEFEND ANYONE WHO NEEDED IT.
HE DOESN'T LOOK LIKE IT...
He was super shy in eighth grade.
BUT HE'S CHANGED A LOT SINCE MIDDLE SCHOOL.
HE DIDN'T HAVE IT ALL TOGETHER...
BUT HE TOOK CARE OF OTHERS. I THOUGHT IT WAS SO COOL.
IT'S ALL I CAN DO JUST TO LOOK OUT FOR MYSELF.

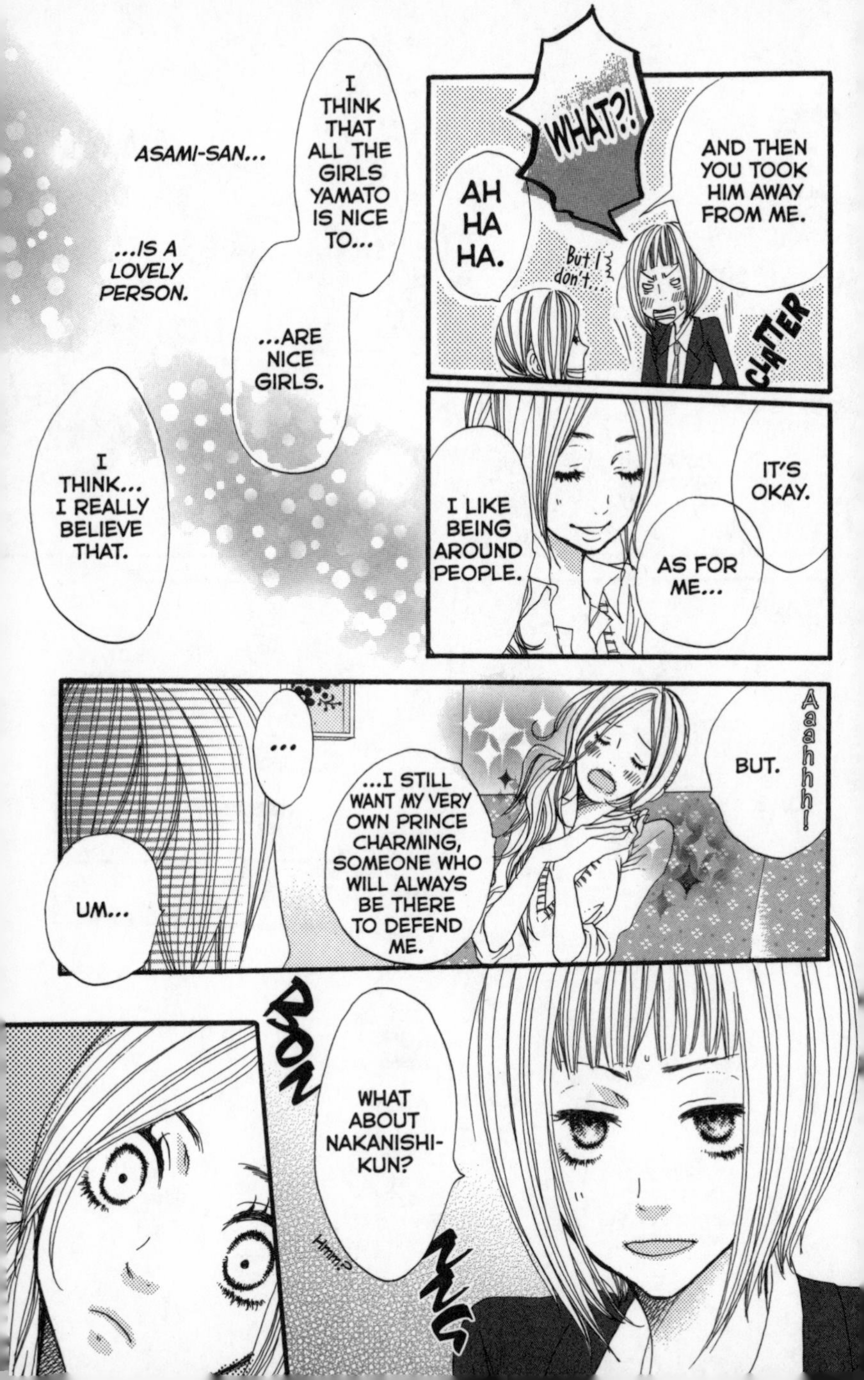
WHAT?!
AND THEN YOU TOOK HIM AWAY FROM ME.
AH HA HA.
But I don't...
CLATTER
IT'S OKAY.
AS FOR ME...
I LIKE BEING AROUND PEOPLE.
I THINK THAT ALL THE GIRLS YAMATO IS NICE TO...
...ARE NICE GIRLS.
ASAMI-SAN...
...IS A LOVELY PERSON.
I THINK... I REALLY BELIEVE THAT.
Aaahhh!
BUT.
...I STILL WANT MY VERY OWN PRINCE CHARMING, SOMEONE WHO WILL ALWAYS BE THERE TO DEFEND ME.
...
UM...
WHAT ABOUT NAKANISHI-KUN?
Hmm?
NNG
BOON

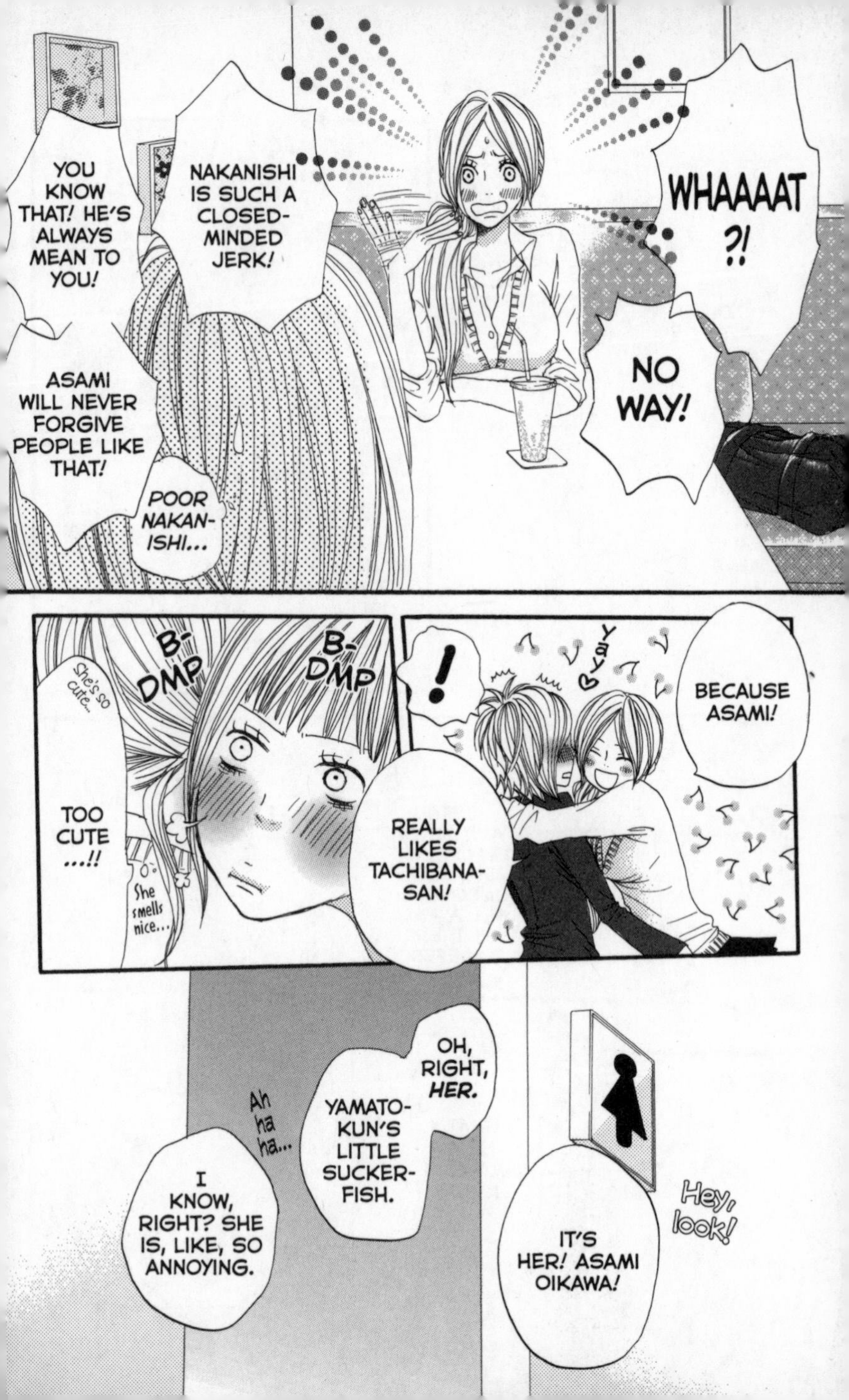

WHAAAAT ?!
NO WAY!
NAKANISHI IS SUCH A CLOSED-MINDED JERK!
YOU KNOW THAT! HE'S ALWAYS MEAN TO YOU!
ASAMI WILL NEVER FORGIVE PEOPLE LIKE THAT!
POOR NAKAN-ISHI...
BECAUSE ASAMI!
Yay
!
REALLY LIKES TACHIBANA-SAN!
B-DMP
B-DMP
She's so cute...
TOO CUTE ...!!
She smells nice...
Hey, look!
IT'S HER! ASAMI OIKAWA!
OH, RIGHT, HER.
YAMATO-KUN'S LITTLE SUCKER-FISH.
Ah ha ha...
I KNOW, RIGHT? SHE IS, LIKE, SO ANNOYING.

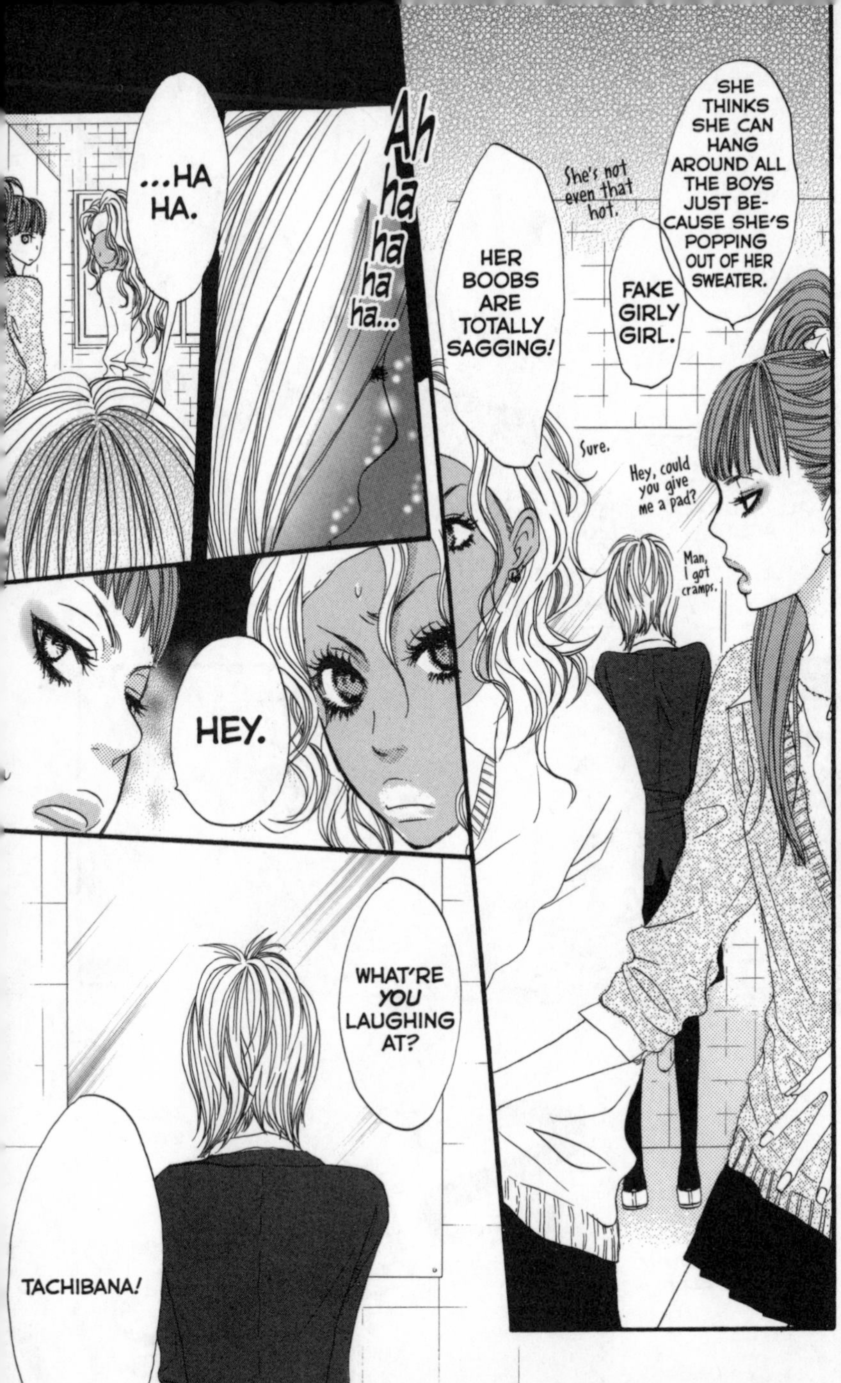
SHE THINKS SHE CAN HANG AROUND ALL THE BOYS JUST BE-CAUSE SHE'S POPPING OUT OF HER SWEATER.
She's not even that hot.
FAKE GIRLY GIRL.
HER BOOBS ARE TOTALLY SAGGING!
Hey, could you give me a pad?
Sure.
Man, I got cramps.
Ah ha ha ha ha...
...HA HA.
HEY.
WHAT'RE *YOU* LAUGHING AT?
TACHIBANA!

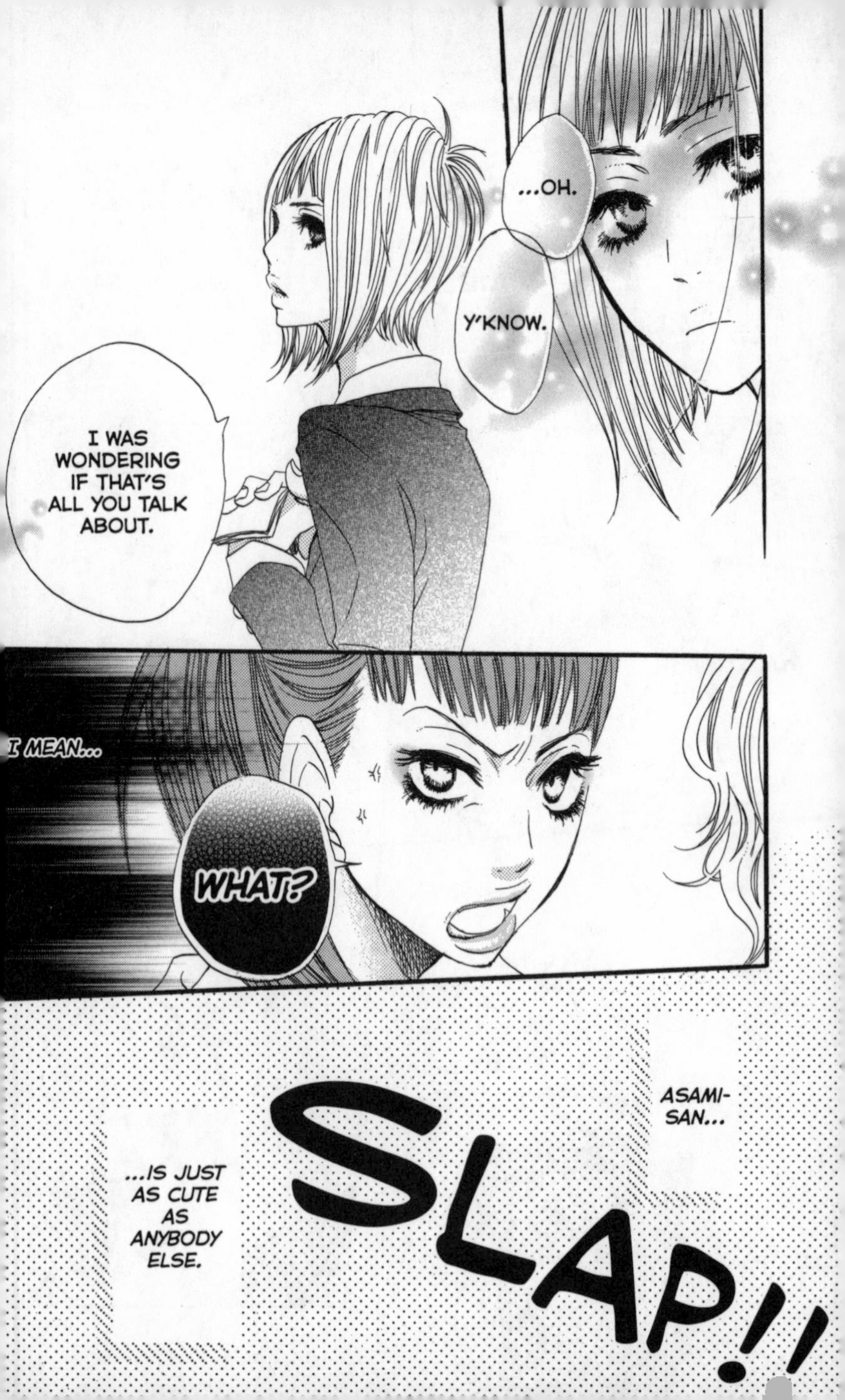

...OH.
Y'KNOW.
I WAS WONDERING IF THAT'S ALL YOU TALK ABOUT.
I MEAN...
WHAT?
ASAMI-SAN...
SLAP!!
...IS JUST AS CUTE AS ANYBODY ELSE.

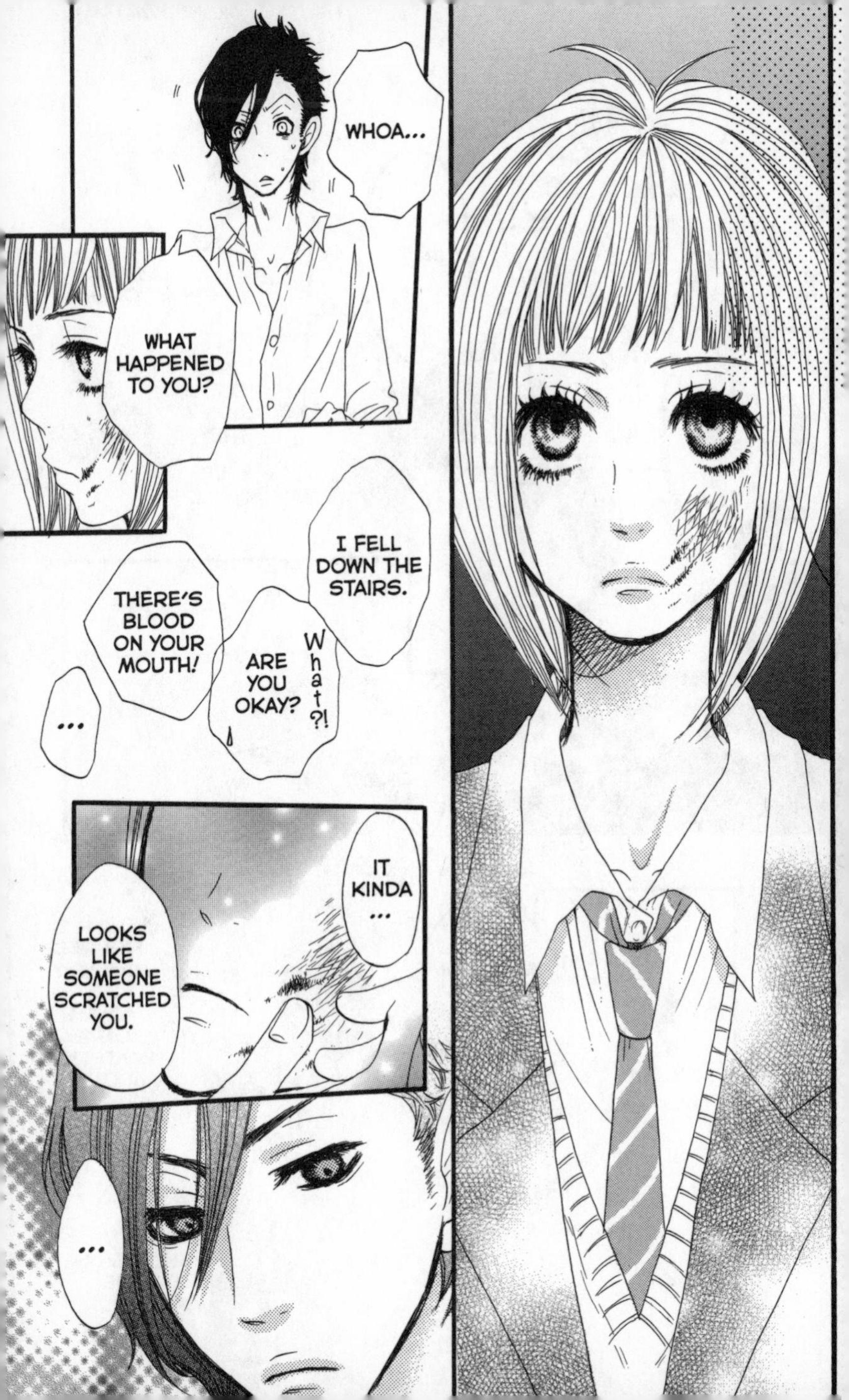
WHOA...
WHAT HAPPENED TO YOU?
I FELL DOWN THE STAIRS.
What?!
ARE YOU OKAY?
THERE'S BLOOD ON YOUR MOUTH!
...
IT KINDA...
LOOKS LIKE SOMEONE SCRATCHED YOU.
...

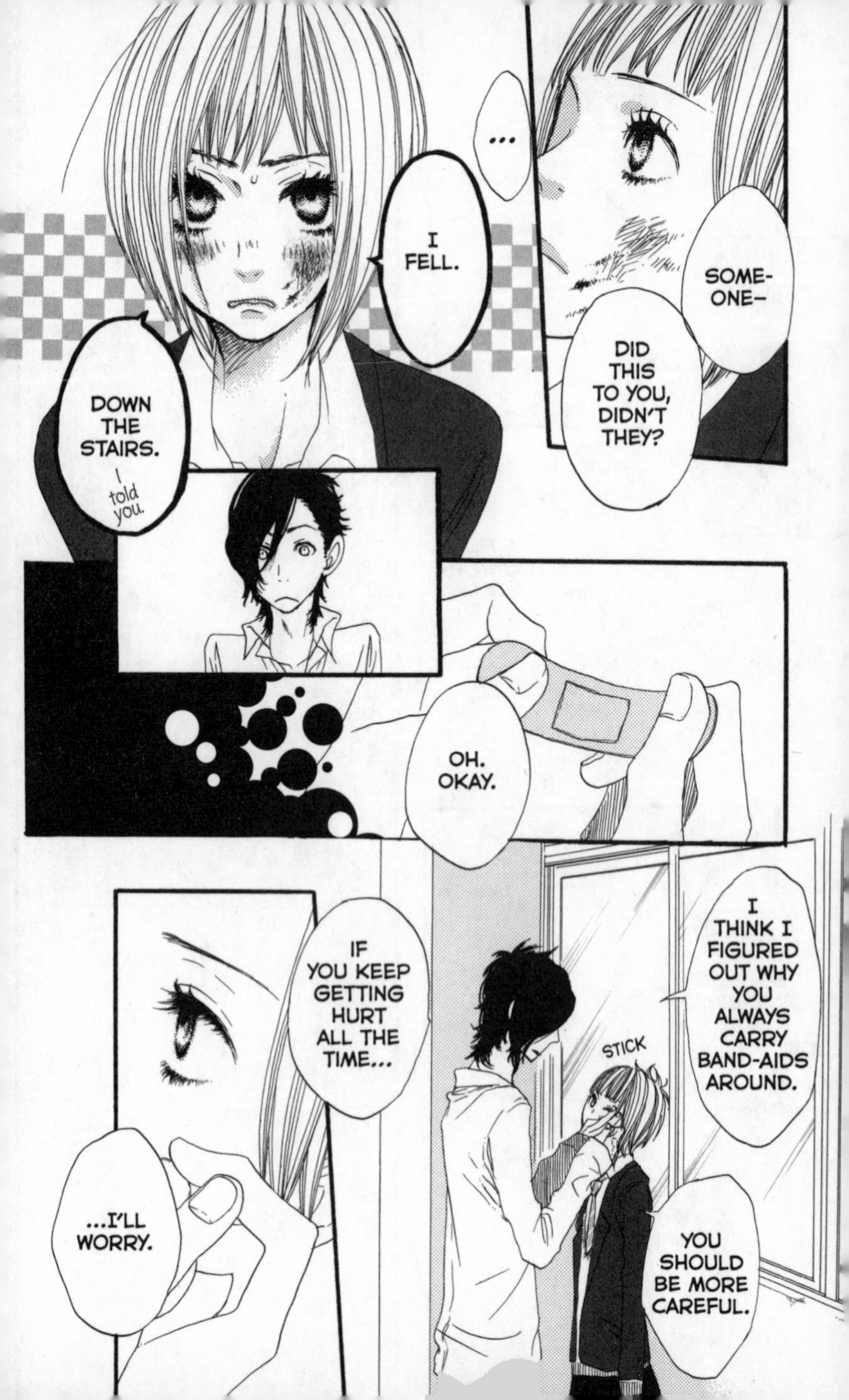
...
SOME-ONE-
DID THIS TO YOU, DIDN'T THEY?
I FELL.
DOWN THE STAIRS.
I told you.
OH. OKAY.
I THINK I FIGURED OUT WHY YOU ALWAYS CARRY BAND-AIDS AROUND.
STICK
YOU SHOULD BE MORE CAREFUL.
IF YOU KEEP GETTING HURT ALL THE TIME...
...I'LL WORRY.

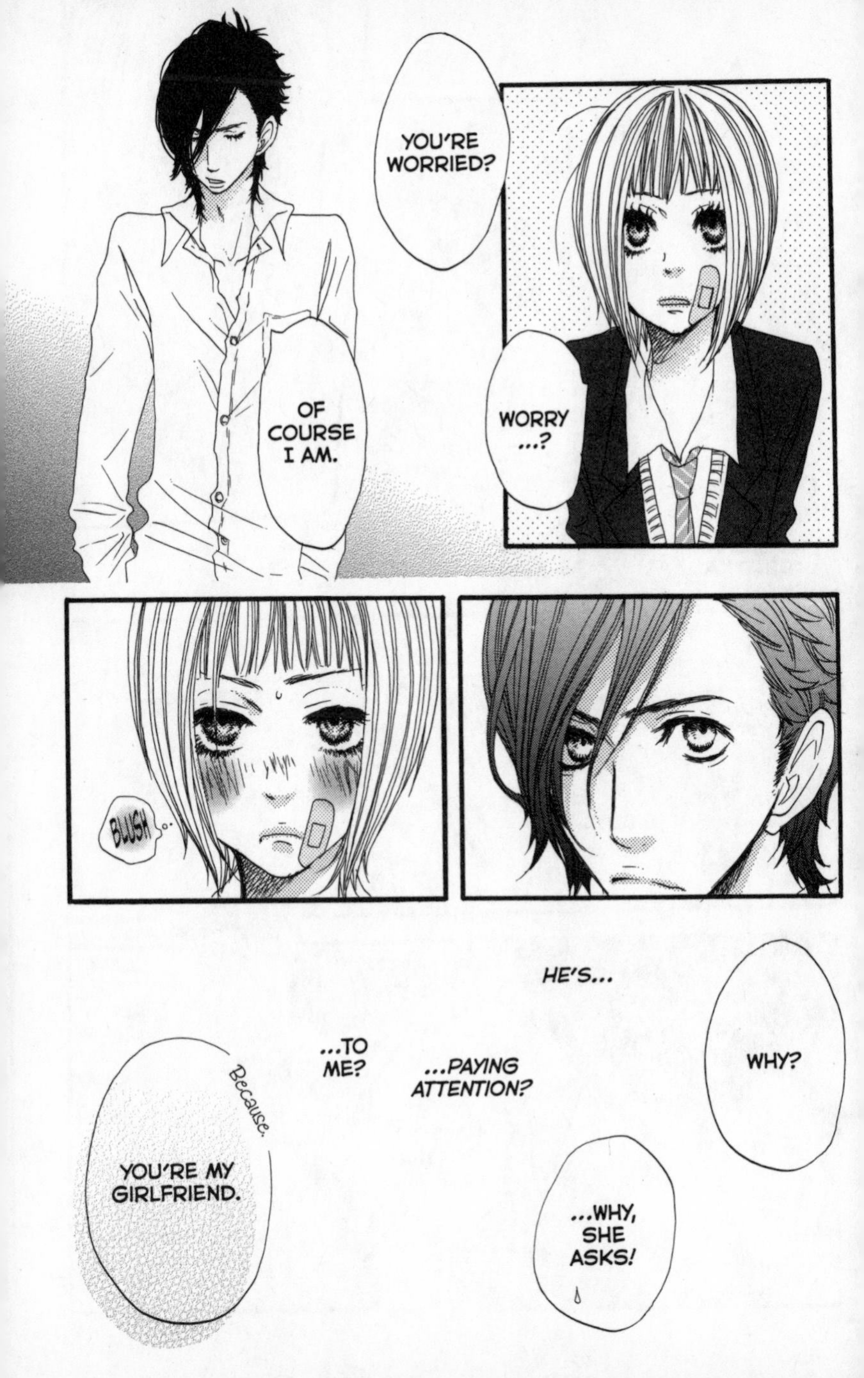
YOU'RE WORRIED?
WORRY ...?
OF COURSE I AM.
BLUSH
WHY?
...WHY, SHE ASKS!
HE'S...
...PAYING ATTENTION?
...TO ME?
Because.
YOU'RE MY GIRLFRIEND.

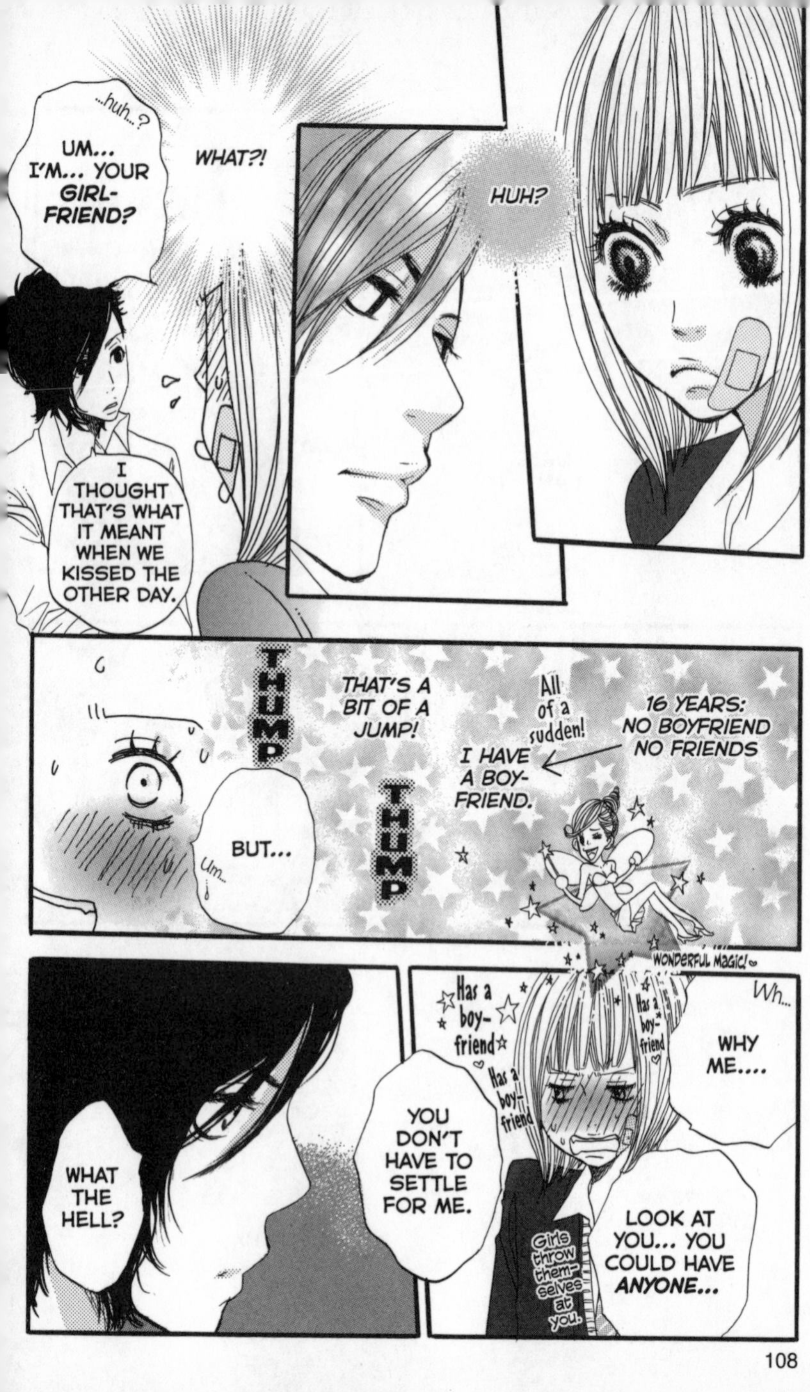
HUH?
WHAT?!
...huh...?
UM... I'M... YOUR GIRLFRIEND?
I THOUGHT THAT'S WHAT IT MEANT WHEN WE KISSED THE OTHER DAY.
16 YEARS: NO BOYFRIEND NO FRIENDS
All of a sudden!
I HAVE A BOYFRIEND.
THUMP
THAT'S A BIT OF A JUMP!
THUMP
BUT...
Um...
WONDERFUL MAGIC!
Wh...
WHY ME....
Has a boyfriend
Has a boyfriend
Has a boyfriend
LOOK AT YOU... YOU COULD HAVE ANYONE...
Girls throw themselves at you.
YOU DON'T HAVE TO SETTLE FOR ME.
WHAT THE HELL?

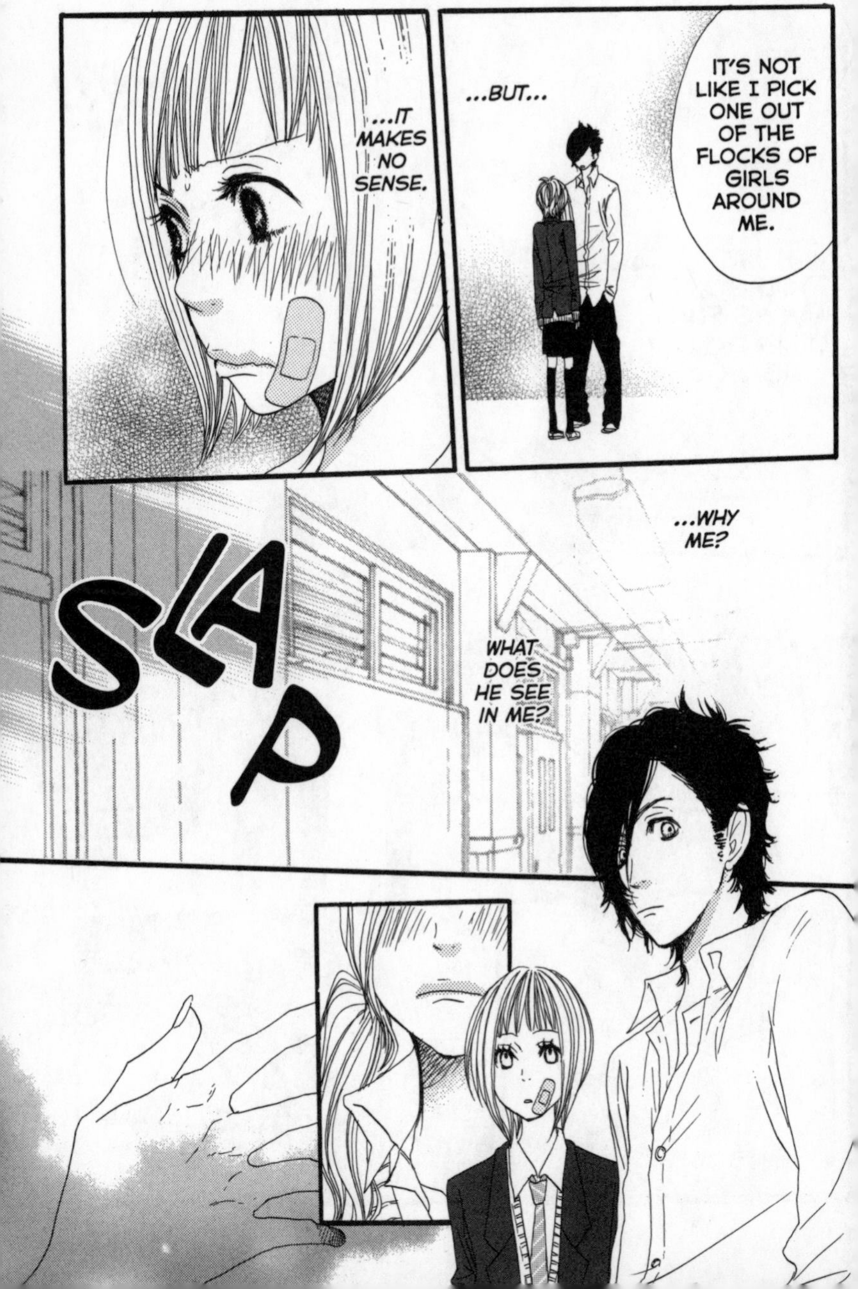
IT'S NOT LIKE I PICK ONE OUT OF THE FLOCKS OF GIRLS AROUND ME.
...BUT...
...IT MAKES NO SENSE.
...WHY ME?
WHAT DOES HE SEE IN ME?
SLAP

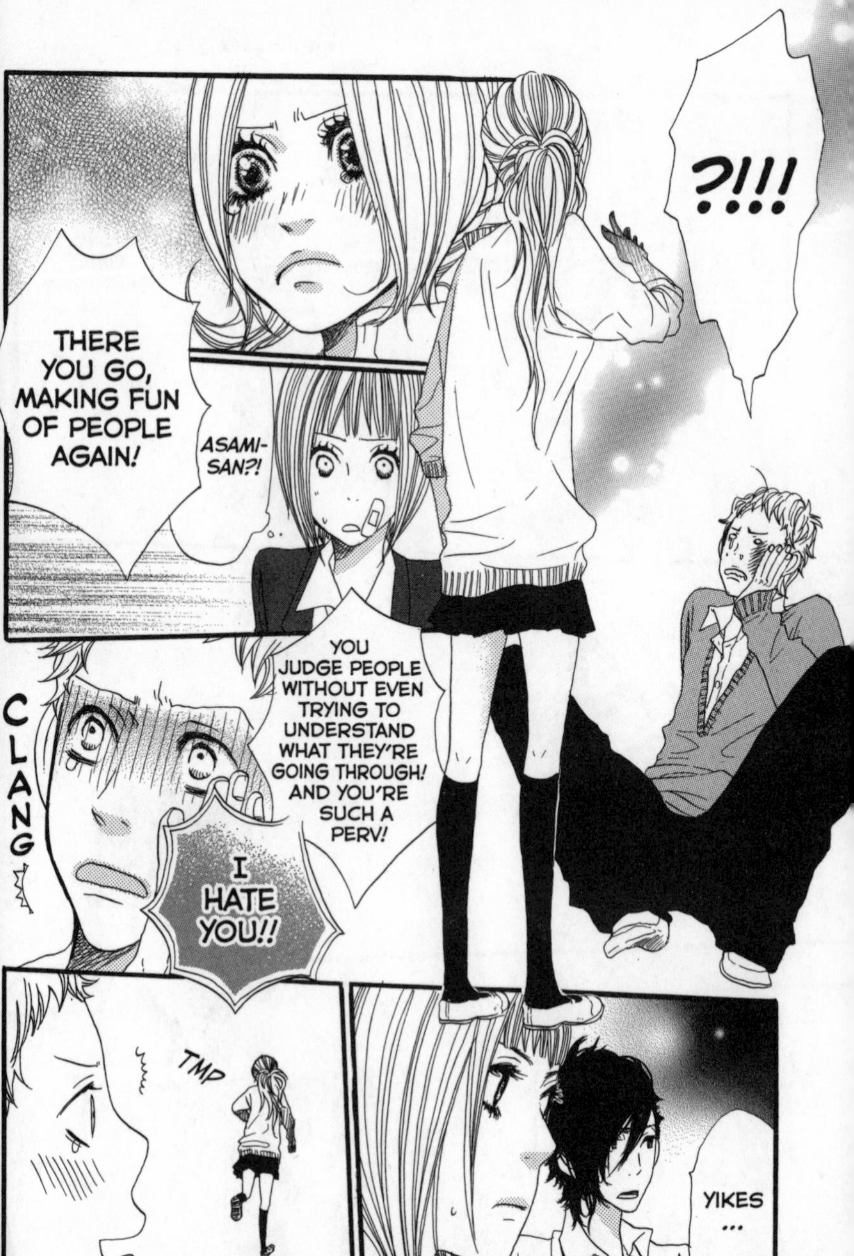
?!!!
THERE YOU GO, MAKING FUN OF PEOPLE AGAIN!
ASAMI-SAN?!
YOU JUDGE PEOPLE WITHOUT EVEN TRYING TO UNDERSTAND WHAT THEY'RE GOING THROUGH! AND YOU'RE SUCH A PERV!
I HATE YOU!!
CLANG
YIKES ...
TMP

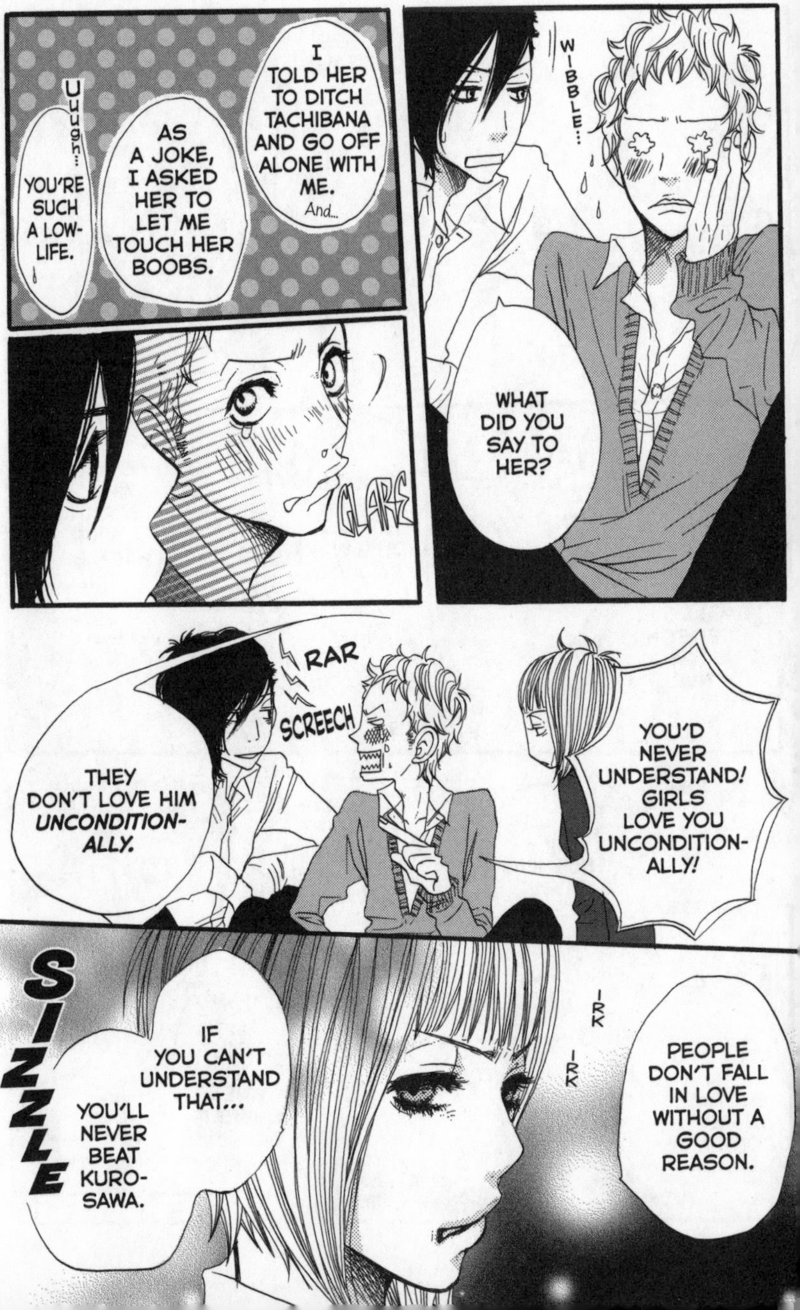
WIBBLE...
WHAT DID YOU SAY TO HER?
I TOLD HER TO DITCH TACHIBANA AND GO OFF ALONE WITH ME.
And...
AS A JOKE, I ASKED HER TO LET ME TOUCH HER BOOBS.
Uuugh...
YOU'RE SUCH A LOW-LIFE.
GLARE
YOU'D NEVER UNDERSTAND! GIRLS LOVE YOU UNCONDITION-ALLY!
RAR
SCREECH
THEY DON'T LOVE HIM *UNCONDITION-ALLY.*
IRK
IRK
PEOPLE DON'T FALL IN LOVE WITHOUT A GOOD REASON.
IF YOU CAN'T UNDERSTAND THAT...
YOU'LL NEVER BEAT KURO-SAWA.
SIZZLE

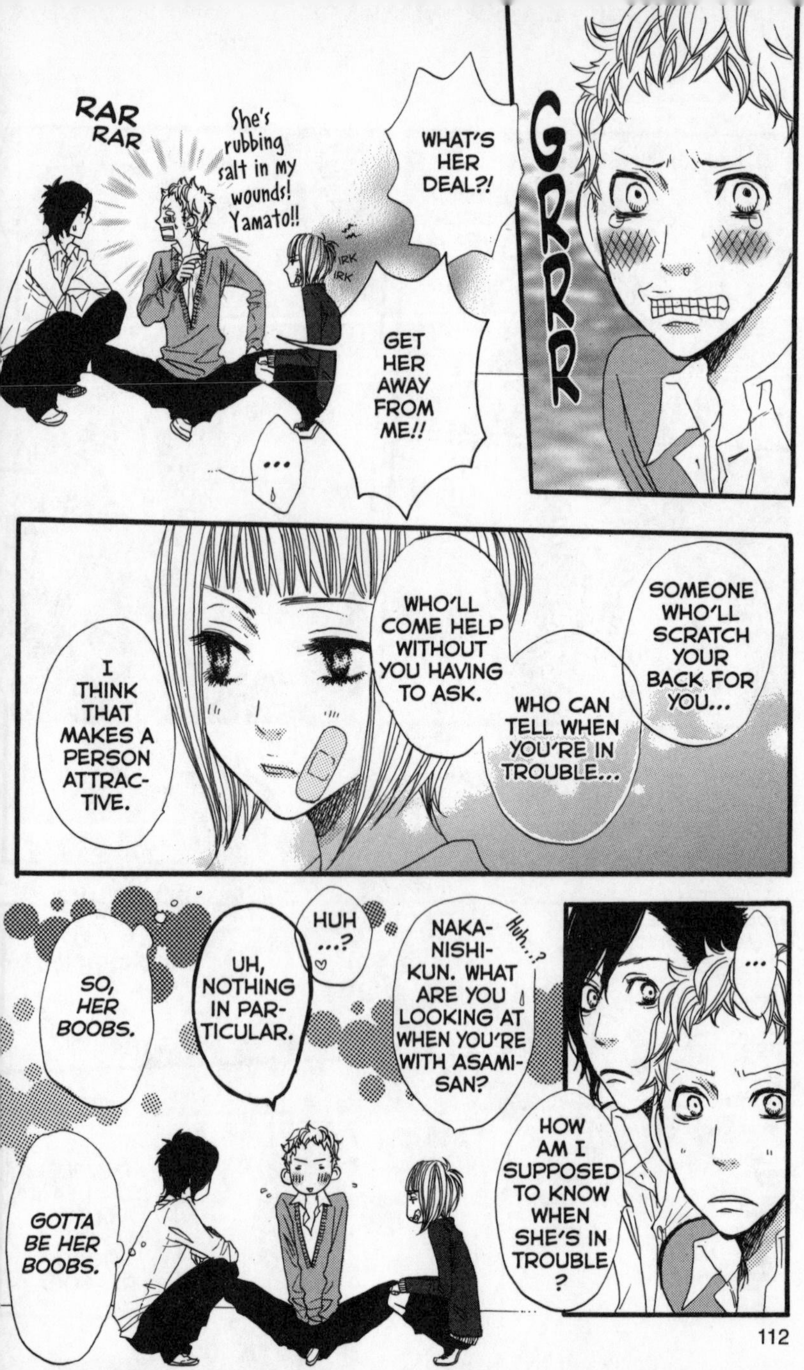
GRRR
WHAT'S HER DEAL?!
GET HER AWAY FROM ME!!
...
She's rubbing salt in my wounds! Yamato!!
RAR RAR
IRK IRK
SOMEONE WHO'LL SCRATCH YOUR BACK FOR YOU...
WHO CAN TELL WHEN YOU'RE IN TROUBLE...
WHO'LL COME HELP WITHOUT YOU HAVING TO ASK.
I THINK THAT MAKES A PERSON ATTRACTIVE.
...
HOW AM I SUPPOSED TO KNOW WHEN SHE'S IN TROUBLE?
NAKA-NISHI-KUN. WHAT ARE YOU LOOKING AT WHEN YOU'RE WITH ASAMI-SAN?
Huh...?
HUH...?
UH, NOTHING IN PAR-TICULAR.
SO, HER BOOBS.
GOTTA BE HER BOOBS.

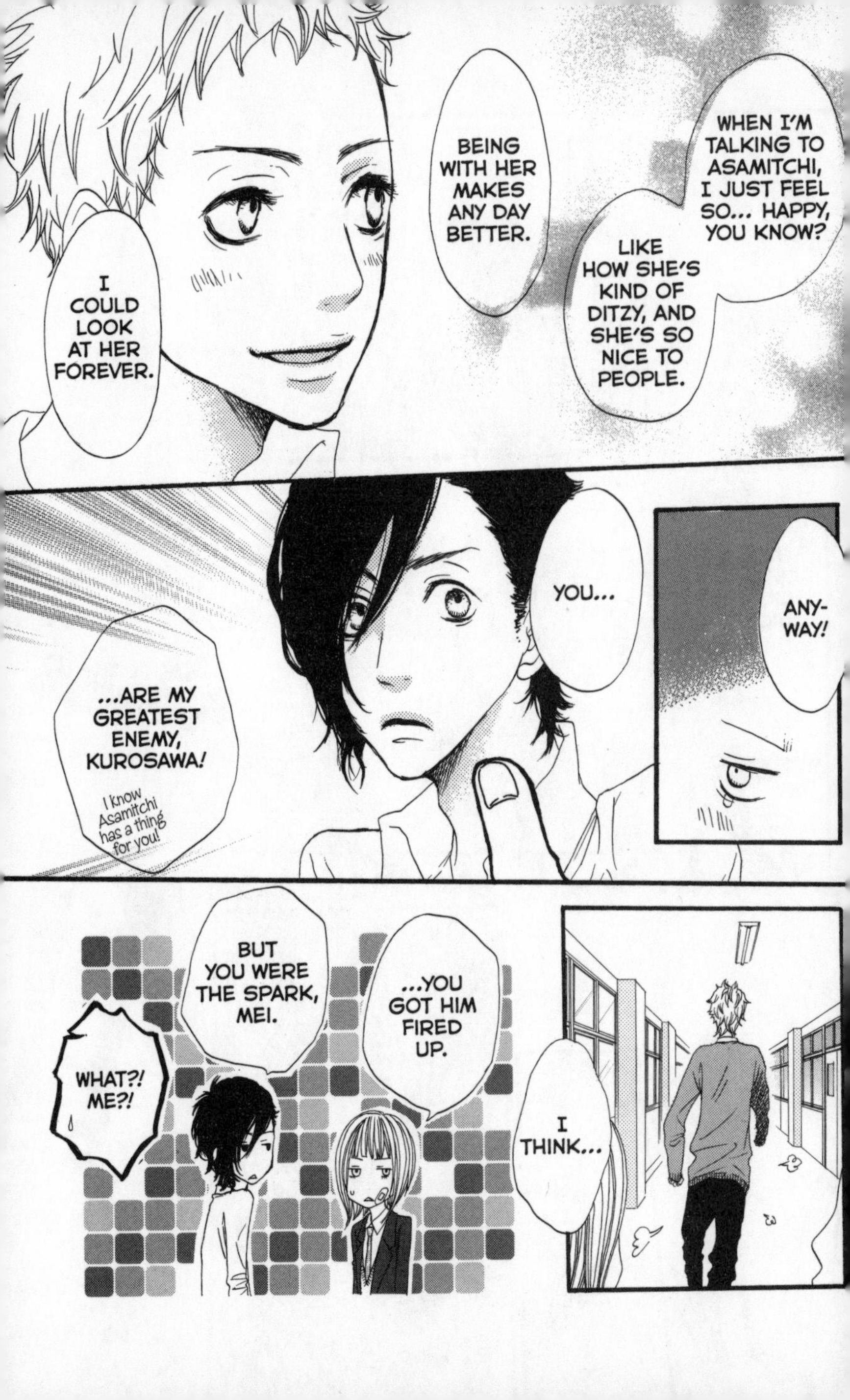
WHEN I'M TALKING TO ASAMITCHI, I JUST FEEL SO... HAPPY, YOU KNOW?
LIKE HOW SHE'S KIND OF DITZY, AND SHE'S SO NICE TO PEOPLE.
BEING WITH HER MAKES ANY DAY BETTER.
I COULD LOOK AT HER FOREVER.
ANY-WAY!
YOU...
...ARE MY GREATEST ENEMY, KUROSAWA!
I know Asamitchi has a thing for you!
I THINK...
...YOU GOT HIM FIRED UP.
BUT YOU WERE THE SPARK, MEI.
WHAT?! ME?!

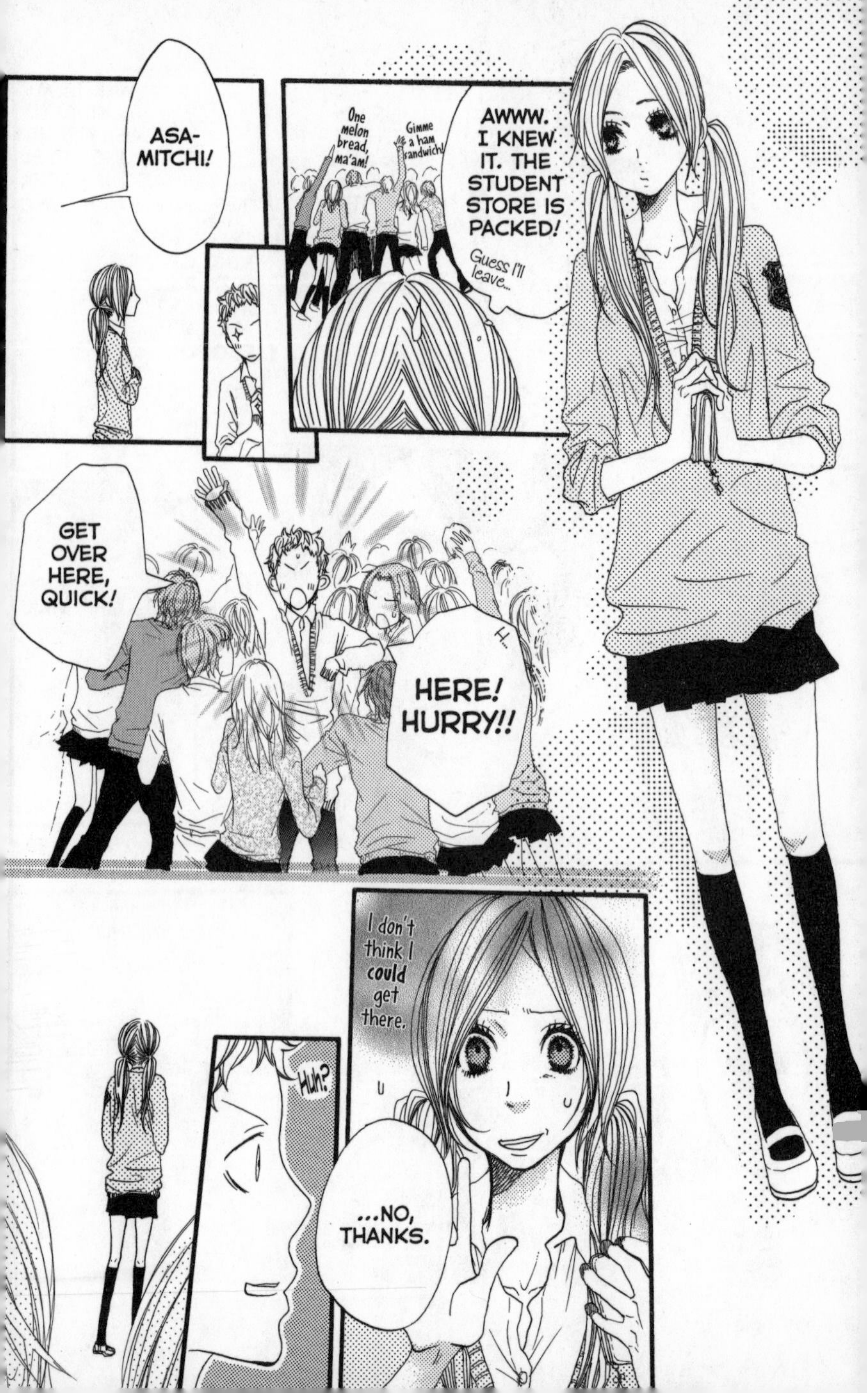
AWWW. I KNEW IT. THE STUDENT STORE IS PACKED!
Gimme a ham sandwich!
One melon bread, ma'am!
Guess I'll leave...
ASA-MITCHI!
GET OVER HERE, QUICK!
HERE! HURRY!!
I don't think I could get there.
...NO, THANKS.
Huh?

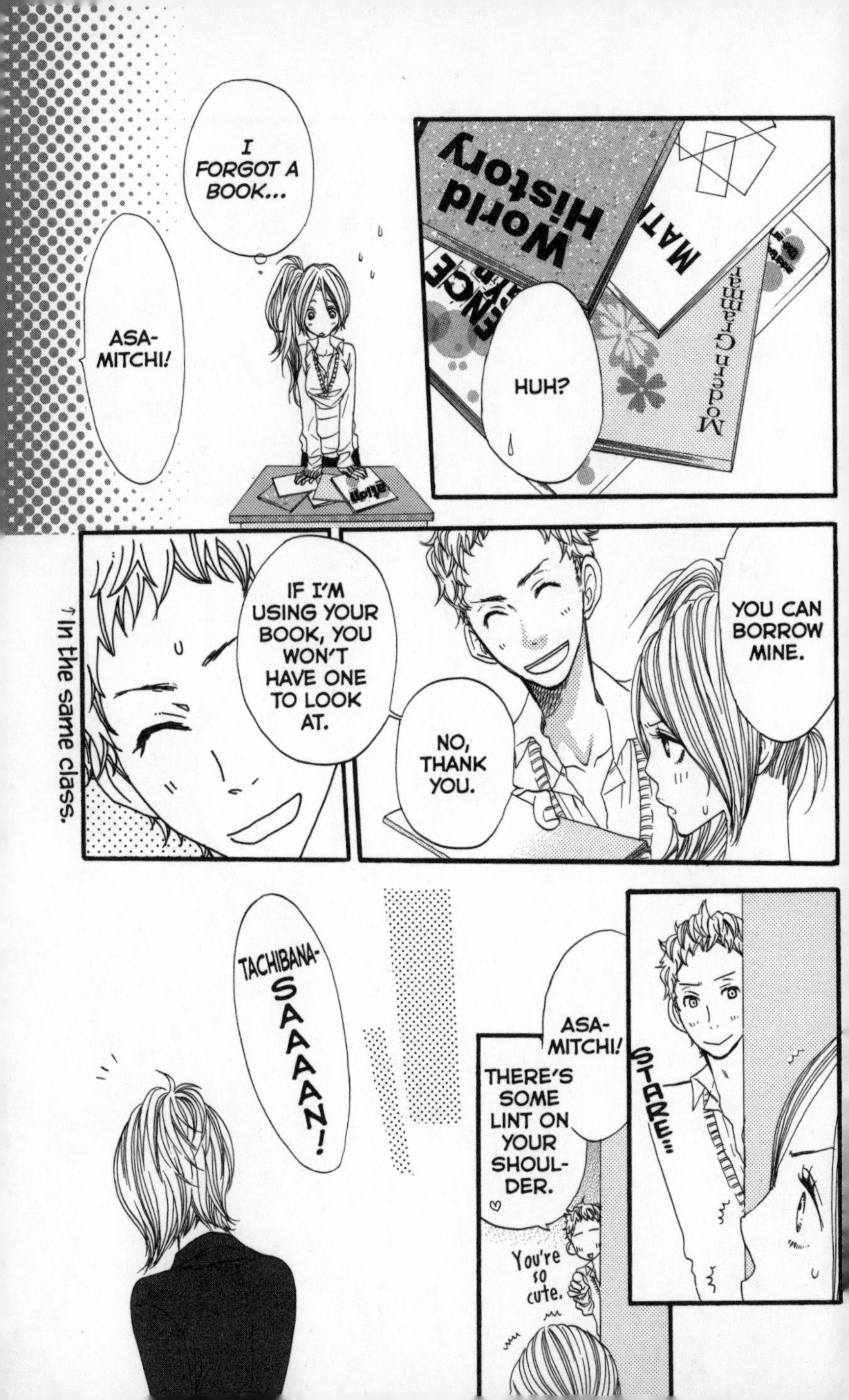
World History
HUH?
I FORGOT A BOOK...
ASA-MITCHI!
YOU CAN BORROW MINE.
NO, THANK YOU.
IF I'M USING YOUR BOOK, YOU WON'T HAVE ONE TO LOOK AT.
↑In the same class.
STARE...
ASA-MITCHI! THERE'S SOME LINT ON YOUR SHOULDER.
You're so cute.
TACHIBANA-SAAAAAN!

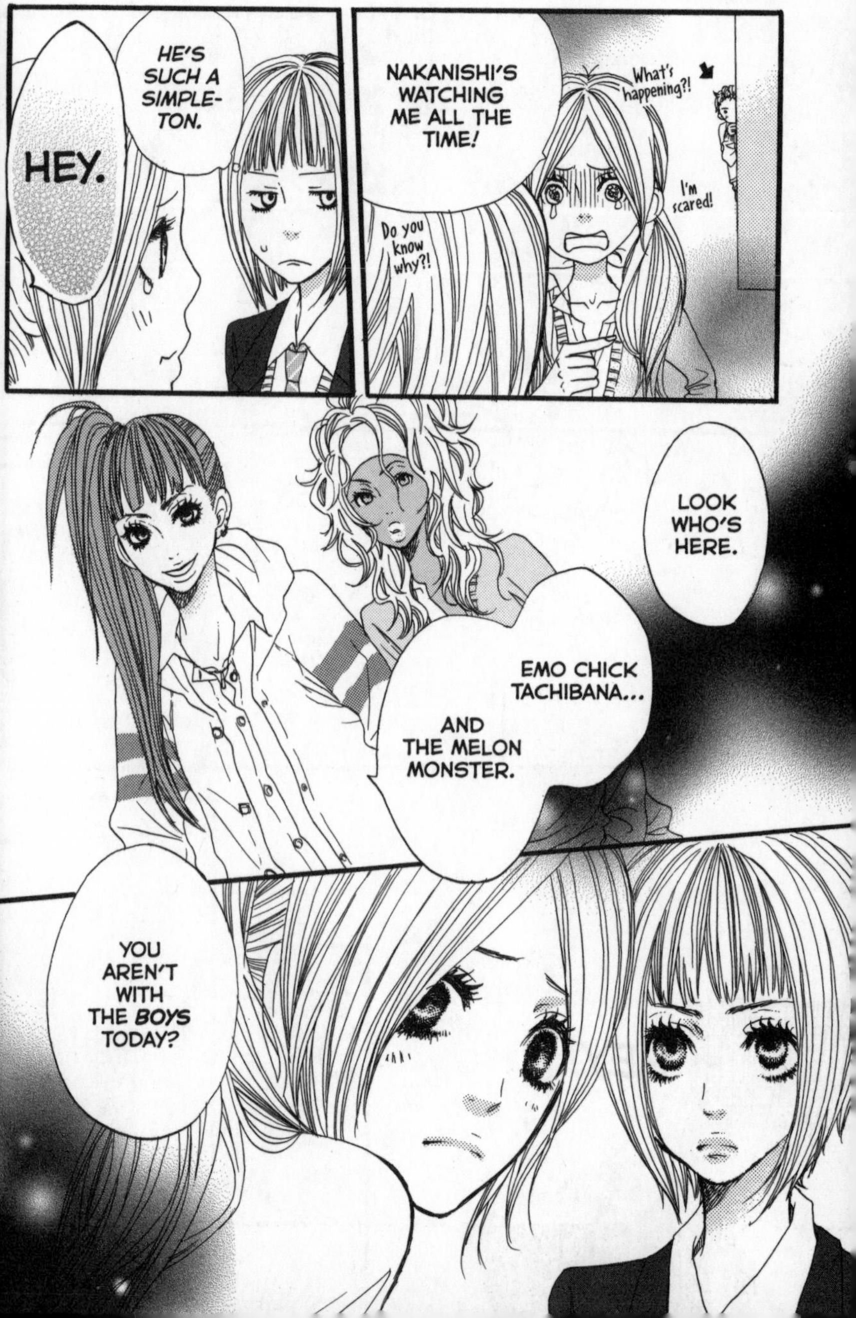
NAKANISHI'S WATCHING ME ALL THE TIME!
What's happening?!
I'm scared!
Do you know why?!
HE'S SUCH A SIMPLETON.
HEY.
LOOK WHO'S HERE.
EMO CHICK TACHIBANA...
AND THE MELON MONSTER.
YOU AREN'T WITH THE *BOYS* TODAY?

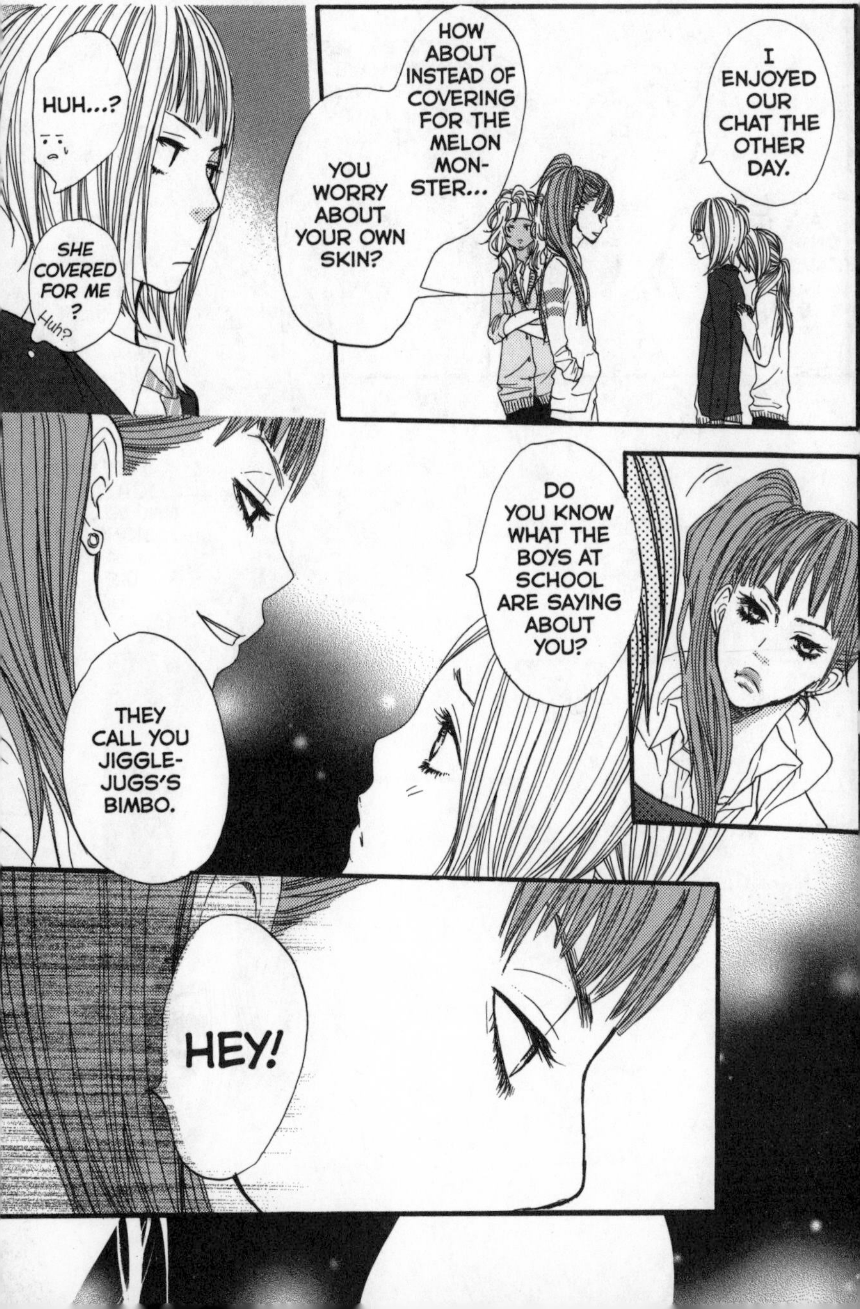
I ENJOYED OUR CHAT THE OTHER DAY.
HOW ABOUT INSTEAD OF COVERING FOR THE MELON MON-STER...
YOU WORRY ABOUT YOUR OWN SKIN?
HUH...?
SHE COVERED FOR ME?
Huh?
DO YOU KNOW WHAT THE BOYS AT SCHOOL ARE SAYING ABOUT YOU?
THEY CALL YOU JIGGLE-JUGS'S BIMBO.
HEY!

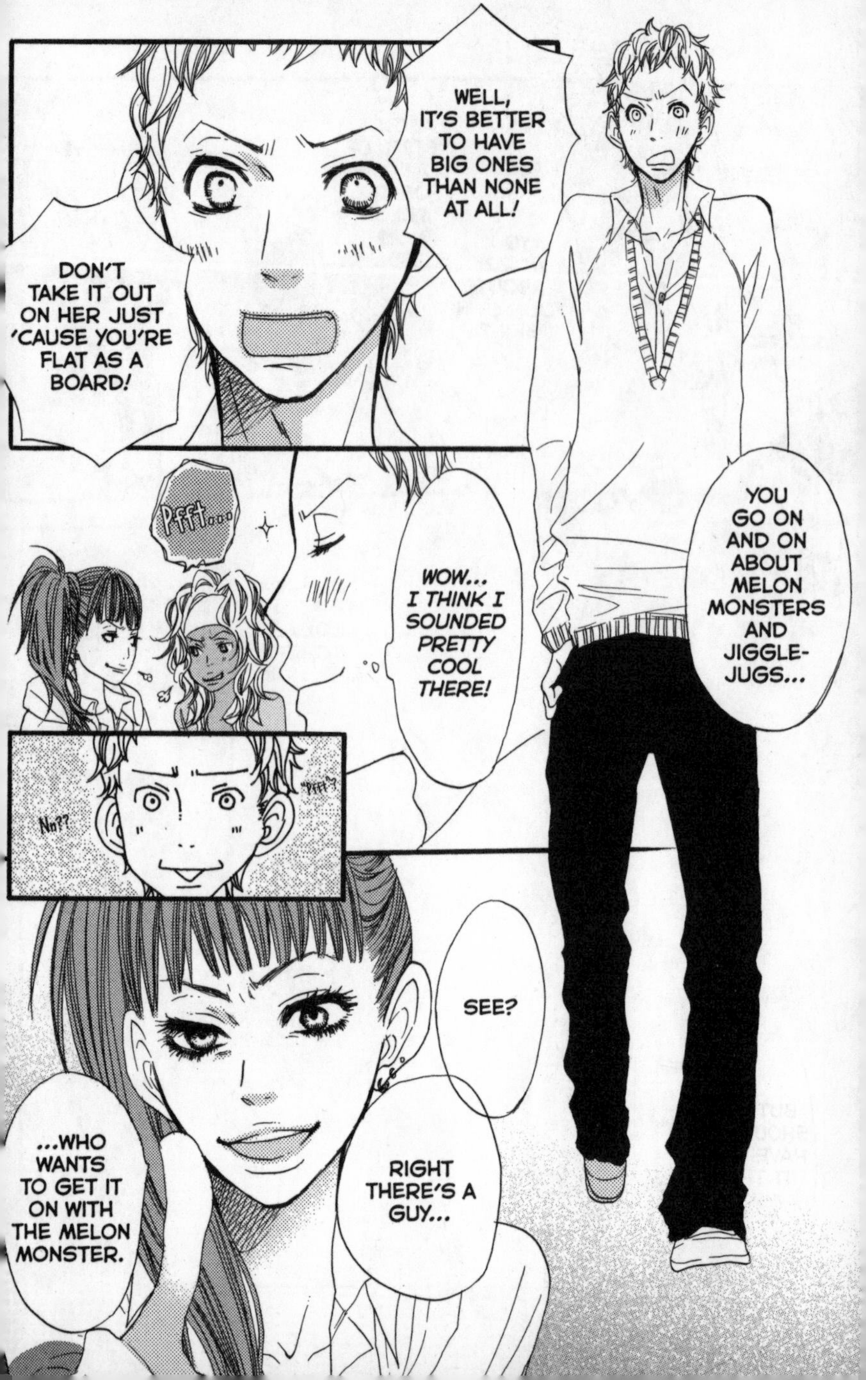
WELL, IT'S BETTER TO HAVE BIG ONES THAN NONE AT ALL!
DON'T TAKE IT OUT ON HER JUST 'CAUSE YOU'RE FLAT AS A BOARD!
WOW... I THINK I SOUNDED PRETTY COOL THERE!
Pffft...
Nn??
YOU GO ON AND ON ABOUT MELON MONSTERS AND JIGGLE-JUGS...
SEE?
RIGHT THERE'S A GUY...
...WHO WANTS TO GET IT ON WITH THE MELON MONSTER.

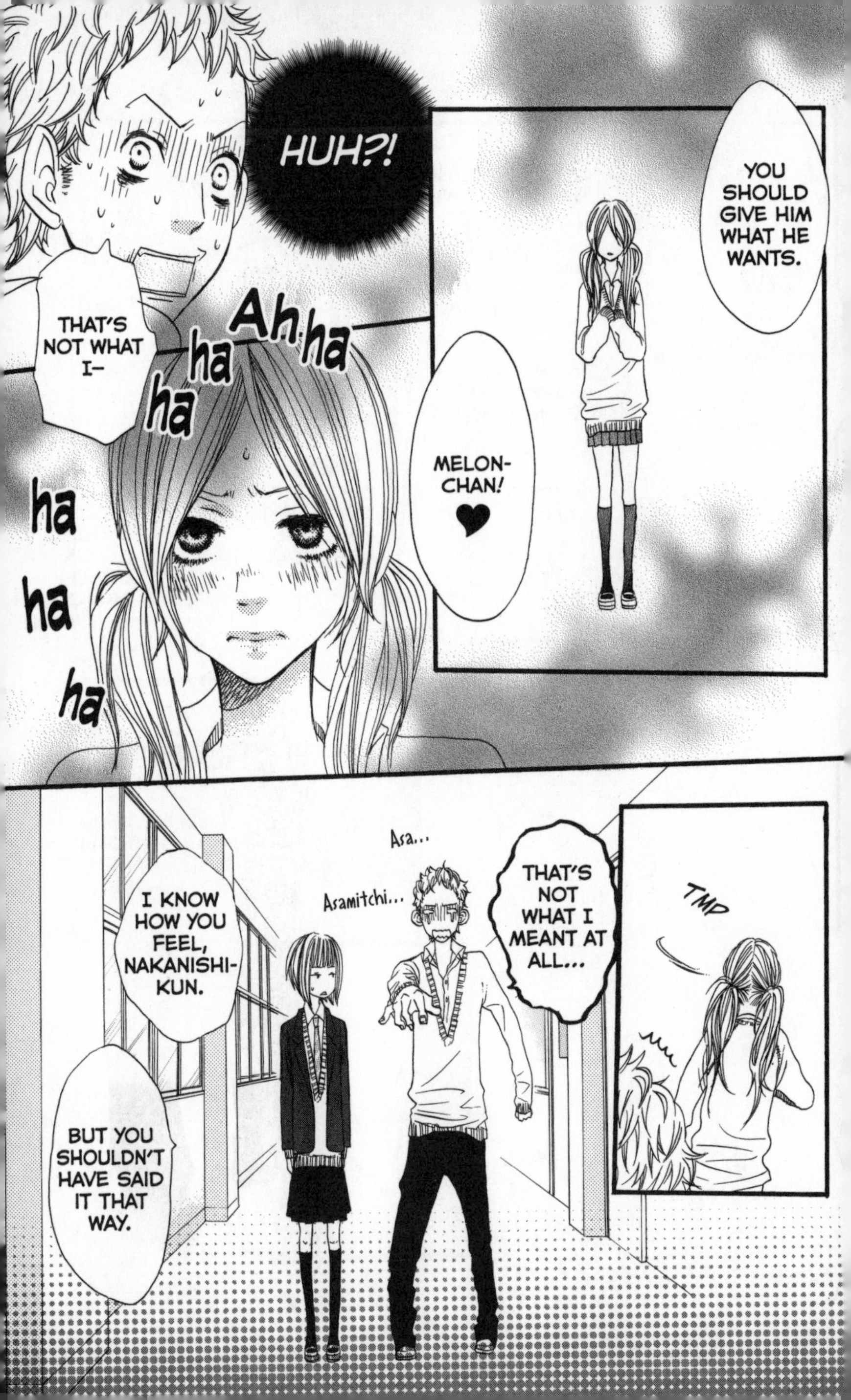
YOU SHOULD GIVE HIM WHAT HE WANTS.
MELON-CHAN! ♥
HUH?!
THAT'S NOT WHAT I–
Ah ha ha ha
ha ha ha
TMP
THAT'S NOT WHAT I MEANT AT ALL...
Asa...
Asamitchi...
I KNOW HOW YOU FEEL, NAKANISHI-KUN.
BUT YOU SHOULDN'T HAVE SAID IT THAT WAY.

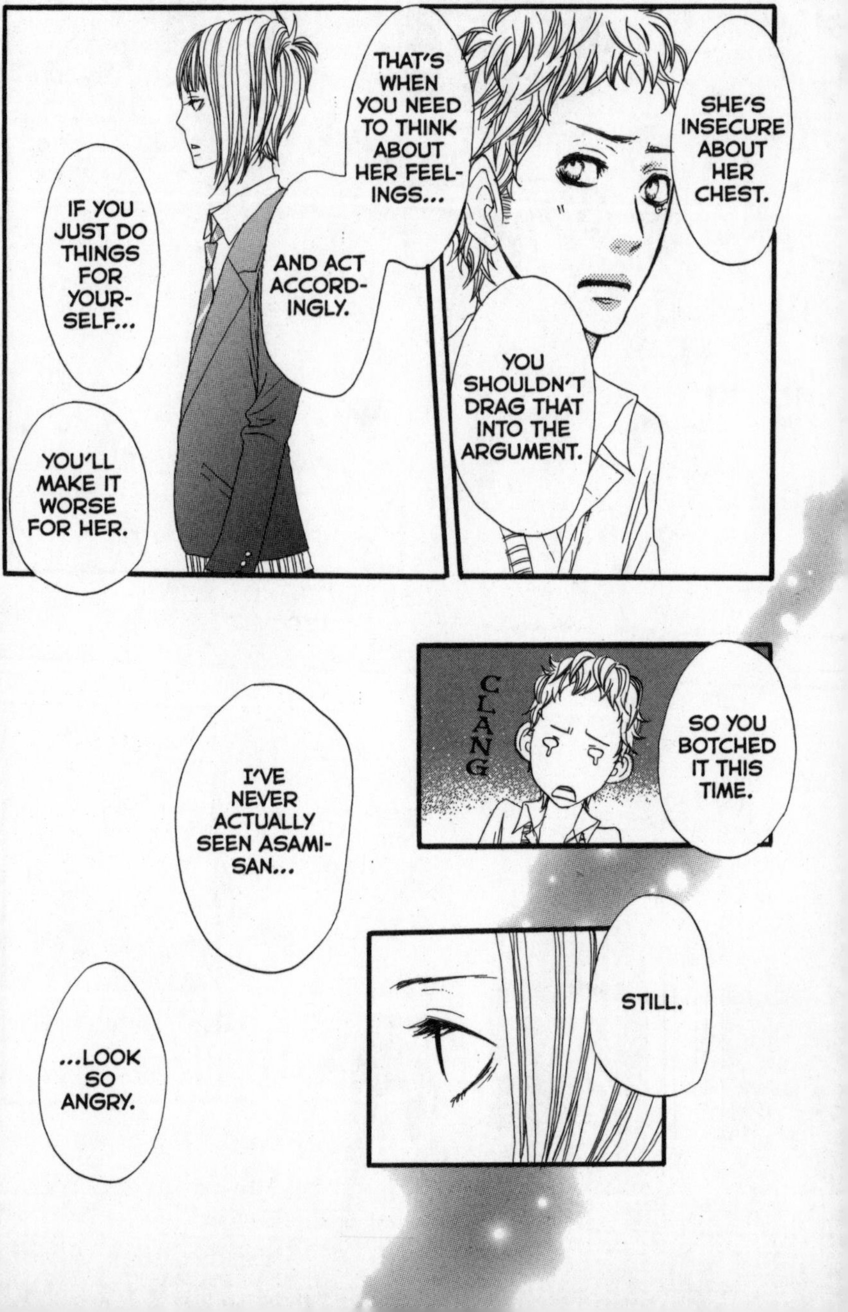
SHE'S INSECURE ABOUT HER CHEST.
YOU SHOULDN'T DRAG THAT INTO THE ARGUMENT.
THAT'S WHEN YOU NEED TO THINK ABOUT HER FEELINGS...
AND ACT ACCORDINGLY.
IF YOU JUST DO THINGS FOR YOURSELF...
YOU'LL MAKE IT WORSE FOR HER.
SO YOU BOTCHED IT THIS TIME.
CLANG
STILL.
I'VE NEVER ACTUALLY SEEN ASAMI-SAN...
...LOOK SO ANGRY.

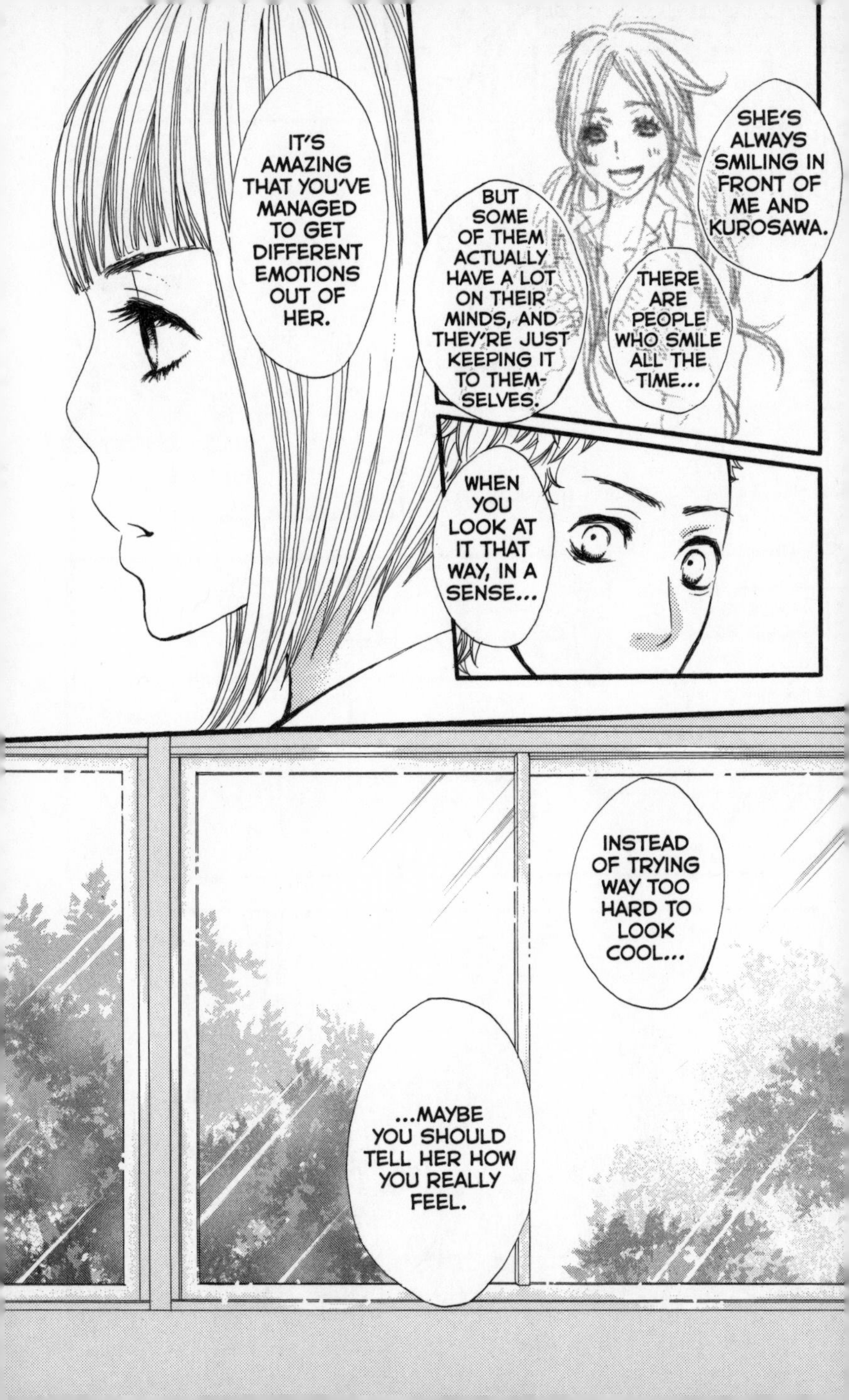
SHE'S ALWAYS SMILING IN FRONT OF ME AND KUROSAWA.
THERE ARE PEOPLE WHO SMILE ALL THE TIME...
BUT SOME OF THEM ACTUALLY HAVE A LOT ON THEIR MINDS, AND THEY'RE JUST KEEPING IT TO THEM-SELVES.
WHEN YOU LOOK AT IT THAT WAY, IN A SENSE...
IT'S AMAZING THAT YOU'VE MANAGED TO GET DIFFERENT EMOTIONS OUT OF HER.
INSTEAD OF TRYING WAY TOO HARD TO LOOK COOL...
...MAYBE YOU SHOULD TELL HER HOW YOU REALLY FEEL.

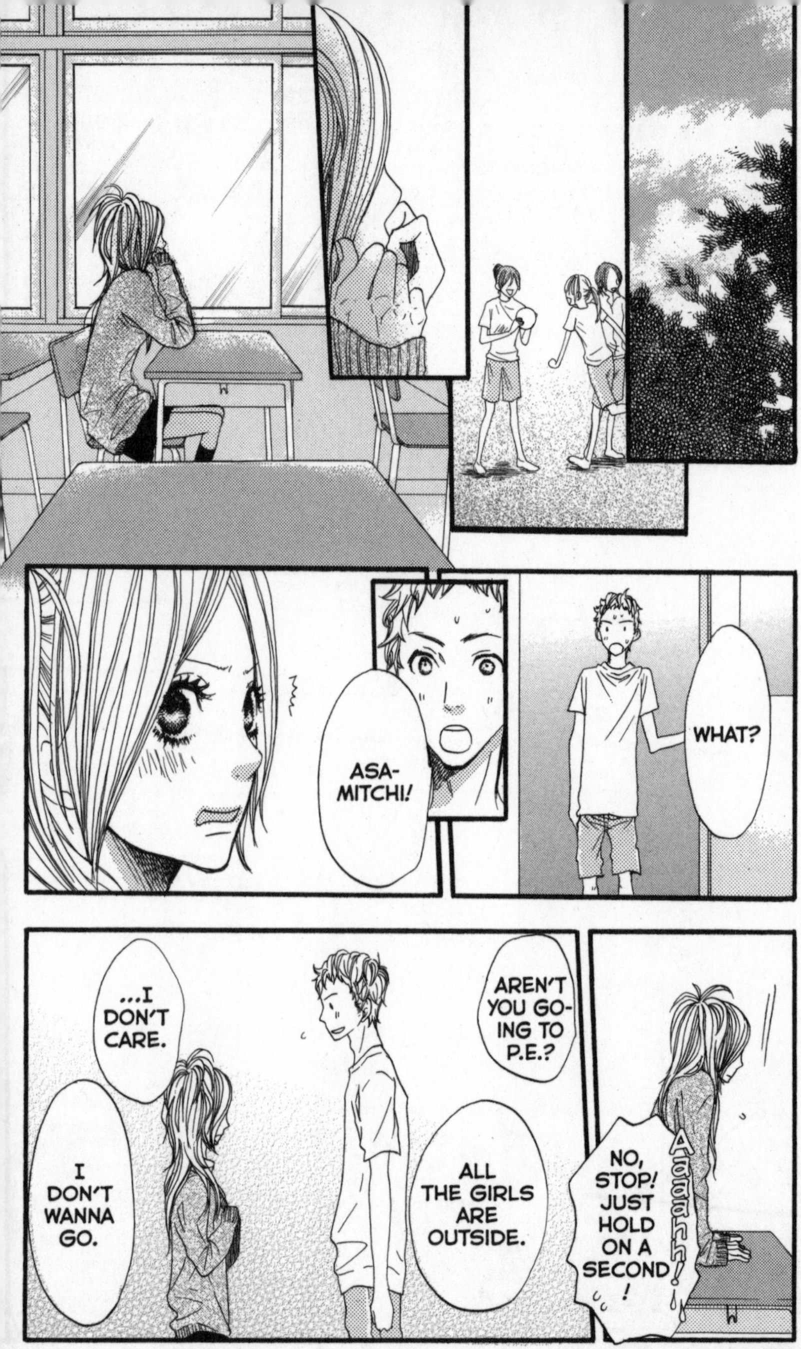
WHAT?
ASA-MITCHI!
NO, STOP! JUST HOLD ON A SECOND!
Aaaaahh!
AREN'T YOU GO-ING TO P.E.?
ALL THE GIRLS ARE OUTSIDE.
...I DON'T CARE.
I DON'T WANNA GO.

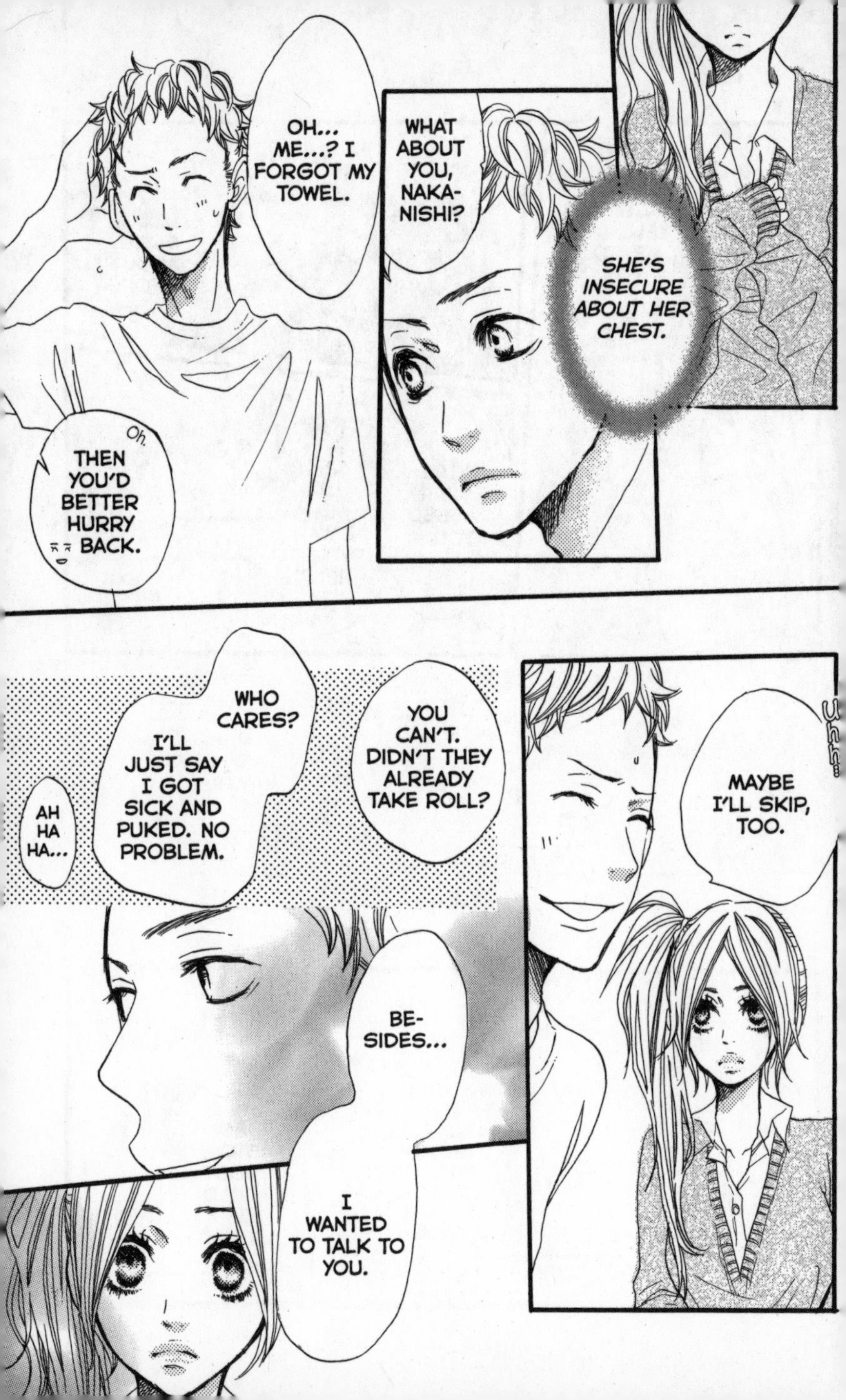
SHE'S INSECURE ABOUT HER CHEST.
WHAT ABOUT YOU, NAKANISHI?
OH... ME...? I FORGOT MY TOWEL.
Oh.
THEN YOU'D BETTER HURRY BACK.
Uhh...
MAYBE I'LL SKIP, TOO.
YOU CAN'T. DIDN'T THEY ALREADY TAKE ROLL?
WHO CARES?
I'LL JUST SAY I GOT SICK AND PUKED. NO PROBLEM.
AH HA HA...
BE-SIDES...
I WANTED TO TALK TO YOU.

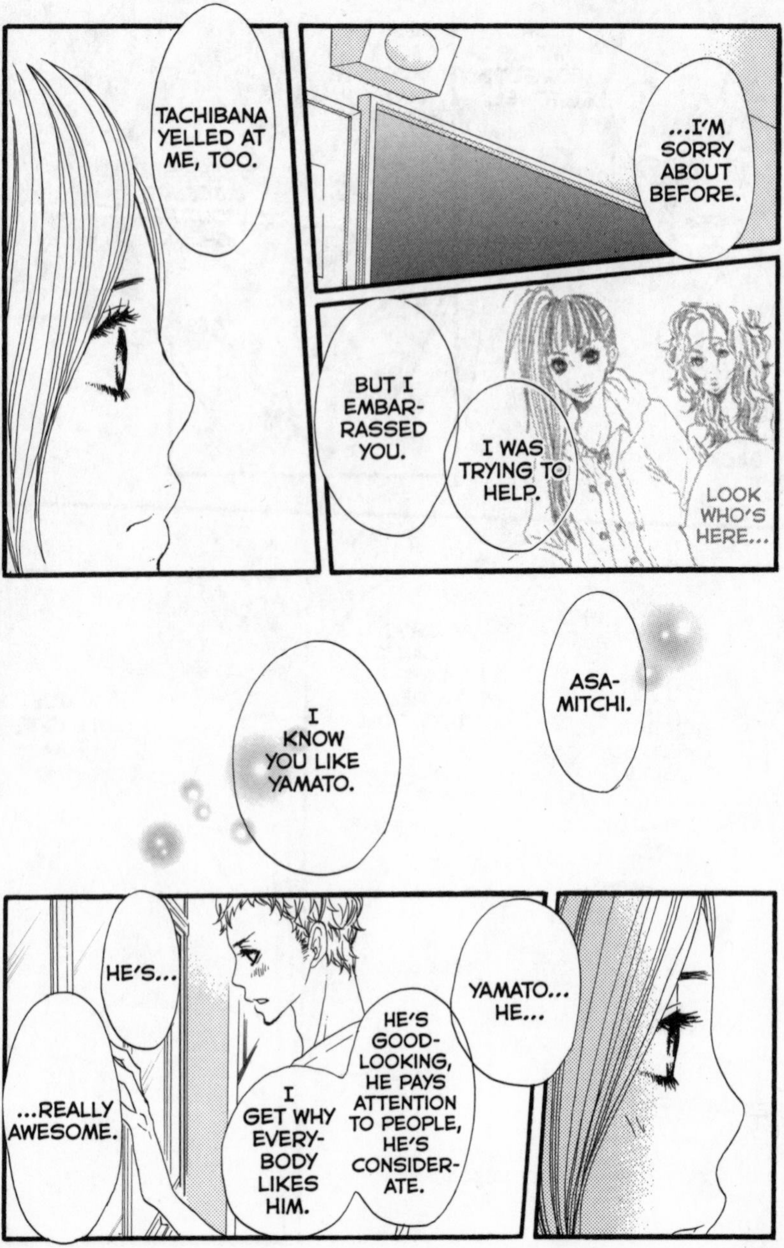
...I'M SORRY ABOUT BEFORE.
LOOK WHO'S HERE...
I WAS TRYING TO HELP.
BUT I EMBARRASSED YOU.
TACHIBANA YELLED AT ME, TOO.
ASA-MITCHI.
I KNOW YOU LIKE YAMATO.
YAMATO... HE...
HE'S GOOD-LOOKING, HE PAYS ATTENTION TO PEOPLE, HE'S CONSIDERATE.
I GET WHY EVERYBODY LIKES HIM.
HE'S...
...REALLY AWESOME.

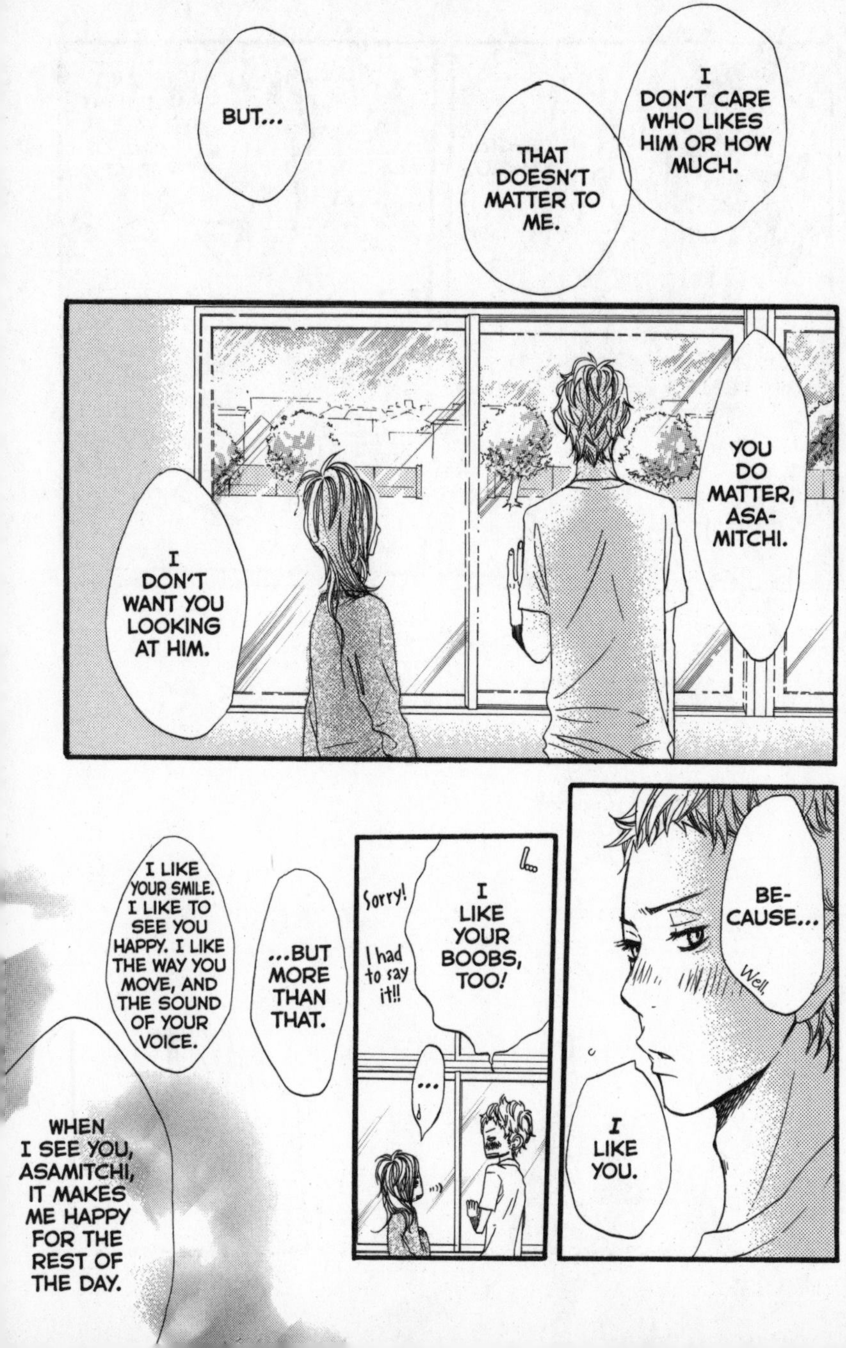

I DON'T CARE WHO LIKES HIM OR HOW MUCH.
THAT DOESN'T MATTER TO ME.
BUT...
YOU DO MATTER, ASA-MITCHI.
I DON'T WANT YOU LOOKING AT HIM.
BE-CAUSE...
Well,
I LIKE YOU.
I...
I LIKE YOUR BOOBS, TOO!
Sorry!
I had to say it!!
...
...BUT MORE THAN THAT.
I LIKE YOUR SMILE. I LIKE TO SEE YOU HAPPY. I LIKE THE WAY YOU MOVE, AND THE SOUND OF YOUR VOICE.
WHEN I SEE YOU, ASAMITCHI, IT MAKES ME HAPPY FOR THE REST OF THE DAY.

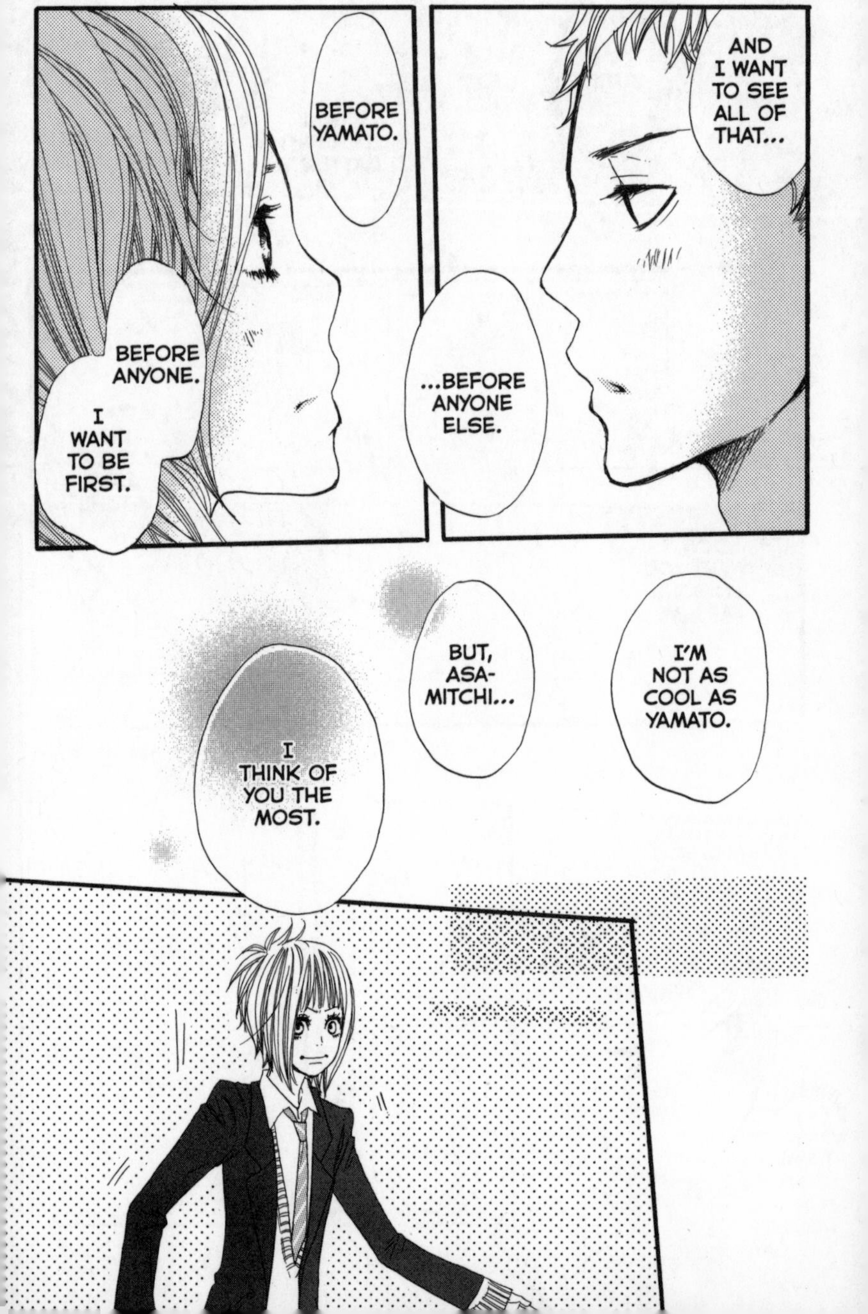
AND I WANT TO SEE ALL OF THAT...
...BEFORE ANYONE ELSE.
BEFORE YAMATO.
BEFORE ANYONE.
I WANT TO BE FIRST.
I'M NOT AS COOL AS YAMATO.
BUT, ASA-MITCHI...
I THINK OF YOU THE MOST.

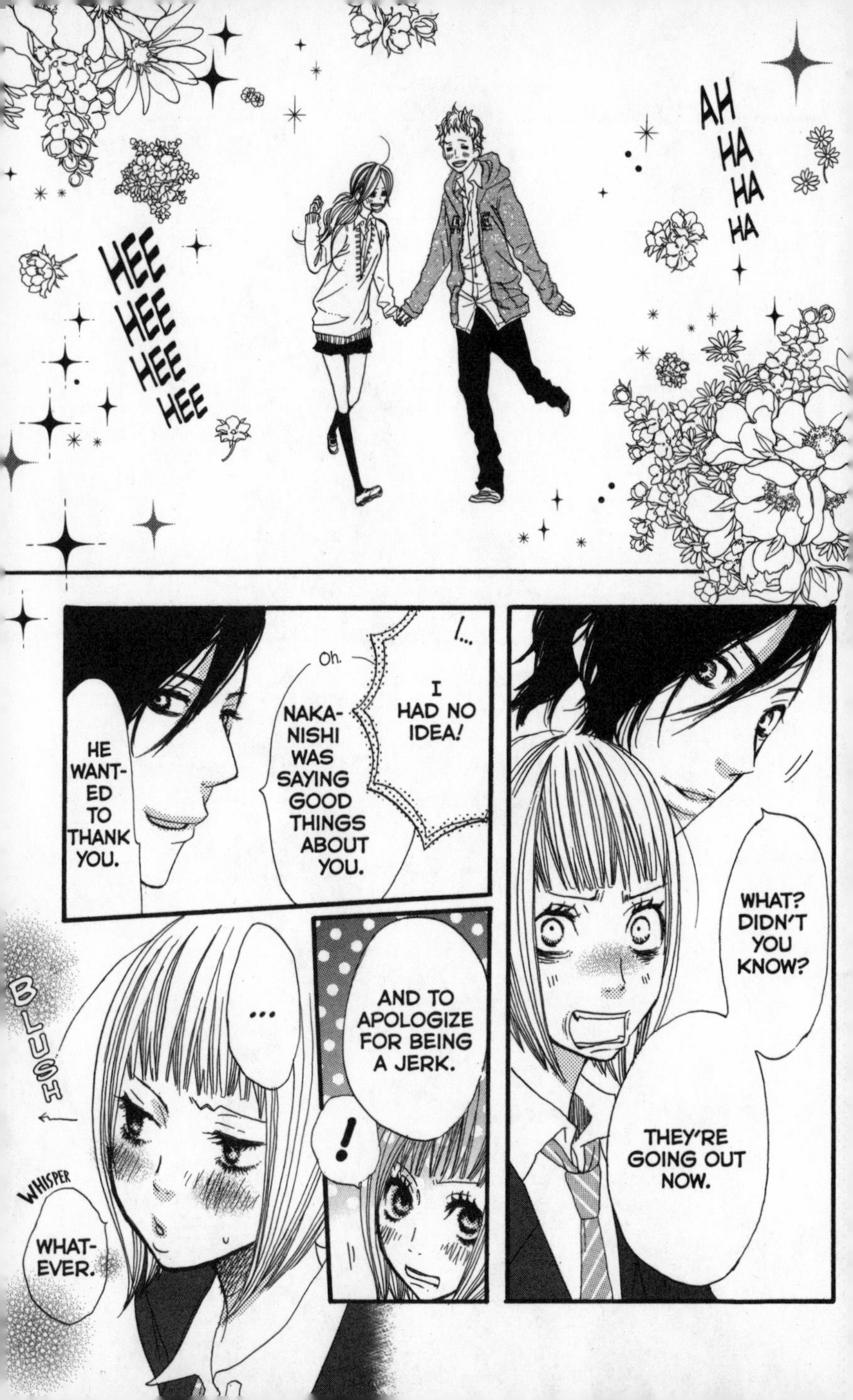
AH HA HA HA
HEE HEE HEE HEE
WHAT? DIDN'T YOU KNOW?
THEY'RE GOING OUT NOW.
I...
I HAD NO IDEA!
Oh.
NAKA-NISHI WAS SAYING GOOD THINGS ABOUT YOU.
HE WANT-ED TO THANK YOU.
AND TO APOLOGIZE FOR BEING A JERK.
!
...
BLUSH
WHISPER
WHAT-EVER.

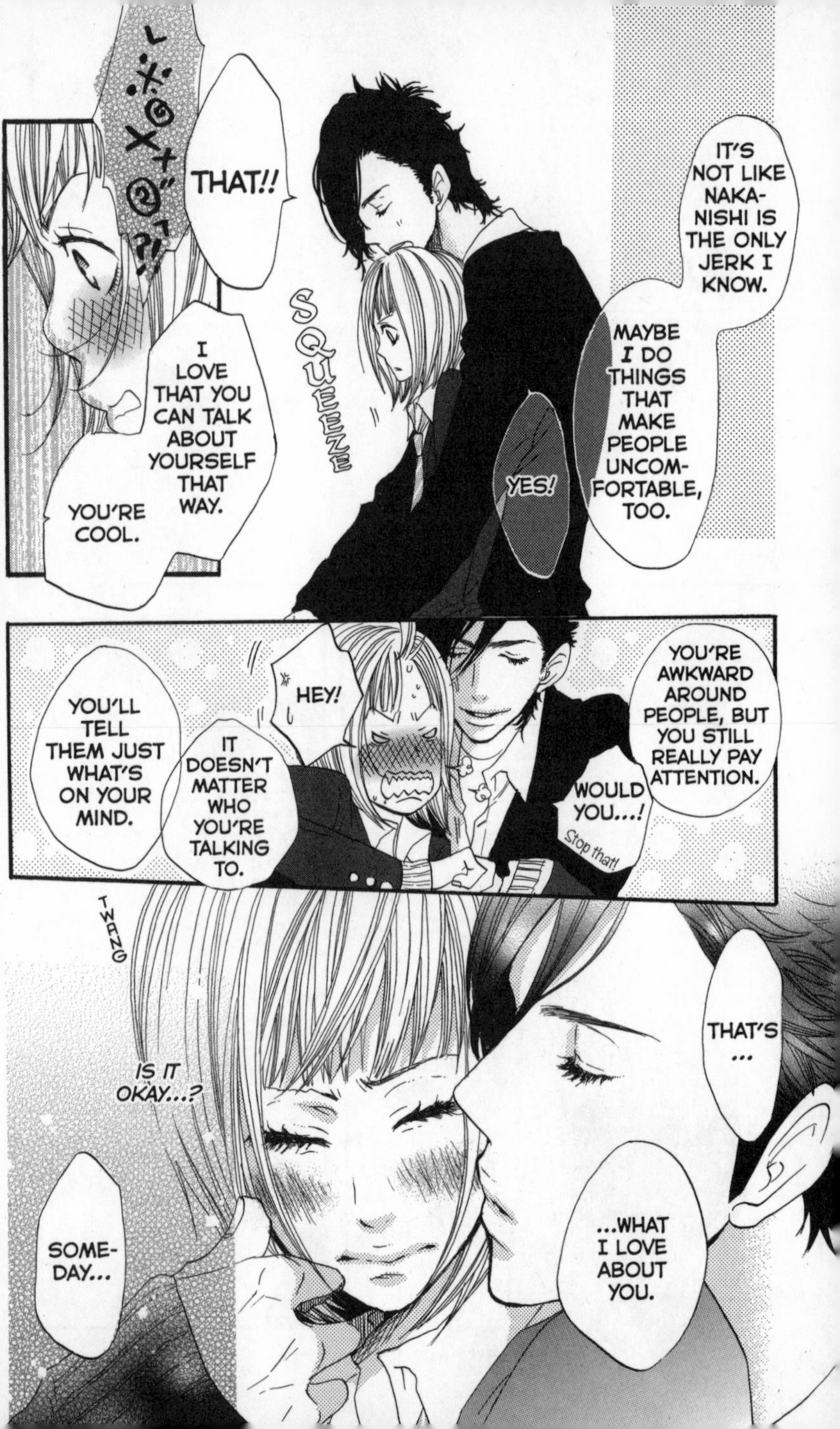
IT'S NOT LIKE NAKA-NISHI IS THE ONLY JERK I KNOW.
MAYBE *I* DO THINGS THAT MAKE PEOPLE UNCOM-FORTABLE, TOO.
YES!
SQUEEZE
I LOVE THAT YOU CAN TALK ABOUT YOURSELF THAT WAY.
YOU'RE COOL.
THAT!!
YOU'RE AWKWARD AROUND PEOPLE, BUT YOU STILL REALLY PAY ATTENTION.
WOULD YOU...!
Stop that!
HEY!
IT DOESN'T MATTER WHO YOU'RE TALKING TO.
YOU'LL TELL THEM JUST WHAT'S ON YOUR MIND.
THAT'S...
...WHAT I LOVE ABOUT YOU.
TWANG
IS IT OKAY...?
SOME-DAY...

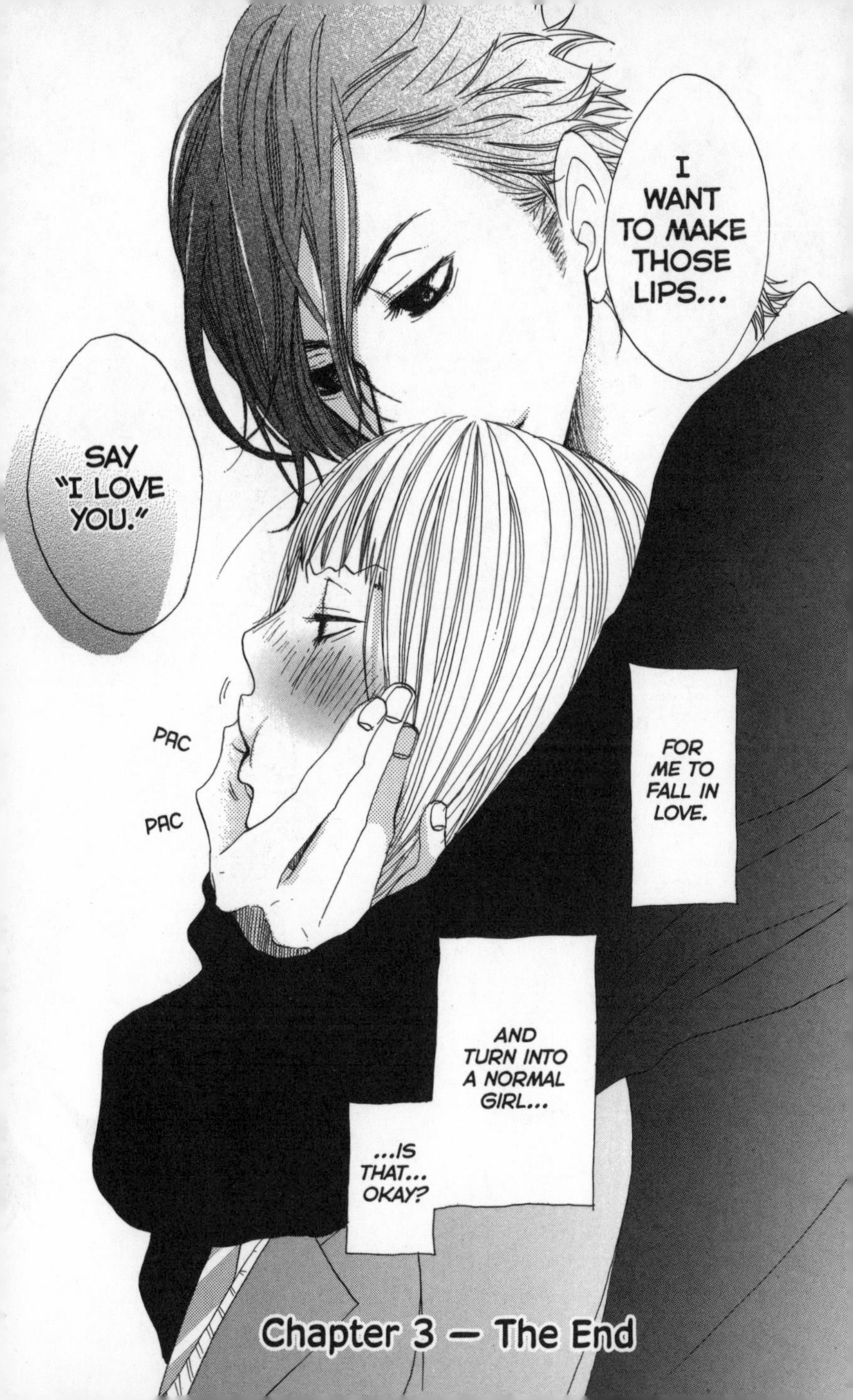
I WANT TO MAKE THOSE LIPS...
SAY "I LOVE YOU."
PAC
PAC
FOR ME TO FALL IN LOVE.
AND TURN INTO A NORMAL GIRL...
...IS THAT... OKAY?
Chapter 3 — The End

Say "I love you".
Kanae Hazuki

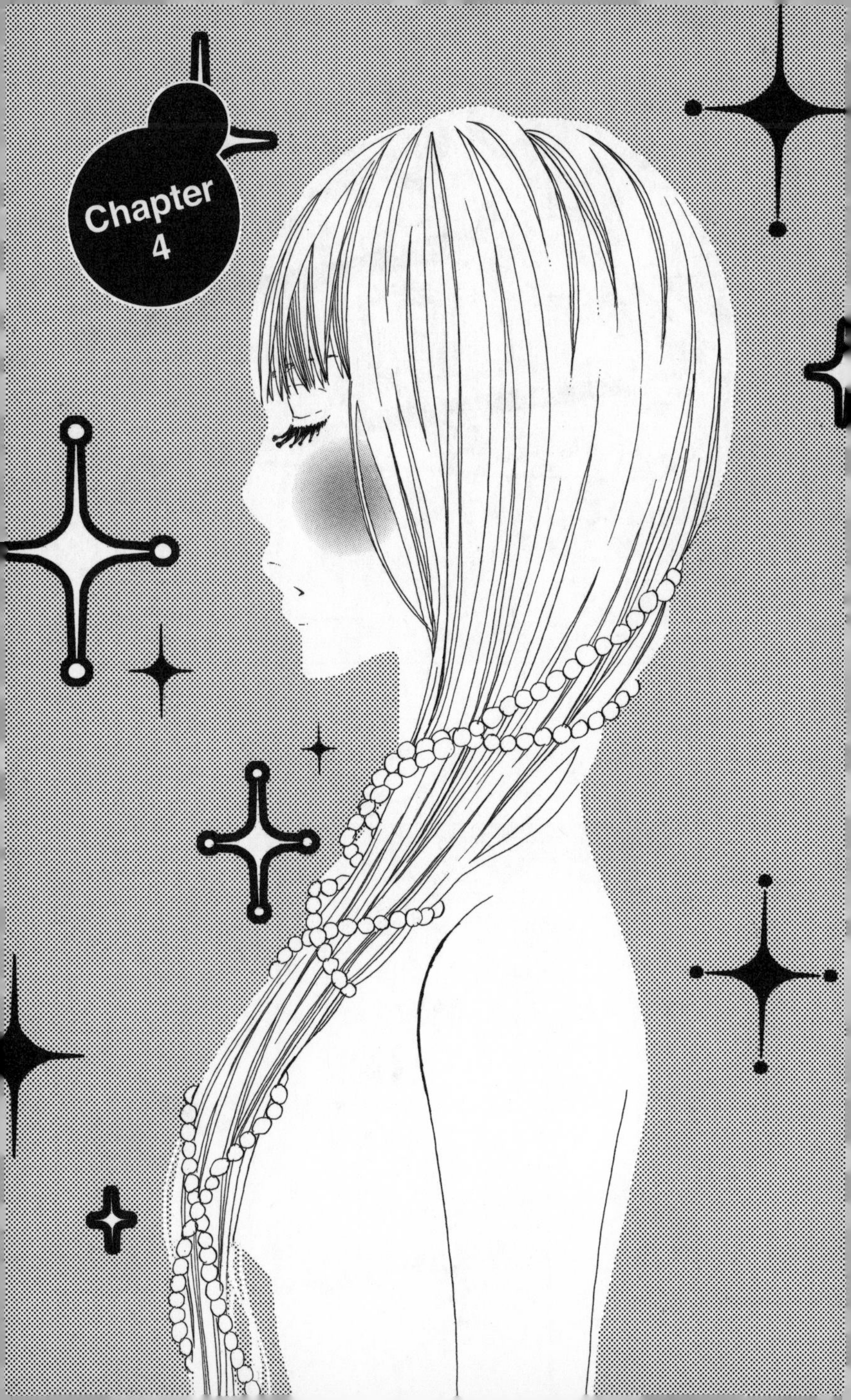
Chapter
4

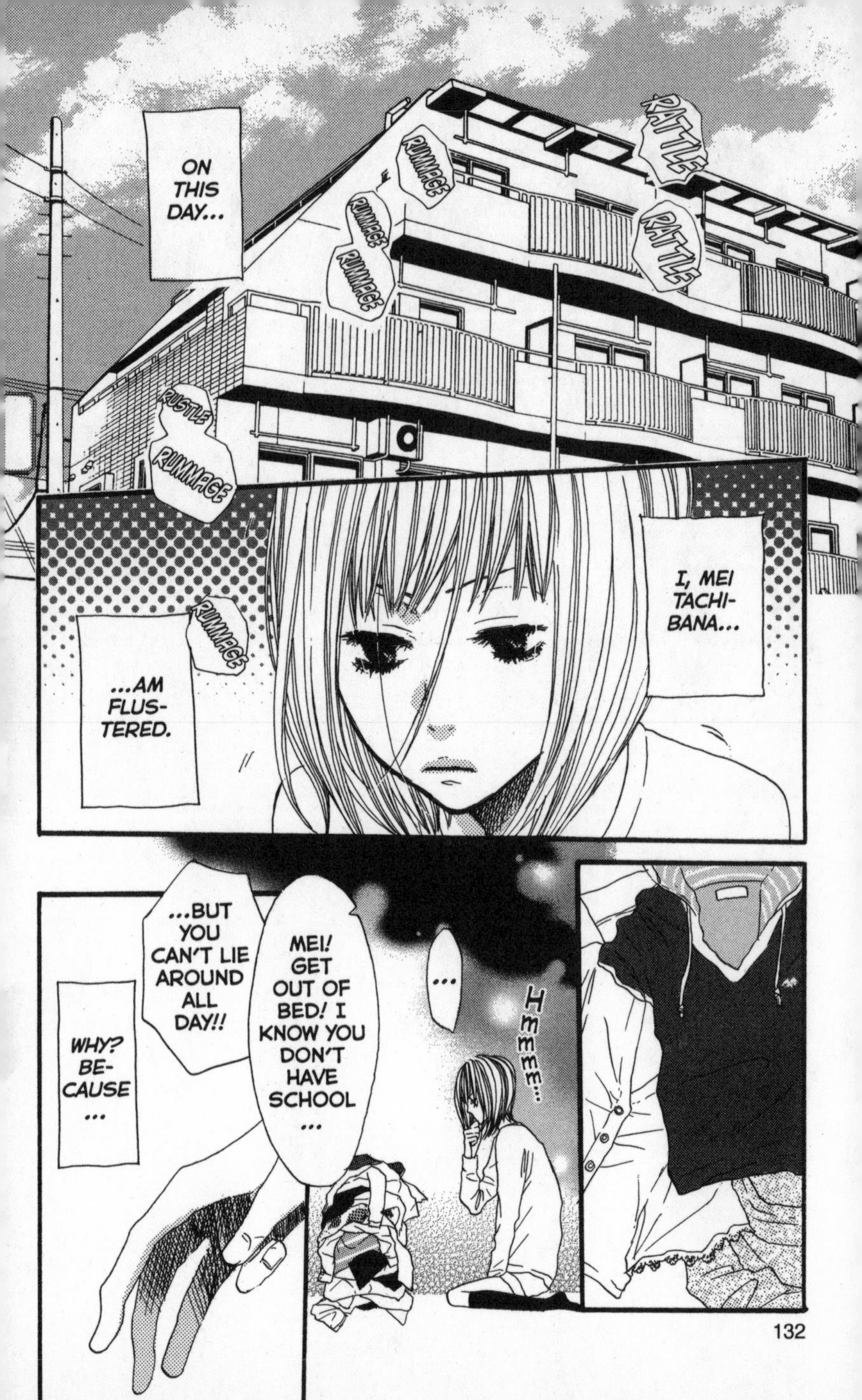
RATTLE
RATTLE
RUMMAGE
RUMMAGE
RUMMAGE
ON THIS DAY...
RUSTLE
RUMMAGE
I, MEI TACHI-BANA...
RUMMAGE
...AM FLUS-TERED.
Hmmm...
...
MEI! GET OUT OF BED! I KNOW YOU DON'T HAVE SCHOOL...
...BUT YOU CAN'T LIE AROUND ALL DAY!!
WHY? BE-CAUSE...

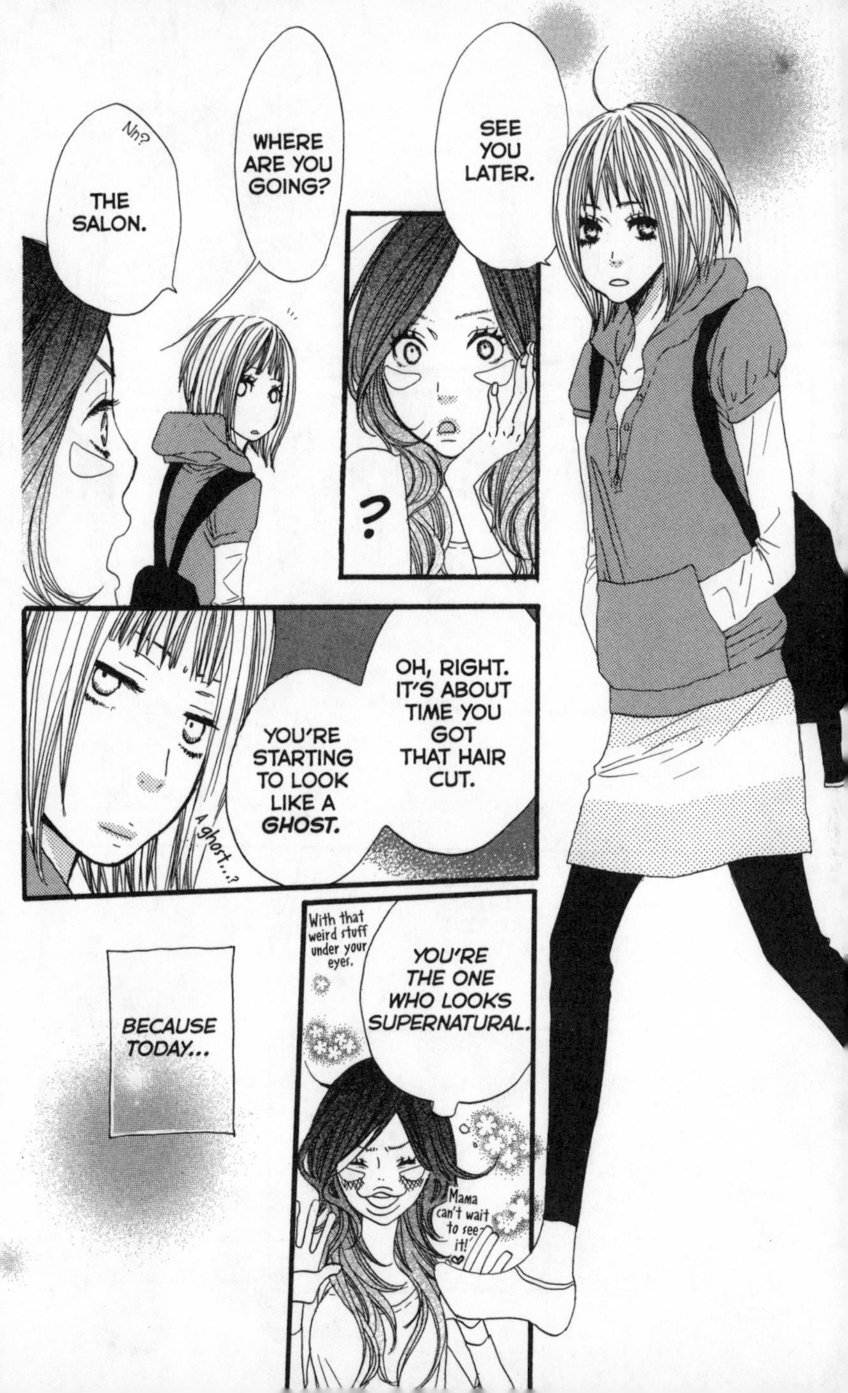
SEE YOU LATER.
?
WHERE ARE YOU GOING?
Nn?
THE SALON.
OH, RIGHT. IT'S ABOUT TIME YOU GOT THAT HAIR CUT.
YOU'RE STARTING TO LOOK LIKE A GHOST.
A ghost...?
YOU'RE THE ONE WHO LOOKS SUPERNATURAL.
With that weird stuff under your eyes.
Mama can't wait to see it!
BECAUSE TODAY...

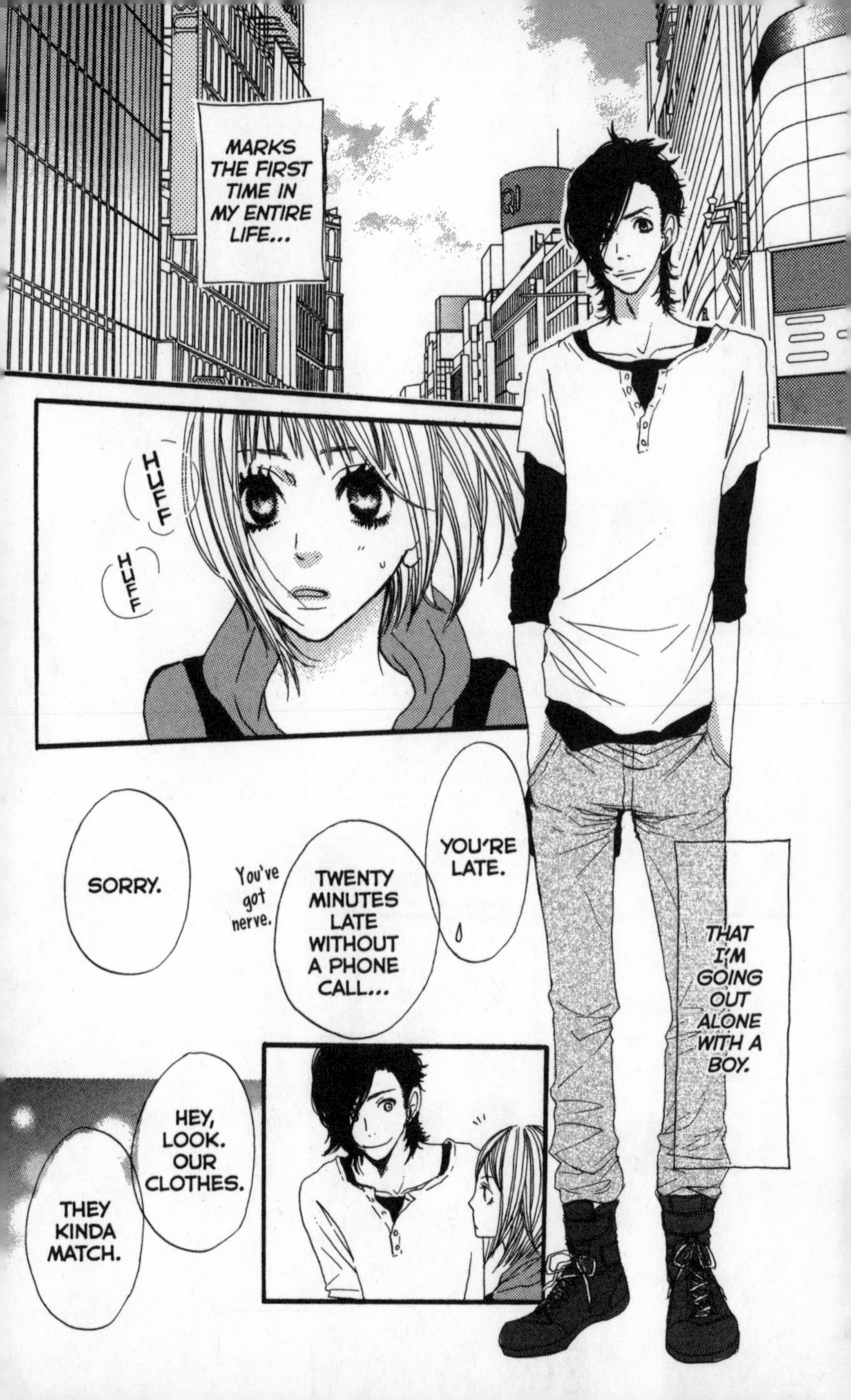
MARKS THE FIRST TIME IN MY ENTIRE LIFE...
THAT I'M GOING OUT ALONE WITH A BOY.
HUFF
HUFF
YOU'RE LATE.
TWENTY MINUTES LATE WITHOUT A PHONE CALL...
You've got nerve.
SORRY.
HEY, LOOK. OUR CLOTHES.
THEY KINDA MATCH.

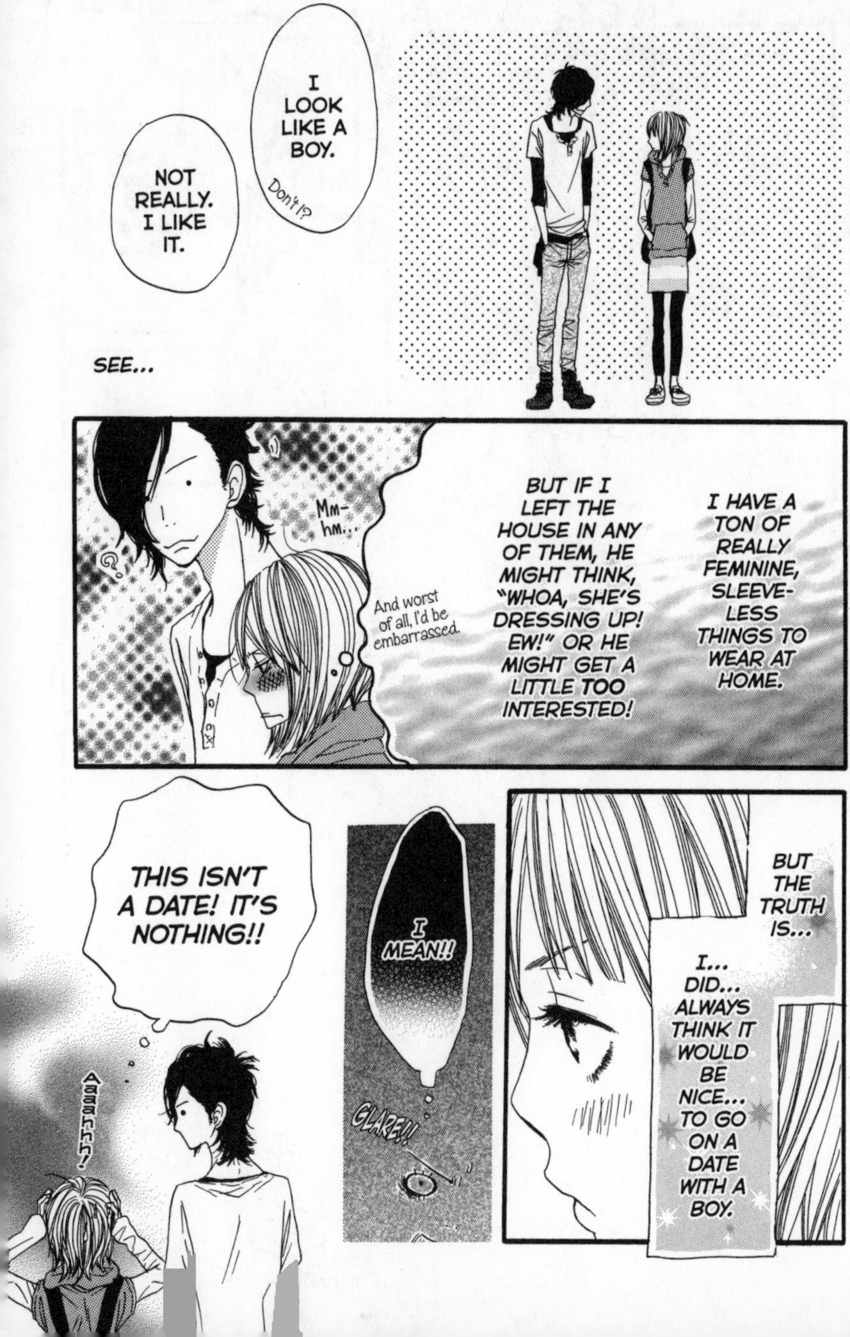
I LOOK LIKE A BOY.
Don't I?
NOT REALLY. I LIKE IT.
SEE...
I HAVE A TON OF REALLY FEMININE, SLEEVELESS THINGS TO WEAR AT HOME.
BUT IF I LEFT THE HOUSE IN ANY OF THEM, HE MIGHT THINK, "WHOA, SHE'S DRESSING UP! EW!" OR HE MIGHT GET A LITTLE TOO INTERESTED!
And worst of all, I'd be embarrassed.
Mm-hm...
BUT THE TRUTH IS...
I... DID... ALWAYS THINK IT WOULD BE NICE... TO GO ON A DATE WITH A BOY.
I MEAN!!
GLARE!!
THIS ISN'T A DATE! IT'S NOTHING!!
Aaaahh!

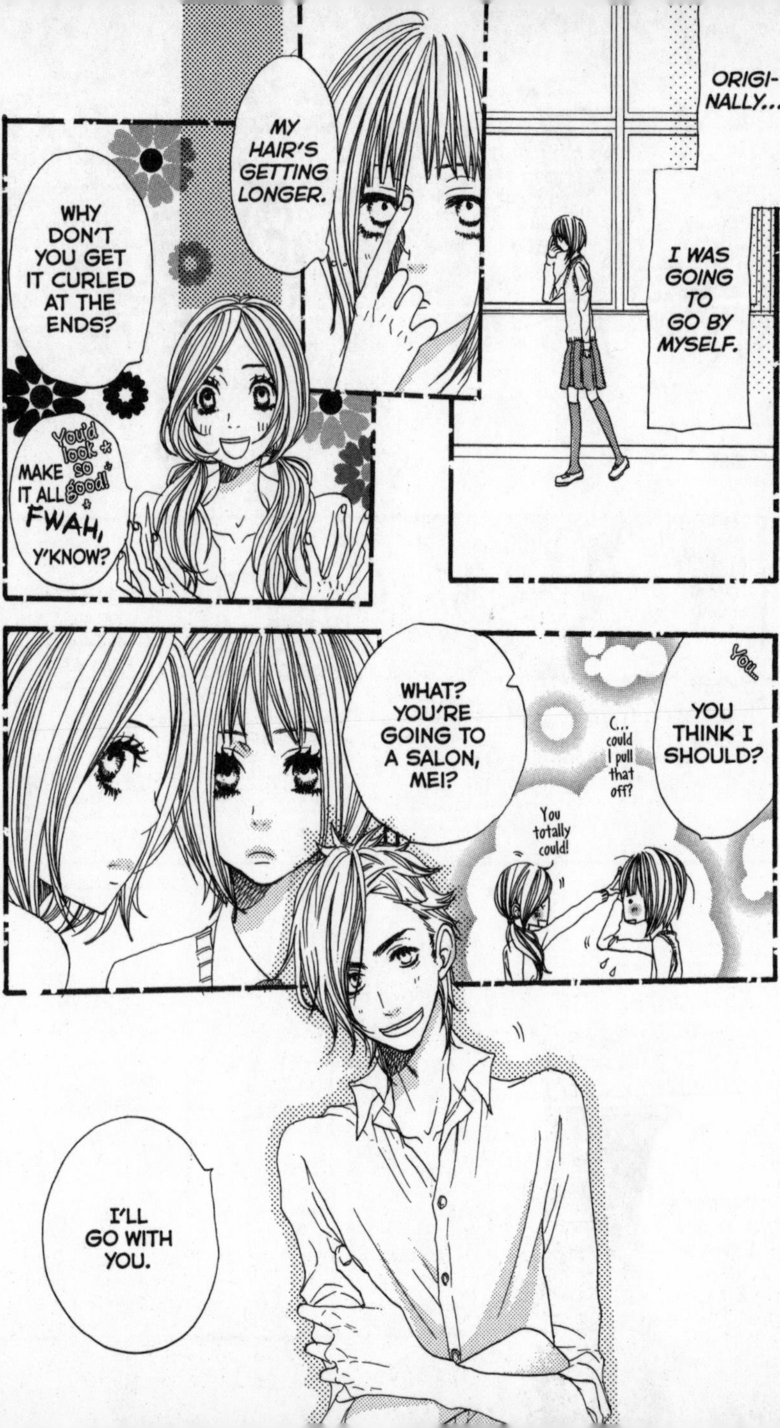
ORIGINALLY...
I WAS GOING TO GO BY MYSELF.
MY HAIR'S GETTING LONGER.
WHY DON'T YOU GET IT CURLED AT THE ENDS?
You'd look so good!
MAKE IT ALL FWAH, Y'KNOW?
You...
YOU THINK I SHOULD?
C... could I pull that off?
You totally could!
WHAT? YOU'RE GOING TO A SALON, MEI?
I'LL GO WITH YOU.

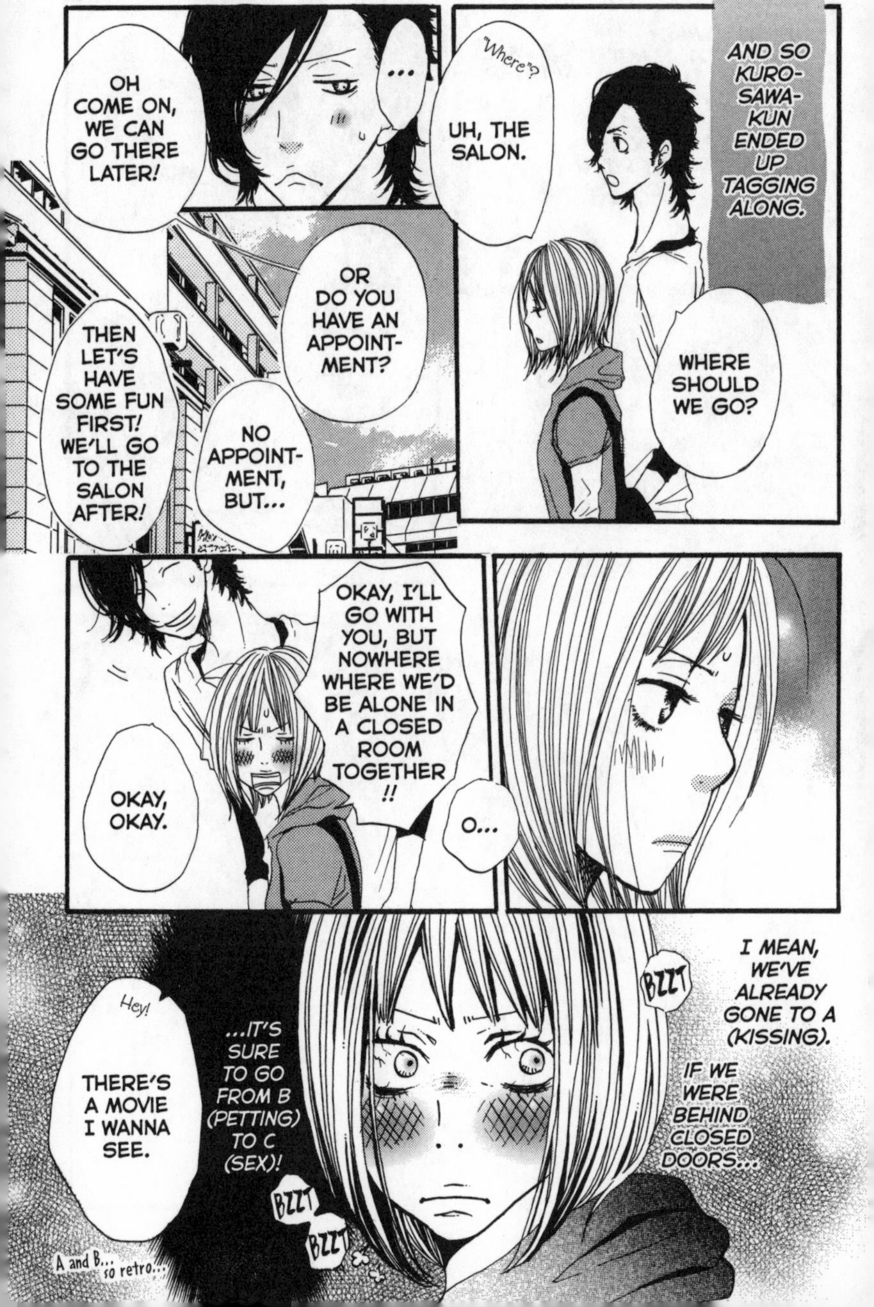
AND SO KURO-SAWA-KUN ENDED UP TAGGING ALONG.
WHERE SHOULD WE GO?
"Where"? UH, THE SALON.
...
OH COME ON, WE CAN GO THERE LATER!
OR DO YOU HAVE AN APPOINT-MENT?
NO APPOINT-MENT, BUT...
THEN LET'S HAVE SOME FUN FIRST! WE'LL GO TO THE SALON AFTER!
O...
OKAY, I'LL GO WITH YOU, BUT NOWHERE WHERE WE'D BE ALONE IN A CLOSED ROOM TOGETHER !!
OKAY, OKAY.
I MEAN, WE'VE ALREADY GONE TO A (KISSING).
IF WE WERE BEHIND CLOSED DOORS...
BZZT
...IT'S SURE TO GO FROM B (PETTING) TO C (SEX)!
BZZT
BZZT
Hey! THERE'S A MOVIE I WANNA SEE.
A and B... so retro...

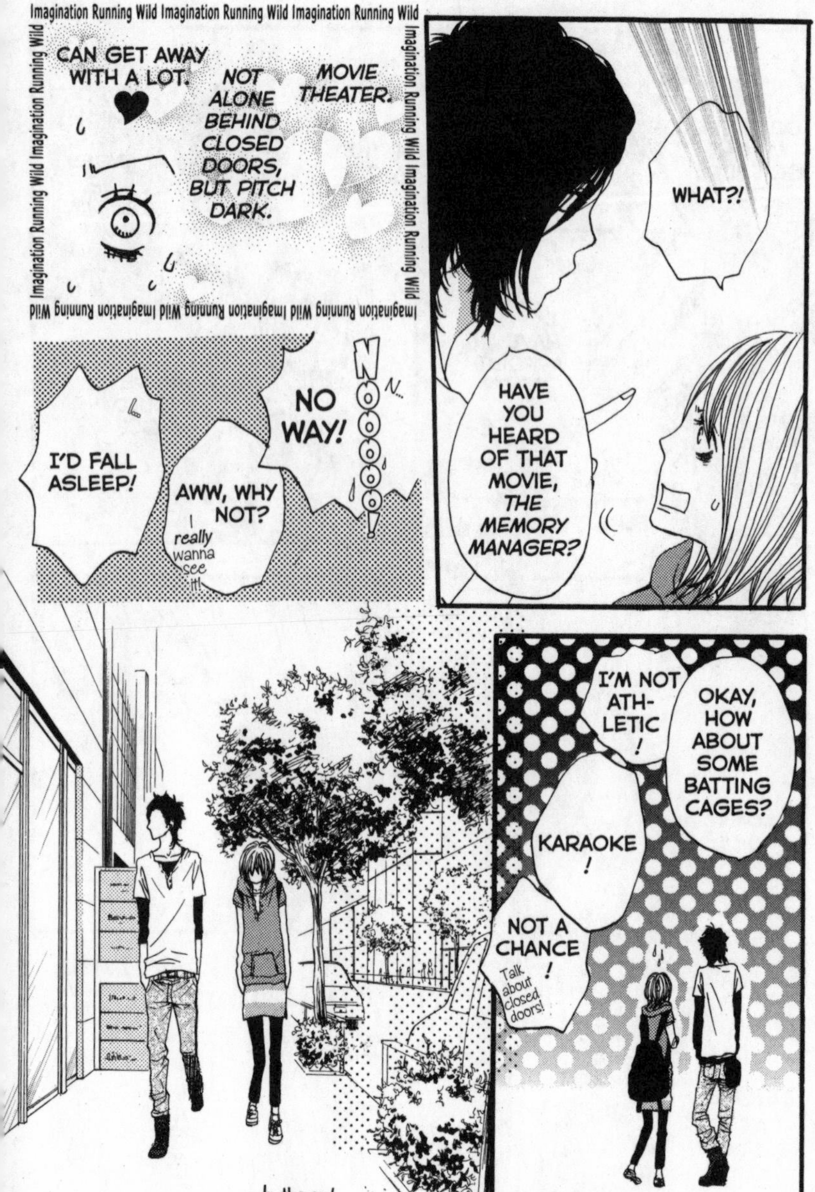
WHAT?!
HAVE YOU HEARD OF THAT MOVIE, *THE MEMORY MANAGER?*
Imagination Running Wild Imagination Running Wild Imagination Running Wild
Imagination Running Wild Imagination Running Wild
Imagination Running Wild Imagination Running Wild
Imagination Running Wild Imagination Running Wild Imagination Running Wild
MOVIE THEATER.
NOT ALONE BEHIND CLOSED DOORS, BUT PITCH DARK.
CAN GET AWAY WITH A LOT.
NOOOOOOO!
N...
NO WAY!
AWW, WHY NOT?
I really wanna see it!
I'D FALL ASLEEP!
OKAY, HOW ABOUT SOME BATTING CAGES?
I'M NOT ATH-LETIC!
KARAOKE!
NOT A CHANCE!
Talk about closed doors!
In the end...

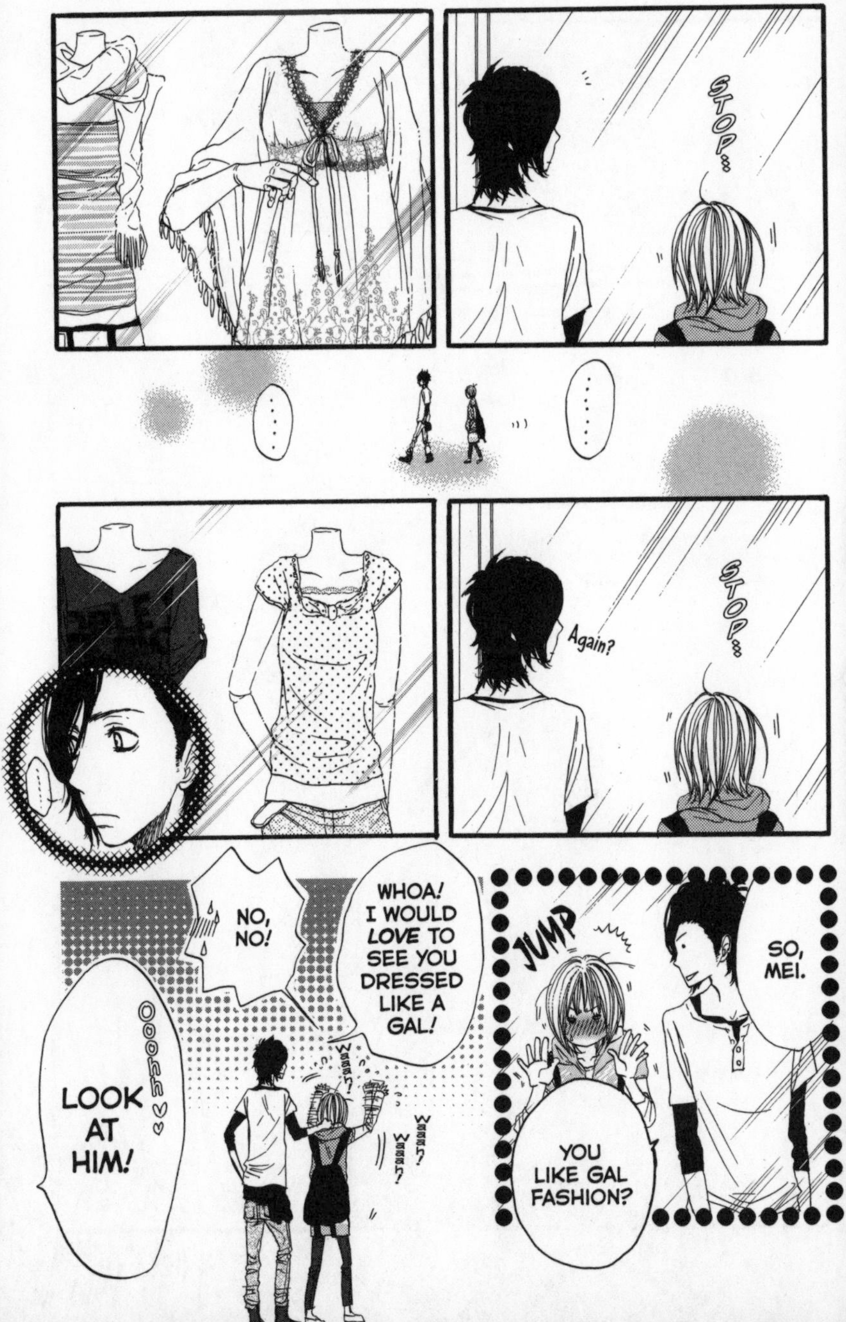
STOP..
STOP..
Again?
SO, MEI.
JUMP
YOU LIKE GAL FASHION?
WHOA! I WOULD *LOVE* TO SEE YOU DRESSED LIKE A GAL!
NO, NO!
Waaah!
Waaah! Waaah!
Ooohh ♡
LOOK AT HIM!

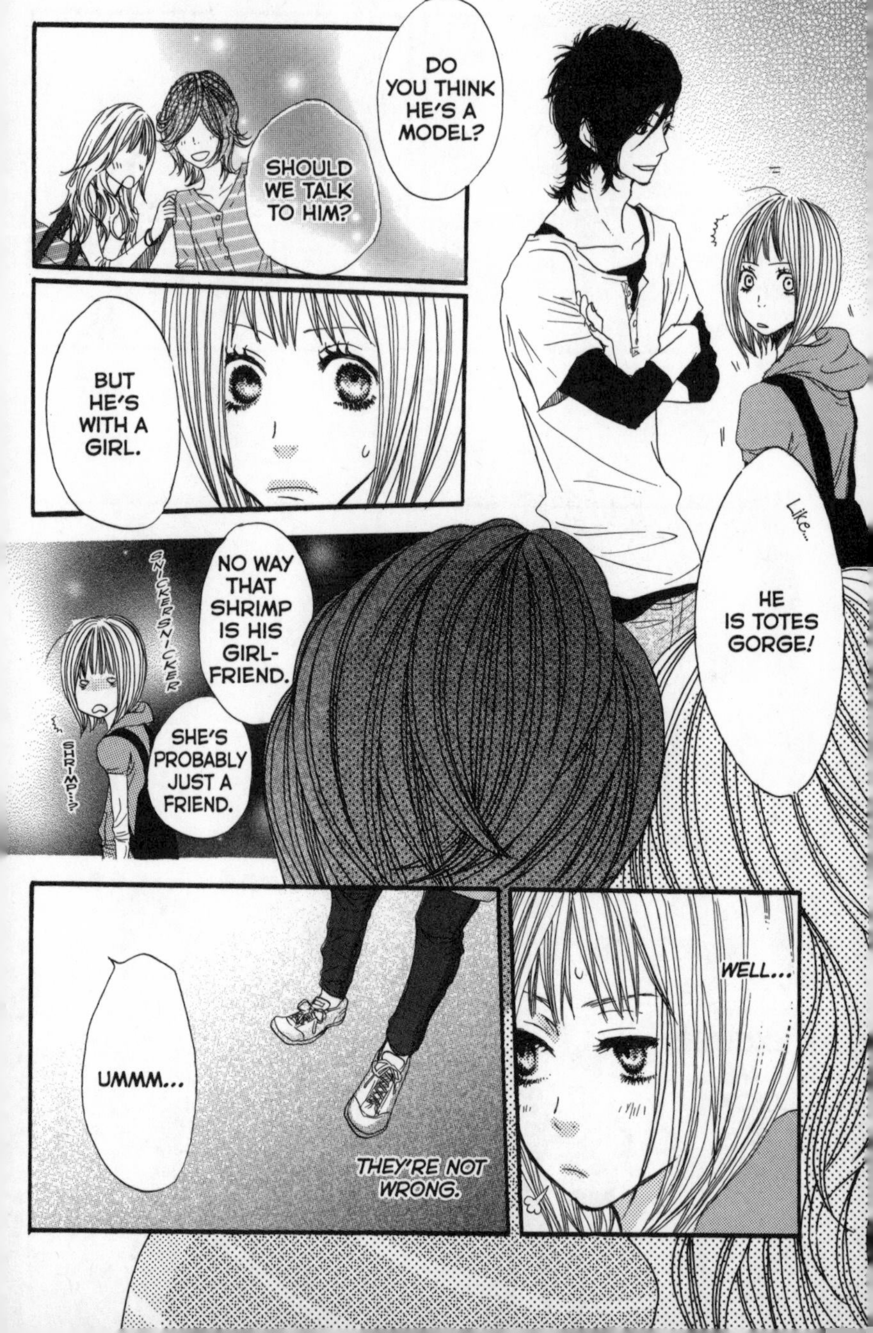

DO YOU THINK HE'S A MODEL?
SHOULD WE TALK TO HIM?
BUT HE'S WITH A GIRL.
Like...
HE IS TOTES GORGE!
NO WAY THAT SHRIMP IS HIS GIRL-FRIEND.
SHE'S PROBABLY JUST A FRIEND.
SNICKER SNICKER
SHRIMP...!?
WELL...
UMMM...
THEY'RE NOT WRONG.

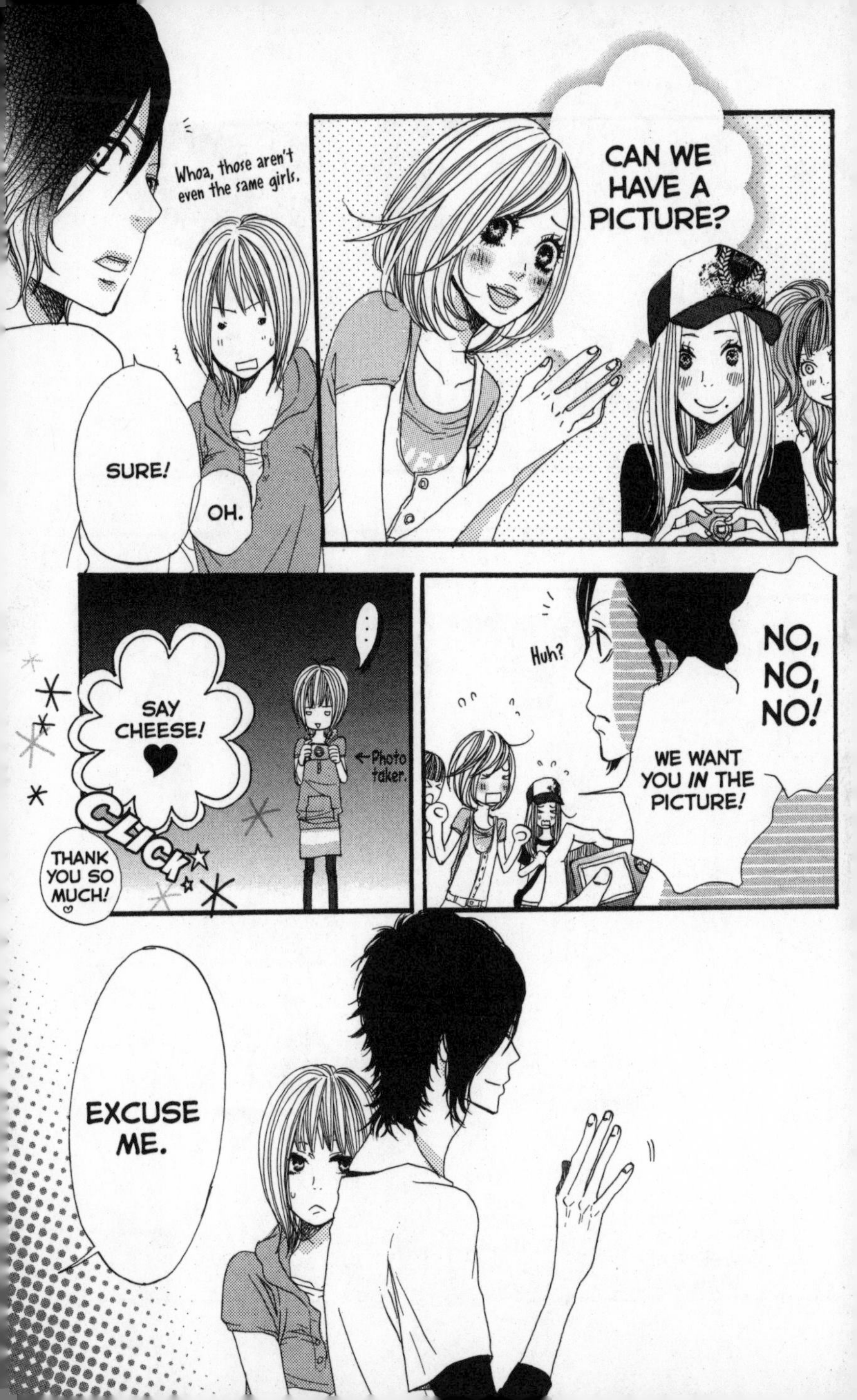

CAN WE HAVE A PICTURE?
Whoa, those aren't even the same girls.
SURE!
OH.
NO, NO, NO!
Huh?
WE WANT YOU *IN* THE PICTURE!
SAY CHEESE! ♥
←Photo taker.
CLICK☆
THANK YOU SO MUCH! ♡
EXCUSE ME.

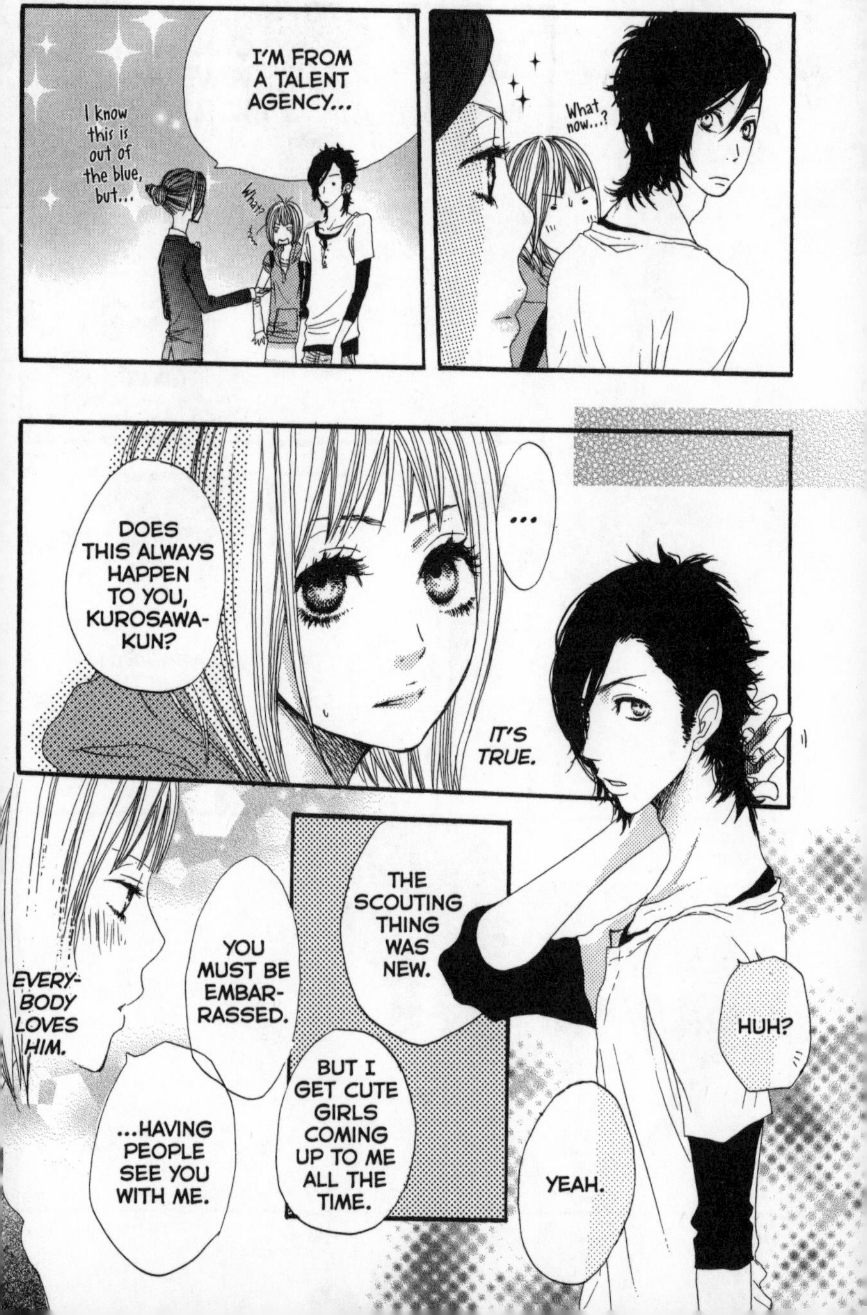
What now...?
I'M FROM A TALENT AGENCY...
I know this is out of the blue, but...
What?
DOES THIS ALWAYS HAPPEN TO YOU, KUROSAWA-KUN?
...
IT'S TRUE.
THE SCOUTING THING WAS NEW.
BUT I GET CUTE GIRLS COMING UP TO ME ALL THE TIME.
EVERY-BODY LOVES HIM.
YOU MUST BE EMBARRASSED.
...HAVING PEOPLE SEE YOU WITH ME.
HUH?
YEAH.

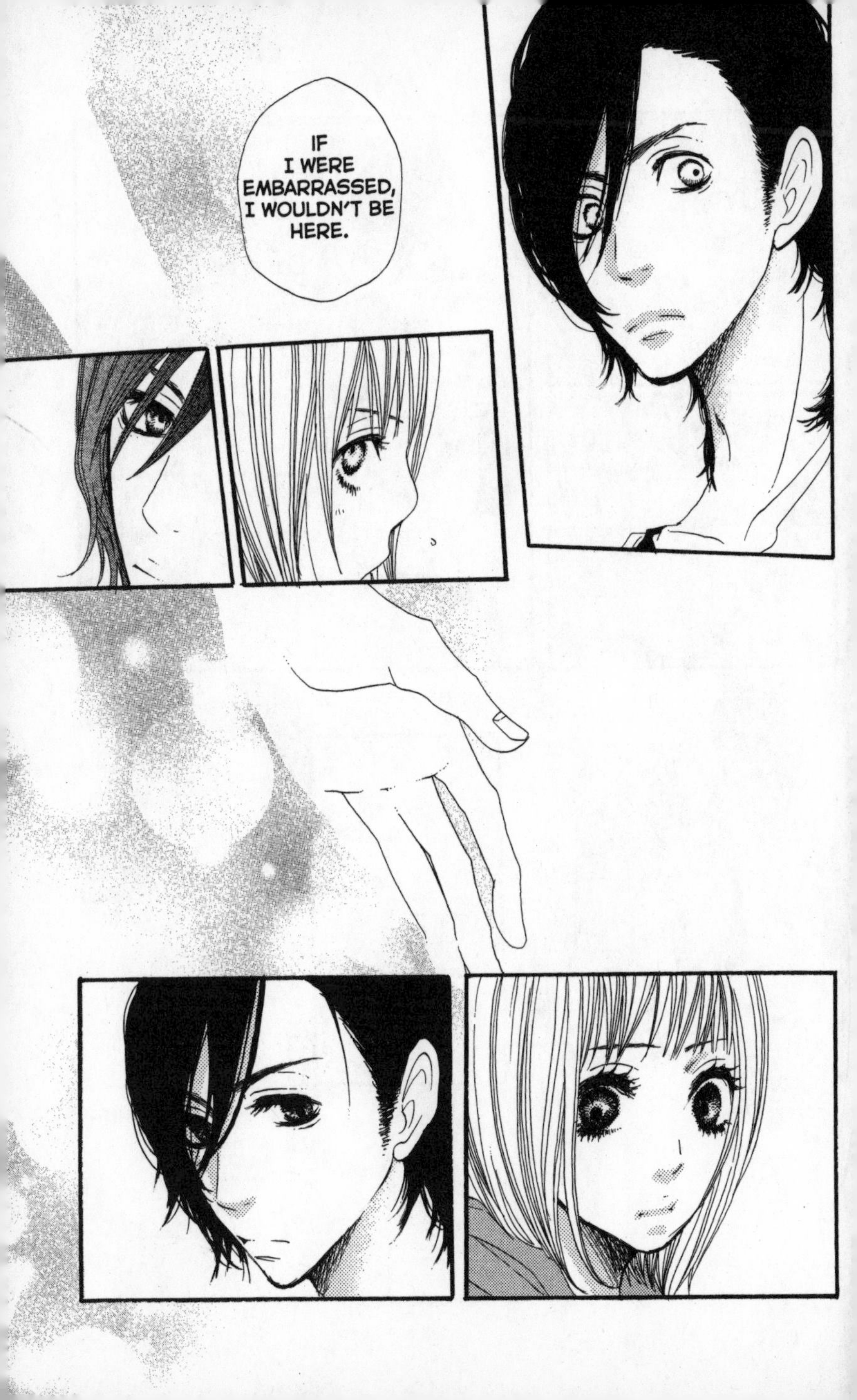
IF I WERE EMBARRASSED, I WOULDN'T BE HERE.

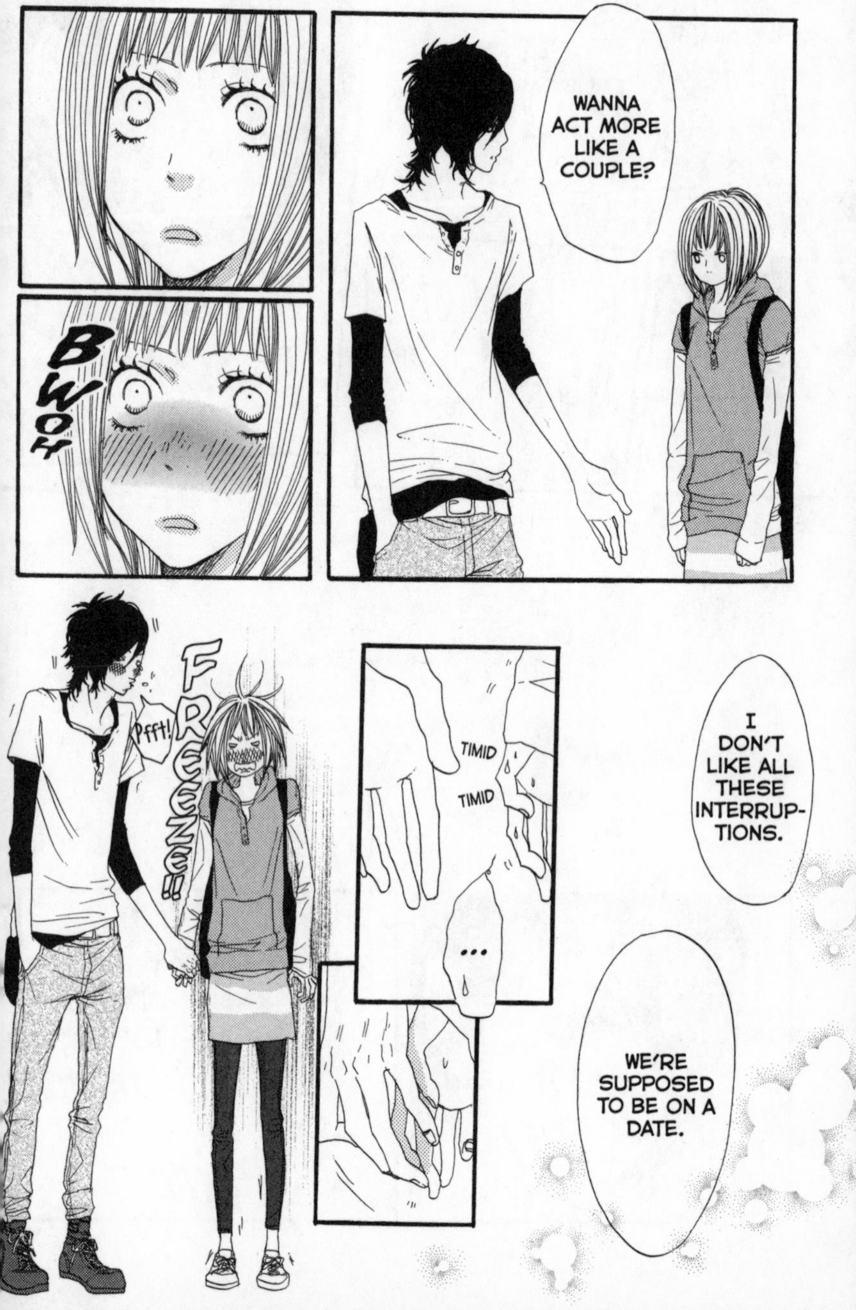
WANNA ACT MORE LIKE A COUPLE?
BWOH
I DON'T LIKE ALL THESE INTERRUP-TIONS.
TIMID
TIMID
...
WE'RE SUPPOSED TO BE ON A DATE.
FREEZE!!
Pfft!

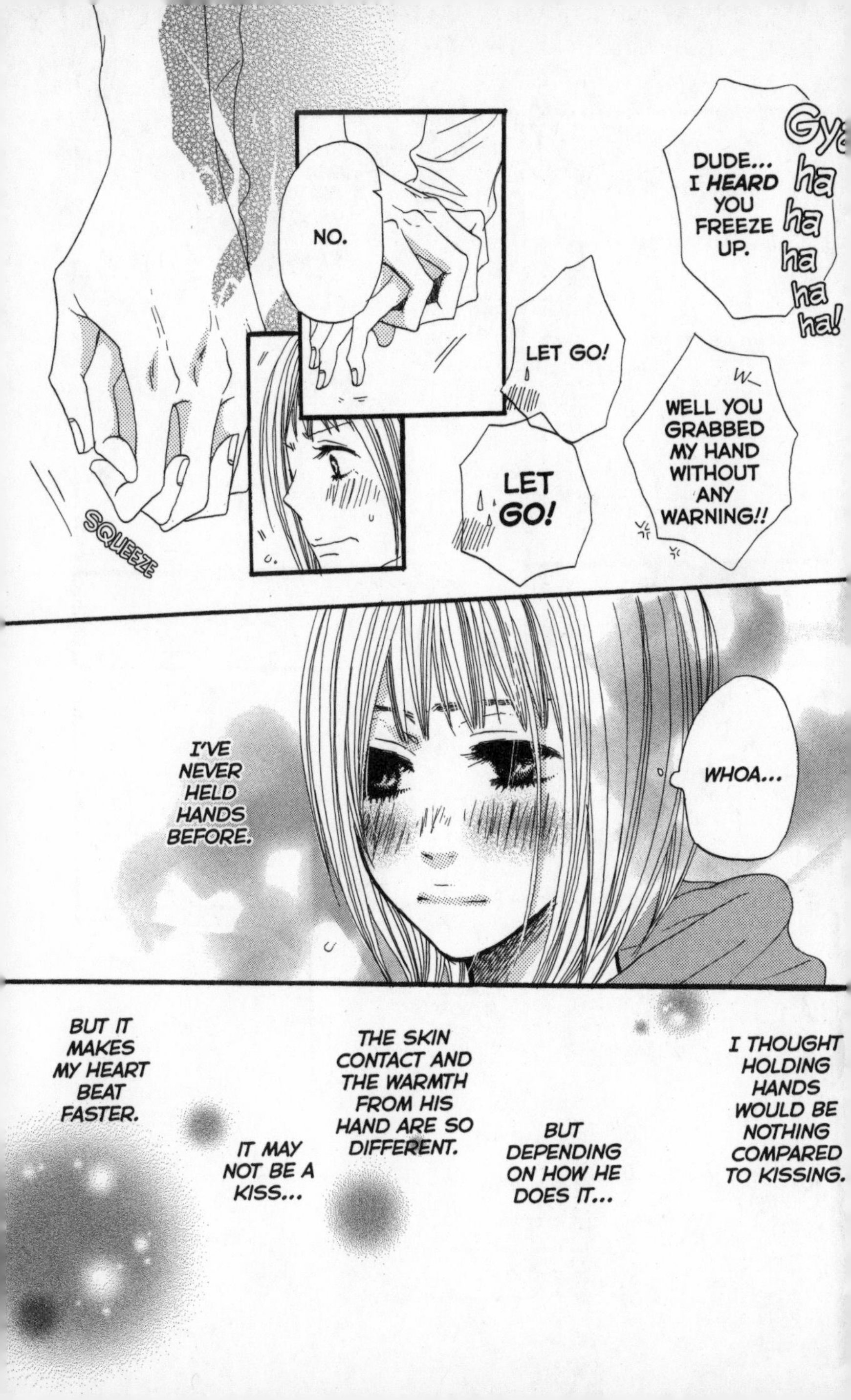
DUDE... I HEARD YOU FREEZE UP.
Gya ha ha ha ha ha!
WELL YOU GRABBED MY HAND WITHOUT ANY WARNING!!
LET GO!
LET GO!
NO.
SQUEEZE
WHOA...
I'VE NEVER HELD HANDS BEFORE.
I THOUGHT HOLDING HANDS WOULD BE NOTHING COMPARED TO KISSING.
BUT DEPENDING ON HOW HE DOES IT...
THE SKIN CONTACT AND THE WARMTH FROM HIS HAND ARE SO DIFFERENT.
IT MAY NOT BE A KISS...
BUT IT MAKES MY HEART BEAT FASTER.

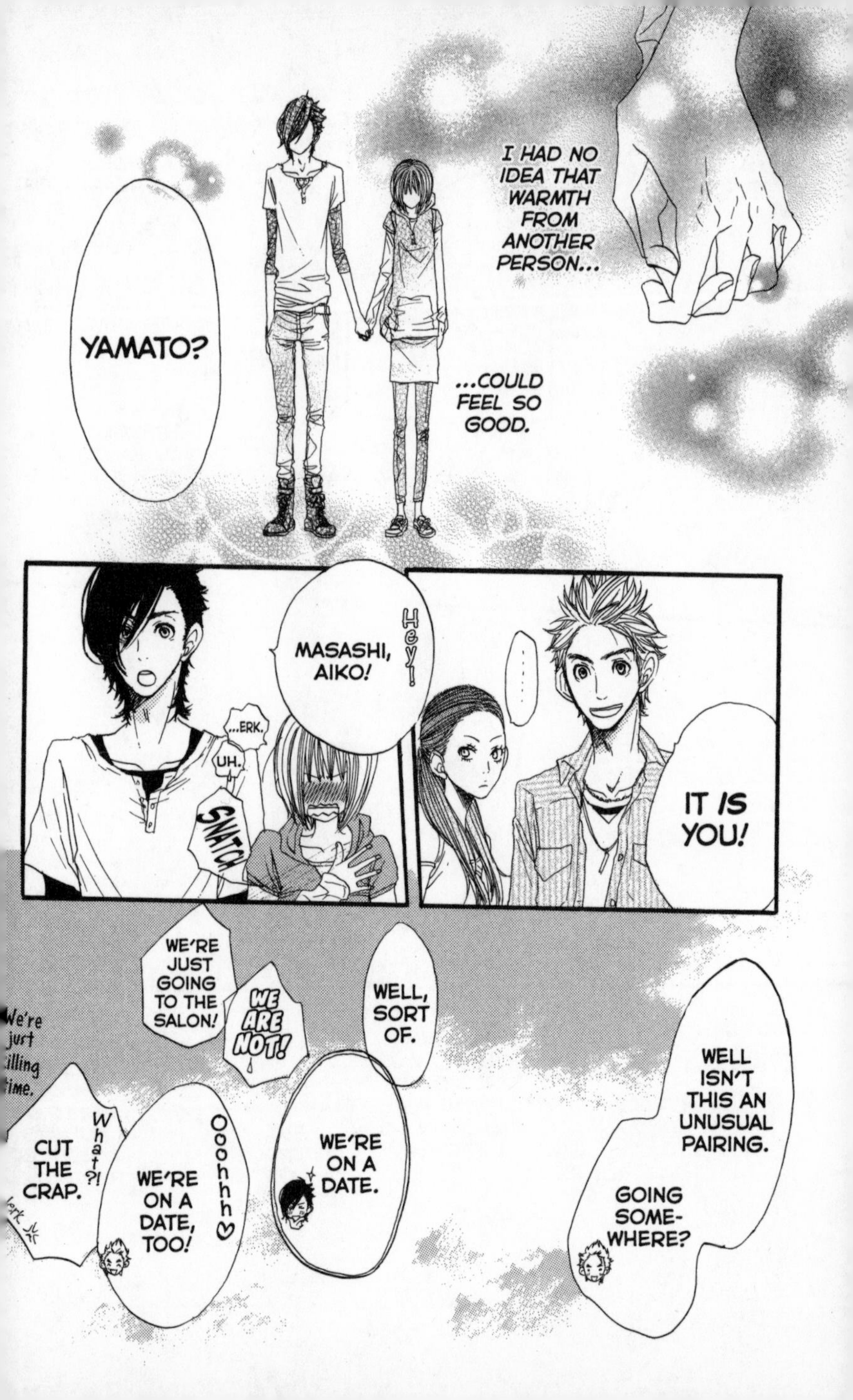
I HAD NO IDEA THAT WARMTH FROM ANOTHER PERSON...
...COULD FEEL SO GOOD.
YAMATO?
...
IT IS YOU!
MASASHI, AIKO!
Hey!
...ERK.
UH.
SNATCH
WELL ISN'T THIS AN UNUSUAL PAIRING.
GOING SOME-WHERE?
WE'RE ON A DATE.
WELL, SORT OF.
WE ARE NOT!
WE'RE JUST GOING TO THE SALON!
Ooohhh ♥
WE'RE ON A DATE, TOO!
What?!
CUT THE CRAP.

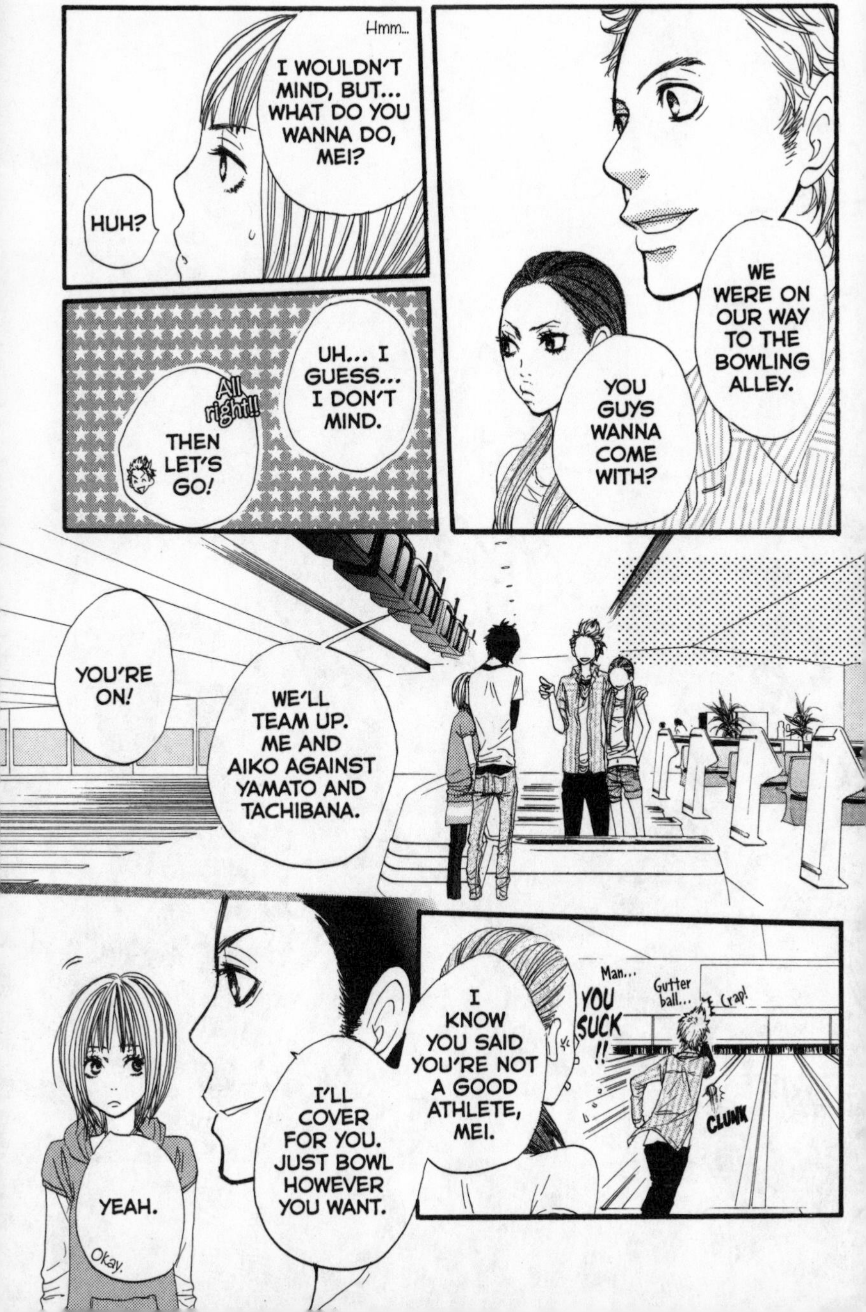
WE WERE ON OUR WAY TO THE BOWLING ALLEY.
YOU GUYS WANNA COME WITH?
Hmm...
I WOULDN'T MIND, BUT... WHAT DO YOU WANNA DO, MEI?
HUH?
UH... I GUESS... I DON'T MIND.
All right!!
THEN LET'S GO!
WE'LL TEAM UP. ME AND AIKO AGAINST YAMATO AND TACHIBANA.
YOU'RE ON!
Crap!
Gutter ball...
Man...
YOU SUCK!!
CLUNK
I KNOW YOU SAID YOU'RE NOT A GOOD ATHLETE, MEI.
I'LL COVER FOR YOU. JUST BOWL HOWEVER YOU WANT.
YEAH.
Okay.

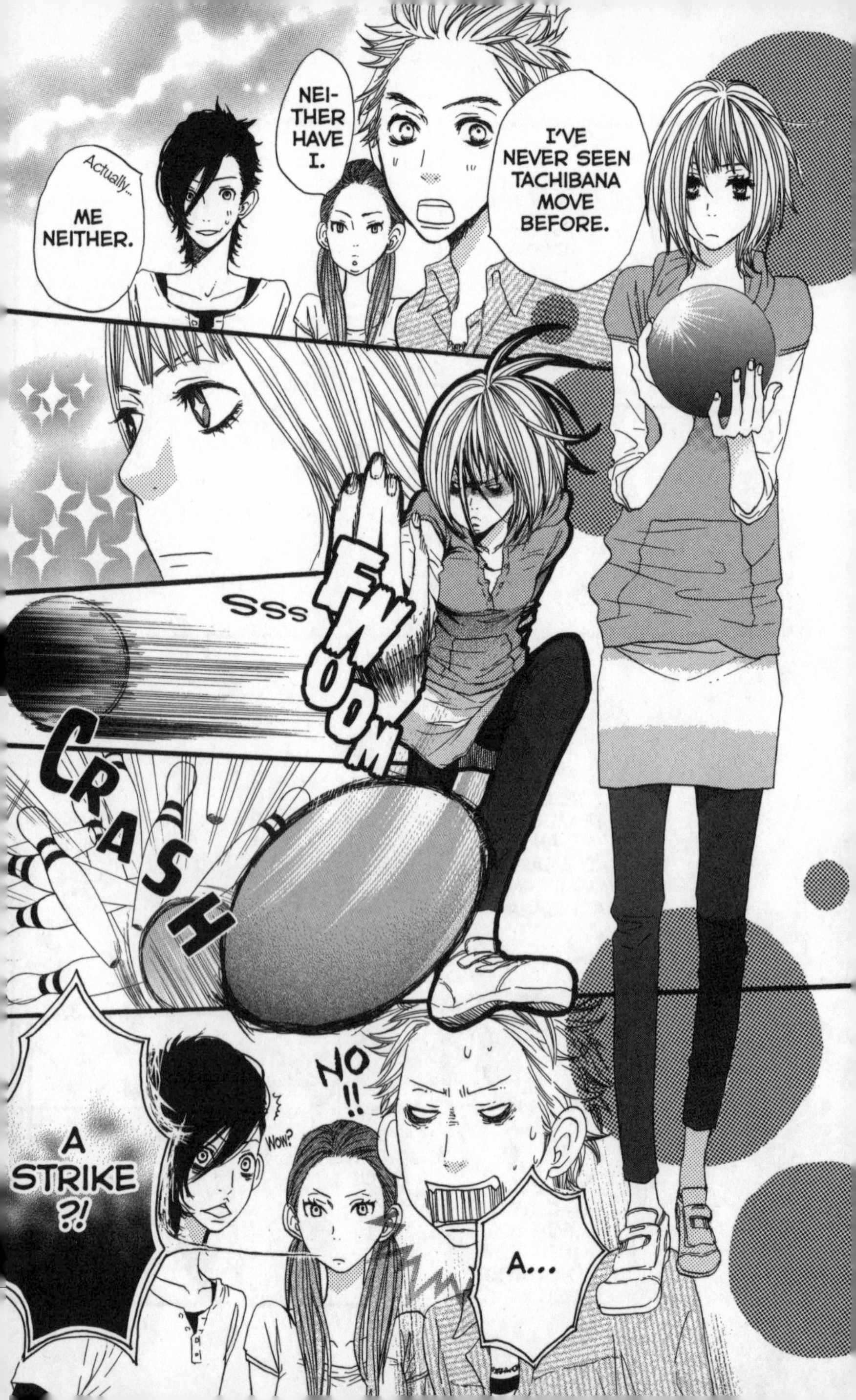
I'VE NEVER SEEN TACHIBANA MOVE BEFORE.
NEI-THER HAVE I.
Actually...
ME NEITHER.
FWOOM
SSS
CRASH
NO!!
A...
WOW?
A STRIKE?!

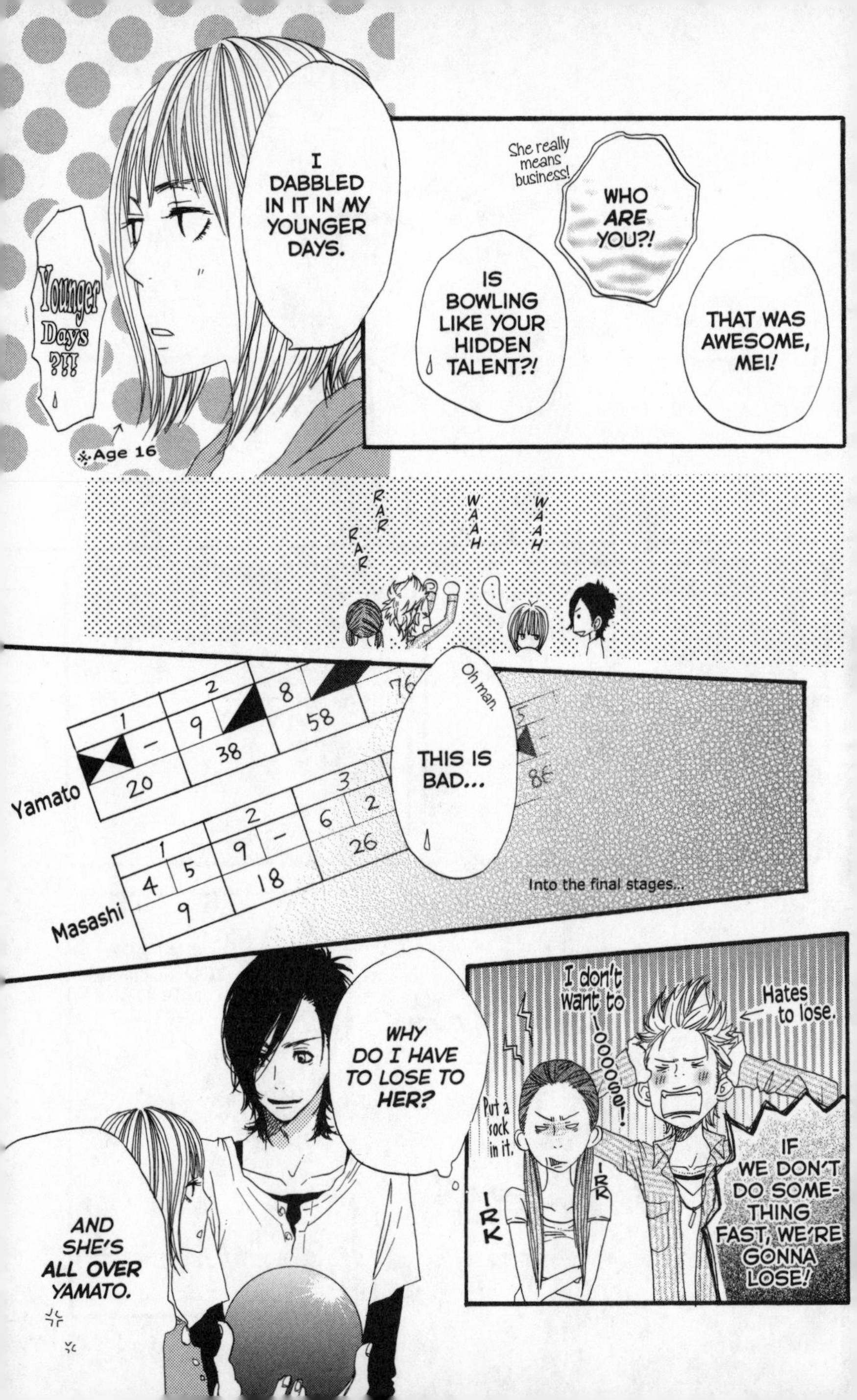
THAT WAS AWESOME, MEI!
WHO ARE YOU?!
She really means business!
IS BOWLING LIKE YOUR HIDDEN TALENT?!
I DABBLED IN IT IN MY YOUNGER DAYS.
Younger Days ?!!
※Age 16
RAR RAR
WAAH WAAH
Yamato
Masashi
Oh man.
THIS IS BAD...
Into the final stages...
IF WE DON'T DO SOME-THING FAST, WE'RE GONNA LOSE!
Hates to lose.
I don't want to looooose!
Put a sock in it.
IRK
IRK
WHY DO I HAVE TO LOSE TO HER?
AND SHE'S ALL OVER YAMATO.

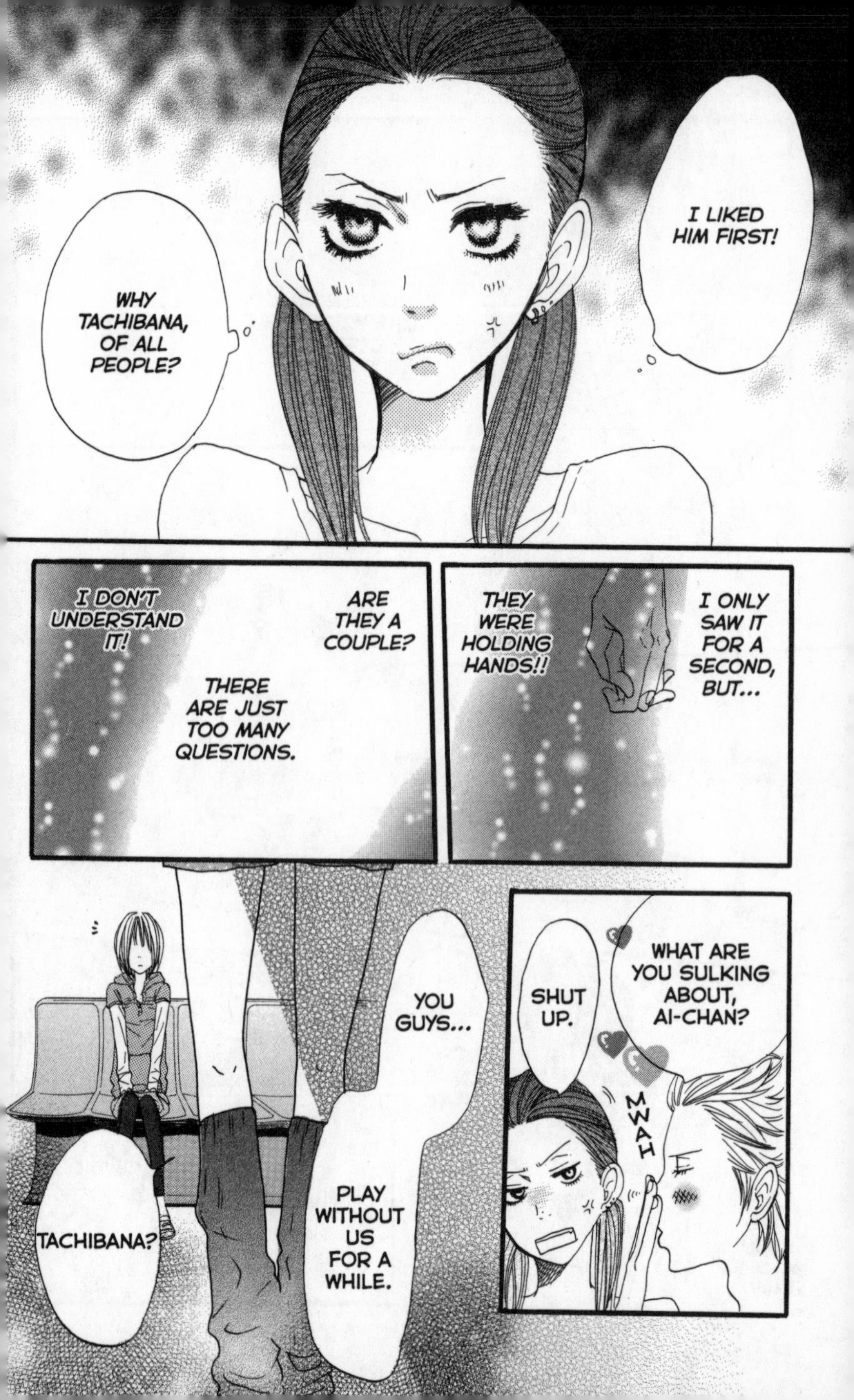
I LIKED HIM FIRST!
WHY TACHIBANA, OF ALL PEOPLE?
I ONLY SAW IT FOR A SECOND, BUT...
THEY WERE HOLDING HANDS!!
ARE THEY A COUPLE?
I DON'T UNDERSTAND IT!
THERE ARE JUST TOO MANY QUESTIONS.
WHAT ARE YOU SULKING ABOUT, AI-CHAN?
SHUT UP.
MWAH
YOU GUYS...
PLAY WITHOUT US FOR A WHILE.
TACHIBANA?

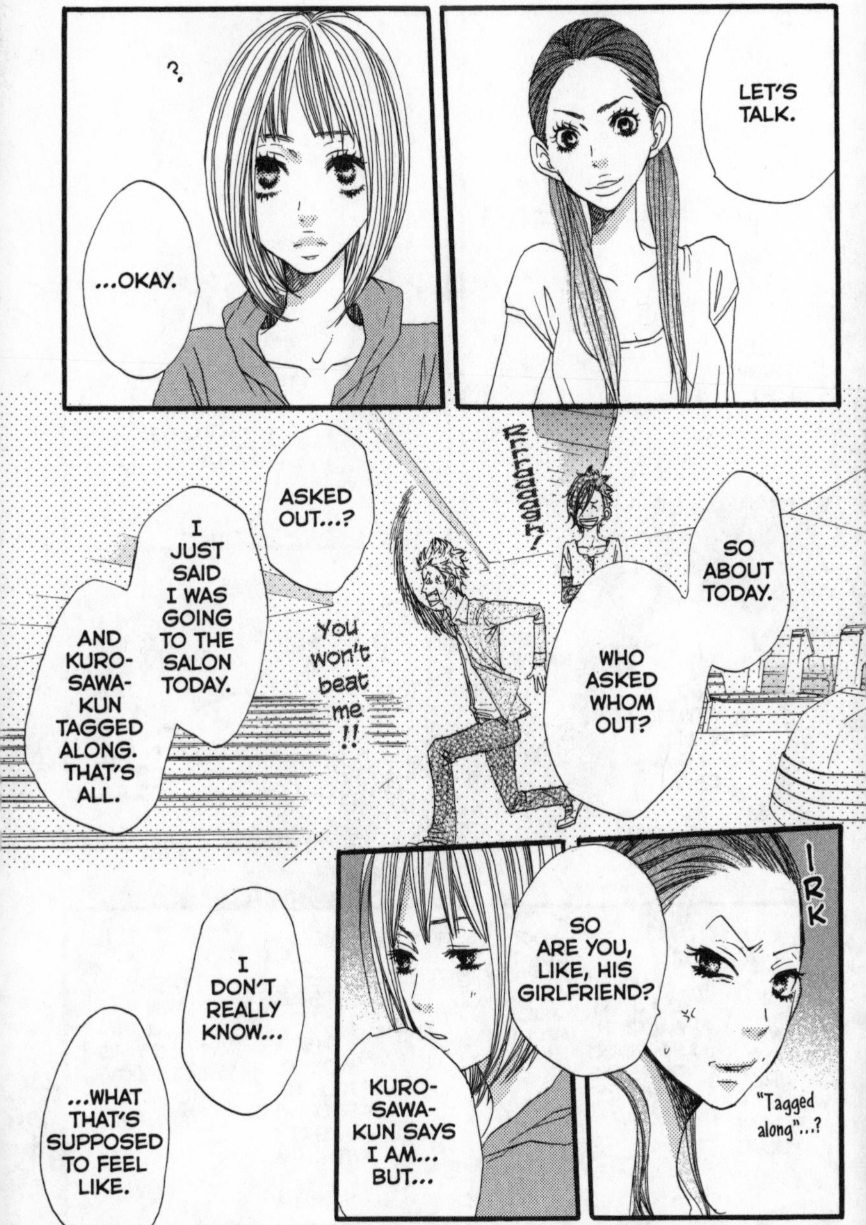
LET'S TALK.
?
...OKAY.
SO ABOUT TODAY.
WHO ASKED WHOM OUT?
You won't beat me !!
ASKED OUT...?
I JUST SAID I WAS GOING TO THE SALON TODAY.
AND KURO-SAWA-KUN TAGGED ALONG. THAT'S ALL.
IRK
SO ARE YOU, LIKE, HIS GIRLFRIEND?
"Tagged along"...?
KURO-SAWA-KUN SAYS I AM... BUT...
I DON'T REALLY KNOW...
...WHAT THAT'S SUPPOSED TO FEEL LIKE.

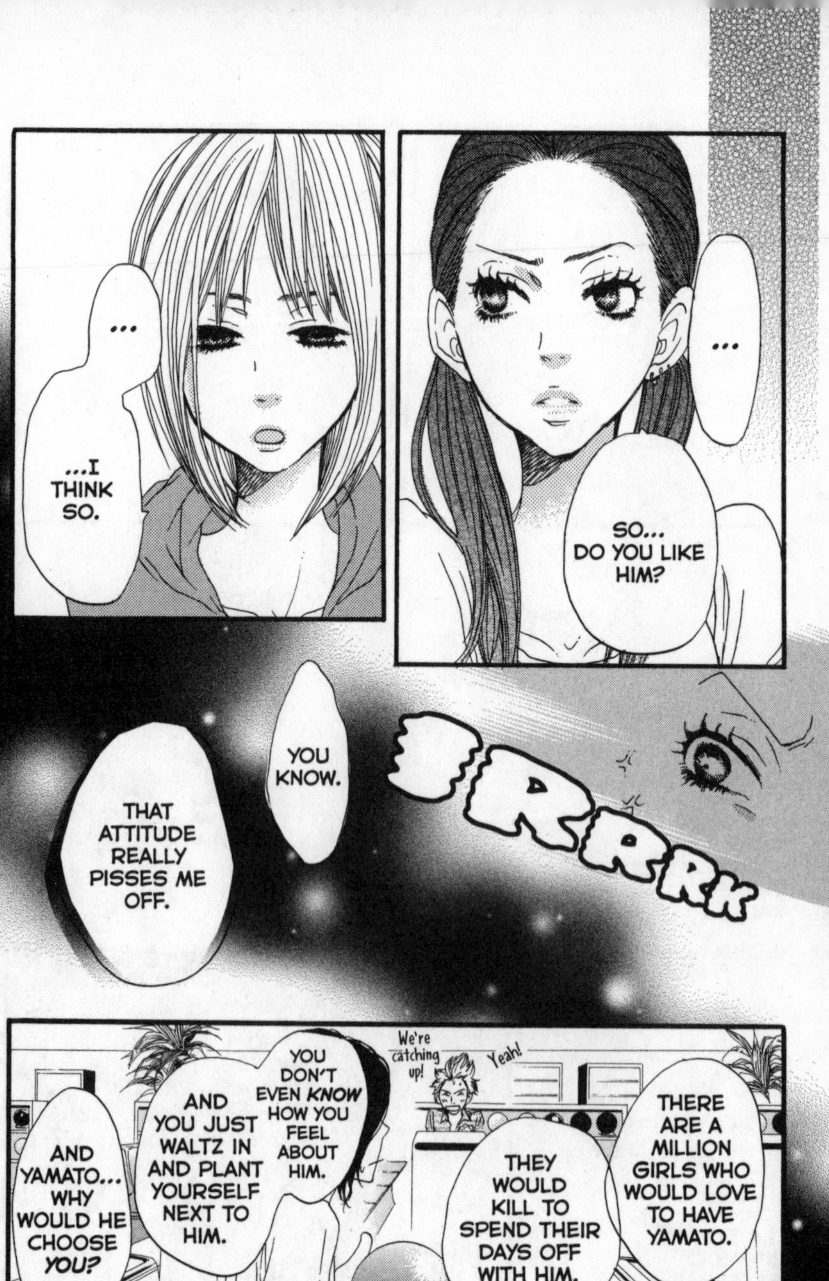
...
SO... DO YOU LIKE HIM?
...
...I THINK SO.
RRRK
YOU KNOW.
THAT ATTITUDE REALLY PISSES ME OFF.
THERE ARE A MILLION GIRLS WHO WOULD LOVE TO HAVE YAMATO.
THEY WOULD KILL TO SPEND THEIR DAYS OFF WITH HIM.
Yeah!
We're catching up!
YOU DON'T EVEN KNOW HOW YOU FEEL ABOUT HIM.
AND YOU JUST WALTZ IN AND PLANT YOURSELF NEXT TO HIM.
AND YAMATO... WHY WOULD HE CHOOSE YOU?

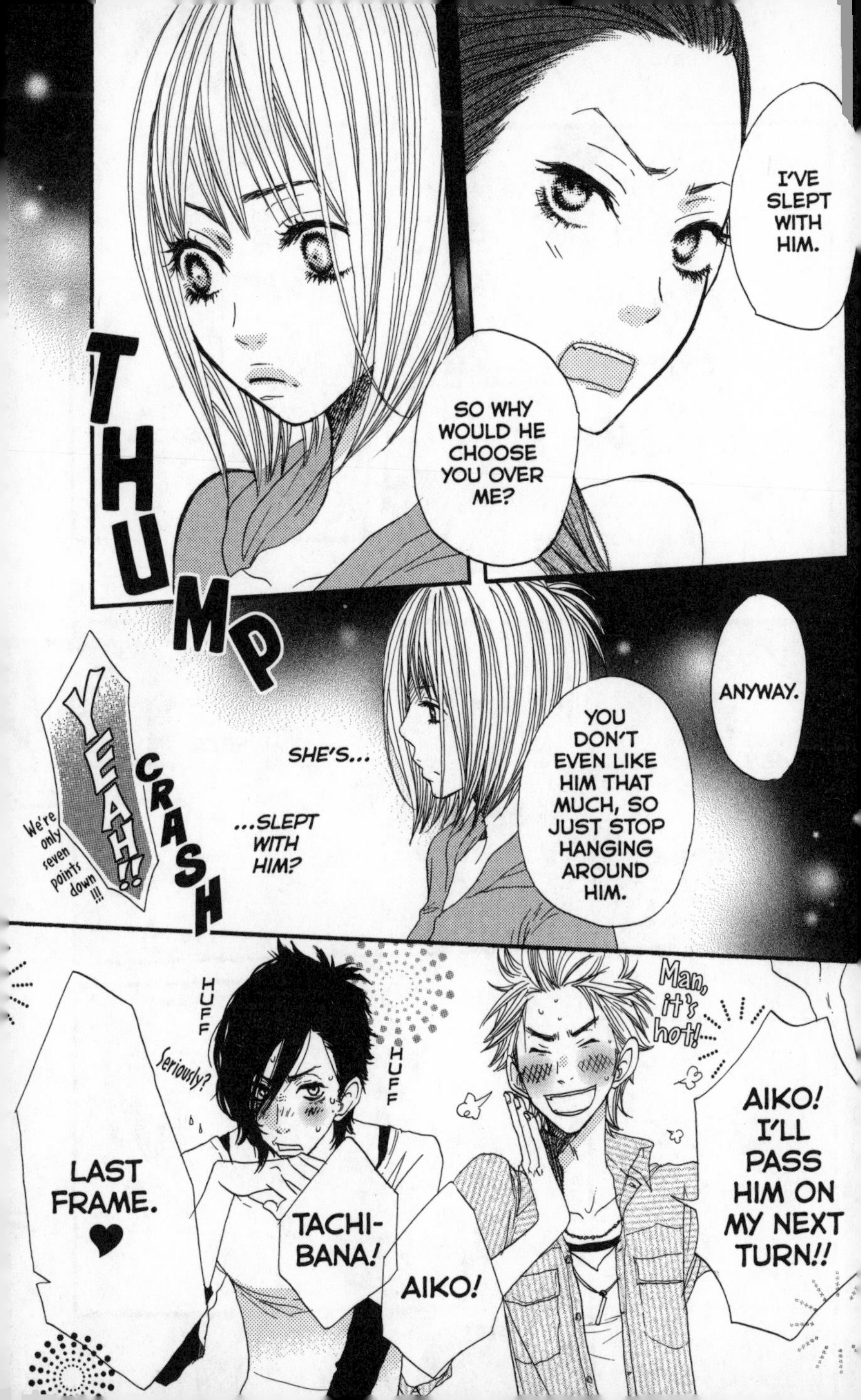
I'VE SLEPT WITH HIM.
SO WHY WOULD HE CHOOSE YOU OVER ME?
THUMP
ANYWAY.
YOU DON'T EVEN LIKE HIM THAT MUCH, SO JUST STOP HANGING AROUND HIM.
SHE'S...
...SLEPT WITH HIM?
CRASH
YEAH!!
We're only seven points down!!!
Man, it's hot!
AIKO! I'LL PASS HIM ON MY NEXT TURN!!
HUFF
HUFF
AIKO!
TACHIBANA!
Seriously?
LAST FRAME. ♥

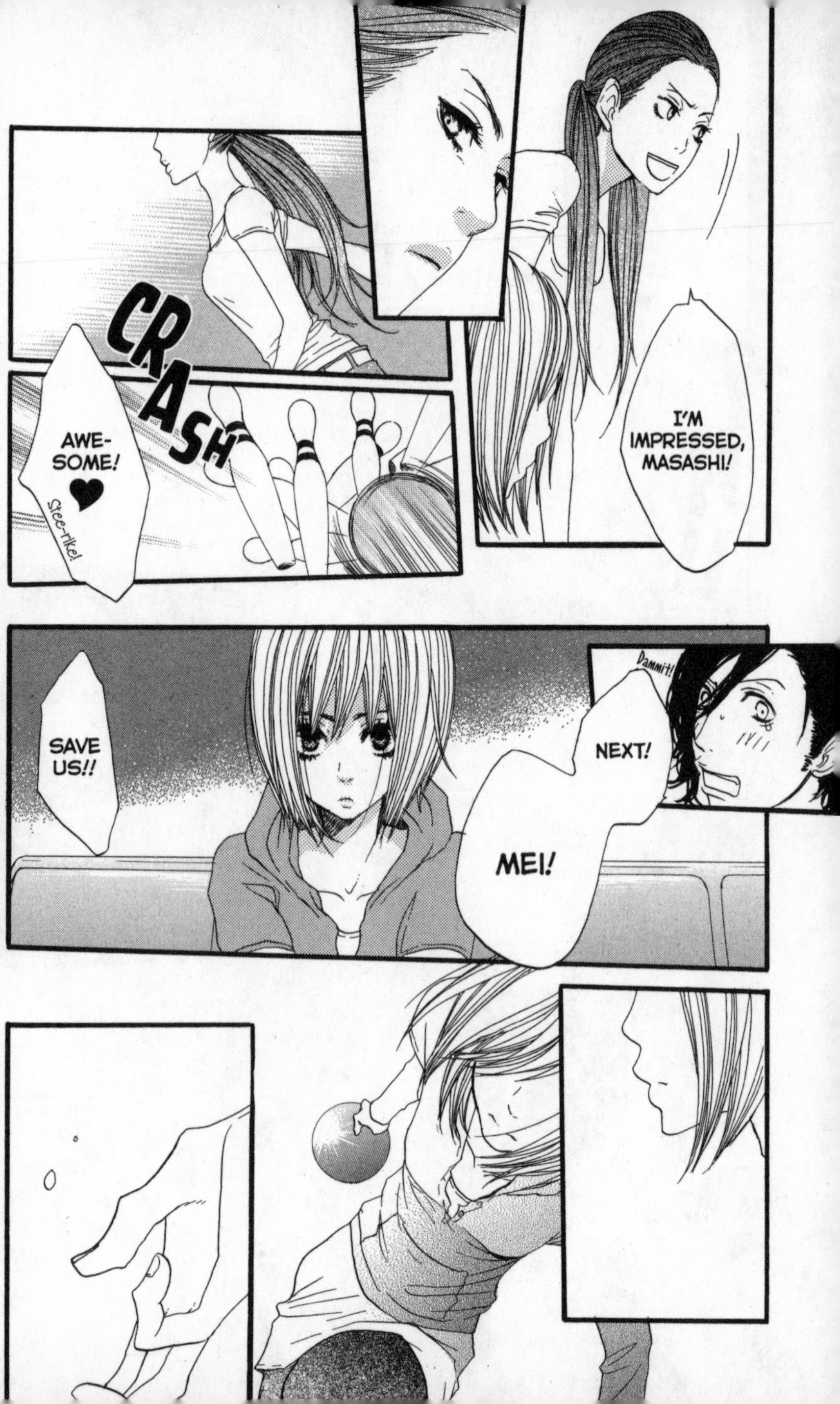

I'M IMPRESSED, MASASHI!
CRASH
AWE-SOME! ♥
Stee-rike!
Dammit!
NEXT!
MEI!
SAVE US!!

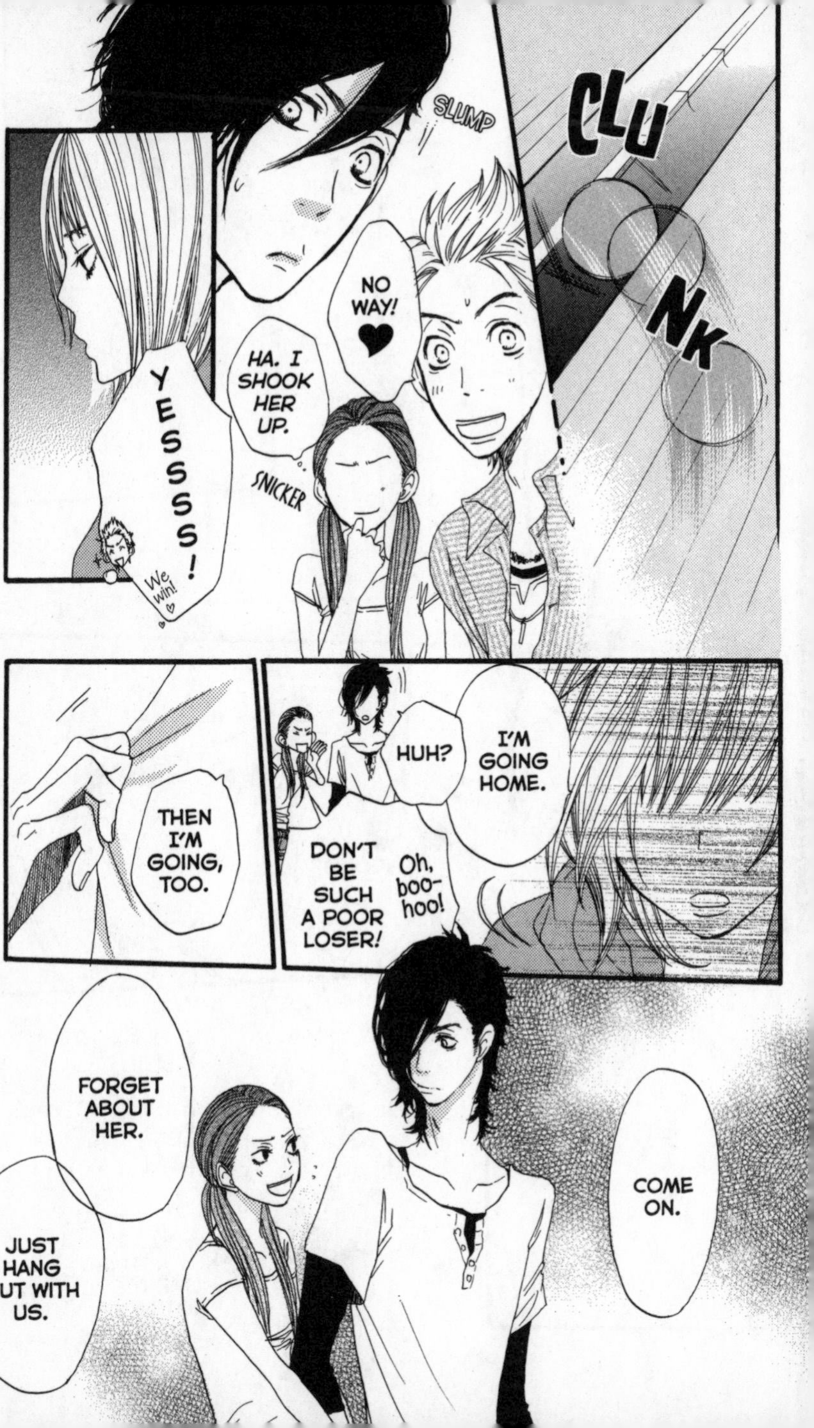
CLUNK
SLUMP
NO WAY! ♥
HA. I SHOOK HER UP.
SNICKER
YESSSS!
We win! ♡
I'M GOING HOME.
HUH?
Oh, boo-hoo!
DON'T BE SUCH A POOR LOSER!
THEN I'M GOING, TOO.
COME ON.
FORGET ABOUT HER.
JUST HANG OUT WITH US.

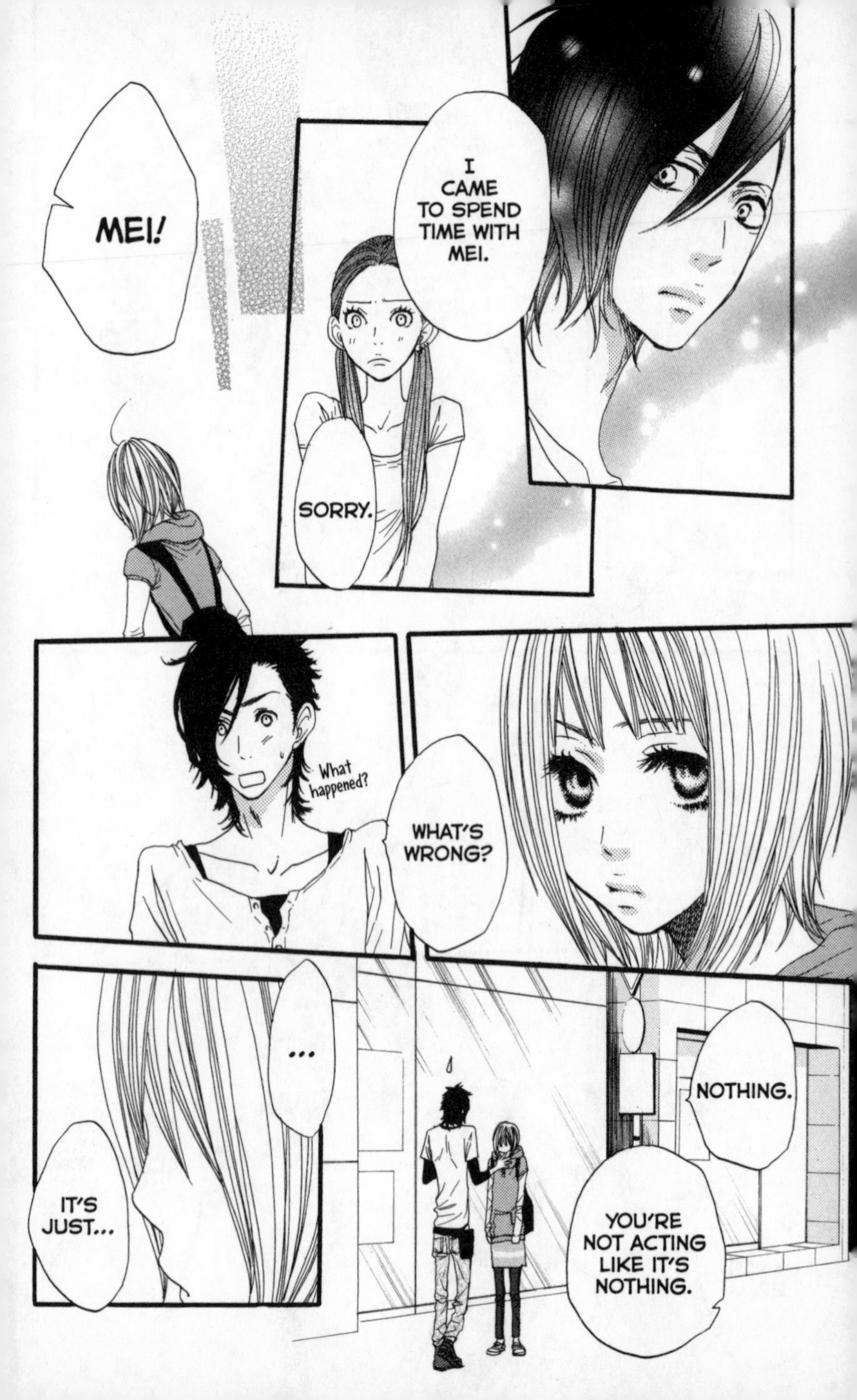

I CAME TO SPEND TIME WITH MEI.
SORRY.
MEI!
What happened?
WHAT'S WRONG?
NOTHING.
YOU'RE NOT ACTING LIKE IT'S NOTHING.
...
IT'S JUST...

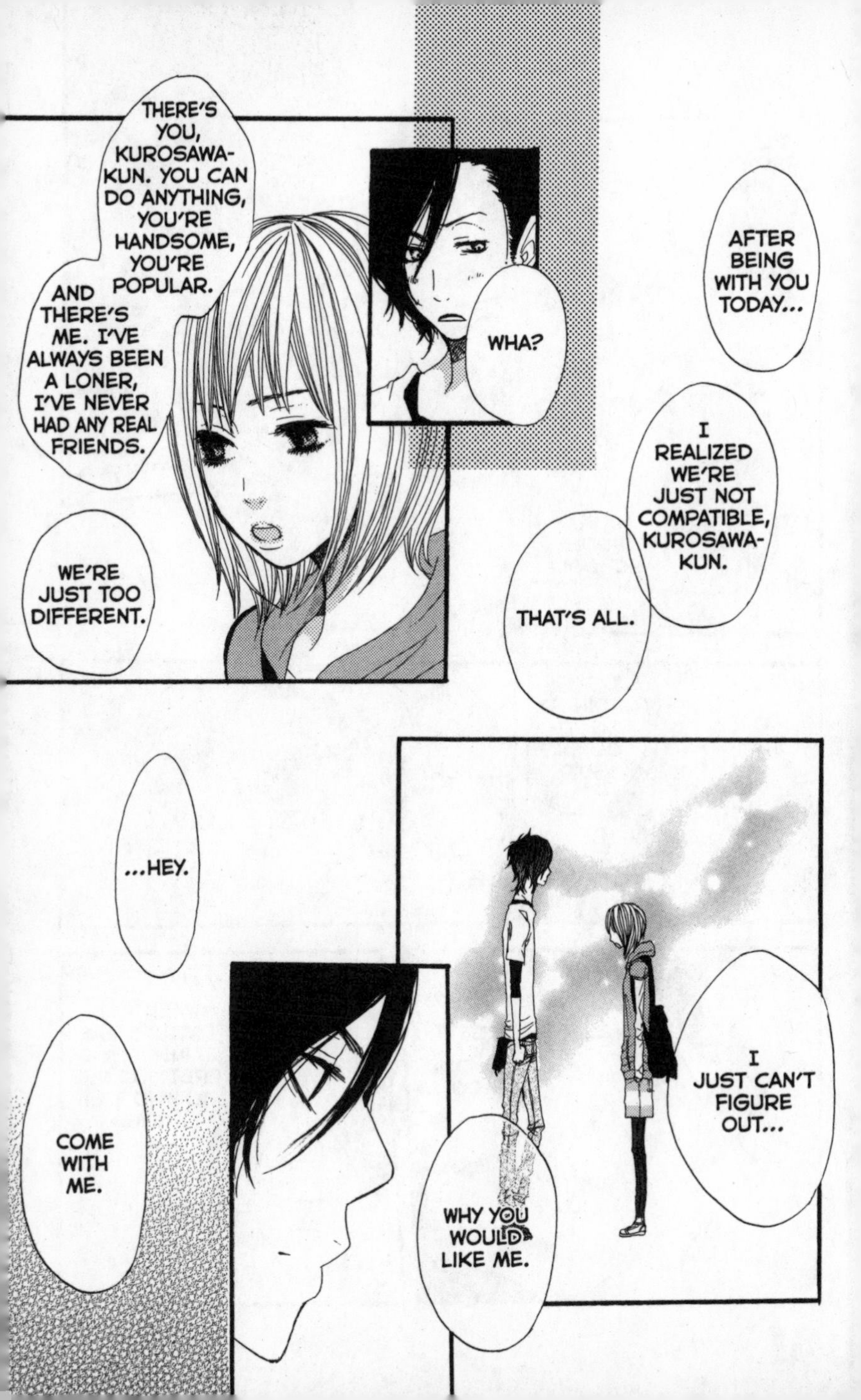
AFTER BEING WITH YOU TODAY...
I REALIZED WE'RE JUST NOT COMPATIBLE, KUROSAWA-KUN.
THAT'S ALL.
WHA?
THERE'S YOU, KUROSAWA-KUN. YOU CAN DO ANYTHING, YOU'RE HANDSOME, YOU'RE POPULAR.
AND THERE'S ME. I'VE ALWAYS BEEN A LONER, I'VE NEVER HAD ANY REAL FRIENDS.
WE'RE JUST TOO DIFFERENT.
I JUST CAN'T FIGURE OUT...
WHY YOU WOULD LIKE ME.
...HEY.
COME WITH ME.

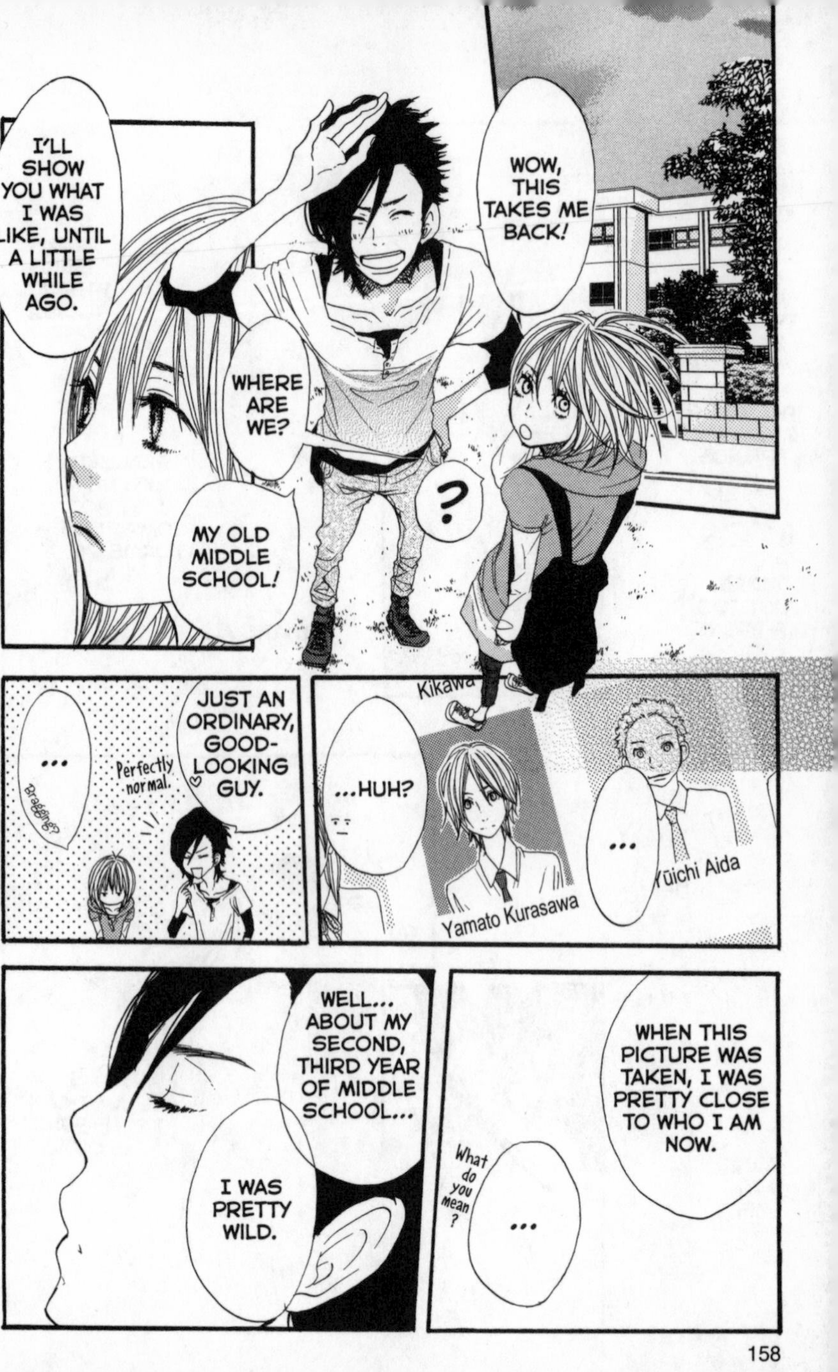
WOW, THIS TAKES ME BACK!
?
WHERE ARE WE?
MY OLD MIDDLE SCHOOL!
I'LL SHOW YOU WHAT I WAS LIKE, UNTIL A LITTLE WHILE AGO.
Kikawa
Yūichi Aida
Yamato Kurasawa
...
...HUH?
JUST AN ORDINARY, GOOD-LOOKING GUY.
Perfectly normal.
...
Bragging?
WHEN THIS PICTURE WAS TAKEN, I WAS PRETTY CLOSE TO WHO I AM NOW.
What do you mean?
...
WELL... ABOUT MY SECOND, THIRD YEAR OF MIDDLE SCHOOL...
I WAS PRETTY WILD.

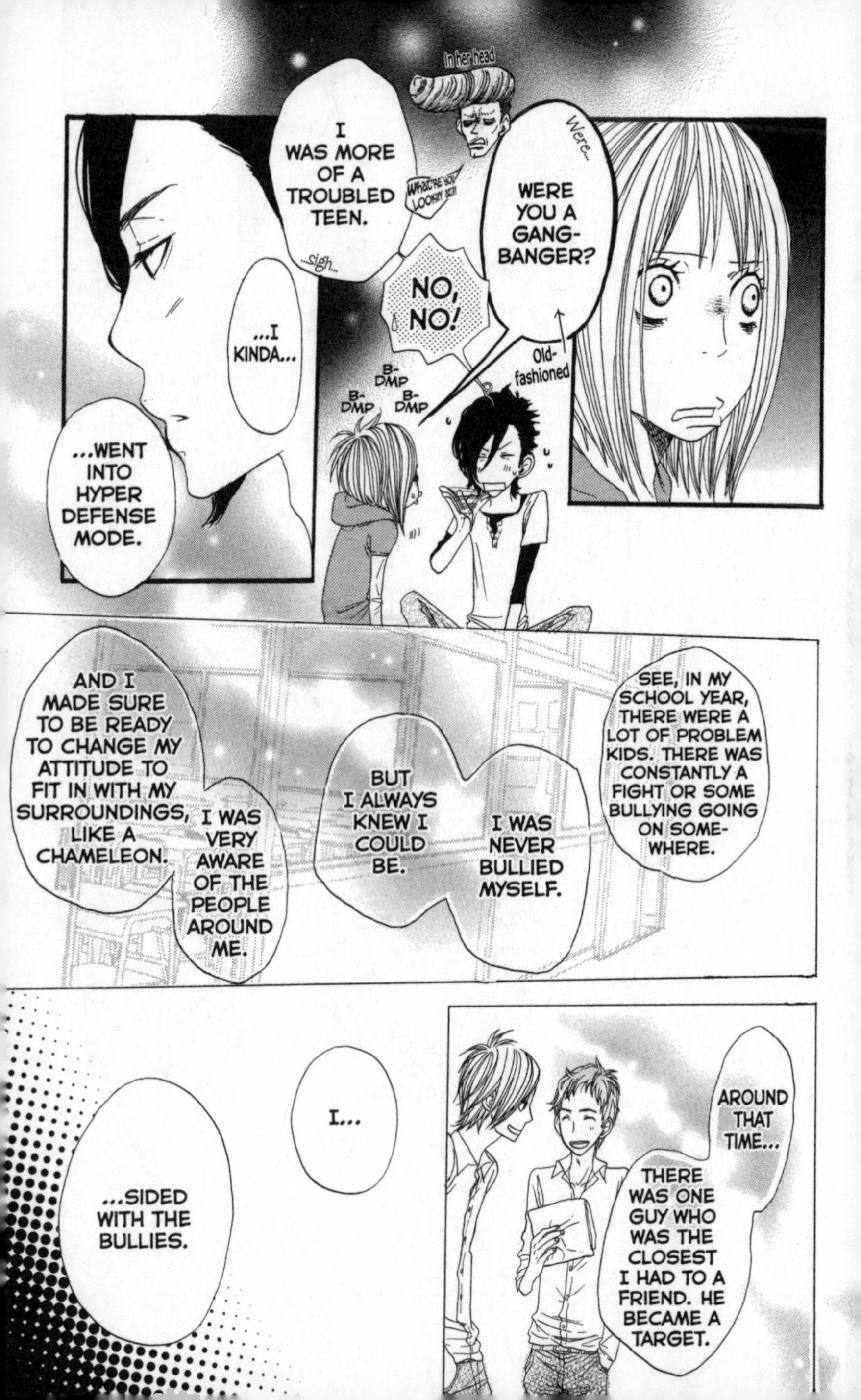
Were...
WERE YOU A GANG-BANGER?
Old-fashioned
NO, NO!
I WAS MORE OF A TROUBLED TEEN.
In her head
WHAT'RE YOU LOOKIN' AT?!
...sigh...
B-DMP B-DMP B-DMP
...I KINDA...
...WENT INTO HYPER DEFENSE MODE.
SEE, IN MY SCHOOL YEAR, THERE WERE A LOT OF PROBLEM KIDS. THERE WAS CONSTANTLY A FIGHT OR SOME BULLYING GOING ON SOMEWHERE.
I WAS NEVER BULLIED MYSELF.
BUT I ALWAYS KNEW I COULD BE.
I WAS VERY AWARE OF THE PEOPLE AROUND ME.
AND I MADE SURE TO BE READY TO CHANGE MY ATTITUDE TO FIT IN WITH MY SURROUNDINGS, LIKE A CHAMELEON.
AROUND THAT TIME...
THERE WAS ONE GUY WHO WAS THE CLOSEST I HAD TO A FRIEND. HE BECAME A TARGET.
I...
...SIDED WITH THE BULLIES.

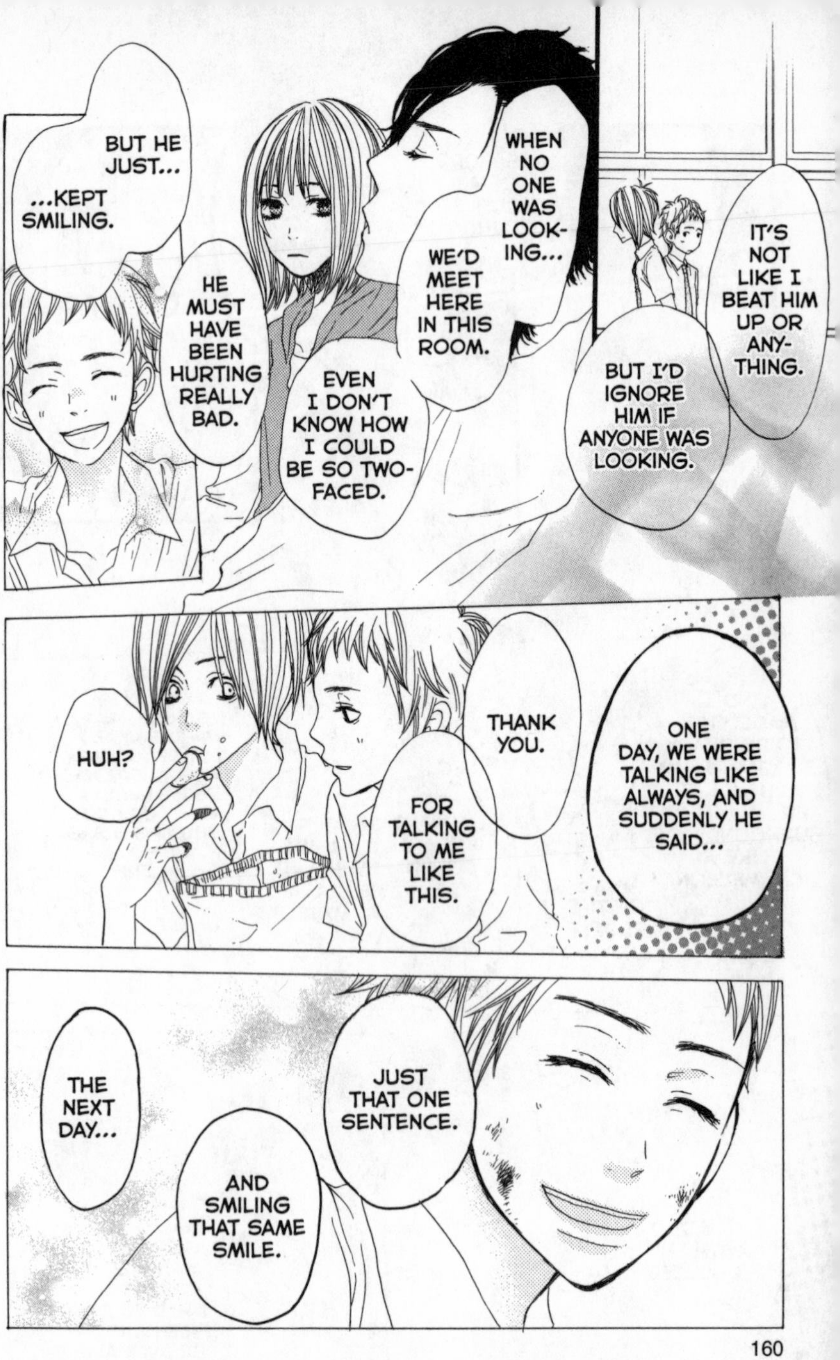
IT'S NOT LIKE I BEAT HIM UP OR ANYTHING.
BUT I'D IGNORE HIM IF ANYONE WAS LOOKING.
WHEN NO ONE WAS LOOK-ING...
WE'D MEET HERE IN THIS ROOM.
EVEN I DON'T KNOW HOW I COULD BE SO TWO-FACED.
HE MUST HAVE BEEN HURTING REALLY BAD.
BUT HE JUST...
...KEPT SMILING.
ONE DAY, WE WERE TALKING LIKE ALWAYS, AND SUDDENLY HE SAID...
THANK YOU.
FOR TALKING TO ME LIKE THIS.
HUH?
JUST THAT ONE SENTENCE.
AND SMILING THAT SAME SMILE.
THE NEXT DAY...

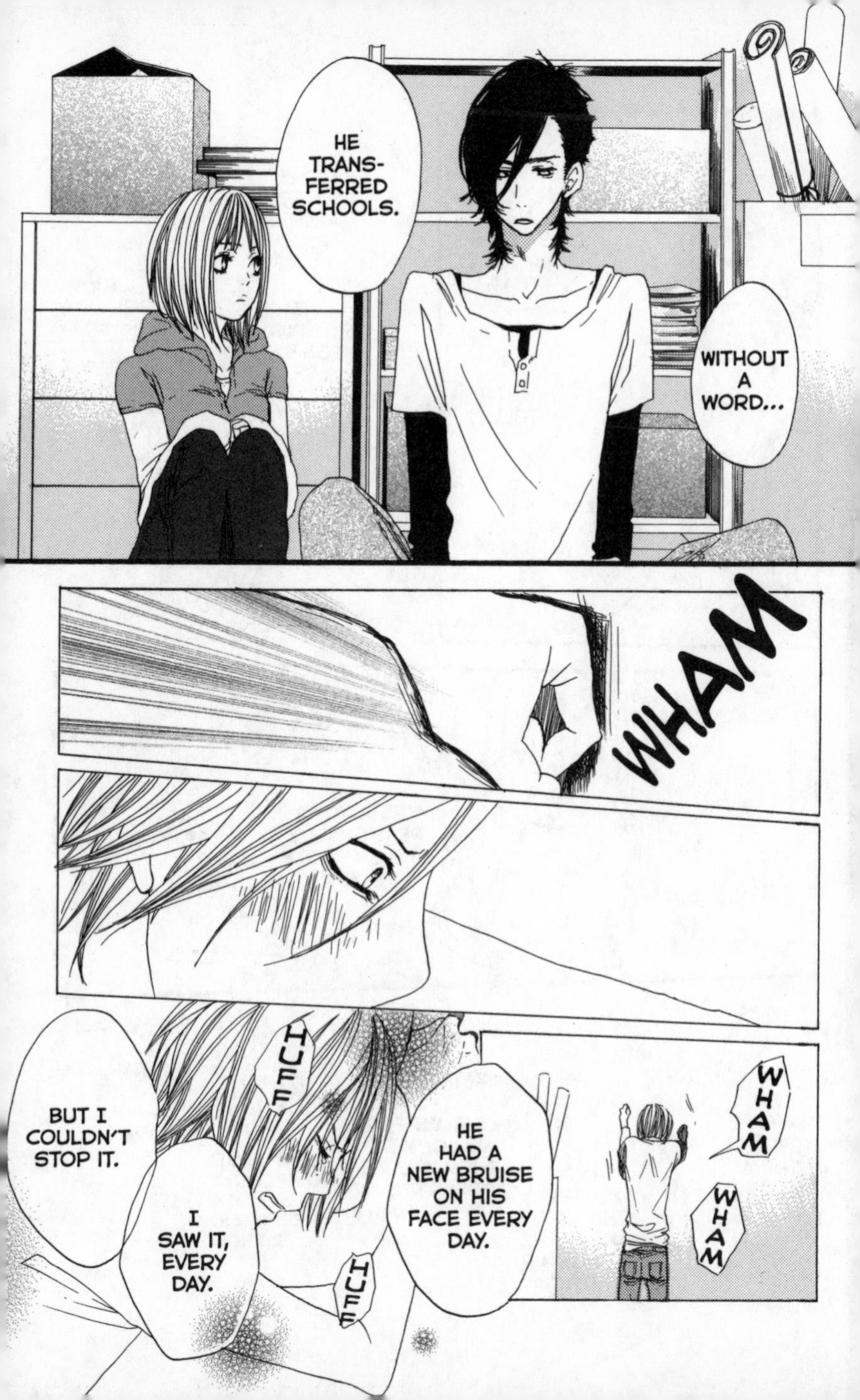
HE TRANSFERRED SCHOOLS.
WITHOUT A WORD...
WHAM
WHAM
WHAM
HE HAD A NEW BRUISE ON HIS FACE EVERY DAY.
HUFF
I SAW IT, EVERY DAY.
HUFF
BUT I COULDN'T STOP IT.

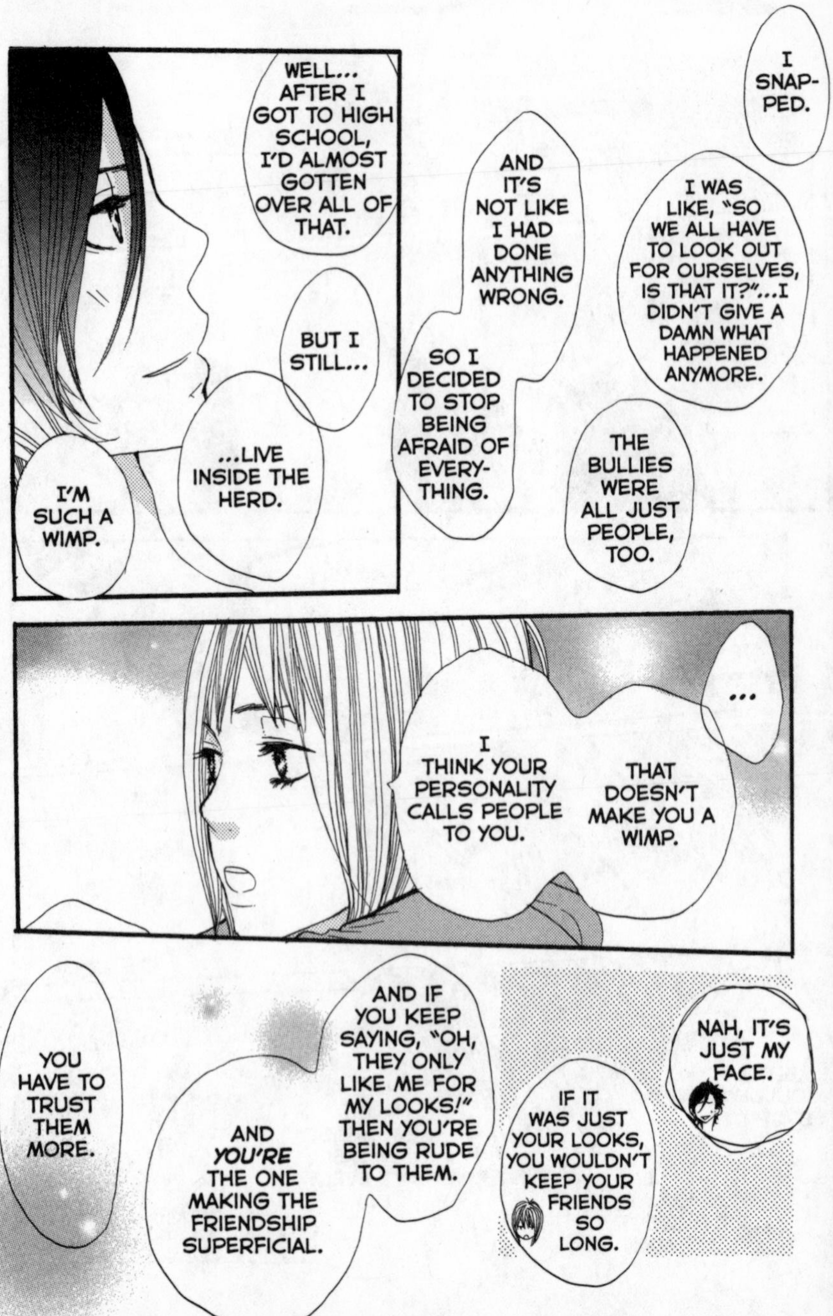
I SNAPPED.
I WAS LIKE, "SO WE ALL HAVE TO LOOK OUT FOR OURSELVES, IS THAT IT?"...I DIDN'T GIVE A DAMN WHAT HAPPENED ANYMORE.
AND IT'S NOT LIKE I HAD DONE ANYTHING WRONG.
THE BULLIES WERE ALL JUST PEOPLE, TOO.
SO I DECIDED TO STOP BEING AFRAID OF EVERY-THING.
WELL... AFTER I GOT TO HIGH SCHOOL, I'D ALMOST GOTTEN OVER ALL OF THAT.
BUT I STILL...
...LIVE INSIDE THE HERD.
I'M SUCH A WIMP.
...
THAT DOESN'T MAKE YOU A WIMP.
I THINK YOUR PERSONALITY CALLS PEOPLE TO YOU.
NAH, IT'S JUST MY FACE.
IF IT WAS JUST YOUR LOOKS, YOU WOULDN'T KEEP YOUR FRIENDS SO LONG.
AND IF YOU KEEP SAYING, "OH, THEY ONLY LIKE ME FOR *MY LOOKS!*" THEN YOU'RE BEING RUDE TO THEM.
AND ***YOU'RE*** THE ONE MAKING THE FRIENDSHIP SUPERFICIAL.
YOU HAVE TO TRUST THEM MORE.

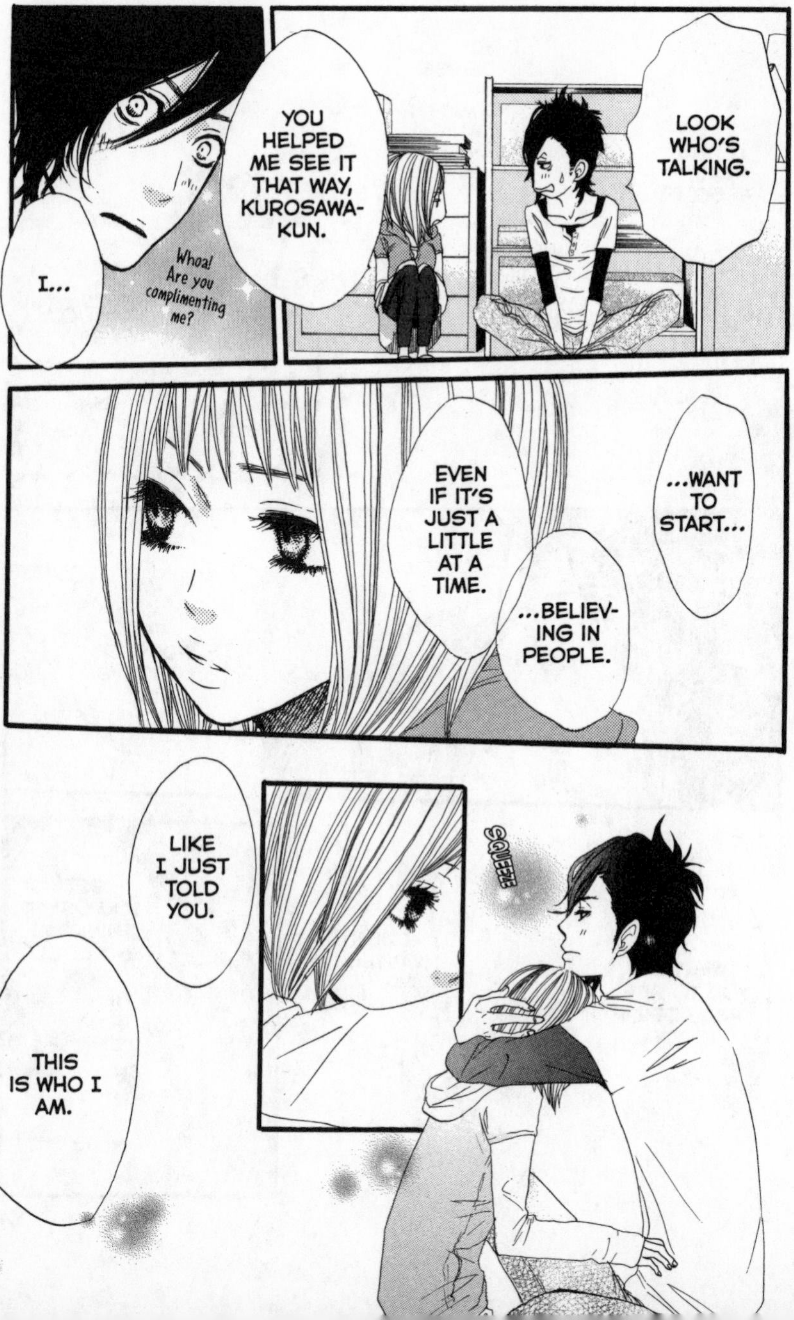
LOOK WHO'S TALKING.
YOU HELPED ME SEE IT THAT WAY, KUROSAWA-KUN.
Whoa! Are you complimenting me?
I...
...WANT TO START...
EVEN IF IT'S JUST A LITTLE AT A TIME.
...BELIEVING IN PEOPLE.
SQUEEZE
LIKE I JUST TOLD YOU.
THIS IS WHO I AM.

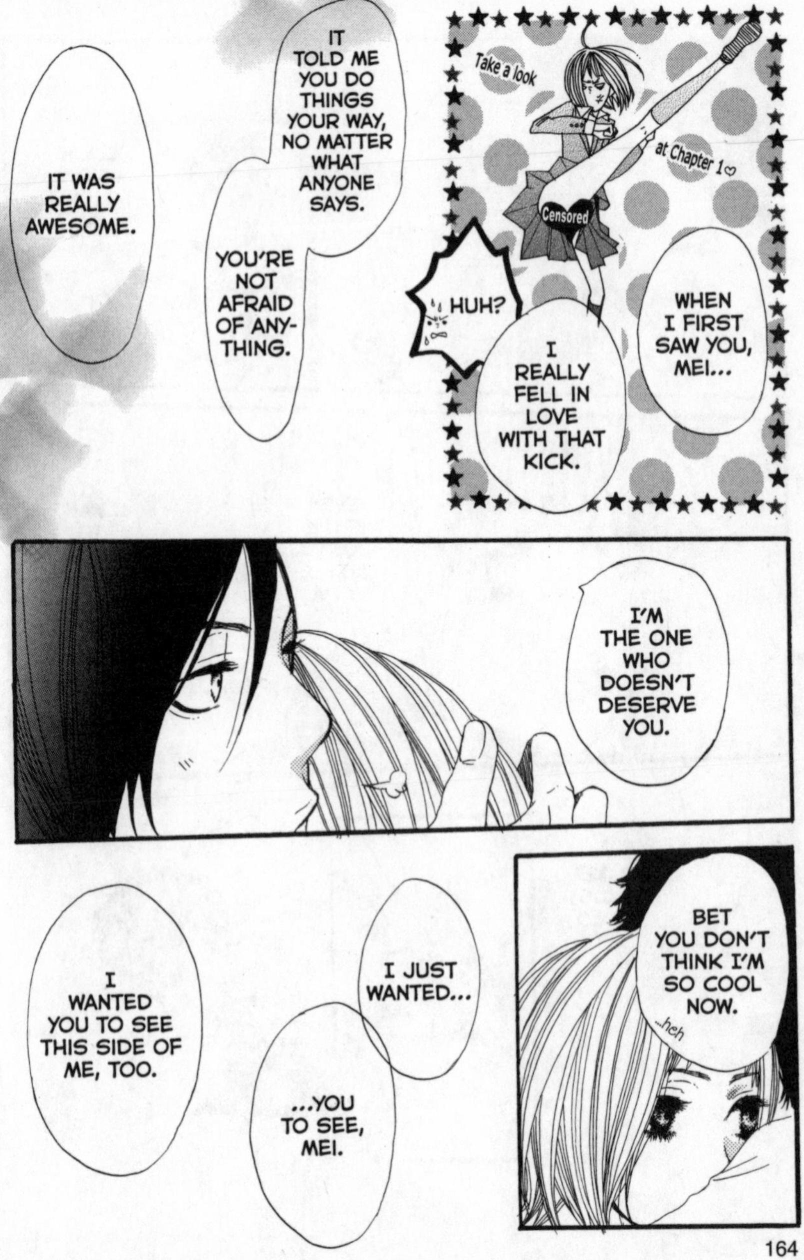
Take a look at Chapter 1♡
Censored
WHEN I FIRST SAW YOU, MEI...
I REALLY FELL IN LOVE WITH THAT KICK.
HUH?
IT TOLD ME YOU DO THINGS YOUR WAY, NO MATTER WHAT ANYONE SAYS.
YOU'RE NOT AFRAID OF ANY-THING.
IT WAS REALLY AWESOME.
I'M THE ONE WHO DOESN'T DESERVE YOU.
BET YOU DON'T THINK I'M SO COOL NOW.
...heh
I JUST WANTED...
...YOU TO SEE, MEI.
I WANTED YOU TO SEE THIS SIDE OF ME, TOO.

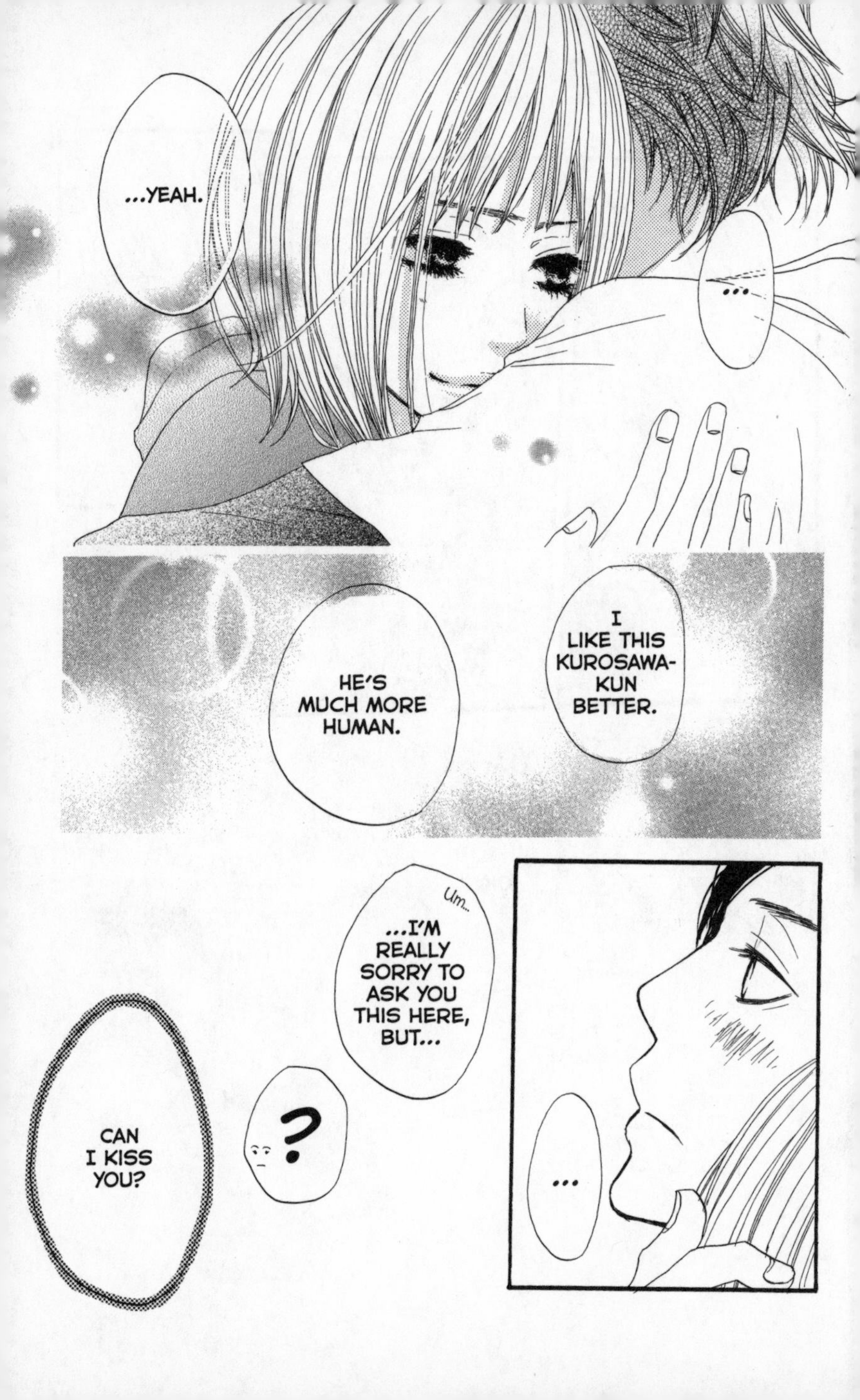
...
...YEAH.
I LIKE THIS KUROSAWA-KUN BETTER.
HE'S MUCH MORE HUMAN.
...
Um..
...I'M REALLY SORRY TO ASK YOU THIS HERE, BUT...
?
CAN I KISS YOU?

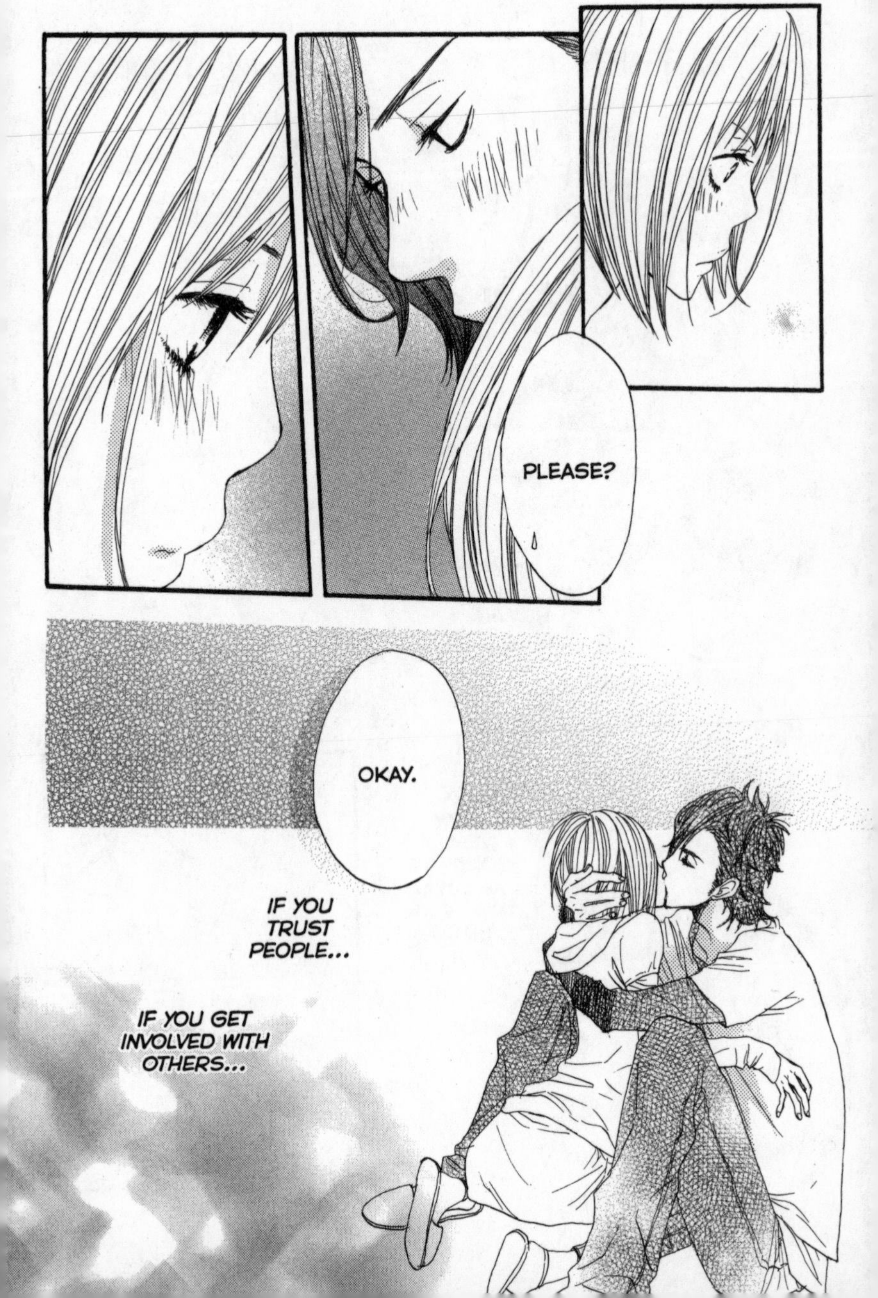
PLEASE?
OKAY.
IF YOU TRUST PEOPLE...
IF YOU GET INVOLVED WITH OTHERS...

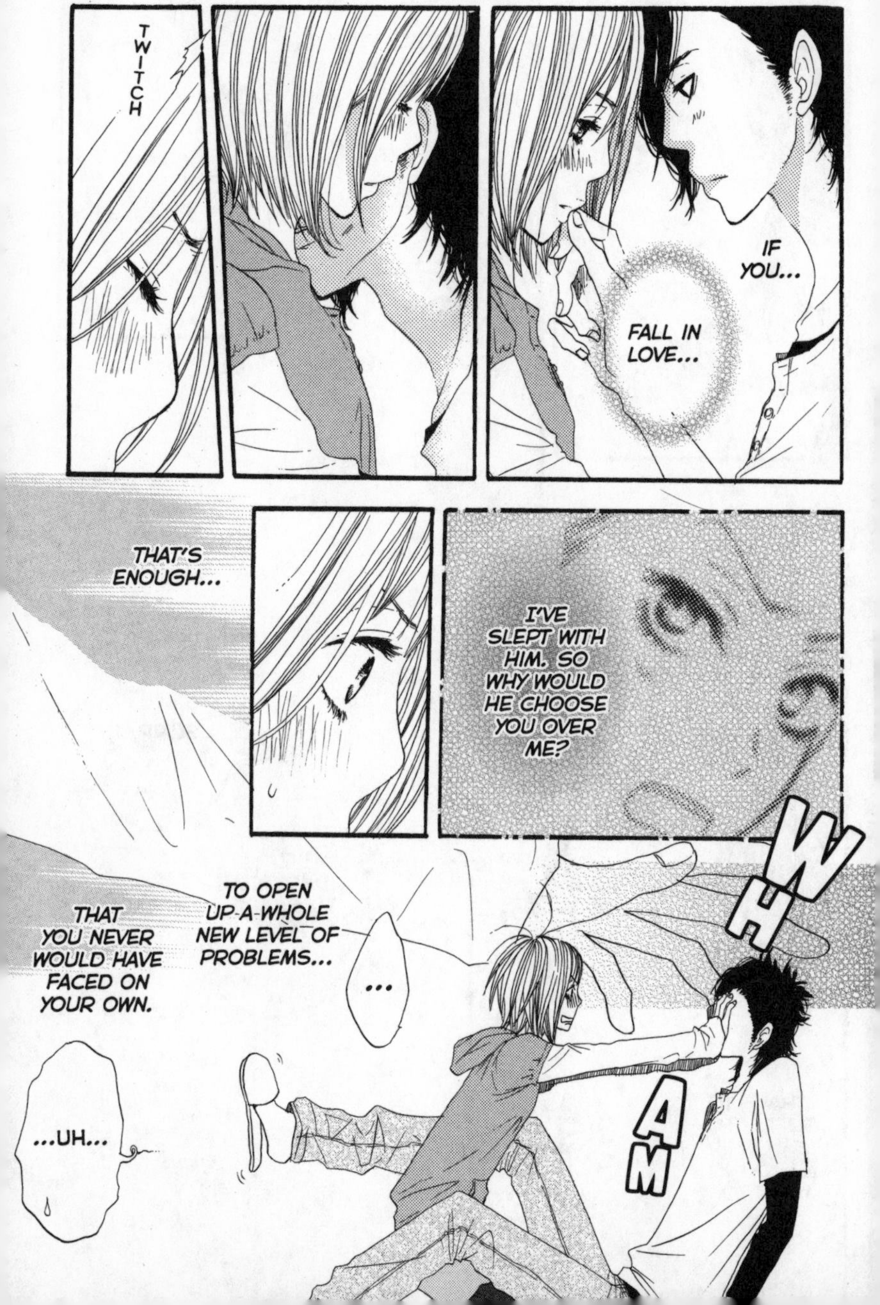
IF YOU...
FALL IN LOVE...
TWITCH
I'VE SLEPT WITH HIM. SO WHY WOULD HE CHOOSE YOU OVER ME?
THAT'S ENOUGH...
WHAM
...
TO OPEN UP A WHOLE NEW LEVEL OF PROBLEMS...
THAT YOU NEVER WOULD HAVE FACED ON YOUR OWN.
...UH...

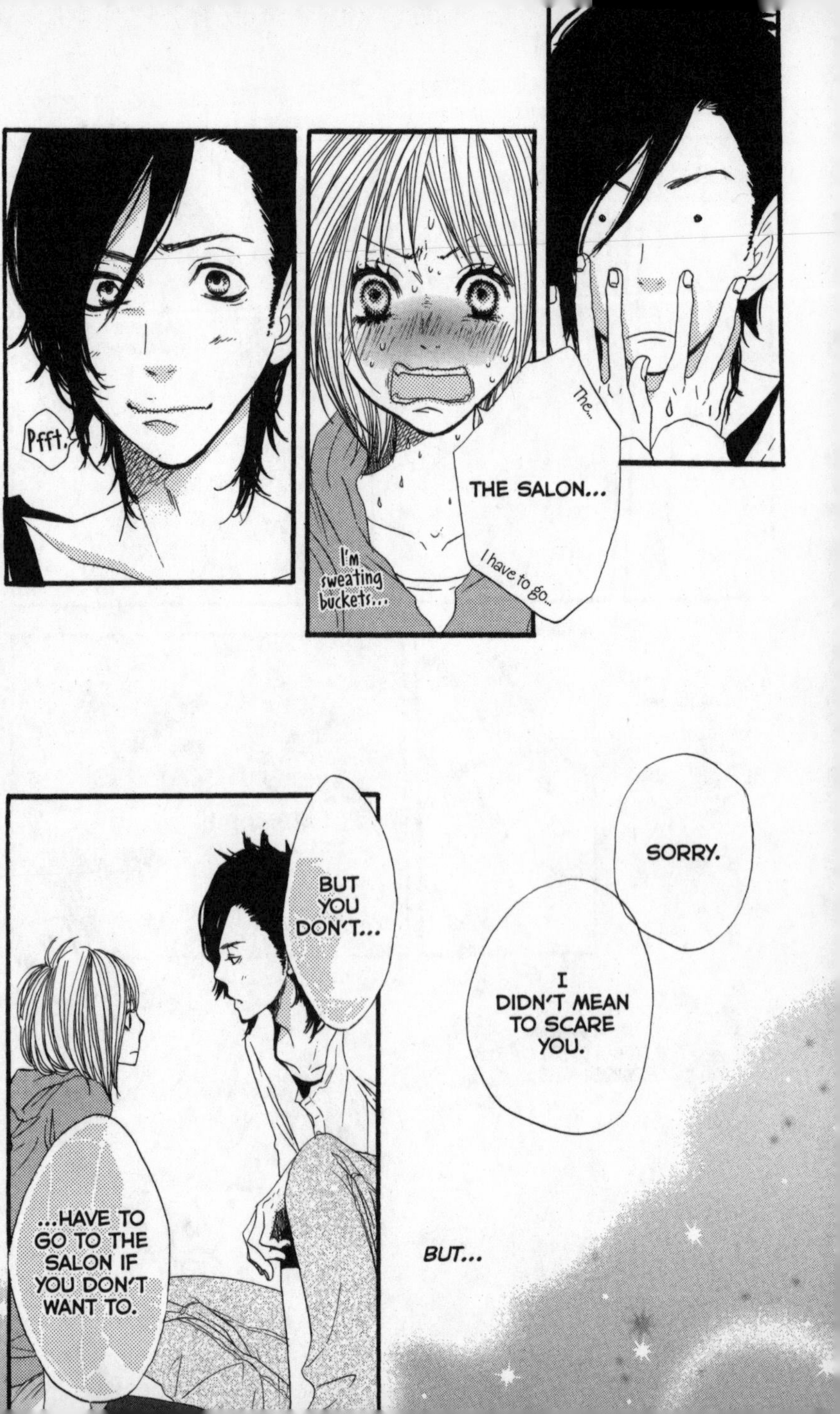
The...
THE SALON...
I have to go...
I'm sweating buckets...
Pfft.
SORRY.
I DIDN'T MEAN TO SCARE YOU.
BUT...
BUT YOU DON'T...
...HAVE TO GO TO THE SALON IF YOU DON'T WANT TO.

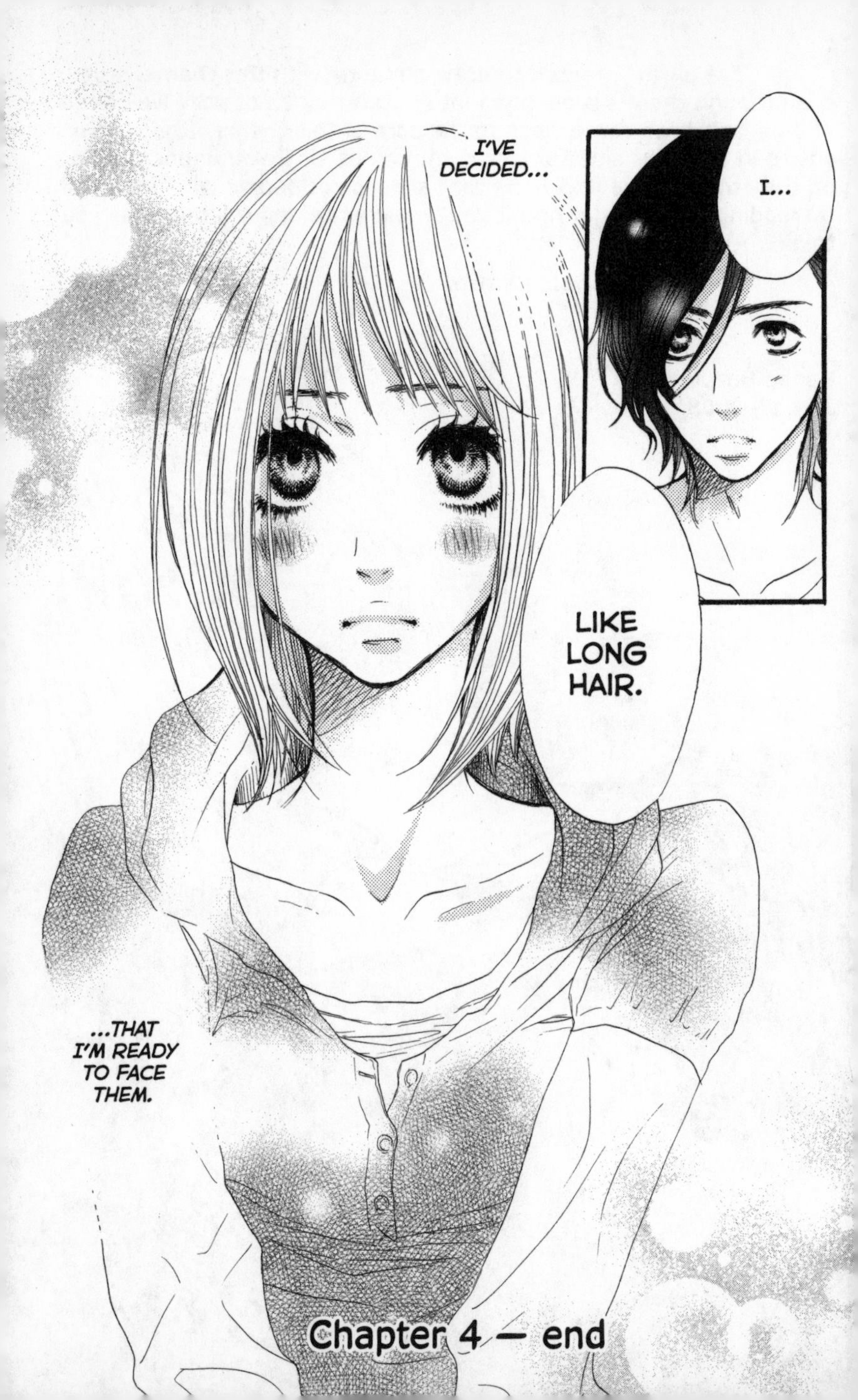
I...
LIKE LONG HAIR.
I'VE DECIDED...
...THAT I'M READY TO FACE THEM.
Chapter 4 — end

I've always wanted to draw a manga with this theme, so, even though there's probably a lot of stuff that's not very well done and doesn't even come close to the core of this theme, I hope that if you're in a similar situation, or if you're not, or if you happen to be on the other side of it...I hope that all kinds of people will be touched by reading this manga. And if you would write and tell me what you think... :-)

I'll see you in volume two.

Kanae Hazuki
July 17, 2008

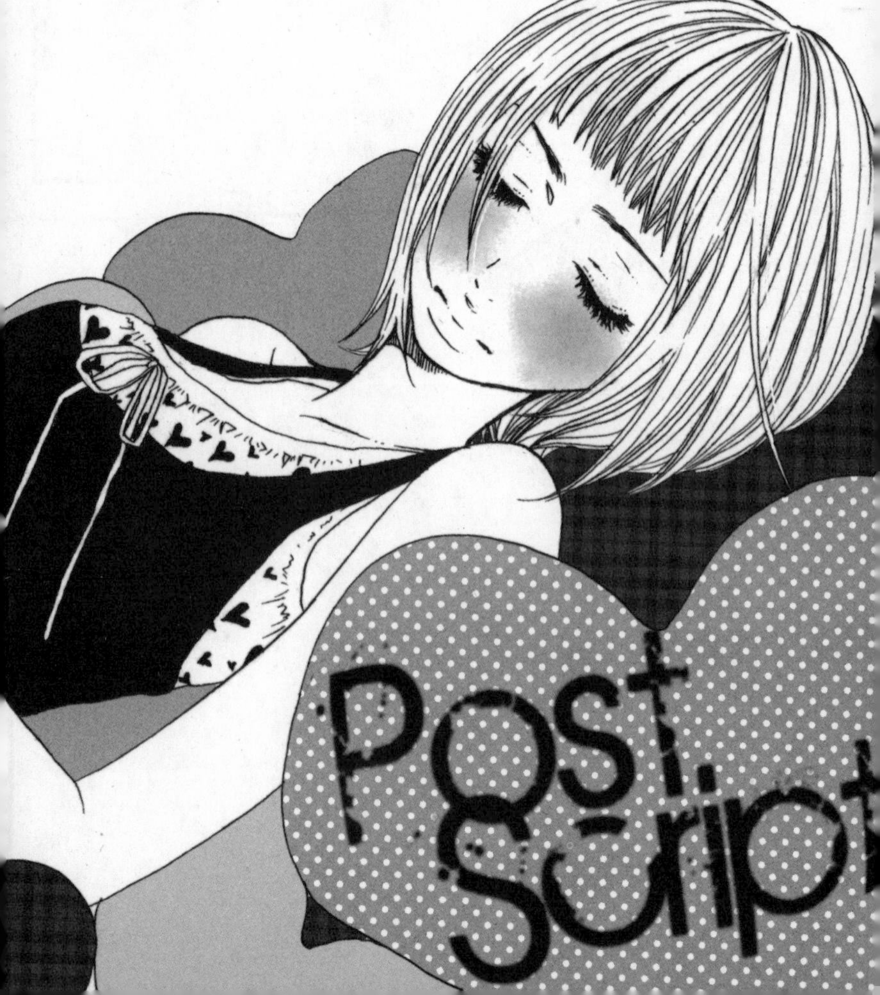
Post script

Hello, Kanae Hazuki here. I feel like I've been out of touch for a long time. (Ha ha.) Thank you so much for picking up volume one of *Say I Love You*.

For this manga, I wanted to draw a romance with a kind of eccentric girl. A girl who used to always be alone learns the warmth of humanity as she gets closer to others... Confused by all these new emotions, she fumbles her way through life with other people. That's the kind of manga I want to draw. Something that you can read and feel all warm and fuzzy inside. I think there are a lot of girls like that out there. I was more of a Mei type myself when I was going to school.

I was really insecure about my body, and of course during adolescence, I heard a lot of hurtful things from people around me. It didn't take long for me to close myself off. It felt like it wasn't worth the effort to talk to other people, and I really couldn't stand it.

But I was the one who closed myself off. I could have changed if I'd wanted to. And when you've got that wall up, then you end up leaving bad impressions on everyone around you. I think that that's another thing you bring on yourself, and you can't blame it on anyone else.

I had a teacher tell me once, "If they get you, pay them back threefold!" No one can understand another's pain unless they feel it for themselves. So do the same thing to them. At first I thought this teacher was nuts. Maybe I only got that advice because nothing I experienced was very bad, but if you truly believe you're not in the wrong, it's okay to hold your ground.

Most people, if they're alone and being bullied, they won't say anything. But what's the point in being afraid of the bully? Don't you hate that they get away with it? If you close yourself off, then you'll get depressed, and you'll see bad in everything around you. It narrows your perspective, and then when good stuff does happen, you don't even notice! It's such a waste!

I started to realize that in my later school years.

Hmm... I'm sorry this sounds so preachy! This is just one person's point of view.

A—actually, the part at the beginning where Nakanishi flips her skirt comes from a real-life experience! (Ha ha.) But there wasn't a roundhouse kick involved. I probably did say straight up, "Go to hell," or something like that: f(^_^;) I was so young.

Page 138: Karaoke and closed doors

Unlike in American karaoke bars, Japanese karaoke is designed only to embarrass you in front of your small immediate group. You rent a private room for you and your friends to sing to your heart's content. It's that privacy that has Mei so concerned.

Page 139: Gal fashion

Gal fashion covers a broad spectrum of fashion trends in Japan, but it generally includes bleached hair, tanned skin, and flashy clothes and makeup.

Page 159: "Were you a gangbanger?"

In Japanese, the word used is "yankee," which refers to a juvenile delinquent type. The stereotypical yankee tries to mimic 1950s American "rebel" styles, including the pompadour hairstyle that Mei imagines when she asks the question. That Yamato might be a yankee is a somewhat old-fashioned idea.

Translation Notes

Page 17: Asamitchi

This is a nickname for Asami. Adding a -tchi at the end of a name is a simple Japanese way of turning almost any name into a nickname. Nakanishi is most likely making it a point to call Asami this as a hint to her that he wants to be on a nickname-basis. Asami, as you may have noticed, talks about herself in the third person. In Japanese, verbs are conjugated the same for first and third person, so it's not uncommon for small children and girls trying to sound cute to use their own name in place of "I" or "me."

Page 98: "Sugar daddies"

What the boy actually guesses is that Asami would have some kind of shady source of income, such as going on compensated dates, or *enjo kôsai*. The basic idea is that an attractive girl will go out with, and sometimes sleep with, an older man in exchange for money or gifts.

Page 102: Yamato's suckerfish

The term that these oh-so-classy young women used to describe Asami's relationship to Yamato translates to "goldfish poop." Anyone who's had fish can probably understand the metaphor—when a fish defecates, the excrement can hang from the fish for some time, like Asami does to Yamato. The translators used the term "sucker fish" as a reference to the parasitic fish that attach themselves to larger sea creatures (sharks, whales, etc.).

The interview starts on the other page!

Creator Kanae Hazuki talks about

Say I Love You.

and the theme I wanted to convey, came together and became *Say I Love You.*

D: What were you going for when you chose the title?

H: It's my way of cheering Mei on, and telling her, "You can do it!" It's me wanting her to go for it with Yamato, her first love. As I draw every chapter, I keep repeating over and over in my head, "I'm going try hard with this manga, so you try, too!"

D: One of the themes of the series is "firsts." Was there one you focused on in particular?

H: I think that people are always really moved when they experience a first. And when you get out of this slump where it's like, "I can't do it, I can't do it—no matter what I do, I'm going to fail!" and then you get to, "I finally did it!", it's even more emotional, you know? It's not just the sense of accomplishment—there was a lot of sweat and tears involved, so the "weight" of the happiness is different. The gratitude you feel to those who helped you, too. And those experiences will always help you in the future. I wanted to draw Mei and company growing little by little, as they feel the joy of working really hard to accom-

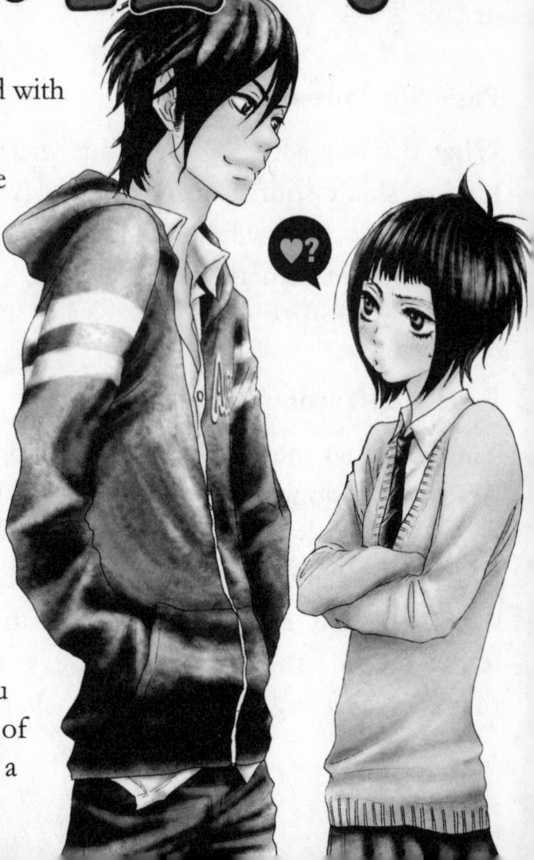
♥?

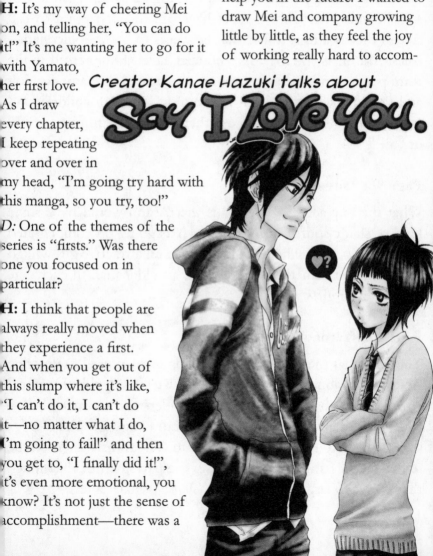

Bonus Interview!

This interview with Say I Love You. *creator Kanae Hazuki originally appeared in the November 2013 issue of Dessert magazine, to celebrate the release of the Japanese live-action* Say I Love You. *movie.*

Dessert: First off, congratulations on having your manga made into a live-action movie! How did you feel when it was made official?

Hazuki: I was sincerely happy. I had three dreams when I started drawing manga professionally, and now the last one is about to come true.

D: So you're really looking forward to it?

H: Yes. I'm looking forward to it as a reader and as the author. I don't want there to be any lies in the words I write, and these are words I wanted to say with all my heart, so I feel very blessed to have them told to the whole country through the actors. Of course it will be new to those seeing my work for the first time, but I think that there are some lines of dialogue that will take on different meanings to those who have been reading my work from the beginning. I hope they'll be able to make new discoveries.

Also, I'm really excited to see some of the things that were pretty difficult to express in manga format. I can't wait to see the scenes in motion, like when their hair is blowing in the wind. Also, all the scenes will have backgrounds now, so I'm interested to see how the characters will look on those backgrounds.

D: What inspired you to draw *Say I Love You.*?

H: I wanted to draw a girl who isn't very good at associating with people, but she doesn't hate them—she wants to make friends, it just doesn't work out. Also, I've experienced bullying in the past, and I wanted to draw a manga that could give a little bit of courage to anyone who's going through the same experience. I've wanted to ever since I started drawing manga. I've always wanted to show those people what I saw and felt when I got out of that situation, and I hope it helps lighten their burden in a small way. The girl I wanted to draw,

The interview continues on the other page!

big emotional support. That's why I try never to forget to be grateful for, and to, the people around me. Also, in that first chapter, when Mei was climbing the stairs and Nakanishi was tugging on her skirt—that happened to me. But of course, I didn't kick anyone in the face or tell him to drop dead!

D: So who is hardest to draw, personality-wise?

H: Yamato. Yamato is this guy who's really good-looking on the outside, but on the inside, he's this totally normal boy. He's actually pretty easily swayed by peer pressure, and he's not much of a go-getter. It's incredibly difficult to draw a character that's nice to everyone and loved by all. But I think it's because he's so normal that it's so easy to believe him when he says something sincere. Yamato is so honest—he's not calculating, he just says what he really thinks—and that's what makes him so attractive. I also think it was very attractive of him to tell Mei about his ugly past without trying to make himself look good. [But] Yamato has no idea how much girls like him. He's an innocent boy who is constantly fighting this question in his mind, "There's nothing special about me—why do they keep coming?", and it's surprisingly hard to draw.

For more Q&A with Kanae Hazuki, check out future volumes of Say I Love You. *from Kodansha Comics!*

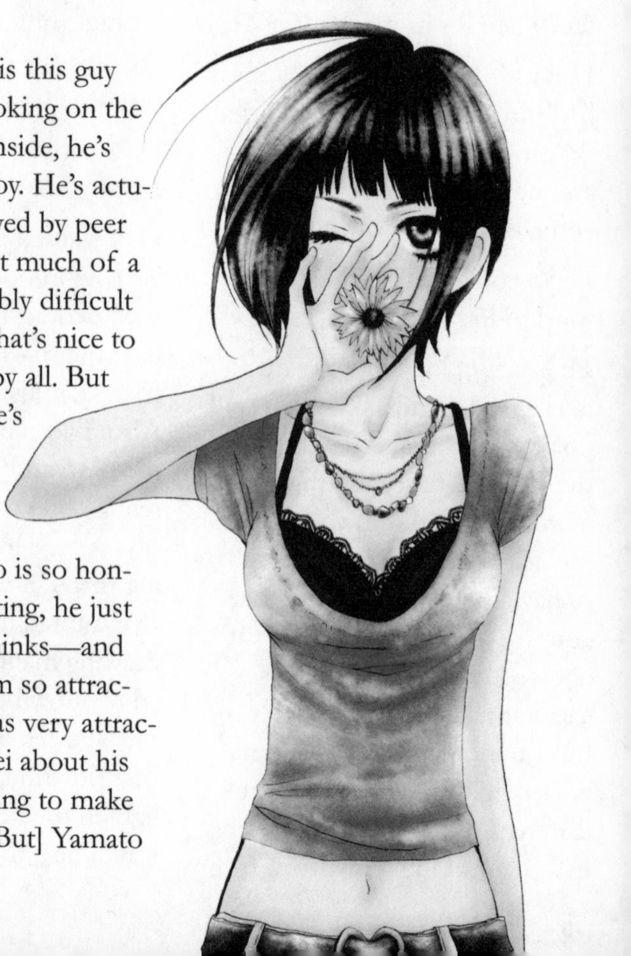

plish something for the first time.

D: Tell us what's most important to you when you're drawing growing characters!

H: First, I was very particular in that I wanted to draw characters that had some kind of insecurities deep in their hearts. And I wanted to respect the side of each character that can't overcome the insecurities, but can still learn to accept them. It was also important to me to have characters that have some small thing the readers can relate to and feel close to.

D: Is there anything in particular that you focused on with the heroine, Mei?

H: I think some people may think that Mei's personality has kind of blurred since the beginning of the series. But I was actually kind of going for that. Mei had some trauma when she was young, and she had built up this wall inside of her; as Mei interacts with others, that wall crumbles, and she's starting to be able to bring out this part of her she had deep inside that always liked people. That change is the "blur" that you're seeing. So I want to

make sure that that part of her, that liking of people, never goes out of focus.

D: Is there anything about yourself, Hazuki-san, that you see in Mei? Do you see her living any of your own experiences?

H: Maybe that we both want to remember how grateful we are for others. When I was being bullied, I had a lot of messed up emotions. But there was a girl who was nice to me anyway, and she was a

Say I Love You. volume 1 is a work of fiction. Names, characters, places, and incidents are the products of the author's imagination or are used fictitiously. Any resemblance to actual events, locales, or persons, living or dead, is entirely coincidental.

A Kodansha Comics Trade Paperback Original

Published in the United States by Kodansha Comics, an imprint of Kodansha USA Publishing, LLC, New York.

Publication rights for this English edition arranged through Kodansha Ltd, Tokyo.

First published in Japan in 2008 by Kodansha Ltd., Tokyo as *Sukitte iinayo.* volume 1.

ISBN 978-1-61262-602-4

Printed in the United States of America.

www.kodanshacomics.com

9 8 7 6 5
Translation: Alethea and Athena Nibley
Lettering: John Clark
Editing: Ben Applegate